THE HISTORY OF SCIENCE IN WESTERN CIVILIZATION

Volume II
The Scientific Revolution

eslie

L. Pearce Williams
Henry John Steffens

University Press
of America™

PREFACE TO VOLUME II

This volume, unlike volume I which dealt with science in classical antiquity and the Western middle ages, is restricted to one
era and topic, the Scientific Revolution of the seventeenth century. What follows is, therefore, but a single (albeit large)
chapter in the history of science in western civilization. The
chapter is organized into a narrative introduction and a collection of documents gathered under various rubrics, as indicated
in the Table of Contents. It is our hope that their variety and
interest will repay serious and close study and offer the reader
real insight into the nature of the origins and content of one
of the most important chapters in the history of man.

Ithaca, New York   L. Pearce Williams

July, 1977   Henry John Steffens

THIS BOOK IS GRATEFULLY DEDICATED TO

HENRY GUERLAC

TABLE OF CONTENTS

Chapter 1. The Scientific Revolution. Narrative   1

Chapter 1. II. Readings on the Scientific Revolution   48

     A. Methodology   48

        1. Aristotelian Method and its Shortcomings . .   49

           a. The case for Aristotle
              John Herman Randall, Jr., "The
              Development of Scientific Method
              in the School of Padua"   49

           b. The case for a new method
              Ernan McMullin, "Medieval and Modern
              Science: Continuity or Discontinuity". .   64

        2. The New Method   80

           a. Francis Bacon, *Novum Organon*   80

           b. René Descartes, *Discourse on Method* . . . 109

           c. Galileo
              Letters on Sunspots 122
              Epistle to the Grand Dutchesse Mother . . 125
              Dialogue on the Great World Systems . . . 137

           d. William Harvey, *De Motu Cordis* 143

     B. The Achievement of the Scientific Revolution . 153

        1. The Birth of the New Physics   153

           a. Nicholas Copernicus, *De Revolutionibus*
              Orbium Coelestium 153

           b. Johann Kepler, *Dioptrics* 170
              Epitome of Copernican Astronomy 175

           c. Galileo, *Dialogue on the*
              Great World Systems 186

           d. Galileo, *Dialogues Concerning*
              Two New Sciences 205

           e. Isaac Newton, *Philosophiae Naturalis*
              Principia Mathematica 219

        2. The Mechanical Philosophy 245

    a. Galileo, *The Assayer* 245

    b. René Descartes, *Principia Philosophiae* . 249

    c. Robert Boyle, *The Excellency and Grounds of the Mechanical Hypothesis* 274

    d. Isaac Newton, *Rules of Reasoning* 284
       Opticks 287

C. The Assessment of the Scientific Revolution . . 304

  1. Robert K. Merton, "Science and Economy of 17th Century England" 304

  2. Frances Yates, "The Hermetic Tradition in Renaissance Science" 312

  3. J. E. McGuire and P. M. Rattansi, "Newton and the 'Pipes' of Pan" 322

  4. A. Rupert Hall, "On the Historical Singularity of the Scientific Revolution of the Seventeenth Century" 339

THE SCIENTIFIC REVOLUTION

I. Narrative

A. The Beginnings of the Revolution

   1. Introduction

     In the sixteenth and seventeenth century, the intellectual map of Europe underwent the most profound transformation in the whole history of Western civilization. This upheaval has been given the name of the Scientific Revolution and it is the fountainhead of our modern scientific and technological society. It was, of course, as well the culmination of the scientific and philosophical traditions of antiquity, the Middle Ages and the Renaissance. Everything seems to have flowed together in this period to produce the creation of modern science. It is a unique event, having never occurred in any other place or time and its effect on the development of Western civilization ranks it among the greatest events of human history.

     Having said all this, it is surprisingly difficult to specify what made the Scientific Revolution and just what the Scientific Revolution actually was. There were of course new ideas injected into Western science, but it is not enough merely to enumerate these and call them a revolution. As modern research has revealed, many of the "new" ideas had been held, in whole or in part, by men before the Scientific Revolution without having disturbed the general intellectual peace. The infinity of the universe, for example, is a clear "revolutionary" result of the Scientific Revolution. Yet, an infinite universe had been suggested by Cardinal Nicholas of Cusa a century before Copernicus without causing a great deal of intellectual stir. Similarly, the "inertial" motion of the planets had been put forward by Nicholas Oresme in the fourteenth century without there being any of the intellectual consequences felt by the similar suggestion by Galileo in the seventeenth century. There was, to be sure, much that was new in the Scientific Revolution but new facts and ideas, of and by themselves, were not enough to create or sustain the Scientific Revolution.

     A generation ago, the answer to the question, "What was the Scientific Revolution?" appeared both simple and sufficient. It was the turn from the barren study of Aristotle in the schools, to the study of Nature in the raw. Subtle logic and semantic hair-splitting was abandoned for the direct inquisition of Nature by experiment. Science emerged from the philosopher's study to the artisan's and engineer's workshop. The great test of a scientific theory was not its logical coherence but whether it "worked" or not. Experiment was merely the result of what the practical manipulator of nature did naturally--trial and error until the "right" result was obtained. The motivation behind the Scientific Revolution was similarly to be found in the needs of practical men. The determination of the number of angels that

could dance on the head of a pin had little urgency for the mer-
chants, explorers and adventurers of the sixteenth and seventeenth centuries. What was important was new machines for
industrial use (mines, particularly), new chemical processes for
the more efficient utilization of natural resources, accurate
laws of motion to guide the aim of the new artillery officers,
accurate star tables to aid the navigators who, in the sixteenth
and seventeenth century began the process of the European con-
quest of the globe. Thus, the Scientific Revolution was a
repudiation, not a continuation, of the philosophical tradition,
accomplished in the name of the practical exploitation of nature.
The archetypal scientist was the engineer.

———Again, this picture of the Scientific Revolution contains an
element of truth but clearly is not sufficient. Copernicus did
no experiments; Kepler's scientific drive came more from a mystical Pythagorean vision of the universe than from any Faustian
urge to dominate Nature. Even Galileo and Newton who were
"practical" in the sense that they understood and appreciated
the engineering tradition, went far beyond the requirements of
the practical arts to construct new philosophies.

———Another interpretation of the Scientific Revolution places
most emphasis upon this philosophical dimension. Its proponents
argue that the Scientific Revolution was first and foremost a
philosophical revolution. Experiment, new facts and the solution
of practical problems were incidental to the construction of a
new philosophical frame of reference which literally re-ordered
the universe. The philosophical stimulus came from the rediscovery and appreciation of Plato in the Renaissance with the
consequent emphasis upon mathematics in nature. The qualitative
physics of Aristotle crumbled before the quantitative, geometrical neo-Platonism of Copernicus, Kepler, Galileo, Descartes and
Newton. The essence of the Scientific Revolution, in this view,
was the re-definition of physical reality in terms of mathematical concepts. The physically real was that (and only that)
which could be expressed in mathematical terms. All else was
subjective and matter for opinion, not science. Thus if one
could but seize hold of a few basic mathematical axioms that also
applied to the physical world, then the whole of physical reality
could be *deduced* mathematically from them. The inspiration was
Platonic; the master to be followed was Archimedes. If physical
qualities could be transformed into geometrical quantities, as
Archimedes had done with weight in his work on hydrostatics, then
the work of the Divine mathematician who created the universe
could finally be opened for all (mathematicians) to read.

Once again, the point is a seductive one but hardly satisfying. Kepler's "discovery" that the orbits of the planets fit
into the circumscribed five regular solids sent Kepler into
Platonic ecstasy but did not have the same "revolutionary" effect
as Galileo's qualitative discovery of sunspots.

Finally, the newest "key" to the Scientific Revolution is
the intoxicating discovery that many of the "revolutionaries"
were mightily influenced by the resurgence of magic in the Renaissance. The demigod here is Hermes Trismegistus, the legendary
originator of alchemy and the Hermetic arts by which men could

call upon the active powers of nature for enlightenment and control. The Hermetic universe was not composed of Aristotelian logical distinctions, Platonic mathematical essences, or engineering machines and models. It was, rather, alive with demons and angels, signs and symbols, all subordinate to but expressive of the Godhead who created it all. God had left His mark on each and every of His creations. If men could but learn to read these Divine signs, they could penetrate the mysteries of creation and, once they knew the divine language, they could hope to use it to gain control of Nature. Faust, not Galileo, is the hero in this view of the Scientific Revolution. Knowledge comes from the study of Nature, but only after one has been initiated into Nature's mysteries by the mastery of the Great Books of Hermeticism. Alchemy and astrology, alike, are branches of Truth if one but knows the way. Moses, who had the great good fortune to be both Egyptian and on intimate terms with the Deity, was the source from which all knowledge came. Hermes was the channel through which mosaic secrets passed. Together, they made up a living fountain of mysteries allowing the initiate to contemplate the Universe in all its mystic glory.

This view of the Scientific Revolution is still battling to gain a hearing. It is so easy to scoff at the mystical extravagances laid bare by modern research. And yet, we had better listen. Copernicus' main argument for a heliostatic system appears to be drawn directly from the Hermetic tradition. Kepler's flights of fancy make some sense within Hermeticism and even Isaac Newton seems to have been touched by its currents. Chemistry, particularly, was affected by its doctrines and, although chemistry did not create the Scientific Revolution, it did contribute to it. The extent of the influence of Hermeticism remains to be determined but what is clear is that it did affect certain aspects of the Scientific Revolution in rather important ways.

This brief examination of interpretations of the cause and meaning of the Scientific Revolution reveals clearly that no one view is sufficient. Nor is this surprising. We should expect that something as complex and imposing as the Scientific Revolution would be explicable only in terms of complex interactions of many different kinds of causes and influences. What we shall do here is to attempt to put the many pieces together. Our narrative will describe what happened. The documents will give some insight into the ways in which scientific innovation appeared in the Scientific Revolution.

2. The Expansion of the Intellectual World

Science and philosophy had developed in the Middle Ages largely as academic disciplines. It was in the great universities that the Aristotelian heritage had first been assimilated and it was among academics that the seemingly endless debates over details of the Aristotelian system raged. There was, to be sure, some awareness of the world without, but by and large, medieval science was bounded by the academic tradition and was worked out within a narrow circle of academically trained and oriented philosophers.

One of the signs of the stirringsof the new science was the breaking down of this academic monopoly and the incursion of non-academic types into the scholarly groves. It will suffice here merely to list briefly the kinds of people who suddenly began to put strains on medieval science by asking it to answer hitherto unasked questions. Primary among such groups is the engineer. Before the Renaissance and the advent of artillery as a fundamental arm of the military, the engineer had practiced his craft within a tradition that extended back to Hellenistic times. He was concerned with the construction and transportation of siege engines and other, rather simple, machines of war. The tradition paid lip service to the likes of Hero of Alexandria, but drew very little from either science or philosophy. It was a practical craft practiced by practical men. If something worked, it was adopted and repeated. If it failed, it was rejected. *Why* something worked or failed could rarely be determined. Correction of error was made empirically. Thus, when a building collapsed during construction, new plans merely thickened the walls and the attempt was made again. Should it fail again, the walls were made thicker until the edifice did stand. There was here no question of the strength of materials, knowledge of statics, stresses or strains, or any other theoretical dimension.

All this changed during the Renaissance, particularly in Italy. The development of despotic city states, dependent for their very existence on the military preparations of the military engineer, elevated the engineer to a new social level. The new city-states also placed new demands on the engineer. City-planning, princely architecture, large-scale irrigation works, building and maintenance of bridges and roads all became the concerns of the engineer. Ideally (from the engineer's point of view) the new city-state should be laid out rationally from both the civil and military point of view. Its walls ought to be designed to resist and counter artillery attack. Its interior should reflect that universal reason which the Italian renaissance worshipped. Hydraulic works should provide the city with copious supplies of water; canals should be constructed for irrigation of the outlying surrounding fields; machines should be devised to aid in the construction of buildings and canals, as well as for the lightening of human labor. All this should lead to a physical and spiritual harmony which would guarantee the well-being of the city-state and its Prince.

This idealized picture of the perfect city (and the perfect engineer), reveals how drastically the function of the engineer had been redefined. He could no longer be a rude empiric, concerned only with supervising the operation of a battering ram or a catapult. He must be a cultivated man, aware of the currents of Humanism swirling about him which defined the new vision of man in order to fit the new city to the new men. He must be an artist capable of creating the physical harmonies of public works upon which the spiritual harmony of the public spirit depended. Above all, he must be of an inventive and mechanical turn of mind. He could no longer merely carry on the technical tradition of his engineering progenitors--he must expand and improve it.

New needs required new ideas and ideas, for the engineer, must be made tangible in new techniques and new machines.

The archetypal figure here is Leonardo da Vinci (1452-1519). We now know that many of Leonardo's "inventions" were common-places among his fellow engineers and it is no longer possible to view him as a lonely, towering genius, born centuries ahead of his time. The discovery that he was more or less typical of the engineers of his day is what makes him important for our under-standing of the beginnings of the Scientific Revolution. We can observe in Leonardo the growing tension between academic learning and the demands of the practical engineer. One simple example may illustrate one aspect. Leonardo was not academically trained but schooled himself in ancient learning. The self-taught man is almost always on the defensive for he is conscious that he proba-bly has missed something that his more carefully educated col-league regards as common knowledge. But, his defensiveness makes the self-taught man more sensitive to contradictions or errors in the traditional corpus of learning and creates a discomfort aris-ing from his inability to explain or explain away what orthodox learning dictates should not exist. The trajectory of a projec-tile was one such problem that caught Leonardo's attention. Aristotelian physics insisted that violent and natural motion could not coexist in the same body. Hence, a projectile must first move violently (in a straight line) until the violent impe-tus was exhausted. Then, natural motion (vertically downward) took over. The trajectory, therefore, was composed of two straight lines meeting at a definite geometrical angle. The question of the trajectory of a projectile was not of central im-portance in the Renaissance since variations in cannon bore, shot size and quality of powder made it impossible to predict the path of any specific cannon ball, most of which were fired at point-blank range anyway to batter down walls. The one exception was mortar fire by which bombs could be lobbed over a defensive wall to explode in the streets of the city. The path of the bomb could be clearly followed, especially at night when the burning fuse traced out the trajectory against the night sky. It was *not* two straight lines as Aristotle and his followers insisted. It was obviously a continuous curve and Leonardo made sketches of mortar trajectories in his notebooks. *What* curve it was, he did not know but he could be certain of two things. Aristotle was simply wrong and the only trustworthy guide here was not academic science but practical experience. We should also notice the social dimension of this observation and conclusion. Precisely because Leonardo was not an academician, it was in his own inter-est to emphasize the difference between Aristotelian theory and military reality. Not all knowledge was in books and the engin-eer could insist that he knew some things too that the academic had better pay some attention to. Thus, in this small instance, we can see one of the ways in which new observations created ten-sions in the intellectual world. And one of the results was the growing emphasis upon the direct observation of nature. *How* does Nature actually work? is a question of fundamental importance to the practical engineer. Only when we know the how in fairly pre-cise terms, can we undertake to answer the *why*. The engineer would insist that observation must always precede theory and there was thus given a considerable stimulus to the accurate observation of nature. Again, Leonardo's notebooks reveal this aspect of the expansion of the intellectual world. Accurate drawings of flowers and plants, not to mention the musculature of the human body, record nature. Only when we have an accurate picture of natural reality, it is implied, can we begin to understand the causes of that reality. Anatomy comes before physiology. Description comes before theory.

It should be noted that the engineers of the Renaissance did little more than raise the question of explanation. Their works could and did serve to cast doubts upon the reliability and completeness of academic science. They did not create a new science to directly challenge the old. They were unable to go beyond the point of saying--orthodox scientific theory does not work in this or that area. We can tell you what does happen, but we cannot tell you why. That "why" was to come from outside the engineering tradition.

There is one further aspect of the engineering component in the scientific revolution that deserves mention. This is the evolution of the "engine" itself. Originally, engines had been war machines. The technological ingenuity of medieval men, however, had vastly expanded the number of engines. There were, by the Renaissance, water mills with intricate gearing mechanisms; wind mills, machines for fulling cloth and clocks for telling time. The Renaissance witnessed another great spurt in engine building. The need for metal, both precious and common, was multiplied exponentially by the new artillery and its importance. It took a lot of money to build an artillery train and money in the fifteenth and sixteenth centuries was gold and silver. The Erzgebirge in central Europe and the silver mines of Mexico and Peru were to provide the bullion required for the modernization of the state's military machine. Other mines were the source of the copper, tin and iron necessary for brass and iron cannon. This was all large-scale exploitation, requiring large power and pumping machines. The result of all this mechanical engineering was growing familiarity with machines and increased (and more common) ability to think in mechanical terms. Two consequences are worth making clear. The first is that mechanical processes could be devised to copy natural processes. The great astronomical clocks of Strasbourg and Lyons used gears and wheels and weights to represent and reproduce the motions of the heavenly bodies. It is still quite a leap from the mechanical representation of the cosmos to the supposition that the cosmos is, itself, a machine whose parts can be isolated and studied just as can the parts of a terrestrial machine. Nevertheless, the first step in the mechanization of the cosmos may be said to be this mechanical imitation of the cosmos. To put it another way, the Aristotelian metaphor for the cosmos was an organic and psychological one. The medieval cosmos was thickly inhabited by angels and other spirits who worked together to keep the cosmos going. The planets moved in their orbits because their orbits were inhabited by angels and circled the earth eternally in holy appreciation of God. All motion was for a purpose, ultimately to be discovered

in the unity of a divinity. Astronomical clocks allowed a different metaphor to emerge. The cosmos could be a well-oiled
machine created by the divine Watchmaker. The whole still might
have a purpose, but the parts were mere mechanical components
working according to mechanical laws. It is difficult to penetrate the motivations of angels, but it is relatively easy to
follow the motion of a gear train. All you need to know is the
laws of mechanics.

The second point follows directly from this one. The
increasing importance of machines could not help but stimulate
interest in how machines work. How is force best transmitted?
What is the mechanical advantage of a system of levers? These
are "theoretical" questions of fundamental importance to the
mechanical engineer. Their answers, however, were not to be
found in the academic science of the day. Nor were the engineers
able, alone, to go much beyond the results of trial and error.
But, there was help available. Greek science had dealt with some
of these questions. If Aristotle was silent on them, Archimedes
was not and Archimedean science might well be worth exploring.

The fact that Archimedes and other Greek scientists were
available to the men of the Renaissance may be attributed to the
rise of Humanism. Gallons of ink have been expended in the dispute between medievalists and Renaissance scholars as to whether
Humanism, defined as the attempt to recapture both the letters
and the spirit of antiquity, was a medieval or Renaissance
phenomenon. There can be no doubt that medieval scholars eagerly
sought out ancient sources, attempted, with some success, to emu-
late ancient writers and thoroughly appreciated the value of the
classics. It remains true, however, that both the tempo and the
direction of the quest for the recovery of antiquity changed markedly in the late fourteenth and fifteenth centuries. In 1397,
the Greek (Byzantine) diplomat Manuel Chrysoloras initiated lectures on the Greek language and literature in Florence which completely turned the heads of Florentine youth. Greek became a
passion and the search for ancient literary remains became a con-
certed one in which monastic libraries throughout Europe were
systematically searched and despoiled by avid Humanists. The
Latin classics, also, were objects of veneration and of passion-
ate appreciation. From 1397 to 1453 when Constantinople fell,
Renaissance Humanists had discovered most of the "new" manuscripts which were to be injected in Renaissance culture. These
discoveries had also prepared them to view the older treasures
with a critical eye and correct or emend texts which had been
corrupted by earlier copyists and translators.

The Humanist emphasis on literature and language has been
viewed by some modern historians of science as detrimental to
the development of science. They argue that the prominence of
grammar, style and the written word tended to obscure the world
of nature and, thereby, dilute the curiosity of those to whom the
Book of Nature was at least as important as the Dialogues of
Plato. There is some merit in this charge. There is no doubt
that one stream of Humanists did serve to choke off interest in
anything but the literary world of antiquity and to become so
involved in grammatical niceties that it could spare no time for

a glance at the Cosmos. But, there is a clear debt to Humanism as well. On the broad philosophical front, the re-emphasis of Plato and the Platonic vision of physical reality offered a meta-physical alternative to the Aristotelian system. It is a common-place that Galileo and Descartes were "Platonists" in that they believed and taught that the physical universe was essentially mathematical in nature. Equally important was the flood of new treatises that were translated and made available by the Human-ists. It was not that Humanists were particularly interested in ancient science, but that one's Humanist spurs could be won only by producing a praiseworthy Latin translation of a Greek original. Not everyone could translate a new Platonic dialogue or Plutar-chian Life. So, especially in the sixteenth century when the manuscript supply was running short, the budding Humanist might have to settle for a medical or mathematical or physical treatise to render into Latin. The science that thus made its way into the West was of particular aptness to feed the new intellectual appetites of the age. Earlier periods had seen the introduction of Greek science from the heroic age of Greek philosophy (5th and 4th century B.C.) and from the twilight (2nd century A.D.). It was in the Renaissance that Hellenistic science came center stage in the West. And Hellenistic science had that same emphasis on the specific and the mechanical which appealed to the Renaissance engineer. Aristotle, when too closely questioned, often failed to give the correct detail although he could still be relied upon for the large picture. Increasingly, people were interested in the details and they could now turn to Greeks who had investiga-ted them. Archimedes' treatises dealt with specific situations and provided specific answers to the questions raised. Hero of Alexandria's *Pneumatics* offered a different perspective on air and air engines from that to be found in Aristotelian generali-ties about air and/or the void. Euclid could be read as intended, not as transmitted through two or more cultural media. The great "higher" mathematicians such as Diophantus and Apollonius of Perga revealed new mathematical techniques of possible utility to the Renaissance scientist. In short, the knowledge of ancient science was considerably expanded and the widening of this intel-lectual horizon offered the Renaissance savant new opportunities for scientific investigation. Two of these deserve special men-tion.

The increasing knowledge and popularity of Plato and Archi-medes provided a counter-balance to the Aristotelian preponder-ance. It should not be forgotten that in the fifteenth and six-teenth centuries, the antiquity of an idea was an important gauge of its validity and respectability. The Renaissance was a "re-birth," not a revolution; its proponents sought to recapture the knowledge of antiquity, not repudiate it. Hence, the existence of alternative metaphysical and physical systems, with claim to equal antiquity to the Aristotelian, forced an opening up of the scientific world. It was no longer enough to cite Aristotle; one also had to deal with non-Aristotelian answers and somehow devise a means to decide *which* of the ancients was right. In such a situation, the result almost has to be a loosening of the effec-tive power of intellectual dogma and a gain in freedom for the presentation of heterodox, even heretical, scientific ideas.

The second effect of the Humanist movement was to enable the earlier medieval harvest from antiquity to be re-evaluated. The force of citing Aristotle as an authority was lessened if it could be shown that the citation was the result of a mis-translation. The Humanist critical spirit was extended to scientific, as well as literary texts. Many obscurities were thereby removed and many contradictions that had puzzled earlier commentators disappeared. We may here merely cite the critical edition of Aristotle over which the great French Humanist Lefevre d'Etaples (ca. 1450-1536) labored for most of his life. This text made it possible to feel some confidence that one knew what Aristotle had really said, and to know precisely what was at issue in any given scientific dispute involving Aristotle.

More importantly, the translation of the Hellenistic mathematicians made it possible to appreciate the earlier translations of such mathematical treatises as Ptolemy's *Almagest*. We know that the *Almagest* was available to the Latin West in the Medieval period. What, we must ask, did medieval scholars make of it? The answer is, very little. They simply did not have the mathematical techniques to handle it with any degree of sophistication. The *Almagest* thus provided a qualitative model of the heavens which medieval astronomers could cite when occasion demanded it. It did not allow them to perform the intricate mathematical computations which were the very heart of the treatise. By the sixteenth century, this had changed. The Ptolemaic system could be fully appreciated and the differences between the reality calculated from the Almagest and that deduced from the Aristotelian physical system emerged with alarming clarity. It is a gross oversimplification to suggest that someone, contemplating the divergent results of Ptolemaic and Aristotelian accounts of planetary motion, must have said that one of these systems *had* to be wrong. It took a long time for the situation to evolve into such a bald confrontation. Yet, the point is implicit and only needed time and the pressure of events to bring it out into the open.

The pressure came from two areas: the development of astrology in the fifteenth and sixteenth centuries, and the expansion of Europe overseas in the same years.

The reasons for the growth of astrology in the Renaissance lie deeply imbedded in the cultural history of the fifteenth century. The Black Plague and the peculiarly vicious wars of the fourteenth and fifteenth centuries, had served to revive belief in the demonic and the supernatural. The particular histories of the Italian city-states also served to call men's attention to the role of fortune and the fickleness of fate in human affairs. The revival of magic and the assumed correspondence between the macrocosm of the universe and the microcosm of man, also tended to influence men to look to external determinants of individual and state fortunes. When all is in flux; when disease and death can strike without warning; when great states can fall (like Byzantium) and new powers can rise (like Sforza's Milan) without rhyme or reason, it is time to turn to cosmic causes if one hopes to be able to understand anything. Astrology had apparently respectable foundations. No one could doubt certain celestial

"influences"--that of the sun, for example, in making the earth
fecund and fertile. It needs little more imagination to identify
certain characteristics with various heavenly bodies and then
assume their influence upon states or upon individual human beings. Just how these influences will actually affect an individual or a state is for the astrologer to decide. He must know
exactly how the influences were at work at any given crucial
moment in order to ascertain what their net effect will be. For
the individual, *the* crucial point in time is the moment of his
birth for the course of his life will be affected by the stellar
influences that focused upon him at that moment. Thus, the
astrologer must be able to calculate the position of the planets
and the stars at any given moment in time. In the fifteenth and
sixteenth century, it became increasingly clear that this could
not be done with the present astronomical data and system. What
could be done, was to fudge results by introducing *ad hoc* correc-
tions, but such a procedure can only be a stop-gap. Increasingly,
it became clear that the old astronomy was insufficient. New,
more accurate data was needed. And, if a new theory were to
appear which would make the astrological task easier, it might be
expected to receive some support.

The same situation obtained in navigation. The European
discovery of the world in the fifteenth and sixteenth centuries
created serious problems. Navigational instruments were extremely primitive and the ability of sailors to hit the same continent
twice was the result more of the size of the continent than
navigational ability. Everyone turned to astronomy in the hopes
that the problem could be easily solved. It couldn't, but that
did not stop people from clamoring for more accurate data and for
more useful and easier means of astronomical computation. Once
again, what emerged most clearly was the insufficiency of the old
systems.

We ought, as well, to add here the other areas where the old
astronomy could not meet the needs of the sixteenth century. The
calendar was out of whack and desperately needed reform. The
date of Easter is determined astronomically and, since this was
the most important religious date in Christian Europe, inaccura-
cies in its determination led the Church to back astronomical
reform. Finally, the attempts at philosophical, mathematical and
physical synthesis clearly revealed the vulnerability of the
traditional astronomy to attack.

Although the main thrust of the scientific revolution was to
come through astronomy, it would be a mistake to confine it to
this subject. At least in its destructive phase when the Aristotelian system was being pulled down, it involved far wider aspects of the intellectual world than the motion of the planets.
Some historians suggest that it was nothing less than a kind of
intellectual class war in which the older theories and beliefs
were undermined by the "new men" of the sixteenth and seventeenth
centuries precisely because these older beliefs threatened to
block the progress of the "new men." Again, some part of this is
true but it will not serve as a general explanation. For the
most part, this type of "class" struggle for the mind was confined to England, but here it did have some importance. It is,

at least, worth noting.

The discovery of the New World and the attempts to plant colonies there may serve as the symbol of the attack on traditional knowledge in England. The first, and most obvious, effect of the new discoveries was the fact that they literally opened up whole new worlds of knowledge unknown to Aristotle, and clearly contradicted some of the dicta of the ancients. The existence of the Antipodes (land on the other side of the earth from Europe) could no longer be doubted after Magellan and Sir Francis Drake had circumnavigated the globe. The sheer number of new plant and animal species that were reported from the newly discovered lands served to weaken faith in the completeness, if not the accuracy, of ancient learning. "There are more things on heaven and earth than are dreamed of in your philosophy, Horatio," said the young student Hamlet at the beginning of the seventeenth century and it represents the new attitude. Even if Aristotle and the ancients were right on some things, they could not be right on all simply because so much had been discovered since they wrote. There was, then, room for new ideas and new men.

In England, those who leaped into the gap between the old and the new learning were eager to exploit the new discoveries both economically and intellectually. They tended to be Puritan in religion and radical in politics. The universities were the seat of privilege and they would have none of them. Learning was not meant to be locked up in the Libraries of Oxford or Cambridge, or kept from currency by confinement to the Latin tongue. Tudor England was the stage for the first real attempt at the popularization of learning. We must be careful to understand the full limits of the word, popular, and to realize that it did not include the lower classes. But, for the literate, there was prepared a scientific feast unknown in the past. Works on astronomy, mathematics, chemistry and medicine appeared in English and most of these challenged the older ideas. Few of these works contained anything of world-shaking originality but they did create an atmosphere in which scientific novelty and speculation could both survive and thrive.

We need mention only one final point to complete our summary survey of the conditions under which the Scientific Revolution took place. It should never be forgotten that the years during which the Scientific Revolution took place were exactly those during which the titanic struggle between the Catholic Church and the Protestant Reformation took place. It was a struggle that touched every aspect of European life and was certainly not without importance in the battle of scientific theories in the Scientific Revolution. Almost anything one could say about the cosmos could have theological significance. The Catholics, in particular, were the guardians of a theology which had included large amounts of Aristotelian science in it. An attack on Aristotle on a purely scientific point often touched a sensitive theological area as well and the scientific argument would have to be suppressed to protect the theology. Protestantism was less vulnerable to scientific novelty. Its major theological foundation was Scripture and, by and large, Scripture did not contain much sophisticated science. In practical terms, this meant that it was probably

easier for a Protestant to publish scientific novelties without
running into opposition from ecclesiastical authorities than it
was for a Catholic. It is important to note that this does not
mean that Protestants were pro-scientific and Catholics anti-
scientific. The focus was *not* on the science but on the effects
of scientific discoveries on theology. Catholicism was more vulnerable than Protestantism and, therefore, tended to be more hos-
tile to new scientific ideas. The debate over Protestantism and
the rise of modern science has raged now for years and we cannot
settle it here. We can say, however, that science tended to
thrive more in Protestant than Catholic countries. The condemnation of Galileo showed what could happen to a Catholic and it
undoubtedly had an inhibitory effect upon the development of
science in Catholic countries.

B.   The Course of the Scientific Revolution

1.   Astronomy on the Eve of the Copernican Revolution

Winston Churchill once remarked that the only successful
revolutions are those made by conservatives. In the case of the
Copernican "revolution," he would have been quite right. The
last thing Copernicus wanted to do was to overthrow the whole
towering structure of Aristotelian learning and traditional
mathematical astronomy. Indeed, his professed motives were to
preserve the ancient system by introducing the idea of the diurnal rotation and annual revolution of the earth.

Before we come to an examination and assessment of the
Copernican "revolution," it is important to examine the astronomical situation rather closely. We shall thereby discover
that what Copernicus did was not so revolutionary as has often
been supposed, but that his system, if taken seriously, opened
the way to the ultimate destruction of the Aristotelian cosmos.
This apparent paradox will be resolved as we proceed.

Let us, first of all, revert to the basic problems which
Ptolemaic astronomy had sought to solve for it was the failure to
achieve exact solutions which created some of the unease amongst
astronomers.

1. Retrograde motion of the planets.
2. Difference in brightness of the planets.
3. The difference in period of the superior planets, i.e.,
    the time for Mars, Jupiter and Saturn to move once
    around the ecliptic and reappear in the same sign of the
    zodiac from which one started to time its period was not
    constant. Some revolutions were significantly more
    rapid than others. It was, therefore, only an *average*
    period that could be given.
4. Although it was not as great a matter for concern, it
    was deemed odd that the inferior planets, Mercury and
    Venus, together with the Sun completed their journeys
    around the Earth all in one year.

5. The difference in speed of the Sun, as well as the planets at various parts of their journey around the Earth. For the Sun, for example, the time for the journey from Vernal equinox to Autumnal equinox was more than that from Autumnal to Vernal equinox.

There were a host of other, minor difficulties, but these five may stand as the major problems that a mathematical astronomy had to wrestle with. The Ptolemaic solutions are worth recalling. 1 through 3 can all be disposed of by use of a deferent circle usually eccentric to the Earth and one or more epicycles. The use of the epicyclette (an epicycle on the epicycle) allowed an astronomer to provide fine adjustments to the system and, thereby, achieve a higher degree of approximation to the observations. 4 was more of a physical or philosophical anomaly than a mathematical problem. All that was necessary was to have the deferent for the sun, Mercury and Venus revolve in one year but it was a matter of some philosophical concern as to why this should work. For the astronomically astute, it surely implied some relationship between the Sun and the inferior planets which was not illuminated by the Ptolemaic treatment. Perhaps 5 was the most embarrassing fact to be explained. It could, theoretically, be attacked in two ways. The apparent difference in speed in different parts of the Sun's orbit could be simply recognized as a difference in speed. This, however, although mathematically simple was philosophically suspect. The heavens, it must be remembered, were perfect and unchanging and the solution to heavenly problems had to be expressed in terms of perfect (circular) and unchanging motion. This meant that accelerations and decelerations were not permissible. This first solution, then, had to be rejected. The second solution was to locate a point within the Sun's orbit about which the angular displacement of the Sun *was* constant. This point, the equant, was *not* coincident with the Earth. Again, mathematically, it is an adequate solution but it could raise physical and philosophical questions. We need note here only the fact that the Earth was not *really* the center of solar motion and had, therefore, already been displaced before Copernicus took up the question.

It should be emphasized that what has been presented here is the barest *qualitative* description of the Ptolemaic system. As such, it had been known since the twelfth century. Its quantitative dimension had not been developed until the fifteenth century. By that time, Arabic refinements, new (and often erroneous) observations had been added to astronomy and the ability of the mathematical astronomer to deal with the "fit" between observation and theory had been greatly enhanced by the revival of Hellenistic mathematics. Thus, at the time that Copernicus began his astronomical work, Ptolemaic astronomy was both old (qualitatively) and new (quantitatively). Copernicus appeared just at the time when it was becoming clear that the old and the new could not be combined. For, no matter what mathematical tricks were tried, theory and observation could not be brought together. There was always a discrepancy between calculated position and position given in the observational tables. Often, the discrepancy was the result of faulty observation but that fact did not become clear until new,

systematic and accurate observations were made.   Thus was created one source of the tension in astronomy which Copernicus
sought to relieve by removing the Earth from the center of the
cosmos.

A second source of concern to astronomers and to those interested in the heavens was the difficulty of reconciling the
Ptolemaic mathematical description of the heavens with the Aristotelian physical explanation of the cosmos.   This aspect should
not be over-stressed since there appears to have been a real
split between mathematical and physical astronomers right up
through the sixteenth century.   That is to say, those who needed
to know exact planetary or solar positions for astrological, cal-
endrical or other reasons mastered the *Almagest*, did their calculations and paid little attention to the physics of the situation.
They did not need to know *why* a planet on an epicyclette moved in
a circle on an epicycle which, in turn, revolved around a point
itself located on a turning deferent.   For the mathematical
astronomer, the planets shrunk into mathematical points and the
cosmos was transformed into a mathematical fiction.   Similarly,
the natural philosopher was content with the Aristotelian system
of nesting spheres, each moving the one nearer to the center
either because of mechanical continguity or, as in Dante, as the
result of angelic commitment to circularity.   The fact that such
movements did not correspond to the actual motions of the planets
was a matter for little or no concern.   It was enough to know that
Aristotle had given the physical explanation for the circular
motions to be found in the heavens without worrying about exact
quantitative determinations of position.

Fortunately for the development of astronomy, not all astronomers or natural philosophers could be satisfied with this theoretical schizophrenia.   In the fifteenth century, the attempt
was made to bring Aristotelian homocentric spheres and Ptolemaic
eccentrics   and epicycles together into a single system.
George Peuerbach (1423-69), who died only four years before
Copernicus was born, tried to bring the two systems together in
his *New Theory of the Planets*.   The diagram below shows what
happens when the Ptolemaic circles are materialized and the
Aristotelian spheres are made subject to mathematical expecta-
tions.*

----

* Diagram and explanation from Marie Boas, *The Scientific
Renaissance 1450-1630*, London, 1962, p. 44.

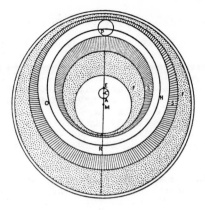

Fig. 1 The Mathematical System of the World
According to Peuerbach

M is the centre of the world, A of the equant, C of the small
circle, E of the eccentric which is movable and describes P,
the epicycle. The two dotted spheres, F,F, carry the apogee
of the equant; the two spheres S,S, carry the apogee of the
eccentric. The deferent is the white sphere lying between S
and S; its eccentric circle is OPHR.

One does not have to be hyper-critical to view this "solution"
with a somewhat jaundiced eye. Peuerbach's collection of eccentric and oddly aligned spheres for *one planet* might be reconcilable both with Aristotelian physics and Ptolemaic calculations
but it must offend anyone who believed that God, as Divine Artist,
meant his creation to be beautiful and, as Divine geometer, meant
it to be simple. Note that not everyone was committed to this
aesthetic or geometrical view. Clearly Peuerbach was happy with
his synthesis or he would not have published it. If an astronomer yearned for physical and mathematical unity in astronomy,
Peuerbach had provided it. One merely had to be willing to accept a rather messy aesthetic and complicated geometrical result.
Fortunately for astronomy, Nicholas Copernicus could not accept
either. His system was intended to be both aesthetically and
geometrically pleasing. It was not, significantly, to be any
more accurate mathematically than Ptolemy's nor was it to be as
physically satisfying as Aristotle's. Therein lay Copernicus'
importance. He provided an alternative cosmological vision,
based upon his own particular aesthetic, philosophical and practical preferences, which raised far more questions than it answered. The conservative astronomers rejected it for this reason.
A few were fascinated by the new questions for reasons of their
own and it was they who turned Copernicus' conservative synthesis
into a revolutionary new world view.

2. Copernicus and the *De Revolutionibus Orbium Coelestium*

The European learned community had indications of what was
to come before the publication of the *De Revolutionibus*. Copernicus had presented the main qualitative results of his system
earlier in a treatise entitled the *Commentariolus*, with only
brief reference to the more quantitative aspects. This manuscript and its copies appear to have enjoyed a fairly wide circulation and also to have failed to stir up significant reaction.
In 1541, Copernicus permitted another, younger astronomer,
Rheticus, to publish a *First Account* (Narratio Prima) of his
system. Again the basic qualitative theory of a sun-centered
astronomy was presented, in a somewhat leisurely rambling style.
Finally, in 1543, the year of Copernicus' death, the full text of
the *De Revolutionibus* appeared. The first book of the work consisted of general discussion and description, with the full mathematical treatment left to the following five books. Thus, by
the middle of the sixteenth century, there were available three
accounts of the new astronomy for those more interested or impressed by concepts and ideas than by calculations. Most of
those who were converted to Copernican astronomy were converted
by these texts rather than by the elaborate and extended mathematical treatment which supplemented them. The reason for this
is simple; the mathematical treatment was not very persuasive.
The mathematics of the *De Revolutionibus* consisted of painstaking
recalculation of all the observed motions of the heavenly bodies
to take into account the heliocentric rather than geocentric universe. Modern historians have shown that Copernicus was not always as adept a mathematician as his ancient predecessor. More
importantly, they have also pointed out that the mathematics of
the Copernican and Ptolemaic systems are very similar and there
is no great mathematical advantage to the Copernican over the
Ptolemaic cosmos. Both systems used complex schemes of eccentrics and epicycles to describe the motion of each heavenly body
separately. The Copernican system did contain a smaller number
of epicycles and Copernicus refused to employ the equant because
he felt this to be an improper astronomical device. There were
no overwhelming mathematical differences between the two systems
and there were no rapid conversions to the Copernican system
among the mathematical astronomers of the sixteenth century.
Those who were concerned with mathematical accuracy found little
improvement in the Copernican system and chose to continue calculations on the basis of the more familiar Ptolemaic system.
Most mathematical astronomers were primarily concerned with calculations, so the qualitative arguments for sun-centered order
and simplicity were not sufficient reasons for change.
Those few sixteenth century natural philosophers who did
become Copernicans converted because they agreed with arguments
about the harmony and simplicity of the universe God created.
On the qualitative level, the Copernican system was impressive.
It resolves all the major observational irregularities described
in such mathematical detail into simple apparently observed irregularities which do not occur in fact but only because of the
visual effects of the earth's motions. The earth has three
motions, the revolution about the sun, the rotation on its axis

and the motion of the earth's axis itself. When these three motions were taken into account, the Copernican astronomer realized that the heavenly motions were indeed regular, circular and eternal; they just appeared not to be because of the earth's motion.

The Copernican system had its most obvious and profound effect upon the consideration of the motion of the planets. Copernicus considered the description of planetary motion to be a major achievement of his astronomy. The Ptolemaic system had treated the motions of each of the planets separately. The motion of each bore no connection to the others. A planet simply performed its own retrograde motion, change in orbital motion and change in brightness alone in its progress in the heavens. The planets were ordered in distance from the earth by the lengths of their periods of revolution around the earth. But there was no explanation for this ordering.

The Copernican hypothesis established a relationship between the planets and between the planets and the earth. The shorter the period of revolution around the sun, the nearer the planet must be to the sun. Thus, the order of the planets from the sun was: Mercury, Venus, Earth, Mars, Jupiter, Saturn. The Earth now separated the inferior planets closer to the sun from the superior planets, further away. This establishment of an order to the planets was essential to a new understanding of the observed phenomena of planetary motion. Retrograde motion was now an appearance, with the earth overtaking a superior planet or an inferior planet overtaking the Earth. (See Diagram) The observed change in brightness of the planets especially of Venus, the morning and evening star, could now be easily explained by the differences in distance between the Earth and Venus, in different positions of the Earth's and Venus's orbit. The variations in periods of revolution of the superior planets was also now dramatically explained in terms of the Earth's own orbital motion.

Qualitatively, then, the Copernican theory provided most of the answers to puzzling astronomical questions in simple terms. More importantly, it restored a sense of wholeness and harmony to the cosmos. One of the great motives for the pursuit of science is the search for wholeness, for that underlying unity that almost every scientist is convinced must exist. And, since it was a toss-up between Ptolemy and Copernicus as far as the mathematics went, we might expect this to have led many astronomers to convert to Copernicanism. But, as we know, this was not the case. The reasons, again, are fairly easy to understand. The wholeness of the Copernican system was purchased at the expense, not of mathematics, but of physics. The questions that now were raised did not involve a contest between Copernicus and Ptolemy, but between Copernicus and Aristotle. For, in order to make his cosmos work, Copernicus had to abandon the old Aristotelian physics. He had little that he could substitute for it. [See Readings, p. 153ff.] We shall, here, only raise some of these questions so that the reader may be alert for Copernicus' answers.

The first question is why should the Earth go around the Sun or turn on its axis? There is no obvious answer and it was a

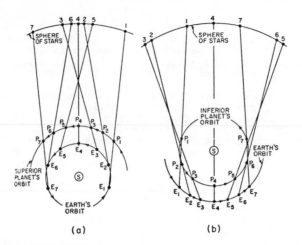

(a)   (b)

Figure 2 The Copernican explanation of retrograde motion for
(a) superior planets and (b) inferior planets. In each diagram
the earth moves steadily on its orbit from E_1 to E_7 and the
planet moves from P_1 to P_7. Simultaneously the planet's apparent
position against the stellar sphere shifts eastward from 1 to 7,
but as the two planets pass there is a brief westward retrogression from 3 to 5.*

question which was not to be answered until the appearance of
Isaac Newton's *Principia* in 1687. More subtle, but of almost
equal importance, were the questions raised concerning terrestrial
physics. Why, for example, should a stone fall to the Earth?
Aristotle, at least, had an answer--because the Earth was at the
center of the cosmos (its natural place) and, therefore, a piece
of earth went to its natural place. But if the Earth were a planet, then there was no natural place for the stone since the Earth
was constantly in motion. This meant that the whole doctrine of
natural places must be suspect. This, in turn, implied the
destruction of the natural hierarchy of the world, by which Aristotle had climbed from formless, inert earth, through the other
elements, the celestial spheres and the heavenly regions to God.
Order and hierarchy were the very cornerstones of sixteenth century orthodoxy, not only in science, but in politics and religion
as well. Was all this to be sacrificed merely because a Polish
Canon was aesthetically and philosophically so inclined? Certainly not until there was a new physics to force the issue--and even
then, only reluctantly. We may here skip ahead a century, to
witness the anguish which such a step entailed. In his *Anatomie
of the World*, another Canon, this time of the English Church,

---

* Diagram from Thomas S. Kuhn, *The Copernican Revolution* (Cambridge: Harvard University Press, 1957), Figure 32.

wrote:
>The New Philosophy calls all in doubt,
>The Element of Fire is quite put out;
>The Sun is lost, and the Earth, and no man's wit
>Can well direct him where to look for it.
>And freely men confess that this world's spent
>When in the Planets and the Firmament
>They seek so many new; then see that this
>Is crumbled out again to his Atomies.
>Tis all in pieces, all coherence gone;
>All just supply and all relation:
>Prince, Subject, Father, Son, are things forgot
>For every man alone thinks he hath got
>To be a Phoenix, and that then can be
>None of that kind, of which he is, but he.

John Donne's reaction, no doubt, was extreme but it clearly reveals that there was far more at stake than a few abstruse astronomical questions. The Copernican system necessarily implied the destruction of Aristotelian physics, and the destruction of Aristotelian physics appeared to involve the dissolution of the intellectual bonds that held the contemporary social and political world together.

Yet, if the Copernican system were true, might it not be best to accept it and its consequences? Was there not some simple observational test that could decide between the rival astronomical theories? The answer was, yes, and it was almost immediately applied. If the earth did move around the Sun then there ought to be a perceptible angle difference when a fixed star is observed from the Earth at opposite sides of the Earth's orbit. This angle, called stellar parallax, would be conclusive proof that the Earth did move and that Copernicus was right. One might assume that the opposite, namely failure to detect stellar parallax would "prove" that the Copernican system was false. No parallax could be detected.* But devout Copernicans (including Copernicus himself) did not find this to be an overwhelming fact. It could be handled simply by assuming that the Universe was a lot larger than had hitherto been supposed. Really radical Copernicans, like the Englishman Thomas Digges (d. 1595) and the Italian Giordano Bruno (c. 1548-1600) went farther than the master himself who had simply moved the sphere of the fixed stars outwards to accommodate the failure to detect parallax. They broke the outer sphere entirely and distributed the "fixed" stars in three dimensions throughout infinite space. The old limited cosmos was destroyed to be replaced by a universe so large that the mind could not encompass it. To the revolutionaries, this was an intoxicating vision; to the orthodox, it was almost more than man could bear. We must not forget that all this astronomical speculation occurred during the century when Protestantism was born and religious wars became common. The old cosmos had been worked into the fabric of Catholic orthodoxy and the new universe appeared to challenge this orthodoxy. Giordano Bruno was burned by the Inquisition for his religious writings, but a new dimension was

---

* Stellar parallax was first measured by Friedrich Wilhelm Bessel in 1838.

added to the debate. It was clear that caution should accompany espousal of the new astronomy.

3. Astronomy After Copernicus

To return to Copernicanism, there were two paths along which astronomy developed in the sixteenth century after the discovery that no observation could either prove or disprove Copernicanism. One was to forget theory for the moment and concentrate on the compilation of accurate observations. Perhaps after that task was performed the data would permit new theoretical adventures. This was the path followed by Tycho Brahe and his young assistant, Johann Kepler. The second path was to promote Copernicanism by attacking and discrediting Aristotelianism. When Aristotelian physics had been destroyed, it might be possible to erect a new physics on the ground thus cleared and, thereby, answer some of the fundamental physical questions the Copernican doctrine had raised. This was the path followed by Galileo Galilei.

Tycho Brahe (1546-1601), a Danish nobleman, was probably the greatest observational astronomer that ever lived. Against his family's wishes, he taught himself astronomy and made his first observations with self-made instruments because his tutor refused him the money to purchase them. These observations, made at the age of 16, were sufficiently accurate to reveal the discrepancies between what he saw and measured and what the best available astronomical tables gave. It was, however, the appearance of a Nova in the constellation of Cassiopeia in 1572 which concentrated all of Tycho's considerable energies on observational astronomy. His account of this phenomenon led the king of Denmark to give Tycho the island of Hveen upon which Tycho built Uraniborg, a castle devoted to astronomy and alchemy. Tycho himself oversaw the construction and mounting of enormous instruments which allowed him to achieve previously unheard-of precision in his observations. At his peak, Tycho could routinely observe to within 4' of arc which is just about the limit of naked eye observational ability.

During the years at Hveen during which he observed and charted the heavens assiduously, Tycho achieved two things. He established the supralunary nature of comets, as he had established the supralunary nature of the new star of 1572. He also piled up a mass of accurate observations which Kepler was to exploit after his death.

Since the time of Aristotle, comets had been assumed to be "meteors," that is, appearances in the air between the earth and the moon, produced by terrestrial exhalations or some other similar vague cause. Aristotle, it will be remembered, following Plato, had insisted upon the perfection and immutability of the heavens, thus forcing comets into a sub-lunary position. In 1577, a comet appeared and Tycho was ready for it. He had already shown that the Nova of 1572 was in the "perfect and immutable" heavens, and he now proceeded to prove that the comet was as well. One blow had been struck at the Aristotelian system for the heavens might be perfect but they could not, henceforth, be considered immutable. By itself, this was a small point but it was later to be joined by other, weightier criticisms whose total force was overwhelming. More important than the proof of celestial mutability was the fact that Tycho also followed the comet in its course and showed that it passed through the orbs of Saturn, Jupiter and Mars. This was really a shock for the orthodox since it meant that the Aristotelian (and Copernican) crystalline spheres in which the planets were assumed to be embedded must be given up. Planets became spheres in space and the Aristotelians were now faced with precisely the same physical problem as were the Copernicans. Why should an isolated ball, like Jupiter or Saturn, circle round the earth? Without the old concentric spheres moved by the *primum mobile*, the Aristotelian found himself unable to give a convincing answer. Tycho did not. He calmly ignored the problem his own observations had created and set forth his own theory. (See diagram.)

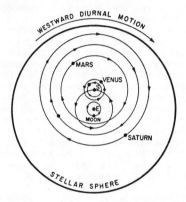

Figure 3 The Tychonic system. The earth is once again at the center of a rotating stellar sphere, and the moon and sun move in their old Ptolemaic orbits. The other planets are, however, fixed on epicycles whose common center is the sun.*

The Tychonic theory was a curious blend of the orthodox and the revolutionary, and it appealed to precisely those who could not accept the clearly ridiculous "fact" that the earth moved but who also had to accept the conclusions of Tycho's work on comets. It was to remain influential well into the seventeenth century.

Tycho began from the common-sense truth that the Earth is stationary. Were it to revolve upon its axis, stones would not fall to the bases of towers, and they obviously did. Similarly, the lack of parallax was sufficient proof for Tycho that the Earth was at the center of the cosmos and did not move. Given this fundamental truth, Tycho went on to shift the center of planetary revolutions from the Earth to the Sun. Thus the Earth

---

* From Kuhn, Figure 37.

remained at rest in the center of the universe; the moon went around the Earth; the Sun went around the Earth; but all the planets revolved around the Sun. It was an ingenious theory for it is mathematically equivalent to both the Copernican and Ptolemaic systems and also solves some of the problems that the Copernican system had solved. Difference in brightness of the planets, for example, was the result of considerable differences in the distances of the planets from the Earth, just as in the Copernican system. Thus one could preserve a small, limited cosmos with all the implications of this for theology and for man's centrality and, at the same time, construct a workable astronomical model. All one had to do was resolutely steer clear of physics and stop worrying about *why* the Sun and the planets revolved and wondering what kept them in their orbits.

Since Tycho's system was equivalent to Ptolemy's and Copernicus', it suffered from the same disabilities. Computations based upon the Tychonic model did not exactly fit the observations. It was to remedy this situation that Brahe's assistant, Johann Kepler (1571-1630), turned to Tycho's observations of Mars determined to find the true orbit of this planet. There is some irony that the laborious task of computation from observations was undertaken by Kepler in 1601. The irony lies in the fact that Kepler was a Neo-pythagorean mathematical mystic who was convinced that God, the divine Geometer, had filled His universe with marvelous mathematical relationships. The natural tendency of such a mind is to "discover" these relationships by deducing them from indubitable axioms, rather than by uncovering them hidden in masses of factual observations. Kepler was not wholly innocent of this practice. One of his greatest discoveries, he thought, was the "fact" that the orbits of the planets fit within the Platonic five regular solids arranged around these orbits. The "fit" here between facts and theory was very loose and Kepler seems to have been content to leave it that way.

The orbit of Mars presented Kepler with a different problem. Here he had ample, accurate data and he had learned from the aged Tycho that he could ignore the data only at the expense of truth. And so he started to calculate. He naturally began by assuming a circular orbit. In order to account for the variation of orbital speed in Mars' journey around the Sun (for Kepler was a convinced Copernican) he assumed an eccentric circle and tried to discover where its center must be for the orbital speed to be constant with respect to the Sun. He came close, at one time finding an eccentric circular orbit in which his calculations differed only by eight minutes of arc from Tycho's observations. But, knowing that the observations were accurate to within four minutes of arc, he rejected this solution and continued his calculations. Convinced that there *must* be some regularity behind the apparently irregular variation in speed in the orbit, Kepler stumbled upon what was later to be known as Kepler's second law. Using an eccentric circle, this relationship was stated by Kepler to be that the radius vector from the Sun to the planet sweeps out equal areas in equal times. Such a relationship, as we shall see, also provided a clue for the physical cause and this Kepler

was to express with real enthusiasm. Meanwhile his search for a
circular orbit went on until Kepler realized that no circle would
fit. The new law of areas enabled Kepler to read his data in a
new light and led him to take the revolutionary step of abandon-
ing circles. After a few more false starts and one heartbreaking
case where he was prevented from discovering the right solution
because of an arithmetical mistake in his calculations, Kepler
finally was able to make the data fit a curve. The curve was not
a circle, but a higher order curve, an ellipse, with the Sun at
one focus. In 1609, he published this result in Prague in a
treatise *On the Motion of Mars*. For the first time since Ptolemy,
there was made available a mathematical theory of planetary
motion which permitted planetary positions to be calculated with
greater accuracy than those estimated by the *Almagest*. Furthermore, much of the cumbersome system of both Ptolemy and Copernicus now simply disappeared. Kepler's first law that planets
moved in ellipses together with the second law of equal areas
removed the need for eccentrics, epicycles, equants and all the
other emergency geometric devices pressed into service by generations of mathematical astronomers. One simple, beautiful curve
ruled all and Kepler could and did celebrate God's wisdom and
mathematical finesse as evidenced in His creation.

There was one element lacking. The first and second laws
testified to the mathematical harmonies of individual planetary
motion but it did nothing to add to the sense of a planetary system. Kepler, like Copernicus, accepted the obvious fact that
planetary periods of revolution were direct indications of their
distances from the Sun. His earlier "discovery" that these distances bore some relation to the spheres within which the five
regular solids could be inscribed provided a rough relationship
tying the planets together. But it was a very rough "fit" and
Kepler was not happy with it. Surely there must be another
mathematical harmony that would reveal the essential unity of the
Solar system. By 1619, when he published his *Harmonies of the
World*, Kepler had found it. The squares of the periods of the
planets were proportional to the cube of their mean radius. Or,
to put it another way,

$$\frac{T_1^2}{T_2^2} = \frac{r_1^3}{r_2^3}$$

This relationship, Kepler's third law, provides the mathematical
tie that binds all six planets together into a single harmonious
whole. Kepler, indeed, was so intoxicated by his discovery of
this harmony that he set out to make it literally audible. If
notes are assigned to the periods and the mean radii according to
the proportions given in the third law, then the harmony of the
spheres may be expressed in straightforward musical terms according to the laws of classical harmonic theory. The Earth, Kepler
found, sang the notes *mi*, *fa*, *mi* standing for misery and famine.
Considering that the Thirty Years' War had just begun, this insight, too, seemed valuable to Kepler.

By 1620, the Keplerian revolution, if we may use this term,

was complete. In many ways, it was far more revolutionary than the Copernican disturbance had been. Copernicus, after all, had only violated a few of the principles of Aristotelian physics while clinging to the central dogma that heavenly motions had to be circular. Kepler's three laws not only blew up the whole of Aristotelian cosmology but also entailed the destruction of Aristotelian physics as well. There was simply *no* Aristotelian explanation for elliptical orbits and *no* Aristotelian way to derive the Law of areas and the Law of periods and radii. And, most importantly, these laws were not mere hypotheses but grounded firmly on the most accurate astronomical data then available. One would think that these facts would have signaled the end of Aristotelianism but it was not that simple. To be sure, Aristotelianism could not deal with Kepler's laws but what these laws were was not immediately apparent. Kepler did not simply derive them from his data. We must not forget that he was a mathematical mystic and his three laws are embedded in a mass of difficult and, to some, incomprehensible Latin prose. It is important to note that although Kepler's laws are empirical, what drove Kepler to their enunciation was his firmly-held belief in the essential mathematical harmony of the world. And, it is this belief that fills his work and gives it its unique character. There were few astronomers in the sixteenth and early seventeenth centuries who were as intoxicated with the idea of God, the Divine Pythagorean mathematician, as was Kepler. Most astronomers simply were not willing to plow through pages of what they must have considered nonsense in the hope of discovering one or two golden nuggets hidden there. The result was that Kepler's three laws and many of his important physical arguments accounting for them were not widely known until after his death. It was not until the mid-1660's, for example, that real knowledge of Kepler's work reached England. The classic case is Galileo. Galileo was vitally interested in the new astronomy and Kepler even went so far as to attempt to strike up a scientific correspondence with him, but Galileo seemingly was not interested. In part, it was probably because Kepler's devotion to ultimate harmonies repelled him, although Galileo was no mean disciple of mathematics himself. But Galileo's hero was Archimedes, not Pythagoras; Galileo was more tough-minded on the role of mathematics in science than was Kepler. Part of his lack of interest in Kepler's work no doubt also was the result of his own attack on the Aristotelian cosmos. It differed appreciably from Kepler's. Where Kepler, by 1620, had proved that Aristotle couldn't be right (nor could Copernicus) when it came to orbits, Galileo used his celestial observations to attack Aristotle's physics and support Copernicus' model. It is possible that Galileo knew Kepler's first Law, but ellipses had no more place in Galileo's heaven than they did in Aristotle's.

Galileo (1564-1642), like Kepler, seems to have been an early convert to Copernicanism for much the same reasons; it was aesthetically more satisfying and it appeared to be more mathematically appealing. One senses in Galileo a further reason, namely a willingness to entertain novelty for its own sake and to use new ideas to bedevil his teachers and his colleagues. There is a certain combativeness about Galileo, absent in Kepler, which was to drive him into polemical disputes and also contribute to his later troubles with the Church.

Be that as it may, Galileo's Copernicanism remained largely an article of faith about which he could argue, but little of which he could support with facts until 1609. It was in that year that he heard that a Northerner had combined lenses together to produce a new instrument which made distant objects appear close up. Galileo immediately set out to duplicate this instrument and was able to construct a telescope of about 30X. When he looked at the heavens, he made a series of startling discoveries. The moon was not a perfect crystalline sphere, but had mountains just like the Earth (1609). The planet Venus displayed phases just like the moon (announced 1612). The Sun had spots on it which moved in such a way that it was difficult to avoid the conclusion that the Sun turned on its own axis (announced 1612). Jupiter was accompanied by four moons which circled it, just as our moon moved around the earth (January 1610). These discoveries were published in two treatises, the *Sidereal Messenger* and the *Letters on Sunspots*. Together they delivered a body blow to the Aristotelian cosmos. The mountains on the moon and the spots on the Sun, unlike a comet or a Nova, were permanent features of these bodies not ephemeral "appearances" which might be explained away. The heavenly bodies were *not* perfect and immutable; indeed, they looked much like the Earth with projections and blemishes. For those who would look and listen, the last Aristotelian sphere was shattered, namely, the one that divided the corruptible, changeable Earth from the incorruptible, immutable heavens. Henceforth, except for the most conservative, there was no spatial hierarchy but uniformity and, by implication, whatever were the physical laws that applied on this planet would be found to apply throughout the Solar system.

The discovery of the rotation of the Sun and of the moons of Jupiter had even more far-reaching implications. If solar rotation were accepted (and not everyone accepted Galileo's arguments here), then a question immediately raised itself--why? There is no Aristotelian answer and one might, then, gain some solace from the Copernican idea that it is the nature of spheres to roll! Similarly, there is no Aristotelian explanation of the revolution of the moons of Jupiter. Celestial bodies were supposed to go around the Earth or, at least in the Tychonic system, first around the Sun and then around the Earth. But the moons of Jupiter clearly went around Jupiter and why this was so was impossible to explain. It should be emphasized that Galileo, as yet, could not give an explanation either but that was no problem. He was using this case to attack the Aristotelian scheme and there was no necessity for him to explain the phenomenon.

The moons of Jupiter, therefore, were a severe embarrassment for Aristotelian theory. They did not "prove" the Copernican theory but they did prepare the way for the acceptance of Copernicanism by those who were willing to settle for less than proven Truth. There was no doubt that the moons of Jupiter *did* revolve around Jupiter even though no one knew why. That fact made it a lot easier to believe that the Earth and the planets went around

the Sun, even though no one knew why. One could believe the fact
without an explanation. Such belief, however, created considerable pressure for an explanation to be forthcoming. Such an explanation, however, required nothing less than the forging of an
entirely new physics. This was to be the second stage in the
acceptance of the Copernican Revolution and was to mark the high
point of the Scientific Revolution.

4. The Birth of a New Physics

Having already noted the conservative features of the Copernican Revolution, we should underline here its revolutionary implications. For some questions, such as the why of the diurnal
or annual revolutions of the Earth, Copernicus could give only
guesses that lacked conviction. He did, however, try to face
squarely the physical consequences of moving the Earth from the
center of the cosmos and, in so doing, suggested an idea which
was to grow in importance until it became the cornerstone of the
new physics. By destroying the idea of natural places, Copernicus destroyed the Aristotelian explanation of gravity. A clod
of earth could not fall to any one "place" in the cosmos since
the Earth was constantly in motion. Hence, the observable fact
that a stone does fall to the Earth must mean that earth goes to
Earth, and not to a specific place in the cosmos reserved for
earth and Earth. That like substances attract like was a doctrine at least as old as Empedocles, but in the Copernican context it took on new dimensions. If earth went to Earth, then
moon material ought to go to the Moon, pieces of Jupiter to
Jupiter, and so on. Each celestial body attracted its own and
for the doctrine of natural places Copernicus substituted a multitude of centers of attraction. Using hindsight, we can make
the enormous theoretical leap that took a century and a quarter
from centers of attraction to universal gravitation. All we need
do is to insist that Earth material, Moon material, Jupiter
material, etc., are not all different but all essentially the
same. Then all matter will attract all other matter and we will
have arrived at Newtonian gravitation. That is the path of
logic, but it was not the path of history, for it was only after
many a twisting, winding and dead end that the principle of universal attraction was reached. Nevertheless, the germ of the
idea--and a revolutionary idea it was--is in the *De Revolutionibus*.

The substitution of a force--dimly and fuzzily perceived--
for a place led to two important developments. Johann Kepler
used it to answer the question of why the Earth went around the
Sun; Galileo used it to answer the question of why the Earth
turned on its axis. Both answers were "wrong" but both contributed to the "right" answer which Isaac Newton gave.

Kepler's attention was drawn to the problem of accounting
for the Earth's annual revolution both by his deep physical intuition and the specific problem of the variation of the Earth's
speed in its orbit. Kepler was forever asking "why?" and, unlike
Tycho Brahe, he could not simply describe an orbit and forget the
physics of it. There must be a reason why the Earth and the

other planets revolved around the Sun and Kepler was determined
to find it. The clue he needed was provided by the English
physician William Gilbert whose treatise *On the Magnet*, published
in 1600, was a model of experimental investigation of this
strange object. Here were to be found attractions and repulsions
which appeared to have cosmic implications. The Earth, Gilbert
showed, was itself a giant magnet and magnetism looked like a
fundamental source of motion in the universe. Suppose, Kepler
argued, that the Earth, as a magnet, were affected by a magnetic
virtue *(anima)* emanating from the Sun. This virtue, sweeping
around the cosmos as the Sun turned, would diminish with distance
from the Sun, thus accounting for the increase in periods of the
planets with distance from the Sun. Then, given the fact that
planets moved in ellipses with the Sun at one focus, it followed
that the planets would move faster near the focus (apogee) than
when they were farther from it (perigee). Qualitatively, this
was a seductive scheme and Kepler was delighted with it. To
others, it looked suspiciously like magic, with its "influences"
and virtues and anima. No one could deny the facts of magnetism
but few were willing to go so far as Kepler. Again, it was not
until the 1660's that Kepler's ideas became well known but this
was in good time for them to be appreciated by Newton.

Galileo took a bolder and more imprecise path in his cam-
paign to replace Aristotelian physics by a new science. His
Dialogue on the Great World Systems, published in 1632, summed up
decades of Galileo's thinking on astronomy and established the
new cosmology. It is, in many ways, a curious book for a cosmological and astronomical treatise. It was, first of all, written
in elegant Italian, not Latin, and this alone announced it as a
work intended for a far wider audience than professional astronomers. As the title states, it is cast in the form of a dialogue
between three Italian gentlemen of good breeding and education.
Salviati clearly presents Galileo's views; Simplicio is an orthodox Aristotelian and Sagredo serves as the questioning interlocu-
tor. This form permitted Galileo to avoid certain problems. It
was obviously not possible, in a "popular" treatise and within
the dialogue form to deal with all the mathematical complexities
of either the Ptolemaic or the Copernican system. Indeed, although the "debate" is supposed to be between the advocate of the
Copernican and the advocate of the Ptolemaic system, there is
little Ptolemy to be found. The real issue is joined over Aristotelian *physics*, not astronomy at all. Thus the reader will
find little mention of epicycles, eccentrics, equants or any of
the complicated mathematical apparatus which makes the *Almagest*
a landmark in the history of mathematical astronomy. Instead,
his attention will be drawn to the fundamental question which
Galileo is determined to answer--namely, can the rotation of the
Earth on its axis and the revolution of the Earth around the Sun
be accepted as true by an intelligent person? If so, how can
these motions be accounted for?

It should here be recalled that the two Copernican motions
of the Earth had been ruled out in Aristotelian physics by the
idea of the strict division of the cosmos into two separate
physical spheres. Above the sphere of the moon, bodies moved

naturally and eternally in circles. Below the lunar sphere straight line motion, to or from the center of the Earth was the rule. Galileo's attack on this system was both bold and imaginative. His astronomical observations had already convinced him of the essential unity of matter and motion throughout the universe and he now attempted to prove this by physical argument rather than observations which could be interpreted in many ways. There were, essentially, two ways to go about this. He could either have extended the terrestrial motions to the heavens or bring the heavenly motions down to Earth. Had he done the former, he would have soon reached an impasse. To have assumed the primacy of straight-line motion would have prevented him from accounting for any of the celestial motions. It was not until the principle of inertia and the concept of force were clarified later in the seventeenth century that curvilinear motion could be deduced from rectilinear motion. So, Galileo chose the other way. He baldly stated that *all* motion was circular and that rectilinear motion was an illusion! His argument is rather delightfully Aristotelian. Salviati first agrees with Aristotle that the cosmos is perfectly ordered and then goes on:

> This principle then established, one may immediately conclude that, if the integral components should be by their nature movable, it is impossible that their motions should be straight or other than circular. This reason is sufficiently easy and manifest; for whatever moves with a straight motion changes place and, continuing to move, moves by degrees farther away from the term from whence it departed and from all the places through which it has successively passed. If such motion naturally suited with it, then it was not, in the beginning, in its proper place; and so the parts of the world were not disposed with perfect order. But we suppose them to be perfectly ordered; therefore, as such, it is impossible that by nature they should change place and consequently move in a straight motion.*

Phase one--the breaking of the dichotomy between celestial and terrestrial motion--has been accomplished by this rather neat circular argument. And, as Galileo promptly pointed out, the Aristotelian distinction between celestial and terrestrial physics was based on this distinction between the natural motions of celestial and terrestrial objects. Therefore, the distinction was invalid and there was but one set of laws for the universe as a whole. Hence, Galileo could agree with Copernicus that there was nothing physically improbable about each planet and star attracting its own parts, just as the Earth did. We are here, again, but a step away from the principle of universal attraction.

The establishment of a universal law of motion had the further effect of destroying Aristotle's hierarchical space. There were, henceforth, no privileged places (with the possible exception of the Sun) and space became Euclidean--that is, indifferent to objects in it. Up and down were no longer absolute directions,

---

* Galileo Galilei, *Dialogue on the Great World Systems*, in the Translation of T. Salisbury, Edited by Giorgio de Santillana, Chicago, 1953, p. 23.

but were to be specified in terms of some particular frame of reference.

All this was very well and very general but what of the "facts"? Could Galileo's universalization of circular motion come to grips with the supposed consequences of, say, the diurnal motion of the Earth? Would not buildings and trees fly off the Earth if it rotated at the required speed? Would not a ball dropped from a tower fall far to the West of the tower as the Earth spins from West to East? Such questions could not be answered by general arguments on perfection or circles. They had to be met squarely head on and this Galileo did. To do so, he had to introduce a concept similar to inertia, but it is a peculiar kind of inertia. Suppose, he argued, that an ideal ball rolled down an ideal inclined plane from any height, h, and then rolled up another such plane. By intuition, if all fractional and resistance forces are removed, the ball would go up the second plane to h and, like a pendulum, would continue forever to oscillate back and forth on the two planes. This movement is not dependent on the angle of inclination of either plane. If the second plane is now made horizontal, then h can never be reached and the ball will roll forever. Horizontal, be it noted, means parallel to the Earth's surface and this makes the ball's path a great circle. Thus we are led back to circular motion and this "natural" motion is now inertial motion. This is why a ball, when dropped from a tower, falls at the foot of the tower and does not fall to the West. When it is let fall, it is as though it were rolling on that ideal horizontal plane and it continued to move around the Earth (with the tower) as it falls. Hence it falls at the bottom of the tower. What looks like straight-line motion is only apparently so. To an observer off the Earth, the motion would be curvilinear. Here, again, Galileo struck a blow against Aristotelian physics by insisting that motions could be combined into a resultant motion. It was this insight that led him to the solution of the problem of projectile motion which had vexed generations of Aristotelians.

This argument, of course, did not answer the objection that objects would fly off a spinning Earth. Galileo, here, asserted another principle, namely that centrifugal force was a function solely of angular velocity. The Earth spun through 360° in a day and if a potter's wheel were to spin that slowly, no one would expect it to throw off pieces of clay. The argument is a convincing one, even if it is totally wrong physically.

The final triumph of Galileo's principle of circular motions is the ease with which it accounts for the revolution of the Earth around the Sun. If the "ball" that rolls down the inclined plane in the beginning is the Earth itself, then it will continue to move in a circle around the Sun eternally. Thus Copernicus was vindicated and the Copernican system shown to be in perfect accord with the new physics. Circular inertia was the key and Galileo built his cosmology around it.

The results of the system proposed in the *Dialogue* are impressive and deserve to be summarized. Space was redefined. It was no longer place—that is, it no longer drew its qualities from the objects that occupied it but became the neutral theater wherein matter moved. Direction was relative, not absolute, and for motion to be correctly described a frame of reference had to be specified. The notion of circular inertia not only provided the answer to the most important questions raised by Copernicanism, but also changed the whole status of motion in physics. In Aristotelian physics, only rest required no explanation. If an object moved, it moved for a reason and the goal of Aristotelian physics was to discover these reasons. In Galileo's physics, some motions were like rest, they required no reasons. Motion in a circle just *was*. What the physicist had to explain were *changes* in motion in a basically dynamic universe. In the *Dialogue*, Galileo could only indicate the qualitative aspects of his physics. Six years later, in the *Discourses Concerning Two New Sciences*, he provided the quantitative basis. [See Readings, p. 205.] Here he derived the law of free fall from strictly dynamic considerations. The *Dialogue* was persuasive but not free from objection. The *Discourses* were axiomatic but narrow. In effect, Galileo asked his readers to accept the new cosmology on the basis of qualitative argument and the hard laws of free fall and projectile motion. Did it necessarily follow that because $S = \frac{1}{2}gt^2$ was both true and incapable of being derived from Aristotle's laws of motion, that the whole of Aristotle had to be rejected and the new cosmology swallowed whole? That was essentially what Galileo was asking and there were still many who could not accept this. The fact that Galileo, himself, refused to bow to Kepler's First Law because it would have destroyed his whole argument was sufficient cause for hesitation. The Galilean cosmology persuaded those who were already converted and it sharpened the arguments between Copernicans and non-Copernicans, but it did not win the battle. There were still many questions to be answered before either the new physics or the new cosmology could become the new science.

5. The Great Syntheses--Descartes and Newton

Kepler and Galileo had delivered fatal blows to the old physics, but they had not succeeded in "replacing" it because they simply had nothing to replace it with. But, if they could not substitute a whole new cosmology for the one they had so successfully attacked, they could argue that they had (finally) established an age-old approach as one that paid off in scientific terms. The old dream of the Pythagoreans, Platonists and apostles of Archimedes now seemed finally on the verge of being realized. Kepler's three laws did seem to prove that mathematics was the key to the cosmos, and Galileo's derivation of certain of the laws of motion also appeared to establish the fertility of the mathematical approach. The seventeenth century natural philosophers were to grasp eagerly at these examples and, by emulating them, attempt to strip the veil from Nature once and for all. The key, of course, lay in the development of mathematics and it is no coincidence that the seventeenth century was one of the great centuries for the progress of mathematics, as well as for the rise of modern science.

The mathematical way to physical truth bears examination

before we speak of the evolution of mathematics itself. There
are essentially two ways in which mathematics may be brought to
bear on physical examination. One is the Keplerian in which the
assumption is simply made that the ultimate relationships in the
world are mathematical. Here, all is grist for the physico-
mathematical philosopher's mill. He will find ratios, harmonies
and mathematical beauties wherever he looks, as Kepler did. The
important point is that he must look. This approach could lead
to the wedding of the empiricist and the mathematician, as it did
in Kepler's case. His three laws, Boyle's Law, Charles' Law, the
Law of Dulong and Petit and a host of others familiar to every
scientist fit into this category. It should be noted that both
the empirical and the mathematical ingredients in the formulation of these laws is crucial. Without the discovery of the
facts of the case, the law could not be enunciated. Without the
firm belief in the existence of a mathematical expression for
these facts, only a "natural history" or Table of Instances in
the Baconian sense would emerge from empirical investigations.
No data are ever perfect. There are always variations from the
"law" because of experimental error, imprecision of instruments
and a number of other causes. It is only the ultimate faith in
the mathematical nature of physical laws that allows one to
smooth out these discrepancies and enunciate a law. The difference between $S = \frac{1}{2}gt^2$ and $S = 1/1.987 \, gt^2$ is more than .013 in
the denominator. The first affirms a faith that nature is ultimately mathematical; the second merely states that certain
things can be represented by numbers. For the seventeenth century, the two were not the same. Had S really involved a factor
1/1.987, it is possible that many men would have lost heart and
reverted to a quasi-Aristotelian qualitative physics.

Galileo's approach differed from that of Kepler's. To be
sure, he had originally derived the law of free fall from measurements with balls rolling down inclined planes but that had
not satisfied him. If, as he insisted more than once, the book
of Nature were really written in the language of mathematics,
then Nature, like mathematics, must be axiomatic. Natural Laws
must not only be expressible in mathematical terms, they must be
derivable from first principles. Galileo's position here is
somewhat more austere than Kepler's. Galileo did not *really* want
to look around at the complexity and beauty and the harmony of
the universe. That can only distract the seeker after truth.
Like the old pre-Socratics, Galileo felt the appearances of the
world were deceptive and the senses, if trusted, could more often
lead the mind astray than guide it to truth. Far better to strip
Nature down to her mathematical essentials. Distinguish between
the mathematical primary qualities of size, weight and figure and
the human secondary qualities of taste, beauty and harmony. When
this distinction was made, it should be possible to derive the
laws of Nature from the primary qualities, just as it was possible to derive Euclidean geometry from a few simple axioms and
postulates. Mathematics, thereby, became more than an expression
of natural Law; it was, as well, a method for the investigation
of Nature. There is only one serious difficulty with this
approach, other than the fact that it may be entirely wrong (as

Aristotle had insisted earlier). It makes progress in physics dependent upon progress in mathematics. The natural philosopher can go only so far and so fast as his mathematical tools permit. By the seventeenth century, some things could be done fairly well. Geometry permitted the study of such subjects as hydrostatics and knowledge of the geometry of conic sections at least allowed Kepler to recognize an ellipse when he saw one emerge from Tycho's data. But, even investigation of the properties of conic sections became extremely difficult when only geometry was available. The problem of constructing tangents, sub-tangents and the understanding of the properties of curves at various points all strained geometry to the breaking point. When the attempt was made to transfer geometry to physics, it required real genius to come up with anything solid. Galileo was unable to give mathematical precision to the shape of a freely-suspended chain in which the links were of equal weight and Kepler solved the problem of finding the maximum volume of a beer keg to be constructed from given materials only after tedious labors. Neither chains nor beer kegs were really at the center of scientific concern in the seventeenth century. The key phenomenon was motion and, except for the simplest cases, the mathematical analysis of motion was impossible. Before a new physics could emerge, a new mathematics had to be invented. This was done in the seventeenth century and the two most influential mathematical innovators were Descartes and Newton.*

Essentially three things happened to mathematics in the seventeenth century: algebra came of age by the adoption of a symbolic form; Descartes invented analytical geometry and Leibniz and Newton invented the calculus.

The sixteenth century was the heroic age of algebra. Men such as Niccolo Tartaglia (1500-57), Jerome Cardan (1501-76), and Francois Viète (1540-1603) took up the old Diophantine tradition and began its transformation into modern algebra. Their work involved essentially the task of discovering and generalizing solutions to algebraic equations. Tartaglia claimed credit for discovering the solution to cubic equations. Cardan was a master at simplifying equations and, by transforming them, finding solutions. Take, for example, the equation $6x^3 - 4x^2 = 34x + 24$. By adding $6x^3 + 20x^2$ to each member and transforming the result he obtained $4x^2(3x + 4) = (2x^2 + 4x + 6)(3x + 4)$. Dividing now by $3x + 4$ he was able to obtain the solution of $x = 3$ from the resulting second-degree equation. When it is realized that Cardan's "equation" was stated in words, not symbols, his mathematical insight may be appreciated. So, too, can the contribution of the seventeenth century. The substitution of x, y, +, -, and = transformed algebra. It became possible to form concrete ideas of a function and of an equation. Algebra leaped to a new level of abstraction.

At the same time that algebra was liberated from words, Descartes freed it from geometry. Diophantine algebra had expressed geometric relations in algebraic terms. Using symbols,

---

* Gottfried Wilhelm Leibniz (1646-1716) invented the calculus independently of Newton and should be ranked with him as a mathematical innovator.

a^2 indicated an area a x a and the expansion of $(a + b)^2$ could be represented by the addition of areas $a^2 + 2ab + b^2$ (see diagram).

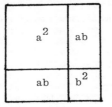

Such a system had certain disadvantages. What, for example, was one to do with powers of greater than 3? Did a^4 have any mathematical meaning when a^4 could not be represented by a geometrical model? And what did a negative quantity represent? The invention of analytic geometry by René Descartes (1596-1650) transformed the study of algebraic functions. Functions were now represented by different kinds of geometric figures--those traced out by the function when graphed. Thus $y^2 = r^2 - x^2$ did not involve squares of sides y, r and x respectively, but was the equation of a circle, given rectangular coordinates of x and y. This new analytical instrument permitted the study of algebraic functions to advance rapidly in the seventeenth century. If an algebraic equation representing a physical process could be written, the equation could be graphed and some of its properties studied. Knowledge of these properties, in turn, offered the prospect of discovering new physical relations. Take, for example, the equation describing the trajectory of a projectile, $y = x \tan a - \frac{gx^2}{2V^2 \cos a}$ where g is the gravitational constant and a the angle of elevation. When y = 0, the projectile will have landed and it is easy to show that x, the range, will be a maximum when $\frac{V^2 \sin 2a}{g}$ is a maximum, which is when a = 45°. Thus, maximum range will be attained when a cannon is elevated 45°. Finally, mathematical conclusions could be drawn sometimes from a physico-mathematical problem. In the above case, since the horizontal and vertical components of the velocity can easily be determined at every point (x, y), the angle of motion of that point can be discovered as $\tan \theta = \frac{2y_1}{x_1} - \tan a$ and this permits one to draw the tangent to the parabola at any point.

The final development in the seventeenth century, was the invention of the calculus by Newton and Leibniz. We can only note here the difference in the two men's approach. For Leibniz, the differential calculus evolved from the problem of finding tangents to curves. His approach was essentially geometrical, involving the construction of a little triangle with two sides Δx and Δy at the site of the point at which the tangent was sought. Δy and Δx shrunk to dy and dx and their ratio became the modern differential $\frac{dy}{dx}$. Newton's approach was more physical, involving the rate of a change of a function. Newton arrived at the same differential, which he wrote $\dot{y}$, but called it a fluxion and it was the method of fluxions which dominated English calculus in the eighteenth century. The calculus permitted natural philosophers to deal with the new dynamic physics by allowing them to treat the rate of change of motion of a projectile or other rates of change of other physical entities. The invention of the integral calculus, which followed hard upon the discovery of the differential, equally opened up new physical vistas. One problem here will illustrate its power. Newton felt it necessary to prove that the inverse square law of attraction held true even when the distance between two masses was small, as when an apple fell to the Earth. To do this, he had to prove that the masses of the two bodies could be considered as concentrated at their centers of gravity. This meant the integration of all the particulate forces of the Earth, a hopeless task without the integral calculus. Once proven, the inverse square law could be accepted as a law of universal application and it became the cornerstone of the Newtonian system.

The development of mathematics in the seventeenth century provided an essential tool to the development of the new physics. It did not, however, provide the fundamental ideas upon which this physics was to rest. These ideas were born from the contemplation of the physical problems inherited from Copernicus, Kepler and Galileo.

By the 1630's when Descartes began his great philosophical venture into the unknown, the old Aristotelian cosmos had been mortally wounded, especially by the attacks of Galileo. There was, however, nothing to take its place and it was Descartes' ambition to fill this void. He began with his famous method of systematic doubt by which he submitted every one of his ideas to critical scrutiny. The final term to which he ultimately came was that he could not doubt that he was doubting. From this came his *cogito ergo sum*, I think, therefore I am, which was to serve as the firm rock of his system.

Having established his own undoubted existence, Descartes deduced from it the existence of God (see Readings, p. 109) and, with God, he was able to establish an epistemology that, he hoped, guaranteed success in the philosophical venture upon which he was about to set out. The senses were untrustworthy and therefore could not serve as the basis for a true science. The unguided reason, too, was fallible because it so often started from false premises. The only source of reliable knowledge was what Descartes called clear and distinct ideas. These were innate in the human mind, planted there by God, and were, therefore, the stuff from which a new cosmology could be made with confidence. The ultimate test of philosophic truth for Descartes was whether or not the ideas involved were clear and distinct or drawn by logic from such clear and distinct ideas. It was a seductive vision and the Cartesian system did, in fact, seduce large numbers of natural philosophers in the seventeenth century. Moreover, as a complete system, it fit nicely into the intellectual hole left by the collapse of the Aristotelian cosmos.

It was in his *Principia philosophiae (Principles of Philosophy)* that Descartes laid out the main ideas of his new cosmos. (See Readings, p. 249ff.)   The first scientific "clear and distinct" idea was that of substance which had as its only essential quality, extension.   If substance is extension, then no void could exist for an extended void is a contradiction in terms. If no void could exist, then the atomic doctrine must be false for atomism necessarily implied vacua between atomic particles. Matter, therefore, must be infinitely divisible and Descartes recognized three levels of divisibility.   Gross matter was the matter of everyday life.   When this matter was divided until it was sub-sensible, it formed the moleculae of chemical science. Chemical qualities were produced by the shape and motion of these particles--acids being able to dissolve other substances, for example, because their particles were endowed with sharp points which permitted them to chisel away the particles of other bodies. The lowest level of division produced the "subtile" ether which permeated space, filling in all the voids left by grosser particles.   Pressure transmitted instantaneously through the ether produced light.

Besides extension, matter possessed the ability to move and motion was an essential aspect of material existence.   From this clear and distinct idea, Descartes deduced two consequences of fundamental importance.   The first was the enunciation of the "true" principle of inertia in which a body in motion in a straight line continues in motion in that line unless acted upon by some other body.   The second was that the total quantity of motion in the universe remained constant.   To these fundamental conditions, Descartes added the further one that all changes of motion took place by the impact or pressure of material bodies upon one another.

With these principles established to his own satisfaction, Descartes now turned to the problems raised by the Copernican system.   He found no trouble accounting for the infinite (or as he preferred to call it, the indefinite) size of the universe for to assume less would be to limit God's creative power.   The actual revolution of the planets of the solar system was accounted for by assuming an etherial hydrodynamic model.   If water is swirled around rapidly in a pail, particles of dirt and stones will be pushed to the center.   So, Descartes assumed whirlpools of ether (*tourbillons*) in space which carried the planets around the Sun and also pressed material bodies to the planets.   Gravity was simply this etherial pressure.   By the end of the *Principia,* Descartes could exclaim *voilà*!   The system was complete, and composed of elements that were beautifully clear and distinct. Furthermore, each step had been logically deduced from the previous one and so *must* be correct.   No wonder that so many seized upon the Cartesian universe as the ultimate answer to the basic cosmological question of the structure and principles of the cosmos.   How, it might be asked, could such a beautiful, simple and rational system be anything but the truth?   There were few who doubted and Cartesianism became the new orthodoxy, almost as tenacious and strong as that of Aristotle.   So long as Descartes' fundamental criteria of truth were accepted, his system appeared invulnerable. It was only when the problem of the cosmos was approached from a different direction that its weaknesses became apparent. It was Isaac Newton who first perceived the flaws in the Cartesian system and who first proceeded (with some glee) to its demolition.

All the many streams which flowed into the Scientific Revolution were united in the person of Isaac Newton (1642-1727). He was a better mathematician than any of his predecessors; a philosopher who could appreciate what Galileo and Descartes were attempting at the same time that he could see how far short of the goal they fell. He was to establish a new metaphysics that permitted him and his successors to probe the sub-sensible world of the atomically small. His experimental genius was manifested in his optical researches which were, literally, epoch making. The combination of mathematical, philosophical and experimental genius was both unique and extraordinarily fruitful. Newton found a fragmented cosmos and left behind him a coherent system of the world based solidly on experience and described elegantly in mathematics.

Our purposes will best be served if we return, once again, to the cosmological problems raised by Copernicus and, now, seemingly solved by Descartes. It would appear that Descartes was probably the single most important influence on Newton. Descartes' *Geometry* and Euclid's *Elements* were what started Newton on his mathematical career. Descartes' *Principia* was what first provided him with an overall picture of the cosmos. All this occurred in Newton's last year as a student at Trinity College, Cambridge. Then, in two short years (1665-6) Newton seems to have had most of the brilliantly original ideas whose later elaboration and publication were to guarantee his pre-eminence in the history of science.

One fact must have struck the young Newton as he carefully read and re-read Descartes. This was the difference between what Descartes wanted to do and what he actually did. Descartes, like Galileo and Kepler, had insisted time and again on the importance and superiority of mathematics in the description of Nature but, unlike Galileo and Kepler, Descartes had not been notably successful in creating a mathematical physics. With the exception of the derivation of Snell's law in optics, it is almost impossible to find a mathematical law in Cartesian physics. The omission was particularly glaring in astronomy. By the 1660's, knowledge of Kepler's laws was becoming more widespread and Galileo's contributions offered some hope for the mathematization of Nature. Newton was fully aware of all this, having just made the acquaintance of Kepler's astronomy and Galileo's physics. Thus, when Newton began to think about cosmology and physics, his framework had been sharply defined and he could not rest content with Descartes' qualitative account.

We can, fortunately, separate the elements that entered into Newton's grand cosmological synthesis. Available to him were a number of important principles and laws. Descartes had enunciated a quite clear principle of inertia in which a body in motion in a straight line would preserve that motion unless pushed out of it by another body. Kepler's three laws described the actual motion of the planets and, in particular, had revealed that the ratio between the square of the periodic time and the cube of the distance from the Sun is the same for every planet ($T^2/r^3 = k$ - Third Law). Furthermore, Kepler had envisioned something *like* a force emanating from the Sun which pushed the planets around in their orbits. Finally, Galileo had provided a law of uniformly accelerated motion which showed that the total distance traveled depended upon the square of the time. Once again, it was possible to view this as a process in time during which a constant *force* acted. Although the concept of force was implicit in both Kepler and Galileo, it was more clearly defined even in Newton's earliest speculations. Force produced a *change* in motion. Newton did not now concern himself with how the force acted.

For once, a familiar story told of the great seems to be true. Newton later related to an early biographer that he had been sitting in the orchard at his family farm in Woolsthorpe, Lincolnshire, when an apple fell. His alert mind immediately leaped to the question of what force would be necessary to hold the moon in its orbit if it, too, fell like the apple (or was accelerated towards the Earth) in accordance with Galileo's law of free fall. Assuming that the moon circled the Earth, Newton discovered that the centrifugal force of this motion neatly balanced the gravitational force of the Earth, *if* the force exerted on the apple were *really* the same as that exerted on the moon. If the same analysis were applied to the planets, moving in circular orbits, it was equally clear that the force emanating from the Sun which counteracted *their* centrifugal force varied inversely as the square of the distance of the planets from the Sun. So far, so good. By the end of 1666 Newton had derived the inverse square law and had computed results which were more or less in agreement with the facts. But, as a modern historian of science, Alexandre Koyré, has remarked, the deepest aim of the Scientific Revolution was to get rid of the world of "more or less," and substitute a world of precision. To achieve this precision, Newton had considerable work to do. He had (most simply) first to get more accurate dimensions, especially for the Earth. Then he had to adjust his calculations for elliptical, not circular orbits. Finally, he had to prove, not merely assume, that Earth, Moon, Sun and Planets acted like point masses. Finally, there was the fact that the solar system was a complex one, involving more than the two bodies (Sun and planet, Earth and Moon) Newton had used for his initial calculations. He could not know that the rigorous solution of the problem of the motion of three or more bodies interacting according to the law of universal gravitation was (and still is) impossible.

Facing these difficulties, Newton put the problem aside and immersed himself in his optical researches. These investigations contributed directly, however, to his ultimate solution of the cosmological riddle. His work on light convinced him of the fundamental truth of the corpuscular hypothesis. This conviction permitted him to sum up particulate forces to arrive at his proof that masses could be considered point masses. And, his own dis-

coveries in optics further convinced him that Descartes' whole
system was wrong, the necessary pre-condition for his later attack on Descartes in Book II of the *Principia*. But, while
Newton's mind was occupied elsewhere, other natural philosophers
began to close in on the problem of planetary motion. G. A.
Borelli (1608-1679) published a work on the *Theory of the Medicean Planets* in 1666 which implied a centripetal force clearly
attractive in nature. More importantly, Newton's contemporary
and colleague in the Royal Society, Robert Hooke, came even
closer to enunciating a theory of universal gravitation. Hooke
had a fine physical intuition but he lacked Newton's mathematical
finesse and so he was able only to come close. Hooke's theory,
although confused and inchoate, nevertheless influenced Newton.
Unfortunately, Hooke's earlier criticism of Newton's theory of
light had deeply offended Newton, so that he never acknowledged
this debt. In 1679, however, a letter from Hooke to Newton did
appear to stimulate Newton to pick up his earlier work and the
road to the *Principia* began.

By 1679, the road had been made somewhat easier to discern.
There were more accurate figures available for calculating
gravitational forces and Newton's mathematical tools had been
considerably developed. He was ready to prove the theorem that
masses acted like points and he was also able to show that an inverse square law of attraction could be adapted to elliptical as
well as circular orbits. All that was now necessary was for
Newton to be pushed into the publication of his results. The
occasion arose in 1684 when Newton was visited by the astronomer,
Edmond Halley. By this time, the idea of an inverse-square law
of gravitation was "in the air." Halley remarked to Newton that
neither he nor Christopher Wren nor Robert Hooke could calculate
the curve that would result if an inverse square law of attraction were assumed for planetary motion. Newton told Halley that
the curve would be an ellipse and when asked how he knew, replied,
"Why, I have calculated it." Then, alas, he could not produce
the calculation leading one historian to remark that when some of
the greatest scientists in Europe were looking for the law of
gravitation, Newton had already lost it!

Halley's visit had served its purpose for Newton now decided
to devote his lectures for the coming term to the motions of
bodies. During the next two years, the final version of the new
work gradually took shape as Halley encouraged and cajoled the
often difficult Newton. A bitter quarrel with Hooke almost persuaded Newton to abandon science, but Halley's good sense prevailed and Newton returned to his labors. In 1687, the great
work appeared, paid for in part by Halley and seen through the
press by him as well. Its title was forbiddingly severe, *Philosophiae naturalis principia mathematica (Mathematical Principles
of Natural Philosophy)*. The title itself announced both a new,
comprehensive framework for physics and a fundamental attack on
Cartesian physics as enunciated in his *Principia philosophiae*.
For the main thrust of what Newton had to say was that the fundamental principles of Nature were mathematical, not philosophical.
That being so, the *Principia* was presented in axiomatic form.
Book I established and proved the theorems upon which the whole

rested. These included the famous three laws of motion (see Readings, p. 219ff.)   and the definitions of mass, momentum, inertia, force and centripetal force upon which the new mechanics was to rest. Book II, among other things, demolished the Cartesian theory of vortices by demonstrating mathematically that Cartesian vortices could not account for the observed planetary motions. Book III uses the results of Book I to solve (finally) the cosmological problems first raised by Copernicus.

The result is truly astonishing and impressive. Not only does Newton account for the paths of the planets, but he also concerned himself with the extremely complex theory of lunar motion and provided a satisfactory theory of the tides. He showed that the orbits of comets were either parabolas or very eccentric ellipses. Experiment, observations, calculations, mathematical proofs, and even advice on proper method were blended in the *Principia* into a single whole which represented a new science. The Newtonian universe was simple and comprehensible. The synthesis had been made and a new age was ushered in. We may end this section, however, on a cautionary note. The new age did not quite know that it had been ushered in. The *Principia* is a work of great difficulty to read. The mathematics is hard and the argument often above the heads of even the "intelligent reader." It took some time for the *Principia* to be assimilated but when it was, it and its author were recognized as the creators of a new intellectual stage in the history of Western Civilization. The famous couplet by Alexander Pope in the eighteenth century represents the next generation's view of its   debt to Newton:

> Nature and nature's laws lay hid in night:
> God said, Let Newton be! and all was light.

6. The Mechanical Philosophy

The *Principia* did more than establish the new cosmology. It also provided a firm foundation for a new philosophy of Nature. Interpretations of the *Principia* were based on the assumption of atomic particles acting upon one another by forces in empty space. This looks superficially like the old atomic theory but it had specific differences from it. Most important was the action of forces across space which later received the name of action at a distance. The implication that a body could act where it was not violated one of the oldest philosophical principles in Western science. Part of Newton's greatness lay in the fact that he could temporarily accept such a notion without agonizing over it to the point of intellectual paralysis. He was willing to accept the fact that he could not account for gravity hence his famous remark, *Hypotheses non fingo* (I feign no hypotheses). And he was also willing to speculate that it *might* be caused by a subtle ether, but it was not essential to know the cause of gravity to be able to give the mathematical laws by which it acted. That forces did act at a distance could be accepted as a fact; how they acted was given by the laws of motion. It was even possible that the active powers of Nature were not mere material emanations but something even close to Divinity itself (see Readings,

p. 322ff.).

In Newton's other great book, the *Opticks*, which first appeared in Latin in 1704, Newton permitted himself somewhat greater freedom in explanation of physical effects. He does present the *laws* of optics but he also tries to come to grips with the causes of these laws. In the *Queries* which he appended to the *Opticks* he even went so far as to speculate on the ultimate realities of physics [see Readings, p. 287ff.]. It was in the *Opticks*, with the laws of motion in the *Principia* as background, that Newton laid out the principles of the mechanical philosophy. Reality consisted of fundamental particles of ponderable matter and other [imponderable] effluvia such as light. These traveled through space which was either empty, as assumed in the *Principia*, or filled with a very subtle ether which affected optical phenomena. The various particles acted on one another by means of forces and physical reality consisted of particles, forces and motion. Particles could clump together to form agglomerates whose properties were a function of their form. From this aspect, one could hope to create a rational chemistry. Effluvial particles obeyed other laws, but the *Opticks* was living proof that these laws could be made comprehensible. Experiment and mathematics together could lay bare the laws of Nature and the Newtonian testament was to provide the basic scientific program for the eighteenth century. The Newtonian achievement was, as well, the culmination of the evolution of the mechanical philosophy of the seventeenth century and before we move to the Enlightenment, it will be fruitful to look at the way in which the mechanical philosophy had contributed to science in other areas than physics.

7. Medicine, Biology and Mechanisms

There is a coincidence in the history of the Scientific Revolution that has often been noted. 1543 marked the appearance of Andreas Vesalius' (1514-64) *De Humani Corporis Fabrica (On the Fabric of the Human Body)* as well as Copernicus' *De revolutionibus*. By implication, this marked the Scientific Revolution in biology but the character of Vesalius' work is considerably less revolutionary than that of his Polish contemporary. What it was was an attempt to map out the structure of the human body using the works of Galen as an almost infallible guide. Vesalius took full advantage of the possibilities offered by human dissection which had become almost standard practice in the Italy of his day. And he was superbly served by the artist who drew the anatomical plates. But, he was also very much under the influence of Galen and often "saw" anatomical structures that Galen said were there but which, to put it mildly, Vesalius had great difficulty in perceiving. The most important anatomical feature (in terms of the history of anatomy in the seventeenth century) that Vesalius "saw" were the pores in the septum of the heart which were essential in Galenic physiology. It was through these "pores" that venous blood was supposed to seep into the right side where it was endowed with vital spirits and pushed out into the arteries. Galen said the pores were there; Vesalius could not find them but also could not bring himself flatly to deny their existence. Until they were denied, however, the true action of the heart would remain a mystery.

Where Vesalius did go beyond his master was in finding and describing anatomical structures that had escaped Galen. And, more importantly, the *De Fabrica* put the results together into an anatomical whole. Here was the first real anatomical atlas of the human body and, as such, it deserves its place as a scientific classic. (See Illustration.) It is not, however, a revolutionary work except insofar as it stimulated further anatomical work.

This it did. The second half of the sixteenth century is a period of great fertility in anatomical discovery. Most of this work was done in Italy and we can here merely mention a few names. Eustachio (1520-74) of Rome did important work in comparative anatomy in which, for example, he indicated that Vesalius had operated upon animal, not human, kidneys and had thereby been led into error. His work on the anatomy of the ear was immortalized by giving his name to the tubes that run from the tympanum to the pharynx. Fallopius (1523-62), professor of anatomy at Padua, described the female generative organs. Fabricius of Aquapendente (1537-1619), another professor at Padua, paid particular attention to the anatomy of the veins. His work, especially in revealing the structure of the valves in the veins, was the necessary preliminary to William Harvey's discovery of the circulation of the blood.

Interest and discoveries in anatomy almost inevitably generated curiosity about physiology. What purpose did organs and anatomical features serve in the life of the body? Galen's physiology was, of course, the dominant one but as anatomists probed deeper into the structure of the human body, it became increasingly unsatisfactory. It was not so much that it was wrong--there was little evidence for that conclusion--as that it was inadequate. The case of the circulatory system may here be used as an example. The discovery and description of the valves in the vein necessarily raised the question, what are they used for? It was this question, as Harvey later admitted, that started him on the train of researches that culminated in the discovery of the circulation of the blood.

Some questions about the Galenic account of blood flow had already been raised by the time that Harvey began his work. Michael Servetus (ca. 1511-53) had earlier suggested, strangely enough in a theological treatise, that the blood circulated from the heart to the lungs and back. He was, incidentally, burned in John Calvin's Geneva for his theological views and his treatise followed him into the flames. His view, therefore, did not gain great currency. Realdus Columbus (1516-59) at Padua published a much more popular work in 1559, *Fifteen Books on Anatomical Matters*, which challenged Galen's statement on the pores of the septum and also insisted that the blood is carried by the pulmonary artery to the lungs and returns to the heart through the pulmonary vein. But, he was unable to make much physiological sense of this discovery except to try and account for it in terms of heat loss of the blood. All it really did, therefore, was to

PRIMA FIGVRA EARVM QVAS OSTENDENDIS MVSCVLIS POTISSIMVM PA
RAVIMVS, IN CVIVS DEXTRO LATERE MVSCVLI MOX SVB CVTE RECONDITI, ANTERIORI IN
facie conspiciuntur: in sinistro autem illis resectis obuij sunt, qui in dextro latere apparentibus proxime succumbunt. Vt verò præsen-
figura redderetur copiosior, eorum quæ caluaria complectitur ima ginem sectionis ordine proponere incepimus, humi oculi musculos, uti
characterum index docebit, delineantes.

From *The Epitome of Andreas Vesalius*, Trans. from the Latin with Preface and Introduction by L. R. Lind, with Anatomical Notes by C. W. Asling, Foreword by Logan Clendening. (Cambridge: The MIT Press, 1949)

suggest a possible way for the blood to get from one side of the heart to the other without passing through the septum.

It was William Harvey (1578-1657) who came to grips with the problem of the motion of the blood as a whole. As he later told Robert Boyle, it was the valves in the veins which led him to the hypothesis that the blood in the veins flowed only towards the heart. The rest of the doctrine of blood circulation followed logically from this fact, for if blood flowed unidirectionally into the heart, it must flow out, as well and come back, eventually, into the veins.

It was one thing to conceive of circulation and quite another thing to prove it. It was here that Harvey showed his genius. In order to understand the motion of the heart, he simplified the experimental situation in various ways. He observed the hearts of animals near death when their rate of heart beat was considerably slower. The action of the heart in systole (contraction) and diastole (relaxation) was then clearly visible. To avoid confusion arising from the complex contractions and dilations of a four-chambered heart, he dissected snakes with two-chambered hearts. Last, but not least, his experiments were greatly aided by his mechanical conception of the circulatory system. [See Readings, p. 143ff.] The heart Harvey considered as a pump, the arteries and veins as pipes and the valves as mechanical blocks to reflux in the veins. (See Illustration.)

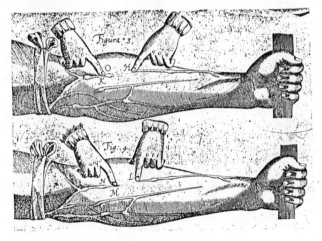

The one part of his system that he could not discover was the connection between the arteries and the veins. [With the newly invented microscope, Marcello Malpighi discovered the capillaries and described them (in the lung) in 1661.] Harvey's *De Motu Cordis (On the Motion of the Heart)* described a wonderfully ingenious hydraulic system by means of which the blood flowed through the body. Although Harvey did not attempt to reduce the system to constituent corpuscles, it was as nice an example of the triumph of the mechanical philosophy as one could wish. This, in spite of the fact that Harvey was more Aristotelian than mechanical in his approach to life. But, at least for the circulatory system, the mechanical approach seemed to work.

As in cosmology, the great proponent of mechanism in the treatment of living matter was Descartes. The human and animal body was, for Descartes, nothing but an intricate machine. What differentiated the human from the animal was the presence of a soul. The human soul acted on the human body through the pineal gland and it was the action of the soul in the body that made man more than a machine. But, as far as physiology was concerned, Descartes was a thorough-going mechanist. Matter and motion were sufficient to account for all physiological processes. Descartes' treatment of the heart is an excellent example of the mechanical philosophy applied to physiology. It might be supposed that Harvey's account could not be improved upon. There was, however, one point that was unacceptable to Descartes. According to Harvey, the active part of the heart's action occurred in systole when the heart contracted to pump the blood through the arteries. Diastole represented the relaxation of the heart during which it filled with blood again. Such an account did not explain the origin of the heart beat. Just as a mechanical pump was activated by a human agent, so, too, might this explanation open the way to a non-mechanical origin of systole. Therefore, Descartes turned the explanation around. Diastole, he insisted, was the active phase and it was caused by the heat (demonstrable) of the heart. As Descartes saw it, when the blood (cooled in the lungs) entered the left auricle of the heart, the heat of the heart caused it to expand greatly. This expansion is what pushed it out of the heart into the arteries. The heart, so emptied, relaxed into systole until a new gout of blood entered it, to be expanded in turn. Thus, *every* aspect of the circulation was mechanical and there was no place through which non-mechanical causes could enter. It was in many ways a daring conception and men, like Giovanni Borelli (1608-79), tried to apply it to other areas. Borelli managed to account for the movements of human and animal limbs by reducing them to cables and levers, but by and large, the attempt failed. (See Illustration.) As with the heart, it was an unproductive view of this complex question.

The example of Descartes and Borelli explains why the life sciences were not revolutionized in the Scientific Revolution. Harvey had shown that experiment could be applied to at least some aspects of physiology but when the attempt was made to encompass living nature in a general, overall philosophy, it failed. There was, then, nothing else for it but to fall back on observation. The seventeenth century witnessed the accumulation of data on living things but not the reduction of this data to order. We cannot linger long here but there are some developments that are worth citing.

Perhaps the most dramatic novelty of the seventeenth century was the opening up of the microscopic world. The microscope, like the telescope, was invented early in the century and, again

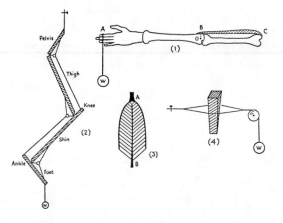

Fig.5 Borelli's static analysis of muscles. (1) If W = 28 lbs.,
the pull sustained by the arm-muscle through the small level

$OB = \frac{OA}{20}$ is 560 lbs. (2) Model of forces in muscles of leg.

(3) Though the muscle-fibres do not act so efficiently in an
oblique as in a direct pull, the number of fibres is much increased; A, B, tendons. (4) Contraction of strings when a wedge
is inserted.*

like the telescope, contributed to the destruction of the old
mode of thought. Here, after all, was a realm of living creatures that Aristotle and his followers had never seen and had not,
therefore, ever attempted to work into their philosophy. The
intricate structure of so simple a beastie as a flea could not
help but astonish and puzzle the mind. The wee animals that the
extraordinary single-lens microscopes of Antoni van Leeuwenhoek
(1632-1723) revealed could not easily be assimilated to Aristotelian categories. The microscope expanded the seen world downwards as the telescope expanded it upwards. Beyond wonder, however, there was little the men of the seventeenth century could
do with the new observations. Except in one field, embryology.
There it was possible to suggest a "mechanical" theory that
appeared superior to the older Aristotelian account. Aristotle
had theorized that the conception of an animal involved the union
of matter provided by the female menstrual blood with form which
came from the male semen. William Harvey, in his work on Generation was able to support his doctrine of blood circulation by
expanding upon this Aristotelian doctrine. According to Aristotle, the (material) basis of form was that fifth essence (quintessence) of which the stellar spheres were made. Harvey argued
from observations that the first thing to appear in the ferti-

* From A. Rupert Hall, *From Galileo to Newton (1630-1720)*
(New York: Harper & Row, 1963), Figure 9, p. 199.

lized egg was blood and, since the natural motion of the quintessence was circular, so, too, was that of the blood--hence the blood moved in circles. Other than noting this very unmechanical aspect of Harvey's thought, we should note that the blood and other organs *developed* from the fertilized egg. This doctrine of epigenesis almost inevitably involved the idea of some guiding hand or entelechy, forming and putting organs together to create the mature embryo. Microscopic observations provided an alternative to this view. The fact that even small insects like the flea had a complex organization suggested that the "miniaturization" of organs could be carried down to the microscopic realm. The spermatazoa, discovered by Leeuwenhoek, were held by him to contain the embryo, although others insisted the embryo was pre-formed within the egg. Both sides agreed, however, that fertilization was merely the beginning of the process by which the pre-formed embryo began to grow. It might appear that this was a triumph for the mechanical philosophy since development became merely nutrition, but it was not for no one was willing to insist that the transmission of life was a purely mechanical process. Yet, the theory of "emboitement" was a mechanical one and, as such, appealed to those who were taken with the new philosophical currents of the day.

The expansion of biological knowledge was caused by more than the invention of the microscope. New realms were opened up by the explorers of the sixteenth and seventeenth centuries. New plant and animal species were discovered and these discoveries threatened to swamp European botanists and zoologists. There was little men could do except write natural histories and hope to arrange their specimens in some kind of order. The magnitude of the task can be seen by the fact that there were some 18,000 known plants. The older system of arrangement by initial letter or in terms of utility to man was no longer adequate. And so, natural historians turned to other characteristics.

Two naturalists will serve to illustrate the results. Joseph Pitton de Tournefort (1656-1708), Professor at the *Jardin des Plantes* in Paris, attempted to group plants according to their flowers and fruits. In the process, however, he failed to distinguish between flowering and non-flowering plants. He also considered other aspects of the plant--root, leaf, stem--as worthless from the taxonomic point of view. His results were less than satisfactory. He could broadly distinguish families within which species were only dimly visible. Tournefort's system was useful only until something better came along, as it did with Linnaeus in the eighteenth century.

John Ray (1627-1705) in England cast his net more widely. He classified plants but also took on birds, fishes, animals and insects. In his *Historia Plantarum (History of Plants)* which appeared in 1686, 1688, and 1704 he tried to provide a reasonable guide to plant life. Nature, he remarked, makes no jumps so one should not expect neatly separated species but rather a continual shading of one species into another. He classified by using seed types, distinguishing between mono- and di-cotyledons although he took other characteristics into account as well. He managed to define many of the natural families of modern taxonomy and this he did by *not* trying to find a single distinguishing characteristic. For animal classification, Ray turned to comparative anatomy and morphology. Some idea of his results may be gleaned from the appended diagram classifying the vertebrates. (See diagram.)

Little more than this could be accomplished before the fact of evolution permitted one to perceive the true, genetic, connections between species. What the seventeenth century left as its legacy in this area was a large body of rather carefully determined facts with little insight on how to make sense of them.

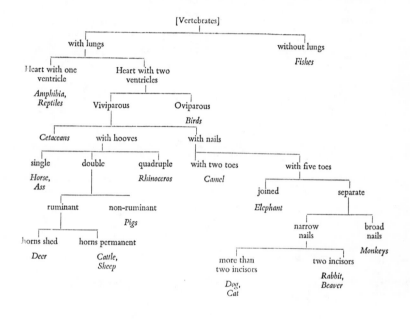

Fig.6 Ray's classification of animals.*

* From A. Rupert Hall, *From Galileo to Newton (1630-1720)* (New York: Harper & Row, 1963), Figure 9, p. 199.

II. Readings on the Scientific Revolution

A. Methodology

Introduction:

The Scientific Revolution is now an accepted term in the historical literature. But, though historians agree that there was an enormous change in knowledge and theories of Nature in the seventeenth century, they are not all in agreement on the cause. As the text has emphasized, there were many medieval elements in the great synthesis of the Scientific Revolution and many ancient and medieval ideas were incorporated into the new science. In what sense, then, was the Scientific Revolution revolutionary?

One of the areas in which there *might* have been a revolution was in the method used to arrive at scientific truth. By and large, medieval science had remained true to the letter and the spirit of Aristotle. It is also true that Aristotle was subjected to intense criticism in the sixteenth and seventeenth centuries and was eventually repudiated. Did this repudiation extend to his method, as well as his results? or were the spectacular results of the Scientific Revolution the effects of a refined Aristotelian method, brought down to earth by generations of logicians and scientific scholars? It is around this question that the documents in this section are arranged.

1. Aristotelian Method and its Shortcomings

a. The Case for Aristotle

(1). John Herman Randall, Jr·, "The Development of Scientific Method in the School of Padua"

J. H. Randall, Jr·, is a philosopher at Columbia University. His article, first published in 1940, presents the case for Aristotle's method as an instrument for the creation of the new science of the seventeenth century.

The Aristotelian science, which the thirteenth century had so eagerly worked into its Christian philosophy of life, aimed at an understanding of nature divorced from power over things. But during the sixteenth century more and more men began to hold that science should be directed, not merely to understanding and vision, but to a kind of understanding that might give power, action, and an improvement of the practical arts. A leading intellectual enterprise of the time was the search for a fruitful method that could serve this new aim to which knowledge was turning. Those thinkers, whose energies were not wholly absorbed by the theological issues in terms of which the major battles were still being fought, concentrated on this problem of method as the paramount scientific task of the day.

Ironically enough, when the fruitful method was finally "discovered" and proved in practice, it turned out to be the

* John Herman Randall, Jr·, "The Development of Scientific Method in the School of Padua," *Journal of the History of Ideas, 1* (1940), Pp. 177-8; 180-94; 199-206.

least novel of all the elements that went into the formation of the new science. After exploring many a blind alley, men came to realize that one of the great medieval intellectual traditions had already made an excellent beginning at just the kind of practical and useful knowledge they now wanted. In the thirteenth and fourteenth century schools, there had been worked out the idea of an experimentally grounded and mathematically formulated science of nature, and since then much had been done in the way of actual achievement. In Leonardo the penetrating, in the Italian mathematicians and physicists of the sixteenth century, in Copernicus, Kepler, and Galileo, such a science had indeed come of age.

Into this science there entered many different strands, each with its own history. And the powerful stimulus imparted during the sixteenth century by the recovery of the techniques of the Greek mathematicians is not to be minimized. But the conception of the nature of science, of its relation to the observation of fact, and of the method by which it might be achieved and formulated, that was handed on to his successors by Galileo, was not the work of the new seekers after a fruitful method. It appears rather as the culmination of the cooperative efforts of ten generations of scientists inquiring into methodological problems in the universities of northern Italy. For three centuries the natural philosophers of the school of Padua, in fruitful commerce with the physicians of its medical faculty, devoted themselves to criticizing and expanding this conception and method, and to grounding it firmly in the careful analysis of experience. It left their hands with a refinement and precision of statement which the seventeenth century scientists who used it did not surpass in all their careful investigation of method.

*   *   *   *   *

Aristotle's logic, his theory of science and method, was discovered in the *Analytics* during the first half of the twelfth century; his basic concepts and principles of natural science were learned from the *Physics* in the second half. The coming of Aristotle introduced a body of materials too impressive to be ignored. Thereafter for centuries the Aristotelian physical writings were taken as the starting-point for all natural science, however far men might eventually depart from them; and the Aristotelian theory of science, however men might interpret it, remained dominant till the time of Newton. From the beginning of the fourteenth century, however, there set in a persistent and searching reconstruction of the Aristotelian tradition, which, when directed to the *Physics*, led by gradual stages to the mechanical and mathematical problems of the Galilean age, and when directed to the *Logic* led to the precise formulation of the method and structure of science acclaimed by all the seventeenth-century scientists.

There were two main critical movements during the later middle ages. The Ockhamites began in Oxford in the thirteenth century, and while persisting there found a new stronghold during the next hundred years in the Faculty of Arts at Paris. The

Latin Averroists began in Paris in the thirteenth century, and
shifted their seat to Padua early in the fourteenth. Both set
out by expressing a secular and anti-clerical spirit, and by
undertaking a destructive criticism of Thomism and Scotism, the
thirteenth century syntheses of science and religion. But both
soon advanced beyond mere criticism to the constructive elaboration of natural science: they became the two great scientific
schools of the later middle ages. The original work of the
Ockhamites belongs to the fourteenth century, that of the Paduans,
to the fifteenth and sixteenth. The former was done in dynamics,
kinematics, and the logic of continuity and intensity; the latter,
in methodology and in the further development of dynamics. Both
turned from the earlier religious syntheses to the purely natural
philosophy of Aristotle himself; and both developed primarily by
a constructive criticism of the Aristotelian texts and doctrines.
The Ockhamites were at first the more "progressive" and "modern";
they were interested in the free development of the Aristotelian
physics, and their works take the form of questions and problems
suggested by Aristotle's analyses. The Averroists, though much
more secular and anti-clerical, were originally more conservative
in their attitude toward Aristotle and his interpreter Averroes:
their works are characteristically commentaries on the texts.
From 1400 on, however, they knew and taught all the Ockhamite
departures from Aristotelian doctrine: Paul of Venice (1429) is
remarkably up-to-date, and his *Summa Naturalis* contains an exposition of all the ideas of the dynamics of the Paris Ockhamites
and the Oxford logicians.

   *   *   *   *   *

The question whether the operation of causes was to be formulated mathematically or qualitatively (whether the "first accident" of substance was to be taken as quantity or not--which
happens to be also the way in which Kepler expressed his view
that a cause is a mathematical law) was vigorously debated at
Padua toward the end of the fifteenth century, and the notion of
"cause" as a mathematically formulated formal cause won many adherents. In the next century there broke out another great controversy among the Paduans as to whether the "cause" of natural
motion was to be sought in a form or in a force, that is, in a
definite way of behaving or in something that acted in a definite way. Galileo joined those who identified "cause" with a
"force"; but since he also defined force in terms of its way of
acting, his divergence was not great. And towards the end of the
same century there occurred another dispute, as to whether final
causes had any place in natural philosophy. The outcome of these
successive debates was to delimit the conception of cause, and to
make the Galilean position inevitable. They are here mentioned
to suggest certain other strands in the development of Italian
Aristotelianism which this study does not presume to set forth in
detail, and which in particular illuminate the change from a
qualitative to a mathematical treatment of natural operations.
It has become a recent fashion to view the whole "Renaissance," and indeed the very "birth" of modern science itself, as

philosophically a turning from the Aristotle of the Schools to
Platonism; and Italian thought of the fifteenth century has been
represented as dominated by that turning. But it must not be
forgotten that the vigorous intellectual life of the Italian
universities remained loyal to the Aristotelian tradition. Now
in most countries the fifteenth century saw the teaching and
refinement of the earlier philosophies, Scotism, Thomism, and
Ockhamism, with little basically new. But in northern Italy, at
Padua, Bologna, and Pavia, and to a lesser extent at Siena, Pisa,
and the brilliant new university of Ferrara, Aristotelianism was
still a living and growing body of ideas. What Paris had been in
the thirteenth century, what Oxford and Paris together had been
in the fourteenth, Padua became in the fifteenth: the center in
which ideas from all Europe were combined into an organized and
cumulative body of knowledge. A succession of great teachers
carried that knowledge to the point where in the next century it
could find fruitful marriage with the new interest in the mathematical sciences. In the Italian schools alone the emerging science of nature did not mean a sharp break with reigning theological interests. To them it came rather as the natural outcome of
a sustained and cooperative criticism of Aristotelian ideas. If
in the sixteenth century the more original minds were led to a
formal break with the Paduan teaching, we must not forget that
even Galileo occupied a chair there from 1592 to 1610, and that
in method and philosophy if not in physics he remained a typical
Paduan Aristotelian.

*   *   *   *   *

If the concepts of a mathematical physics were arrived at by
a long criticism of Aristotelian ideas, the "new method," the
logic and methodology taken over and expressed by Galileo and
destined to become the scientific method of the seventeenth century physicists, as contrasted with the many noisy proposals of
the sixteenth century "buccinators" down to Francis Bacon, was
even more clearly the result of a fruitful critical reconstruction of the Aristotelian theory of science, undertaken at Padua
in particular, and fertilized by the methodological discussions
of the commentators on the medical writers. For three hundred
years, after Pietro d'Abano brought the problems to the fore, the
Paduan medical teachers were driven by their texts, especially
Galen, to a careful analysis of scientific procedure. The great
commentators on Galen, Jacopo da Forlì (1413), who incidentally
wrote widely on the methods of the Paris physicists, and Hugo of
Siena (1439), gradually built up a detailed theory of scientific
method which the Aristotelian scholars, themselves holders of
medical degrees, incorporated into their version of the nature of
science. It is possible to trace step by step in rather beautiful fashion the gradual elaboration of the Aristotelian method,
in the light of the medical tradition, from its first discussion
in Pietro d'Abano to its completed statement in the logical controversies of Zabarella, in which it reaches the form familiar in
Galileo and the seventeenth-century scientists.

*   *   *   *   *

These men were concerned with the discovery and use of "principles" in science. Like all thinkers from the twelfth century to Newton, they understood *principium* as Aristotle understood ἀρχή, as that from which a thing proceeds and has its origin in any way whatever; specifically, in science a *principium* is that which is in any way a source of understanding. The particular character of "priority" and origin, of which both Aristotle and the scientific theory deriving from him distinguished various kinds, depends upon the specific character and context of the problem under consideration. The distinctions between the different kinds of order and method, therefore, running through all the men here considered, are *ipso facto* distinctions between different kinds of "priority," that is, between different meanings of *principium*.

The question of method was raised, and the terms in which it was to be treated for three centuries were clearly formulated, by Pietro d'Abano in his *Conciliator differentiarum philosophorum, et praecipue medicorum*, written in 1310. In discussing the question whether medicine is a science he points out that "science" is used in two senses.

> Science in the most proper sense is that which infers the conclusion through causes which are proximate and immediate, like that science defined in *Analytica Posteriora*, L.I., c. 2 [71b]; "We think that we know a thing unqualifiedly (*simpliciter*) and not in a sophistical and accidental manner, when we think we know the cause on account of which (*propter quam*) the fact exists, that it is the cause of that fact, and that it could not be otherwise"; and this kind of science is gained from "demonstration *propter quid*" (demonstration *wherefore* or *why*) or what Galen called "*doctrina compositiva*" (the compositive way of teaching). There is a second sense of science that is also proper, and indeed can be said to be for us most proper; since for us the natural way is to proceed from what is more knowable and certain for us to what is more knowable in the order of nature: see the beginning of the *Physica* [184a]. When, in cases where effects inhere in their causes according to an essential order of priority, we arrive by the opposite order at the cause we are seeking, through proximate and logically immediate middle terms; or when we conclude an effect from more general causes, omitting certain intermediate causes, we acquire knowledge by "demonstration *quia*" (demonstration *that*) or what is called "*doctrina resolutiva*" (the resolutive way of teaching).

Pietro is here making his central distinction between two kinds of science and demonstration in terms of the theory of science developed in the *Posterior Analytics*. Science is defined as a demonstrative knowledge of things through their causes; its instrument is the demonstrative syllogism, which establishes the relations between causes and their effects. The problem of forming such syllogisms is the problem of discovering causes and defining them in such a way that they can serve as the middle terms of demonstrations. Pietro is thus distinguishing between two kinds of *proof*: that of effects through causes, and that of causes through effects.

The transformation of the demonstrative proof of causes into a method of discovery is precisely the achievement of the Paduan theory of science. That change of context is already suggested, in the above passage, in Pietro's identification of the two kinds of demonstration with the various ways of teaching, or *doctrina*, and of *order* or dependence. These terms are drawn from other sources than Aristotle, and they bring with them an interest that is methodological as well as purely logical. Pietro treats them at length in Difference 8. The *Tegni* (*Techne*) or art of medicine of Galen commences with a prologue in which three *doctrinae* or ways of teaching medical science are distinguished: by *resolution*, by *composition*, and by *definition*.

> In all the ways of teaching (*doctrinae*) which follow a definite order there are three orders of procedure. One of them is that which follows the way of conversion and *resolution* (*dissolutio*); in it you set up in your mind the thing at which you are aiming, and of which you are seeking a scientific knowledge, as the end to be satisfied. Then you examine what lies nearest to it, and nearest to that without which the thing cannot exist; nor are you finished till you arrive at the principle which satisfies it. . . . The second follows the way of *composition*, and is the contrary of the first way. In it you begin with the thing at which you have arrived by the way of resolution, and then return to the very things resolved, and put them together again (*compone eas*) in their proper order, until you arrive at the last of them. . . . And the third follows the way of analysing the definition.

*   *   *   *   *

The physician Jacopo da Forlì (1413), who occupied in turn the chairs of medicine and of natural philosophy at Padua, followed Hali and Pietro in their distinction between the two *doctrinae*, compositive and resolutive. He added, however, a further analysis of the method of resolution which brings it closer to a procedure of investigation.

> Resolution is twofold, natural or real, and logical. Real resolution, though taken improperly in many senses, is strictly the separation and division of a thing into its component parts. Logical resolution is so called metaphorically. The metaphor is derived in this fashion: just as when something composite is resolved, the parts are separated from each other so that each is left by itself in its simple being, so also when a logical resolution is made, a thing at first understood confusedly is understood distinctly, so that the parts and causes touching its essence are distinctly grasped. Thus if when you have a fever you first grasp the concept of fever, you understand the fever in

general and confusedly. You then *resolve* the fever into its causes, since any fever comes either from the heating of the humor or of the spirits or of the members; and again the heating of the humor is either of the blood or of the phlegm, etc.; until you arrive at the specific and distinct cause and knowledge of that fever.

This is a clear case of the method of medical diagnosis; Jacopo illustrates most of his distinctions with a number of examples drawn from medicine. The methodological sense of the traditional terms seems to have crystallized in his usage.

Hugo of Siena (1439), teacher of medicine at Padua, Ferrara, and Parma, is still more concerned with methodology. . . . A proper scientific method will begin with the effects, seek the cause, and then explain the effects from which it started by that cause.

In the discovery of the middle term or cause we proceed from effect to cause. . . . Such a way of acquiring knowledge we call resolutive, because in that discovery we proceed from an effect, which is commonly more composite, to a cause which is simpler; and because by this discovery of the cause we certify the effect through the cause, we say that demonstration *propter quid* and *of cause* is the foundation of resolutive knowledge. . . . But I myself see in the discovery of a science of effects through their cause a double form of procedure, and likewise in the discovery of a scientific knowledge of causes through their effects. The one procedure is the discovery of the middle term or cause, the other is the setting forth of its consequences or effects. And the process of discovery in the case of demonstration through causes is resolutive, while that of setting forth the consequences is compositive. In demonstration through effects it is just the other way around.

Thus Hugo refuses to separate the two procedures: in any science and in any demonstration, discovery or *inventio* and setting forth the consequences or *notificatio* both enter as successive phases of the method to be employed. Discovery and proof are both essential moments in all method.

This notion of a "double process" in scientific method had already been set forth by Urban the Averroist in his large commentary on the *Physics* in 1334. Following Averroes, he distinguishes three modes of demonstration: the demonstration *simpliciter* of mathematics, in which the principles do not have to be sought after; demonstration *of sign*, proceeding from observed effects, by which the physicist learns the causes of natural things; and a third kind,

demonstrations which proceed from causes which, though they are always prior and more known *quoad naturam*, are often posterior and less known to us. This occurs in natural science, in which from those things prior for us, whose modes are effects, we investigate their causes, which are

posterior and less known to us. And this is the way of the
method of resolution. But after we have investigated the
causes, we demonstrate the effects through those causes;
and this is the way of the method of composition. Thus
physical demonstrations follow after mathematical demonstrations in certainty, because they are the most certain after
those in mathematics.

Paul of Venice (1429) examines still more closely this
double procedure in physical demonstrations, defending it against
the charge of being what Aristotle called a circular proof.

> Scientific knowledge of the cause depends on a knowledge
> of the effect, just as scientific knowledge of the effect
> depends on a knowledge of the cause, since we know the cause
> through the effect before we know the effect through the
> cause. This is the principal rule in all investigation,
> that a scientific knowledge of natural effects demands a
> prior knowledge of their causes and principles.--This is not
> a circle, however:--In scientific procedure there are three
> kinds of knowledge. The first is of the effect without any
> reasoning, called *quia*, that it is. The second is of the
> cause through knowledge of that effect; it is likewise called
> *quia*. The third is of the effect through the cause; it is
> called *propter quid*. But the knowledge of why (*propter
> quid*) the effect is, is not the knowledge that (*quia*) it is
> an effect. Therefore the knowledge of the effect does not
> depend on itself, but upon something else.
> The Commentator [Averroes] recognizes a double procedure
> in natural science. The first is from what is less known to
> nature to what is more known to nature, and is from effect
> to cause. The second is from what is more known to nature
> to what is less known to nature, and is from cause to
> effect. . . . Natural science begins both from the causes
> and from what is caused, but in different senses. It be-
> gins from the causes "inclusively," that is, by knowing
> them; but from the things caused "exclusively," that is, by
> knowing by means of them. . . . There is thus a twofold
> knowledge of every cause, the one kind by the procedure *quia*
> and the other by the procedure *propter quid*. The second
> kind depends on the first, and the first is the cause of the
> second; and thus the procedure *quia* is also the cause of the
> procedure *propter quid*.

During the fifteenth century attention was increasingly
focused on this "double procedure" involved in scientific method.
It came to be known by the Averroistic term "regress"; the dependence of all strict demonstration on the prior investigation and
establishment of the appropriate principles was strongly emphasized, and the details of that establishment were carefully
examined. The outstanding natural philosopher of the middle of
the century, Cajetan of Thiene (1465), repeats Paul's treatment.

The fullest account of these problems is to be found in the
commentary of Agostino Nifo on the *Physics* (1506). After

explaining the three kinds of demonstration in Averroes's *prohe-mium*, and assigning the natural philosophy the two procedures, "the one from the effect to the discovery of the cause, the other from the cause discovered to the effect," Nifo takes up at once the question whether this is a circular proof, and cites Philoponus, Themistius, and Averroes in defense of such a *regressus*.

> Recent writers (*recentiores*) maintain that there are four kinds of knowledge. The first kind is of the effect through the senses, or observation; the second is the discovery (*inventio*) of the cause through the effect, which is called demonstration *of sign*; the third is knowledge of the same cause through an examination (*negotiatio*) by the intellect, from which there first comes such an increased knowledge of the cause that it is fit to serve as the middle term of a demonstration *simpliciter*; the fourth is a knowledge of thatsame effect *propter quid*, through that cause known so certainly as to be a middle term.

Since the second knowledge of the effect differs widely from its initial observation, this is no circle, but rather a "regress." Nifo then asks, what is this examination or *negotiatio* by the intellect? It is clearly neither a demonstration nor a definition, nor is it induction.

> This *negotiatio* is composition and division. For when the cause itself has been discovered, the intellect composes and divides until it knows the cause in the form of a middle term. For though cause and middle term be the same thing, they differ in their form (*ratio*). For it is called the cause in as much as the effect proceeds from it, whether it be better known than the effect or not. But it is a middle term in as much as it is a definition. From effect to cause is thus the procedure of discovering the cause; *negotiatio* is directed toward the cause as a middle term and a definition. But since a definition is discovered only through composition and division, it is through them that the cause is discovered in the form of a middle term, from which we can then proceed to the effect.

Nifo later added a further *recognitio* in which he suggests another view of what he calls "demonstrative regress."

> It is customary to treat at length the regress in physical demonstrations; I say "physical," because there is no regress in mathematics. In this difficulty the most recent writers (*iuniores*) conceive three kinds of knowledge in the demonstrative regress. The first is knowledge that the effect is (*quia*), *i.e.*, that the proposition signifying the effect is true; and this knowledge comes from the senses. For instance, that man has the capacity for science is known by sense. The second kind of knowledge is of the reason why (*propter quid*) what is observed by sense is so.

> Thus we consider the reason why man has the capacity for
> science, and not the brute; and we say, because he has a
> rational soul. Therefore of the effect, or of the proposi-
> tion signifying the effect, there are two kinds of know-
> ledge: the one, that it is true, and this is clear to
> sense; the other, why it is so, and this is known to us
> through the discovery of the cause. Of the cause, or of
> the propositions signifying the cause, there is but one
> kind of knowledge, and this is discovery (*inventio*), which
> is nothing else than that it is the cause, or that the
> propositions signifying the cause are true. Hence these
> writers conceive that through this knowledge which is the
> discovery of the cause, or that the propositions which sig-
> nify the cause are true, there is learned the reason why
> the effect is so, or why the conclusion which signifies the
> effect is true. Thus in the regress in physical demonstra-
> tion there are three kinds of knowledge, of which two are
> of the effect while the third is the discovery of the cause.
> When the last is related to the effect, it is the reason
> why the effect is so; but when it is related to the cause,
> it is the fact that it is the cause. And this discovery
> is made through the effect.

It is significant that Nifo cites his examples from the *History
of Animals*, the most empirical of the Aristotelian writings.

> From this it is clear that there is no need of any
> *negotiatio* to render greater our knowledge of the cause, as
> we formerly held; for the mere knowledge that it is the
> cause is the reason why the effect is so. Yet when I more
> diligently consider the words of Aristotle, and the commen-
> taries of Alexander and Themistius, of Philoponus and
> Simplicius, it seems to me that in the regress made in
> physical demonstrations the first process, by which the
> discovery of the cause is put into syllogistic form, is a
> mere hypothetical (*coniecturalis*) syllogism, since through
> it the discovery of the cause is syllogized in a merely
> conjectural fashion. But the second process, by which is
> syllogized the reason why the effect is so through the
> discovered cause, is demonstration *propter quid*--not that it
> makes us know *simpliciter*, but conditionally (*ex conditione*),
> provided that it really is the cause, or provided that the
> propositions are true that represent it to be the cause, and
> that nothing else can be the cause. . . . But you object
> that in that case the science of nature is not a science at
> all. We must say that the science of nature is not a sci-
> ence *simpliciter*, like mathematics. Yet it is a science
> *propter quid*, because the discovery of the cause, gained
> through a conjectural syllogism, is the reason why the
> effect is so. . . . That something is a cause can never be
> so certain as that an effect exists; for the existence of an
> effect is known to the senses. That it is the cause remains
> conjectural, even if that conjectural existence is better
> known than the effect itself in the order of knowledge *prop-
> ter quid*. For if the discovery of the cause is assumed, the

reason why the effect is so is always known. Hence in the
Meteors Aristotle grants that he is not setting forth the
true causes of natural effects, but only in so far as was
possible for him, and in conjectural or hypothetical fashion.

Here, then, at the beginning of the sixteenth century we
find plainly set forth a formulation of the structure of a science of hypothesis and demonstration, with the dependence of its
first principles upon empirical investigation. This was the one
element in the Aristotelian theory of science that had remained
obscure. The *Posterior Analytics* had seemed to say that while
the principles and causes in terms of which a given subject-
matter might be understood were to be discovered through sense-
experience, they were seen to be true by νοῦς, by sheer intellectual vision. The scholastic theologians, like Thomas and Duns
Scotus, had been led by their Augustinian Platonism to emphasize
this power of *intellectus* to recognize the truth of principles.
It is significant that at no time do the Paduan medical Aristotelians attribute any such perceptive power to intellect. The
method by which principles are arrived at is rather the guarantee
of their validity; they are "dependent" on that method, and it is
the "cause" of their explanatory power. Nifo has merely made
explicit what is implicit in the long previous discussion.

          *   *   *   *   *

The originality of Zabarella, and of the whole development
of which he is the culmination, is to set off a "scientific experience" from mere ordinary observation, the accidental or plan-
less collection of particular cases. The weakness of the logic
of the Schoolmen had lain precisely in their acceptance of first
principles established by mere common observation. In contrast,
Zabarella, and with him the whole new science, insisted that
experience must first be analyzed carefully to discover the precise "principle" or cause of the observed effects, the universal
structure involved in them. After this analytic way of discovery
has been pursued, we are then in a position to demonstrate deduc-
tively how facts follow from this principle or cause: we can
pursue the way of truth. Scientific method, that is, proceeds
from the rigorous analysis of a few selected instances or illustrations to a general principle, and then goes from that principle back to the systematized and ordered body of facts, to the
science itself formally expressed. Zabarella calls this the
combination of the resolutive and the compositive methods; and
such were precisely the procedure and the terms of Galileo.
The presupposition of this method is of course that there exists
an intelligible structure in the subject-matter under examination,
of which the particular cases observed by the senses are instances; Zabarella makes this perfectly plain.

Demonstrative induction can be carried on in a necessary
subject-matter, and in things that have an essential connection with each other. Hence it does not take all the particulars into account, since after certain of them have been

examined our mind straightway notices the essential connection, and then disregarding the remaining particulars proceeds at once to bring together the universal. For it knows
that it is necessary that the same relations should be embodied in the rest.

No clearer statement could be made of the procedure of the seventeenth-century scientists.
     This double method, and particularly the analysis of in-
stances, Zabarella considers more fully in his little work *De
Regressu.*

     The regress is between cause and effect when they are
     convertible and the effect is better known to us than the
     cause. For since we must always set out from what is better
     known to us, we first demonstrate from the known effect the
     unknown cause, and then return (*regredimur*) from the cause
     so known to the effect to be demonstrated, that we may know
     the reason why it is so.

Zabarella does not bring in "nature," like Aristotle; for it is a
logical and not a metaphysical question he is considering. "Both
demonstrations are made by us and for us ourselves, not for
nature." In our way of discovery we are following the order of
knowledge, not that of things. Like Nifo, Zabarella finds four
stages in the procedure that is the regress. First we observe
the particular effect. Secondly, we resolve the complex fact
into its component parts and conditions. Thirdly, we examine
this supposed or hypothetical cause by a "mental consideration"
to clarify it and to find its essential elements. Finally, we
demonstrate the effect from that cause.

     When the first stage of the procedure has been completed,
     which is from effect to cause, before we return from the
     latter to the effect, there must intervene a third interme-
     diate process (*labor*) by which we may be led to a distinct
     knowledge of that cause which so far has been known only
     confusedly. Some men [Nifo] knowing this to be necessary
     have called it a *negotiatio* of the intellect. We can call
     it a "mental examination" of the cause itself, or a "mental
     consideration." For after we have hit upon that cause, we
     begin to consider it, so that we may also understand what
     it is.--Zabarella then proceeds to a further analysis of
     this "mental consideration."--But what this mental consider-
     ation may be, and how it is accomplished, I have seen ex-
     plained by nobody. For though some say that this inter-
     mediate *negotiatio* of the intellect does play a part, still
     they have not shown how it leads us to a distinct knowledge
     of the cause, and what is the precise force of this *nego-
     tiatio.* . . . There are, I judge, two things that help us
     to know the cause distinctly. One is the knowledge that it
     is, which prepares us to discover what it is. For when we
     form some hypothesis about the matter (*in re aliquid prae-
     noscimus*) we are able to search out and discover something

else in it; where we form no hypothesis at all, we shall
never discover anything. . . . Hence when we find that
cause to be suggested, we are in a position to seek out and
discover what it is. The other help, without which this
first would not suffice, is the comparison of the cause
discovered with the effect through which it was discovered,
not indeed with the full knowledge that this is the cause
and the effect, but just comparing this thing with that.
Thus it comes about that we are led gradually to the knowledge of the conditions of that thing; and when one of the
conditions has been discovered we are helped to the discovery of another, until we finally know this to be the cause
of that effect. The regress thus consists necessarily of
three parts. The first is a "demonstration that" (*quod*),
by which we are led from a confused knowledge of the effect
to a confused knowledge of the cause. The second is this
"mental consideration," by which from a confused knowledge
of the cause we acquire a distinct knowledge of it. The
third is demonstration in the strictest sense (*potissima*),
by which we are at length led from the cause distinctly
known to the distinct knowledge of the effect.

These three phases may indeed occur simultaneously: they are
logically rather than psychologically distinct. "The end of the
regress is a distinct science of effects, which is called science
propter quid."
 The theory of science set forth in the *Analytics* is a theory
of proof, not a theory of discovery. Here within the school of
Paduan Aristotelians, there has been worked out what was so sore-
ly needed, a logic of investigation and inquiry. No longer are
the first principles of natural science taken as indemonstrable
and self-evident: they have become hypotheses resting upon the
facts they serve to explain. If Zabarella did not follow up the
suggestion of Nifo that all natural science therefore remains
conjectural and hypothetical, it was because he believed that an
examination of particular instances would reveal an intelligible
structure present in them; and this was precisely the faith that
inspired seventeenth-century science.

 Principia essendi are not propositions but things, nor
are they of necessity known beforehand. But often they are
unknown; and they can be demonstrated *a posteriori*, though
not *a priori*. For if they themselves had prior principles
they would not be principles.

But these principles of existence are no mere conveniences of
knowledge; they belong to their subject-matter, and are part of
the intelligible structure of the world.

 Propositions accepted in demonstrations from effects, if
we consider them in themselves, are no less necessary, less
per se, or less essential, than the propositions of strict
demonstration. But if we consider our minds, they are not
so clearly known by us to be necessary as the propositions

of strict demonstration. Still we recognize a certain kind
of necessity in them; if not so much as is really there, at
least so much as suffices for that syllogism to deserve the
name and nature of demonstration.

It is not surprising that Galileo should so often sound like
Zabarella. For he arrived in Padua in 1592, while the echoes of
the great controversies over method between Zabarella on the one
hand and Francesco Piccolomini and his disciple Petrella on the
other, fought in the 1580's, were still resounding.

       *   *   *   *   *

Zabarella's version of the Aristotelian logic, though interpreted and colored in terms of each of the three great theories
of knowledge inherited and reconstructed by the seventeenth-
century thinkers, and though receiving in practice wide variations of emphasis on its several parts, remained the method and
ideal of science for all "natural philosophers" until the fresh
criticisms of Locke and Berkeley. For though the language is
diverse, the whole great literature on method that fills the
scientific writing of the seventeenth century is at bottom a
series of footnotes to the *Organon* of Aristotle. Indeed, the
more fully the record of late medieval and Renaissance thought is
studied, the clearer it becomes that the most daring departures
from Aristotelian science were carried on within the Aristotelian
framework, and by means of a critical reflection on the Aristotl-
lian texts--however various the sources of the ideas that fertilized that criticism. The "father" of modern science, in fact,
turns out to be none other than the Master of them that know.

       *   *   *   *   *

There was but one element lacking in Zabarella's formulation
of method: he did not insist that the principles of natural science be mathematical, and indeed drew his illustrations largely
from Aristotle's biological subject-matter. Though he had studied mathematics under Catena and Barocius, and was accounted
expert in optics and in astronomy, these studies failed to leave
any fundamental impress on his thought. The gradual emergence
of mathematics into the dominant position it held in the seventeenth century is due to its cultivation by a small group of
men working on the periphery of the main intellectual movements
of the sixteenth century. There is a conventional view that this
shift to mathematical interests was powerfully furthered by the
Renaissance revival of Platonism and its number mysticism, derived from Proclus, from the Pythagorean tradition, and from the
Cabala. In the Germanies this has some basis in fact, and Kepler
may stand as its consummation. But it is difficult to find any
support for the view that attributes the great achievements of
the Italians in mathematics and mechanics to the influence of
Neoplatonism. On the one hand the Italian Platonists had almost
no scientific interest in mathematics, and their "numbers" led
them at once to the mazes of theology and theosophy. And on the

other, with rare exceptions the Italian mathematicians down through Galileo, when they possessed a philosophical interest at all, were not Platonists but Aristotelians in their view of mathematics, of its relations to physics, and of the proper method of natural knowledge. What they found in the ancients and what they worked upon themselves was no mathematical vision of the world, but effective techniques and practical problems of procedure and discovery. What they constructed as "new sciences" it remained for Descartes to interpret in the light of the tradition of Augustinian Platonism.

Indeed, the one contribution the Humanists can fairly claim to have made to the rise of modern science was to send men to the study of the original ancient sources in mathematics. In reestablishing connection with the mathematics and mechanics of the Hellenistic Age, the appeal to the ancients introduced Archimedes and Hero, as well as Apollonius, Pappus and Diophantus. The mathematical methods of analysis and synthesis of Archimedes, of whom Tartaglia published the first Latin edition in 1543, were the one element which neither the fourteenth-century Ockhamites nor the sixteenth-century Paduans possessed. From them the mathematicians took their start, and carried the day for the quantitative side of the Paduan discussion, to which reference has been made above.

With this mathematical emphasis added to the logical methodology of Zabarella, there stands completed the "new method" for which men had been so eagerly seeking. By the analysis of the mathematical relations involved in a typical "effect" or phenomenon we arrive at its formal structure or "principle." From that principle we deduce further consequences, which we find illustrated and confirmed in experience. Science is a body of mathematical demonstrations, the principles of which are discovered by the resolution of selected instances in experience. This is the method called by Euclid and Archimedes a combination of "analysis" and "synthesis," and by the Paduans and Galileo, "resolution" and "composition." It is traditional and Aristotelian in regarding the structure of science as dialectical and deductive, and in seeing all verification and demonstration as inclusion within a logical system of ideas. It has altered the scheme of the medieval Aristotelians in making the principles of demonstration mathematical in character; and to the scholastic empiricism it has added the insistence that the way of discovery is not mere observation and generalization, not mere abstraction from common experience, but a careful and precise mathematical analysis of a scientific experience--what the medical tradition of Padua called "resolution" and what Archimedes called "analysis." And to that experience demonstration must return, in a "regress," for confirmation, illustration, and the guarantee of the existence of the deduced consequences. But the return to experience is not for the sake of certain proof: for throughout the seventeenth century it is almost impossible to find any natural scientist maintaining that a mere fact can prove any certain truth.

b. The Case for a New Method

(1). Ernan McMullin, "Medieval and Modern Science:
Continuity or Discontinuity?"*

*Ernan McMullin is a philosopher who teaches at Notre Dame.
Rather than a continuity of method from the medieval to the
modern period, Professor McMullin sees a change of fundamental
importance.*

The question asked in my title is, of course, badly posed,
because there was obviously *some* continuity and *some* discontinuity between the empirical natural science of the medieval period
and that of the seventeenth century. The problem is, rather, one
of emphasis: are we to regard the advent of "modern" science as
a relatively smooth and continuous development from the thirteenth-century restoration of Aristotelian thought? Or is the
conventional phrase 'scientific revolution' the more appropriate
way of describing what happened in the seventeenth century?
In short, which are we to stress: evolution or revolution?

1. Historical Introduction.

*   *   *   *   *

The seventeenth-century scientists themselves emphasized the
novelty of what they were doing: Bacon, Galileo, Descartes, all
insisted that they had found a *new* method of approach to the natural world which would yield far more fruit than anything known
hitherto. Little explicit allusion was made to earlier writers,
except to disagree with them. One gets the impression that Aristotelian physics is being rejected *en bloc*. For these men, it
was not a matter of building on the older physics; it seemed to
them necessary to replace it entirely. In their eyes, it would
no longer have even *approximate* validity, not even of the sort a
physical theory of the last century, now outmoded, might still be
said to have today; it was simply an otiose and no longer interesting way of discussing nature, now (in their view) to be wholly
given up.

*   *   *   *   *

If one were to ask Bacon or Galileo or Descartes *why* they
rejected the older physics, the answer would in all cases have
been the same. They would have criticized its *method* as defective, a method of exposition at best, rather than one of discovery or even of proof. Each had his own conception of what the
new method would have to be. Bacon and Newton would reject the
idea of a science of "necessary" truths whereas Descartes (and to
some extent Galileo) still accepted this. Descartes and Galileo
insisted upon singling out the quantifiable aspects of physical
beings as primary, and rejected Aristotle's qualitative essence-
to-property inferences as being purely verbal, conveying no real
insight into the motions of, or distinctions between, bodies.

---

* Ernan McMullin, "Medieval and Modern Science: Continuity or
Discontinuity?" *International Philosophical Quarterly*, 5 (1965),
pp. 103-5; 107-29.

What constituted *evidence* for the "new" scientists seemed to them to be altogether different from what counted as evidence in the *Posterior Analytics*. They would have readily admitted a continuity of *concept* with the Greek scientific tradition: concepts like *matter*, *energy*, *force*, *impetus*, all of which had a long previous history, were still central to the "new science." But they would have insisted (had they adverted to this point) that the continuity with the past indicated by the presence of such conceptual ties was simply a minimal linguistic one which dwindled into insignificance by comparison with the massive discontinuity between the old and the new methodologies.

*   *   *   *   *

Granted that there was a renaissance of natural science at the end of the sixteenth century, to what extent did this *depend upon* a previous tradition? To what extent did it *resemble* the natural science of the thirteenth century? Taking the first of these questions, it is clear that Galileo was far more influenced by his Paduan predecessors and especially by the great Italian savants of the generation just before him (Cardano, Bonamico, Benedetti, Tartaglia) than was once thought. Furthermore, *their* work in turn had been affected by the far-ranging research in mechanics at Oxford and Paris two centuries before. It cannot be said that their work *developed out of* the earlier in some simple sense; the lapse was too long, the new influences coming from technology, from mathematics, from alchemy and astrology, were too powerful. But, nevertheless, the earlier works were well known to them, and were reprinted in countless editions on the new presses; some continuity of problematic and of terminology would not, then, be hard to establish.

The second question, about the de facto *resemblance* between medieval and modern science, is more important, and can be answered with more confidence. What Ferguson has called the "revolt of the medievalists" had led for a time to an exaggeration of the resemblance. Crombie's thesis, that seventeenth-century science is no more than "the second phase of an intellectual movement in the West that began when philosophers of the thirteenth century read and digested in Latin translation the great scientific authors of classical Greece and Islam," leads him at times to diminish the originality of the later period. It is understandable that the reaction to the "hiatus" view of medieval science should itself tend to go to the opposite extreme. But now that the point has been made, it is surely possible to reassess the question in its entirety.

The position I wish to defend here is that: (1) the new science involved a revolution in the domain of *method*; (2) this revolution required a conscious rejection of the Aristotelian ideal of scientific method outlined in the *Posterior Analytics*; (3) insofar as this revolution had been presaged in medieval thought, it had been by way, therefore, of implicit *modifications* in the accepted Aristotelian approach of the time. I am assuming that the most illuminating way of comparing the old and the new here is on the score of *method* and not of specific scientific results. It cannot be denied that the "new science" had a power and a range to it that the older simply lacked. It seems clear that this power came from a difference of approach and of technique. Crombie notes that "the enormously greater achievements and confidence of the seventeenth century scientists make it obvious that they were not *simply* carrying on the older methods though using them better." There was, in short, a new philosophy of science latent in the new science, one that had only been hinted at in the thirteenth century, and one that was strongly at variance with the prevailing Aristotelian tone of the methodology of the earlier period.

2. From "First Principles" to Hypothetical Approximations

To document this, I shall single out the four aspects of Aristotelian "science" that were most firmly set aside by the "new science": (1) its "demonstrative" and *a priori* character; (2) its qualitative character; (3) its restriction to the concrete "natural context"; (4) its separation from *techné*. In doing this, let me recall once again that a measure of continuity is being taken for granted, a continuity of belief in the generalizing power of the human mind, as well as in the intelligibility of physical nature.

In his formal work on methodology, the *Posterior Analytics*, Aristotle stressed a deductive "Euclidean" ideal for natural science, though apparently not insisting on this difficult standard in other domains of thought such as ethics. Such a science would (once properly formulated) begin from first principles, themselves indemonstrable but self-evident once properly understood, progress via definitions of natural essences that could ultimately be cast as the middle terms of "demonstrations" of properties, akin to the demonstrations of geometry. These essences would be certainly known via induction; hypothesis might play a role in *discovery*, but not in the finished *science*. This *a priori* ideal, relying on the analysis of concepts abstracted from everyday experience as well as on deductive syllogistic logic, was manifestly at variance with the methodology practiced by Aristotle himself in his own scientific work in biology. It was endlessly discussed in the thirteenth century in a whole series of commentaries that added some details (for example, on the method of "resolution and composition") but left the basic *a priori* ideal unchanged. It was not that these writers were unaware of the importance of observation, any more than Aristotle himself had been. It was just that its exact role, the exact nature of the "induction" that led to the knowledge of essence, and above all the evidential status of the principles on which the science was said to depend, were never really adequately clarified.

With the challenge to Aristotelian methodology thrown down by the ecclesiastical condemnation of Averroism in 1277, a new caution entered into the discussion of the status of the "first principles." Many theologians were unwilling to concede to physics the determinate deductive self-evidence of geometry, on the grounds that such a claim would restrict the freedom of the

Creator in fashioning the physical universe. If alternatives
were possible (something that Aristotle would hardly have conceded), then alternative systems of physics were presumably possible, too. Thus the role of observation was strengthened and
the uniqueness of the first principles weakened. In practice,
this meant that natural philosophers were readier to settle for
theories of a hypothetical sort than their more Aristotelian
predecessors had been. Yet it is important not to exaggerate
this shift, as Duhem (who was the first to point it out) somewhat
tended to do. It is not as though a new methodology came to be
explicitly formulated, in which hypothesis was recognized not
only as a temporary expedient of discovery but as a key feature
of natural science itself. Fourteenth-century writings on scientific method still on the whole gave the impression that a
proper natural science should progress from essence certainly
known to property certainly deduced.

On this key point, Descartes was still an Aristotelian, and
it was precisely on this point of method that Cartesian physics
ultimately foundered. Galileo, on the other hand, saw the
necessity for beginning with exact statements of natural regularity, directly based on observation, and (to Descartes' dis-
gust) did not try to warrant them via deduction from higher
principles, nor did he use syllogistic reasoning in his
"demonstrations." It was only with Newton, however, that the
older *a priori* ideal was definitively given up: Newton and
Huyghens emphasized that the theories of science must be seen as
approximations. Even more important was their stress on the fact
that a theory rests solely on the observational grounds it proposes to explain; it does not have an autonomous warrant in
"self-evidence," in intuition, or in any source other than the
individual observations. (On this point, Galileo had tended
occasionally towards the *a priori* side.) Later Newtonians were
to forget this sometimes. In general, successful scientific
theories in the course of time have tended to take on an unduly
a priori air, as though the warrant for them far transcended in
its intuitive immediacy anything that mere observations could
give. Nevertheless, since the time of Newton the point most
emphasized in discussions of scientific method has been the dependence of theory for its validation upon the individual facts,
the necessity to adjust it if it does not fit the facts, coupled
with the flat rejection of the view that theory derives its
warrant from some intrinsic property akin to "self-evidence," or
the like.

Consequently, it seems misleading to describe the
seventeenth-century development in Crombie's phrase as "the recovery of the Greek idea of theoretical explanation in science
and especially of the 'Euclidean' form of such explanation." It
is quite true that many of the classics of seventeenth-century
science were cast into a deductive form reminiscent of Euclid.
But as Newton himself emphasized, a propos of the *Principia*, this
was largely with a view to pedagogical convenience, as well as to
rhetorical effect in dealing with Cartesians. It is also true
that Galileo attributed to the Copernican hypothesis and Newton
to his General Scholion a privileged status of a sort that obvi-

ously transcended the available empirical evidence. Yet nevertheless, there was a growing appreciation of the joint hypothetical and empirical status of scientific theory. Canons of
mathematical simplicity or of philosophic coherence were not so
much *rejected* in the assessment of theory as heavily qualified
by empirical demands of verification and meaning.

Consequently, the relation between Greek, medieval, and
modern views on this question is nowhere near as smooth as Crombie suggests:

> The basic conception of scientific explanation held by
> the medieval natural scientists came from the Greeks and
> was essentially the same as that of modern science. When
> a phenomenon had been accurately described so that its
> characteristics were adequately known, it was explained by
> relating it to a set of general principles or theories
> connecting all similar phenomena.

This is misleading because of the equivocal character of the
notion of "theory." It is true that ancients and moderns agree
that explanation in natural science (or anywhere else) involves
recourse to principles of a higher degree of generality than the
facts to be explained. But this is to say almost nothing: the
Greeks were, of course, the first to attempt to make things
systematically intelligible, and this can *only* be done in universal terms. But to dwell on this is merely to press the unex-
citing point that they, as we, wished to explain Nature. This
is scarcely to establish a continuity of methodology. To do the
latter, one would have to show that the sort of "principles or
theories" they invoked, or the way in which they reached them,
somehow foreshadowed seventeenth-century methodology.

And this is precisely what we are denying. Or more exactly,
we are saying that one of the two competing methodologies of scientific explanation in the seventeenth century *was*, in fact,
faithful in many ways to the Aristotelian ideal, but that this
was just what spelt its doom. The triumph of the Galilean-
Newtonian approach over the Cartesian meant that the "principles
or theories" of physics could *not* be taken as epistemologically
prior (either *quoad nos* or even *quoad se*) to the facts and laws
they purported to "explain." The warrant for the theory is *not*,
in the first instance, some intrinsic character of self-evidence,
some relation of conceptual necessity, but its ability to account
for the extrinsic empirical evidence. The theory itself is, in
fact, open to constant modification in the light of later extrinsic evidence, even though scientists, through a natural inertia,
may sometimes be unduly reluctant to make such modifications.

It cannot be too much emphasized that this involved a complete reversal of the Aristotelian notion of "demonstration."
For Aristotle, to "demonstrate" meant to go from something in
some sense better-known to something less-known, from something
which carried its own intrinsic warrant (as a Euclidean axiom or
a philosophical principle did) to something which received its
scientific warrant from its being derived from the first principle or definition. The geometrical axiom was not accepted

because of the truth of the theorems derived from it; rather, the theorems were true because they were derivable from the axioms (which were "seen" to be true). Observation had a heuristic role in leading the mind to the principles, but once the principles were discovered, they no longer rested upon the observations which had occasioned them.

The Newtonian method goes in just the opposite direction. There is no *demonstration* here, strictly speaking. That is left in the future to mathematics. The observations lead the scientist to the formulation of laws and ultimately of theories. The "leading" here is of a highly intuitive and non-formal sort, depending largely on long familiarity with the matter involved. The laws and theories will be approximate and hypothetical; their warrant comes mainly from outside, i.e., from the observations from which the "retroduction," as Peirce called it, began or which have since been added. The theory can be used to predict (in mathematical or logical fashion) consequences not yet tested, whose verification constitute an additional warrant for the theory. Such a prediction could not be called a "demonstration," since it does not *prove*, i.e., add to the warrant of its conclusion. The reverse, in fact is the case: it is only when the prediction is verified in terms of canons of observation not themselves part of the deductive structure of the theory that it becomes fully acceptable. And it will then be the prediction which helps to verify the theory and not the theory which verifies the prediction. One must carefully distinguish *demonstration* from *explanation* and *verification*.

The modification of scientific method that came about at the hands of Galileo, Newton, and their followers must be regarded as *empiricist* by comparison with either the Cartesian or the earlier Aristotelian views. . . .

3.   The "Mathematicization" of Physics

Aristotle drew a sharp distinction between mathematics and physics; the latter is less abstract, less removed from matter and motion, than the former. Physics is the science of mobile-being-in-general as well as of the essential differences between types of mobile beings (e.g., the elements). It tells us what sort of beings there are in the world around us. Mathematics is the science of quantified things, considered only in their quantitative aspects. It tells us about the physical world only at two removes; first, it concerns only the accident of quantity, not any essential factor; second, physical objects usually only approximate to the perfect figures of the geometer. Quality, not quantity, is the clue to physical natures. . . .

In the medieval period, this highly phenomenalist approach to physics gradually began to be modified under the insistent pressures of Platonist successes. Research on the rainbow by Grosseteste, Theodoric, and others, showed the ability of a structural model of light refraction to account for many of the properties of the rainbow, to describe which the language of geometry seemed, therefore, best fitted. Likewise in mechanics, it began to seem that something better than Aristotle's rather vague assertions about the speed of falling bodies could be achieved if mathematical language were used. The Merton School gave a new precision to statements about natural motion by bringing to bear the best mathematical skills of the time. Discussions of statics, too, harked back to the geometrical methods of Archimedes. All of this meant that the older ideal of a non-quantitative physics began to be seriously challenged. It began to seem as though quantity, and the science which treated of it, had somewhat more to do with essence than had been suspected by Aristotle. Yet within the Aristotelian camp so great was the distrust of Platonic mathematizing that the most that could be conceded was that there could be "middle sciences," mathematical in form, physical in application, between physics and mathematics. They would not be part of "physics," strictly speaking: the only valid road to physical essences must still be through the perceptual qualitative. Yet even on this point some scepticism was beginning to make itself felt: *did* "physics" give us the knowledge of even a *single* physical essence? It did not seem so, even though knowledge of such essence seemed to be the natural goal of the human mind.

The way was, in a sense, prepared, then, for the transition later to Galileo's famous dictum that "the Book of Nature is written in the language of mathematics." This represented the entire abandonment of the Aristotelian ideal of non-mathematical physics. Galileo made the necessary distinction between mathematics as a *language* or syntax, and mathematics as a locus of truths about some subject matter. He was not returning to the Platonism of the *Timaeus*, where the physicist had to look to the mathematician not only for his language but for the evidence he needed about the nature of the physical universe. When Plato says that the universe is composed of atoms of certain shapes, the warrant he urges for this claim comes not from physics, not from observation, but from pure geometry. It is this methodological confusion that Aristotle effectively refuted. But in refuting it, he went too far and refused the help of mathematics to the physicist even in the much more restricted role of syntax. It was this latter refusal that Galileo categorically rejected. He rejected it because of the practical success that his predecessors and he himself had been achieving by the use of mathematical syntax in mechanics, and also, presumably, because of the general preference he often expressed for the philosophy of Plato.

It was no longer clear to him why mathematics should not be used as the syntax of physics. The findings of his telescope had broken down the boundary between the celestial order (where even Aristotle had conceded the utility of mathematics) and the terrestrial one. If nature manifests itself through motion, and if motion is best described with the help of mathematical formulae, then there is no need to think of mathematically expressed mechanics as a "*scientia media*"--it *is* physics, or part of physics. It is a surer road to the knowledge of physical essence than any which lies exclusively through qualities perceptible to contingent human senses. Indeed, Galileo and many of his successors will go further and say that it is the *only* road.

*   *   *   *   *

Galilean science thus works a sort of metamorphosis of the
Aristotelian categorial scheme. The "substance-quantity-quality"
triad is no longer helpful to the scientist. His structural
models and mathematically expressed equations of motion are the
only adequate means available, in most cases, for understanding
the *differences* between natural kinds. (The *samenesses* are
another matter, but Aristotle always assumed that the "science of
physics" treated samenesses and differences in methodologically
the same way.) Despite its mathematical form, this science is
not concerned simply with some "accident" of physical bodies,
called quantity. It bears equally on quantity and quality,
whichever of the many meanings of these terms one chooses. And
it reaches out for substance too, unless one is to hold for an
inexpressible *Ding an sich*. The concepts of physics, so understood, are not purely mathematical: they are mathematical in
their *syntax*, physical in their *semantics*.

*   *   *   *   *

4.   Idealization and the Natural Context

A third point of cleavage concerns an issue closely related
to the one just discussed. Aristotle assumed that the degree of
"abstraction" that was proper to physics was one which simply
left aside the individuality of things, but otherwise considered
them in their entirety, and in their natural context. This was
quite central to his notion of *nature* itself. One got to understand the essence of a physical thing by seeing what it "normally" did, disregarding the occasional chance event, disregarding
too the instances where motion was imposed non-naturally upon it.
The natural motion of earth is downwards, because in its natural
context it will either be at rest or falling directly down.

With this view of nature as starting point, it would have
seemed wrong to Aristotle to seek knowledge of nature by artificial simplification of the natural context, by putting something
in a context foreign to it in order that the profusion of relevant
factors in the familiar causal sequences of everyday life might
be reduced to manageable proportions. Aristotle was too much of
the biologist, concerned with problems of ecology and natural
history, to concede much virtue to a method so foreign to the
search for "natural habitat" and "natural behavior." Nature was
to be discovered, not by asking what this particular kind of
thing would do in every conceivable context, but rather: what
would it do in its "natural" context?

There is a close relationship here between nature and tele-
ology: to discover nature, one had to consider the being itself
in a certain specified "always-or-for-the-most-part" setting.
Since such a setting, and all that pertains to it, is part of a
natural order which, taken as a whole, has a considerable stability, indeed an essentially unchanging character in Aristotle's
view, whatever behavior is evinced in a "normal" context of the
kind will guide us to the *goal* of this being's activity, its

telos as part of the natural order. Action within this pattern
is directed towards the continuation of the order, and is thus
the locus both of intelligibility and of good in the operation
of nature. (Aristotle, like Plato, would see in stability or
non-change the evidence of form, not only as intelligible but
also as good; the possibility of finding pattern in the very
change itself, no matter of what sort it is, is never really
explored, so strong is the Platonic *a priori*.) An action which
takes place *outside* the normal pattern cannot thus tell us anything about the finality of the nature; it may indicate how it
reacts to unusual circumstances and thus help to define for us
its "passive potencies," but it will not tell us anything of its
form, strictly speaking.

Physics must be carried on, therefore, by examining things
in their normal complex contexts; by implication, it would seem
as though we must not contrive any sort of non-natural situation,
if the information we seek is to be truly "scientific." It is
not surprising in view of this that the notion of *experiment* is
not discussed by Aristotle in his account of scientific method,
and could hardly have been conceived to be a legitimate part of
this method in any event. As a biologist, he did of course carry
out numerous dissections and exact observations. But that was
not quite the same thing: though dissection *might* conceivably
have suggested to Aristotle a liberalizing of the types of questions that could be posed to nature, it did not in fact do so.
Indeed, his account of "science" in the *Posterior Analytics*, as
we have already remarked, owes little or nothing to his practice
as a biologist.

It is notable that appreciation of the importance of *experimental* techniques in natural science was far slower in developing than was the realization of the importance of mathematics.
Whereas the latter had a strong backing in one half, at least, of
the Greek scientific tradition (and specifically in the Platonic
tradition that was the first to come to the fore in the medieval
period), the notion of experiment was much more novel. Experiment involves two rather different strands: it requires *idealization* and it requires *contrivance*, or actual interference with
the natural order. We shall see more of the latter strand in the
next section. But here it may be noted that the "idealization"
suggested by Plato was not really of an experimental sort. What
he did was to postulate highly simplified models or principles
from which the over-all lines (though not the details) of the
natural order might be understood. The complexity and obscurity
of the physical universe proceeded, he thought, from the imperfection and instability of its image-relation with the world of
form. Such complexity can safely be disregarded in the search
for true "science"; it is not dependent upon intelligible principles in the first place. The "idealization" here is a conscious effort to transcend the world of image, and grasp the
unchanging sources of natural regularity in a direct insight.

It is important to distinguish between two somewhat different sorts of "idealization" in science. One, let us call it
"theoretical idealization," involves the setting up of a simplified model of what is in fact a complicated situation with a view

to giving at least a partial understanding of the situation. The other, which we can call "experimental idealization," is the simplification of an actual physical situation with a view to asking questions about it that can, in consequence of the simplification, be unambiguously answered. It is the latter that we are principally concerned with in this section. The former has already been indirectly discussed, to some extent, in § 2 where we enquired into the *a priori* factor in scientific discovery. The type of "idealization" suggested in Plato's writings is of the theoretical, not the experimental sort. And it is not suggested as an "idealization" in the later sense of an *artificial* simplification in the interests of a manageable theoretical structure. Plato's ideal-world is the *true* world for him, not a temporary and constantly modified device. It is the active *source* of intelligibility, not the hypothesis of a scientist. Nevertheless, Plato's metaphysics is part of the lineage of the theoretical idealization so central to natural science today.

Returning once more to experimental idealization, we note that historians of thirteenth-century science are wont to cite occasional instances of such idealization from that period. Theodoric, for example, experimented with flasks of water in his attempt to discover laws and models of refraction that would illuminate his discussion of the rainbow. Indeed, there is reason to suppose that part of the motivation behind his experimental work was a methodological one: he wanted to show the role of experiment in physics by means of concrete examples. One even finds instances of "thought experiments," where the notion of simplification has actually been detached from that of observational warrant and the "thought-experiment" is used to analyse, in conceptual fashion, the relations between factors that in any everyday situation would be jumbled inextricably with a multiplicity of irrelevant features.

Nevertheless, it should not be supposed that experiment became a central feature of natural science during the medieval period. Very few actual instances of its use are recorded. What is more surprising is that those who did talk about experiment quite frequently did not perform the experiments they describe, or the results would undoubtedly have been quite different. The scholastic method of "resolution and composition" (which developed out of some remarks made by Aristotle) suggested the idea of breaking complex problems into simpler components, but this was applied primarily to the simplifying and isolating of concepts, not to the planning of experimental techniques. On the whole, it can be said that fourteenth-century writing on method still shows very little appreciation for experimental idealization.

Its use, however, gradually increased, as its value came to be realized. A century before Galileo, Marliani was rolling balls down inclined planes in order to clarify some disputed statements in mechanics, though he did not measure any of the quantities involved. Cusa, da Vinci, and many others used experiment more and more. But it was Galileo who first made it the center of physics, a position it has since retained. He saw clearly that if he wished to "put nature to the question" in a fruitful way, it had to be by means of carefully planned and accurately designed experiments. Random or complicated questions would never lead to useful results. Thus, he reduced frictional

and resistance factors virtually to zero in order to discover the
relations between the space and time variables in that complex
phenomenon known as "free fall," which had so baffled the sustained efforts of natural philosophers over centuries. To plan
the experiment, one had in a sense to know what one was looking
for; in particular, one had to have some idea which factors in
the situation were relevant to the question being asked; finally,
it required considerable practical ingenuity to manipulate those
factors in the desired way. What Galileo quite consciously was
doing here was shaping a technique which until then had been
relatively incidental to the method of science, a method of considerable technical sophistication and unlimited applicability.
It might well be said that this was Galileo's own most important
contribution to natural science. Galileo also used theoretical
idealization, but this belonged to a different facet of his
thought. He acknowledged his debt to Plato for it, and, of
course, he was well aware of its widespread use in later medieval science. But his experimental idealization relied mainly
on a quite different source of inspiration: the technical work-
shops he knew so well and the practical demands they imposed on
theoretical knowledge. This leads us to the last of the strictly
"non-Aristotelian" aspects of modern science.

5. Theoria and Techné

One of the most striking aspects of ancient Greek civilization was the separation within it of the theoretical and technical dimensions of life. The Greeks almost singlehandedly invented the notion of theoretical understanding, and made it an
attainable ideal for man that he has never since lost. They
were proficient in technology, though not notably more so than
some other ancient peoples, like the Egyptians and the Babyloni-
ans. But the two scarcely interpenetrated one another at all.
In Greek life it did not seem as though *techné* in any sense contributed to *theoria*, nor *theoria* to *techné*. *Theoria* was an
ideal for the leisured, cultivated, speculative mind. It involved not the grubby manipulation of matter, but the unhurried
ordering of ideas with a view to leading man to transcend the
material order, so far as this was possible to him. *Techné*, on
the other hand, was a skill handed on in an unwritten unstudied
way from craftsman to apprentice; it helped man to dominate matter in a practical way, but its goal was definitely within the
material order itself.

        *   *   *   *   *

In the medieval period, partly because of Roman traditions,
the division between theory and practice never ran quite so deep.
In medicine, in agriculture, in mining, in military technology,
in the vast encyclopedias which were so much a hallmark of the
age, theory began to illuminate technique in a way it had never
done before. Not only that, but the early writers on methodology,
like Hugh of St. Victor and Gundissalinus, insisted on relating
each science with a corresponding art, and made the art heavily
dependent upon the science. Even in the universities, practical

subjects were incorporated to a surprising degree in the general
course requirements. The actual techniques available were not
notably in advance over those of Greece and Rome until after
1300, but where they had frequently been regarded as curiosities
in the earlier period, the Christian medieval world took them
very seriously as a means to transform the temporal order.
    Despite all of this, one looks almost in vain at this time
for any trace of *theoria-techné* interpenetration in the domain
of physics. Part of this was due to the enormous authority of
Aristotle in matters of method; part of it was due to the bookish
character of nearly all university teaching. There was no
laboratory work in the curricula; the final appeal was most often
to an ancient work or a commentary on an ancient work. Direct
appeal to observation, though not unknown, was overshadowed by
the citing of authorities. The universities were simply not in
living touch with the progressing technology nor did it seem to
them to be any of their business to aid in this progress. The
liberally educated student had to know a little about the "ser-
vile arts" in order to be well-rounded, but the prosecution of
these arts lay far outside the interests and competence of the
university as such.

                *   *   *   *   *

    What was needed by 1400 was some new ferment that would
break the old bottles. And that could come only from outside
the university milieu. When it came, it came mainly from the
engineers, the artists, and the *virtuosi* whose curiosity led them
to tread new paths and whose technical training caused them to
keep theory as closely bound to practice as possible. Da Vinci
would be the most obvious example of this: his art led him to
stress the necessity for exact observation, while his engineering
problems forced him to look outside the conventional university
science of his day for guidance in matters of theory. Technology
(unlike theoretical science) continued to develop steadily
throughout this period; as it developed, it became more complex
and more aware of its need for the wider horizons of theory.
Da Vinci and people like him were forced to try new theoretical
approaches, since the traditional physics could not help them.
It was this above all that prepared the way for Galileo, both by
forcing change upon physics from a source outside its traditional
methodology and by giving it a new empirical temper that it had
never before possessed.
    In Galileo's science, there was a new insistence upon opera-
tional definition of the key concepts, a new demand for exactness
in the stating of laws, a new suspicion of "first principles"
remote from the exact specification of the motions of bodies, a
new willingness to try alternative hypotheses, a new reluctance
to talk of "causes," at least until the effects were fully explored. All of these derived largely from the technological
context within which the new science was shaped, and which imposed many of its own characteristics upon it. These characteristics had developed slowly in a hit-or-miss fashion over the
centuries, but by now their pragmatic success in manipulating

the material order attested to the presence in them of a considerable implicit insight into that order itself. The explicit
methodological discussions of science, on the other hand, had
up to this time derived in all cases from prior metaphysical
positions. There was a remoteness from the pressure both of
observational verification and of practical application.

Now the two streams flow together for the first time. The
power of their union was perhaps most clearly shown in the new
stress upon *instrumentation*. Galileo saw quite clearly that
exact instruments would be necessary for the work of experimental
science. He himself was responsible for developing or encourag-
ing the development of several of them. In this development,
theory suggested to the technician not only what instruments
would be required but also how they might be constructed, while
the instruments, once constructed, provided results that often
led to a modification of the theory.

It is this union of theory and *techné* that most of all,
perhaps, marks off "modern" science from its Greek and medieval
ancestors. It came about not so much by an evolution within
natural philosophy itself, as was to some extent the case with
the other changes we have discussed, but much more because of the
impact upon natural philosophy of an external agency quite independent of it, whose own evolution had been governed rather by
socio-economic-religious forces than by criteria of purely
intellectual origin.

6. Conclusion.

It is now time to draw together the threads of our theme.
Discussions of the origins of modern science once tended to a
"total discontinuity" thesis: it was as though the new science
sprang, without progenitor, from the heads of Galileo, Bacon,
and the others. The second, more realistic, thesis was that
modern science was in direct continuity with Greek science, but
that the medieval period had contributed nothing in the mean-
time--the thesis of "medieval hiatus." This thesis was destroyed
by the labors of the medievalists, some of whom then produced
their own antithesis: a claim of more or less total continuity
running from Greek to modern science, with medieval science as a
half-way house. Lastly, the renewed interest in Aristotelian
philosophy in recent decades, particularly in scholastic circles,
has occasionally tended to result in the thesis that modern science is in its essence more or less similar to Aristotelian
science, despite the fact that its pioneers so strenuously
denied this.

The thesis defended in this paper (as already noted) has
three parts: (1) there is a fundamental discontinuity between
Aristotelian and modern science regarding nearly all questions
of method; (2) insofar as the medieval period formed a bridge to
the modern one, it was precisely to the extent that it saw the
modification, or the beginnings of rejection of, some central
Aristotelian themes; (3) nevertheless, medieval science remained
basically Aristotelian in its approach; the transition from it to
modern science was not a gradual evolution due to internal re-

working, but much more a *revolution* in which the literary Renaissance, the growth of technology, as well as many other agencies outside the domain of science itself, contributed to a change of intellectual climate in which the Aristotelian approach to natural enquiry no longer made sense.

1) Aristotle insisted upon the intrinsic evidential character of the "first principles" from which physics was to be derived; he excluded mathematics as a means of reaching out to natural essence; he situated science in the context of "normal" behavior, thus implicitly making experiment an unlikely way to physical insight; he saw no direct relevance of *techné* to the pursuit of physics, nor of physics to the betterment of *techné*. On all four of these scores, his approach was set aside by the Galilean scientists. It is true that he *was* himself a great biological scientist, and that the rediscovery of his work was an important historical step in the reestablishment of the scientific ideal itself. He was the first to vindicate in detail the claim of the human mind to discover intelligible permanent patterns intrinsic to physical behavior. He stressed the importance of observation more than anyone else had done up to his time. But the methodology he laid down for natural science in his *Posterior Analytics* was incapable of doing the job, in the domain of physical natures, at least. It was too dependent on a geometrical ideal, too remote from the experimental and technical order, too much wedded to a verbal-phenomenal notion of forms. If one is to assess the continuity-discontinuity theme in this context, one is forced to say that there is almost no methodological continuity at all between Aristotelian and Galilean physics, and that if one is to look for continuity, it will have to be in vaguer and more intangible terms of "stress on the intelligibility of the physical universe,""realization of the need for observation," and the like.

2) It follows from the above, then, that medieval science can be regarded as a "bridge" in two ways only. First, the renaissance of interest in the works of Plato and Aristotle *did*, in a general way, turn men's interests once again to the systematic study of the natural world. But, second, insofar as the period was to *prepare* for the scientific renaissance of the seventeenth century, it could only have been by the *modification* it imposed on Aristotelian physical method. . . . So that medieval science is a "bridge," then, almost precisely to the extent that it ceased to be Aristotelian.

3) When all is said and done, however, medieval science--despite the novelties in it here and there--was still Aristotelian in its basic methodology. . . .

In particular, the instances of drift from Aristotelian orthodoxy were not regarded as such at the time; they were implicitly taken to be minor developments, in basic continuity with "the" tradition. Consequently, no effort could be made to rethink the whole approach in the light of the new suggestions. The idea that a much more radical shift was necessary than could be afforded by an isolated and somewhat half-hearted use of mathematics or experiment would not have occurred easily to men who had been led to regard Aristotle as supreme in matters of

method. After all, had he not invented logic and biology almost
single-handedly? Who was to say with assurance that his approach
to the mysteries of nature lacked logic and observational
cunning?

The men of 1300 could not say it. But the men of 1600
could--and did. What made their assertion possible was not primarily the developments in science or in scientific method in the
interim. As we have seen, the interim had been surprisingly
blank as far as scientific advances were concerned. The really
significant change in the centuries between had taken place in
man himself, what in this same context Wightman (adopting
Nietszche's phrase) has called "the transvaluation of values."
In 1600, an "authority" was no longer someone to be accepted, but
someone to be questioned and, if possible, transcended or even
repudiated. Science could no longer be oriented solely to the
order of contemplation. If it were truly knowledge, it had somehow to make a practical difference. Galileo's spokesman in the
Dialogues is impatient with any knowledge which seems merely
verbal, any claim that is inexact or untested, any principle so
general that it seems to have no real illumination for the individual case. There is a new hardness here, an impatience, an
intolerance that sometimes verges on arrogance when the "new"
men look at the work of those who went before them. Where the
men of 1300 had over-stressed their reliance on their predecessors (to the point of concealing or minimizing departures from
them), the "new" men will do just the opposite: they will rarely
concede their dependence on books or teachers even where this
dependence was manifest, and they will magnify their own originality as a matter of course. The humanism of the Renaissance
was part of this change, whether as cause or effect makes no
difference here. So that the Enlightenment historians turn out
to have been not wholly wrong after all; the effect of the
Renaissance was, in fact, a many-sided one: negative first, as
far as interest in natural enquiry was concerned, but positive
later--in *some* respects, at least--in its indirect preparing of
men for a "*new* science."

It is a psychological, almost a moral, change then, one that
was to have reverberations in many domains besides that of natural science. Bacon and Boyle and Galileo took the accumulated
small criticisms of Aristotelian method that dotted medieval science, and wove them into a pattern that was relatively consistent
and altogether new-seeming. The fact that they *wanted* their pattern to seem a new one made a decisive difference to the boldness
with which they tackled the weaving of it. Where Aristotle had
once been "the Philosopher," to the new men he was "the enemy."
This led them frequently to exaggerate their differences with him,
to minimize his achievements in biology and to ridicule his utter
lack of success in chemistry and mechanics. But it also allowed
them to look at the clues with new eyes, to see a new pattern
where before them no one had seen anything more than small departures from an old and familiar path. It was the seeing of this
new pattern that constituted the "scientific revolution," and
which permits us to call it "revolution." Even though its
(usually unacknowledged) roots were firmly in the past, even

though there is scarcely a single element in the new methodological complex that did not have *some* precedent, there is, truly,
something new and revolutionary. And what is new is the whole,
the *gestalt*, the pattern previously unseen that man could never
again unsee.

2. The New Method

(a). Francis Bacon and the *Novum Organon* (New Instrument)
of scientific method.*

Francis Bacon (1561-1626) was trained in the law and a
philosopher by avocation. Early in the seventeenth century he
set himself the task of reforming scientific method and, to this
end, composed his New Instrument, which was first published in
1620. In it, Bacon spelled out both his criticism of earlier
methods, particularly Aristotle's, and laid down his own. In
the process, he was forced to redefine science, as well as its
proper method, and it is both these subjects which the following
selections illustrate.

Translation of that part of the *Distributio Operis* (the outline
of the "Instauratio Magna") which relates to the Novum Organon.

"Now that we have coasted past the Ancient Arts, we will
prepare the human Intellect for its passage to new lands of discovery. And so this second Part has for its end Instruction as
to a better and more perfect use of Reason in discovery of things,
and the true aids of the Intellect: so that (as far as the frail
condition of humanity allows) the Intellect may be raised by it,
and enabled to scale the steep and dark ascents of Nature. This
Art (which we term *the Interpretation of Nature*) is in kind
Logical; although between it and ordinary Logic there is a vast,
immeasurable difference. For the latter does indeed also profess to elaborate and provide help and guards for the Intellect;
and so far only we agree. But ours differs from it chiefly in
three ways: viz. (1) in its end; (2) in the order of its demonstrations; and (3) in the starting point of its inquiries.
"(1) For the end proposed for this Science of ours is the
discovery not of Arguments, but of Arts; not of what agrees with
Principles, but of Principles themselves; not probable reasons,
but the marking out and indication of effects to follow. And so,
the intention of each being different, different results ensue
in each. There the adversary is vanquished and bound down by
Disputation; here Nature by Operation.
"(2) And to an end of this kind correspond both the nature
and the order of our Demonstrations. For in common Logic almost
all men's labour is expended on the Syllogism. As to Induction,
Logicians scarcely seem to have thought seriously about it; passing it over with but light notice, and hastening on to formulæ
of Disputation. But we reject Syllogistic Demonstration, because
it acts confusedly, and lets Nature slip out of its hands. For
although no one can doubt that "quæ in medio termino conveniunt,

---

* *The Novum Organon or A True Guide to the Interpretation of*
Nature, by Francis Bacon, Lord Verulam. A New Translation by the
Rev. G. W. Kitchin, Oxford, 1855. Pp. xxv-xxix; 4-7; 12-14; 18-
22; 25-6; 29-31; 80-85; 113-5; 124-51; 153-65.

ea et inter se conveniunt"--(for this has a sort of Mathematical
certainty), yet there lies under it the fallacy, that the Syllogism is composed of Propositions, Propositions of words, words
are the counters and signs of conceptions. And so if the conceptions of the mind (which are as it were the soul of words, and
the basis of all this structure and fabric) be badly and care-
lessly abstracted from things, be vague, ill defined and circumscribed, and faulty in many ways, the whole thing falls to the
ground. And so we reject the Syllogism; and that, too, not only
for first Principles (to which Logicians themselves do not apply
it), but also for middle Propositions; which Syllogism indeed
produces and brings forth; but which are barren of products,
remote from practice, and clearly useless for the active part of
the Sciences. Accordingly, although we leave to Syllogism, and
such-like famous and boasted kinds of Demonstration, jurisdiction
over popular Arts, and those which depend on opinion (for we make
no movement in this direction), yet for the Nature of things we
make use of Induction throughout, and for minor as well as for
major Propositions. For we count *Induction* to be that form of
Demonstration which defends the Senses, presses on Nature, and is
close to, and almost takes part in, production of results.

  "And so the order of Demonstration is also entirely inverted.
Hitherto things have been carried on as follows:--men fly from
the Senses and particulars direct to most general axioms, as to
fixed poles round which disputations turn; and from these everything else is derived by means of middle terms: a short way,
certainly, but precipitous; one which Nature cannot tread, though
easy and smooth for Disputations. But by our plan, Axioms are
brought out continuously, step by step, so that one does not
reach the most general Axioms till the last: but these when
reached are not conceptional, but well limited; and such as
Nature acknowledges as really more noscible to herself, and such
as reach to the very marrow of things.

  "Moreover in the form of Induction, and the judgment which
takes place by it, we undertake far the greatest matter of all.
For that Induction of which Logicians speak, which proceeds by
Simple Enumeration, is a puerile matter, concludes uncertainly,
is exposed to danger from a single Contradictory Instance, and
only looks into subjects to which we are accustomed; nor does it
discover the end.

  "But for the Science of Induction there is need of a form
which may solve experience, may separate things, and, by means of
due exclusions and rejections, conclude necessarily. But if that
common Judgment of the Logicians is so weighty, and has exercised
such great minds,--how much more should we toil over this kind,
which is drawn not only from the reason of the Mind, but even
from the very bowels of Nature.

  "(3) Nor is the end here. For we also press down more
tightly, and make solid the foundations of the Sciences, and take
a lower point for beginning inquiry than men have done hitherto:
by subjecting those things to test, which common Logic receives
on trust. For the Logicians borrow the principles of each Science from that Science in particular: then worship the first
conceptions of the Mind: lastly, are quite satisfied and rest in

the immediate information of the Senses: but we have determined
that the true Logic ought to enter the province of each Science
with greater Authority than the principles of each possess; and
to make those same imaginary principles render an account of
their real value. As to the first conceptions of the Intellect,
none of those things which the Intellect gathers when left to itself is other than suspected by us, and we do not ratify it,
unless, after new judgment, it stands and is pronounced valid.
Moreover, we try the information of the Senses also in many ways.
For the Senses are also fallacious, but shew their mistakes. The
mistakes are near at hand, but helps against them are sought from
afar.

"The faults of the Senses are two: they either fail or
deceive. For in the first place there are a multitude of things
which escape the Senses even when they are rightly disposed and
nohow hindered; either by the subtilty of their whole body, or
by the minuteness of their parts, or by their distance, or by the
slowness and even the swiftness of their motion, or by the familiarity of the object, or other reasons. And again, where Senses
lay hold of a thing, their grasp is not particularly firm. For
the testimony and information of the Senses always are measured
by Man, and not by the Universe: and it is a great mistake to
assert, that Sense is the measure of all things.

"And so to meet these evils we, with much and faithful service, have sought out and gathered helps for the Senses from
every side; so to supply substitutions where they fail, rectifi-
cations where they vary. Nor do we attempt this with Instruments
so much as with Experiments. For their subtilty is far greater
than that of the Senses, even when aided by exquisite instruments.
And so we do not allow much to the immediate and proper perception of the Senses: but make the Senses judge only of Experiments, Experiments of things."

      *   *   *   *   *

Now our plan is as easy to explain as it is hard to carry
out. It consists in laying down grades of certainty, in defending the senses by reducing them to their proper functions, in
rejecting for the most part that operation of the mind which
follows directly after the operation of the senses; and then in
opening and laying down for the mind a new and certain way from
the perceptions of the senses. And this, undoubtedly, they also
saw who assigned such important functions to Dialectics; and it is
clear they sought for some support for the intellect, while they
respected the native and spontaneously acting process of the mind.
This remedy, however, came altogether too late; for things were
desperate, after that the mind, thanks to the daily habits of
life, was both filled by polluted discourse and teaching, and
possessed by vainest phantoms. And so that Art of Dialectics
taking heed to this too late, and nohow restoring the matter, was
potent rather for the confirmation of errors than for the disclo-
sing of Truth. There remains but one hope for safety and health--
in the entire recommencement of the whole work of the mind; and
in nohow leaving the mind to itself from the very beginning, but

in perpetually guiding it, and in carrying out our object as it were by means of machinery. For truly if men had attempted works which required mechanical means with their bare hands, without the power and aid of instruments, as they have not hesitated to handle intellectual work with little but the bare strength of their minds, very small would have been those things which they would have been able to move and overcome, even though they had exerted strenuous and combined efforts. And let us linger a moment, and look into this same example, as into a mirror; let us suppose the question to be, how perchance some obelisk of remarkable size could be moved from one place to another, to grace some triumph or such-like pageant--would not any sober spectator of the proceeding declare it an act of great madness, were men to attempt it with their bare hands? . . . And yet men are borne along with a like unsound energy and useless combination in matters intellectual, so long as they hope for great results either from the multitude and consent, or from the excellence and acumen of intellects, or even while they brace up the muscles of their minds with Dialectics, which may truly be regarded as a sort of mental gymnastics: but meanwhile, although they use so great diligence and endeavour, yet (if one rightly judges) they cease not to apply only their bare intellect. But it is most clear, that, in every great work which men's hands produce, neither the strength of individuals nor of numbers can be combined without the application of instruments and machines.

*   *   *   *   *

The cause and root of almost all evils in the Sciences is this one; that while we falsely admire and exalt the powers of the human mind, we do not seek its true aids.

The subtilty of Nature far surpasses the subtilty of sense and intellect; so that men's fair meditations, speculations and reasonings are a kind of insanity, only there is no one standing by to notice it.

Just as the Sciences which now prevail are useless for the discovery of results, so the Logic also which now prevails is useless for the discovery of Sciences.

The Logic which is in vogue is rather potent for the confirming and fixing errors (which are based on vulgar opinions) than for the investigation of Truth: so that it is more harmful than useful.

The Syllogism is not applied at all to the principles of Science--is applied in vain to the medial axioms, since it is no match for the subtilty of Nature. And so it constrains Assent, not Things.

Syllogism is composed of propositions, propositions of words, words are the symbols of conceptions. And so if the conceptions themselves (which are the foundation of the whole thing) be confused and rashly abstracted from things, there is no solidity in what is built upon them. And so our only hope is in a true Induction.

In the conceptions both of Logic and Physics there is nothing sound: our conceptions of *substance, quality, action, passion*--and even of *being*--are not good; much less those of *weight, levity, density, rarity, moisture, dryness, generation, corruption, attraction, repulsion, element, matter, form,* and the like--all of them are fanciful and ill-defined.

The conceptions of *Infimæ Species, man, dog, dove,* and of the immediate apprehensions of the senses, *warm, cold, white, black,* do not so very much mislead; and yet even these are sometimes confounded from the flux of matter and the strife of things--All other conceptions, which mankind have used up to this time, are errors, and abstracted and drawn out of things by no due methods.

$$*\qquad *\qquad *\qquad *\qquad *$$

The Phantoms and false conceptions which have hitherto preoccupied man's intellect, and are deeply rooted in it, not merely so besiege men's minds that truth can with difficulty approach; but also, where truth has had a passage allowed her, they will again occur and be troublesome in the Instauration of the Sciences, unless men be forewarned and defend themselves against them as far as is possible.

There are four kinds of Phantoms which lay siege to human minds. To them (for instruction's sake) we give names; and call the first kind *Phantoms of the Tribe*; the second, *Phantoms of the Cave*; the third, *Phantoms of the Market-Place*; and the fourth, *Phantoms of the Theatre*.

The raising of conceptions and axioms by means of true *Induction* is certainly the proper remedy for driving and clearing out Phantoms: yet there is great use in pointing out the Phantoms. For right teaching about Phantoms stands towards the Interpretation of Nature, as the teaching about confutation of Sophisms does to the common Logic.

The *Phantoms of the Tribe* are founded in Human Nature itself, and in the very tribe or race of man. For it is a false assertion, that "human sense is the measure of things"; whereas on the contrary, all perceptions both of sense and of mind are measured by the standard of man, not by the standard of the Universe; and the human Intellect is like an uneven mirror catching the rays of things, which mingles its own nature with the nature of things, and distorts and corrupts it.

The *Phantoms of the Cave* are the phantoms of the individual. For each man has (besides the generic aberrations of human nature) some individual cave or den which breaks and corrupts the light of nature; either by reason of the peculiar and singular nature of each; or by reason of education and conversation of man with man; or by reason of the reading of books, and the authority of those whom each man studies and admires; or by reason of differences of impressions as they occur in a mind preoccupied and predisposed, or even and sedate; or the like. So that evidently the human spirit (according as it is placed in each individual) is a various thing, and altogether disturbed and, as it were, the creature of circumstance. Whence Heraclitus hath well said that "men seek knowledge in lesser worlds, not in the greater and common world."

There are also phantoms arising as it were from the inter-
course and society of men with one another. These we call *Phantoms of the Market-Place*, on account of the commerce and consort
of men. For men associate by means of discourse; but words are
imposed at the will of the vulgar: and so a bad and foolish imposition of words besieges the intellect in strange ways.
Neither do the definitions or explanations wherewith learned men
have been accustomed to fortify and clear themselves in some
cases, in any way set the matter to rights. But words clearly
put a force on the intellect, disturb everything, and lead men
on to empty and innumerable controversies and fictions.

Lastly there are phantoms which have entered into the minds
of men from the different dogmas of Philosophical systems, and
even from perverted laws of Demonstration. These we name *Phantoms of the Theatre*: because we count that each Philosophy received or invented is like a Play brought out and acted, creating
each its own fictitious and scenic world. Nor do we only speak
of those philosophies and sects which are now flourishing, nor
even of the ancient ones, since plenty more such Plays might be
composed and got up; for the causes of errors utterly diverse may
be nevertheless almost common. Nor again do we only understand
this of the universal philosophies, but even of very many other
principles and axioms of the sciences, which have gotten strength
through tradition, credence, and neglect.

*   *   *   *   *

The Human Intellect, from its peculiar nature, easily supposes a greater uniformity and equality in things than it really
finds; and though there are many things in nature unique, and
full of inequality, yet it feigns parallels, correspondents, and
relations which do not exist. Hence the figment "that in the
heavens all things be moved through perfect circles," spiral
lines and eccentrics being cast aside (except merely in name).
Hence the Element of Fire with its Orb is introduced to make up
the quaternion with those other three which are subjected to the
senses--and farther, on the elements (as they are called) is
imposed at their pleasure, the tenfold progression of rarity,
each after other; and fancies of the like kind. Neither does
this vanity only prevail in dogmas, but even in simple conceptions.

The human Intellect, in those things which have once pleased
it, (either because these have been received and believed, or
because they delight,) draws also all other things to vote with
and consent to these--and though the weight and multitude of contrary instances be the greater, yet either it does not observe
them, or despises them, or draws distinctions, and so removes
and rejects them--not without great and pernicious prejudice--in
order that the authority of those previous conclusions may remain
unshaken. And so he answered well, who, when the picture of
those who had fulfilled their vows after escaping the peril of
shipwreck were shown him hung up in a temple, and he was pressed
with the question, did he not after this acknowledge the Providence of the Gods, asked in his turn, "But where are they painted

who, after vowing, perished?" The same is the method of almost
every superstition, as in astrology, in dreams, omens, judgments,
and the like; in which men who take pleasure in such vanities as
these attend to the event when it is a fulfilment; but where they
fail, (though it be much the more frequent case,) there they neglect the instance, and pass it by. . . .

The human Intellect is far most hindered and led astray by
the dulness, incompetency, and fallacies of the senses; so that
those things which strike the sense outweigh those which do not
do so immediately, even though these latter be the more important.
And so thought almost ends with sight; so that there is little or
no observation of things invisible. And so every operation of
spirits shut up in tangible bodies lies hid, and escapes the
notice of men. Every very subtle change, too, in the structure
of the parts of grosser things (which men ordinarily call *alteration*, while in truth it is a conveyance, or movement through the
least space) in like fashion lies unnoticed; and yet, unless
these two, which we have spoken of, were explored and brought to
light, nothing great, as far as regards results, can be done in
Nature. Again, the nature of common air itself, and of all
bodies which in their rarity surpass the air (and these are very
many), is almost unknown. For the sense by itself is a feeble
thing, and errant; neither do instruments avail much for the
increasing the sense or its sharpening; but every true interpretation of Nature is achieved by means of instances, and fit
and apposite experiments; wherein the sense judges only of the
experiment, but the experiment of the nature and the thing
itself.

The human Intellect is carried to abstracts by reason of its
proper nature; and feigns that those things, which are variable,
are constant. Better is it to dissect Nature than to abstract
her, as did the school of Democritus, which penetrated farther
into Nature than the rest did. Matter ought rather to be considered, its structure and changes of structure, and simple
action and law of action or motion; for Forms are fictions of the
human soul, unless it be allowable to call the laws of action
Forms.

*   *   *   *   *

But the *Phantoms of the Market-place* are the most troublesome of all. These have stolen into the Intellect from the associations of words and names. For men believe that their reason
rules over words; but it is also the case that words react and in
their turn use their influence on the Intellect; and this has
rendered Philosophy and the Sciences sophistical and inactive.
But words for the most part are imposed at the will of the vulgar,
and divide things by lines most conspicuous to the vulgar Intellect. When however a sharper Intellect or more diligent observation wishes to shift those lines, to make them more in accordance with Nature, then words cry out against it. Whence it
comes that the great and solemn disputations of the learned often
degenerate into controversies about words and names; with which
(after the manner of foreseeing Mathematicians) it would have

been more advisable to have begun, and to have reduced words to
order by definitions. And yet these definitions (in things
natural and subject to Laws of Matter) cannot cure this evil,
since definitions themselves consist of words, and words beget
words. And so it is necessary to recur to particular instances,
and to their series and orders. This we shall mention presently,
when we have arrived at the manner and plan of framing conceptions and axioms.

Phantoms, which are imposed on the Intellect by means of
words are of two kinds. Either they are the names of things
which exist not, (for as there are things which have no names,
through lack of observation, so too there are also names without
things through fanciful supposition,) or they are names of things
which exist, but are confused and ill-defined, and rashly and
irregularly abstracted from things. Of the former kind are,
Fortune, *Primum Mobile*, the orbits of planets, the element of
fire, and such like fictions, which spring from vain and false
theories. And this kind of Phantoms is the more easily ejected,
because they can be exterminated by constant disowning and rejection of theories.

But the other kind is intricate and deeply rooted; it is
produced by bad and unskilful abstraction. E.g. take some word,
(*moist*, if you like,) and let us see how those things which are
designated by this word agree. You will find that the said word
moist is nought but a confused mark of diverse actions, which
admit of no consistency or reduction to one head. For it signifies what readily surrounds another body; what is in itself
indeterminable, and has no consistency; what readily yields in
every direction; what readily separates and scatters itself; what
readily gathers and collects itself; what readily flows and is
set in motion; what readily adheres to another body, and renders
it damp; what is readily reduced to a liquid state, or melts,
when it was before consistent. And so, as soon as we are come to
the predication and imposition of this name: if you take one
sense, flame is moist; if another, air is not moist: if another,
minute dust is moist; if another, glass is moist: so that it is
clear that this notion is hastily abstracted from water only, and
common and ordinary liquids, and that, too, without any due
verification.

Furthermore, there are in words certain degrees of wrongness
and mistake. Less faulty is the class of names of some substance,
especially of *infimæ species*, and those well deduced (for the
conceptions of *chalk*, or *clay* are good; of *earth*, bad); more
faulty that of actions, as *generation, corruption, alteration*;
most faulty that of qualities (with the exception of immediate
objects of sense) as *heavy, light, rare, dense*, &c.; and yet in
all these it must be that some conceptions are a little better
than others, according as things in greater or less plenty strike
the human senses.

       *   *   *   *   *

The foundations of experience (for we must certainly come
down to this point) have hitherto either been non-existent, or
very infirm; nor has store of material of particulars either in
quantity, kind, or certainty fit to inform the Intellect, or in
any way sufficient, hitherto been sought out and collected. But
on the contrary learned men (idle truly and easy folk) have accepted for the formation or confirmation of their Philosophy,
sundry rumours reports and breaths of experience, and have attributed to these the weight of legitimate testimony. And just
as if some kingdom or state governed its counsels and its business, not by the letters and despatches forwarded to it by its
Ambassadors and trustworthy Messengers, but by the small-talk
and gossip of the streets; so have the affairs of Philosophy been
administered, as far as experience goes. Nothing in Natural
History is found to be duly investigated, nothing verified,
nothing numbered up, nothing weighed, nothing measured. And what
is in observation indefinite and vague, the same in information
is deceitful and unfaithful. If these things seem strange say-
ings to any one, and not far removed from unjust complaint;--
seeing that Aristotle, a man of such powers, and supported by the
wealth of so great a King, has completed so accurate a History of
Animals; and some others with greater diligence, (though with
less noise,) have added much thereto: and again others have
written copious histories and narrations of plants, metals, and
fossils;--he does not seem to attend sufficiently and to see into
what is going on at present. For there is one kind of Natural
History, which is made for its own sake; another kind which is
gathered for the information of the Intellect in order to the
building up of Philosophy. And these two kinds of History differ
on other points indeed, but specially in this; that the former of
them contains the various natural species, the latter the experiments of Mechanical Arts. For just as in civil affairs the
abilities of each man, and the secret sense of his mind and
affections are better drawn forth in positions of disturbance
than elsewhere; similarly the hidden things of Nature more betray
themselves when the Arts provoke them, than when they wander on
in their own course. And so we then shall have good Hope for
Natural Philosophy after Natural History, which is its base and
foundation, has been better arranged;--till then no Hope at all.
   And again; in the very abundance of Mechanical Experiments,
the utter poverty of those which make most for and assist the
information of the Intellect is discovered. For the Mechanician,
nohow solicitous about the inquiry into Truth, neither raises his
mind nor stretches forth a hand to anything which does not sub-
serve his own work. But then shall Hope of the farther progress
of the sciences be well founded, when there shall be received and
gathered into Natural History a multitude of experiments, which
in themselves are of no use, but avail only for the discovery of
causes and axioms. These we are wont to call *Light-bringing*
experiments, to distinguish them from *Fruit-bearing* ones. They
have in them a wonderful virtue and condition; namely, they never
deceive or disappoint. For as they are employed not to effect
any result, but to reveal the natural cause in something, in
whatever way they fall out, they equally satisfy our purpose, as

they settle the question.

But not only is a greater abundance of experiments to be sought for and procured, and of another kind too from those hitherto gathered; but also an entirely different Method, Arrangement, and Process are to be introduced for the continuation and promotion of experience. For vague experience, which follows only itself, (as has been said above,) is a mere groping, which stupifies men rather than informs them. But when experience shall proceed under a fixed Law, in due series and sequence, then we may have better Hopes for the sciences.

But after collection and preparation of such abundance and material of Natural History and Experience as is requisite for the work of the Intellect or for any philosophical work, still the Intellect is in no way sufficient to act spontaneously and by bare aid of memory upon those materials; one might just as well hope to be able to retain in memory and to know by heart the computation of an Almanack. And yet up to this time meditation has done more in discovery than writing has; nor as yet has a "Literate Experience" been collected: and yet except by writing no discovery is to be approved. When however it comes into use, we may hope better things from Experience when it has at length become Literate.

And farthermore, when there is so great a number and host of particulars, and these too so scattered and diffused as to disconnect and confuse the Intellect; no good Hopes can be entertained from the skirmishings, light movements, and transitions of the Intellect; unless there be an arrangement and marshalling of those things which pertain to the subject on which we are making inquiry, by means of fit, well arranged, and, as it were, living Tables of Discovery; and unless the mind be applied to the prepared and digested assistance afforded by these Tables.

But we must not forthwith pass from the abundance of particulars duly and orderly placed under our eyes, to inquiry into and discovery of new particulars, or effects; or at any rate, if this be done, we must not rest there. We do not deny that after collection and digest of all experiments of all arts, and after these have come to the knowledge and judgment of one man, many new things may be discovered, useful for human life and condition, by transferring the experiments of one art to others, by means of that Experience, which we call Literate: still, less things are to be hoped for from it, and greater things from the new light of Axioms, educed by certain way and rule out of those particulars, which in their turn may indicate and mark out new particulars. For the road does not lie on a level; but ascends and descends-- ascending first to Axioms, descending to Effects.

Nor, however, can it be allowable for the Intellect to leap and fly from particulars to remote, and (in name) most general Axioms, (such as are what they call "the principles of Arts and Things,") and by means of their (supposed) immoveable Truth to prove and make out intermediate Axioms. This is the process followed hitherto, thanks to the proneness of the natural impulse of the Intellect to this, and to its being accustomed and trained to it, by means of Syllogistic Demonstrations. But then we may hope well for the Sciences, when ascent is made by the true ladder, by successive steps, not interrupted or broken, from partic-

ulars to lesser Axioms, thence to intermediate ones, one over
another, and lastly, in due time, to the most general. The
lowest Axioms differ but little from bare experience. And those
highest and most general Axioms (as now considered) are conceptional and abstract, and have in them no solidity. But the middle ones are the true, solid, living Axioms, whereon depend man's
affairs and fortunes; and above these, at last, are those really
most general; these however are not abstract, but truly bounded
by the intermediate ones.

And so we must not add wings, but weights and lead, to the
Intellect, so as to hinder all leaping and flying. And this has
not hitherto been done: when it has been, we shall be allowed
to entertain better Hopes for the Sciences.

Moreover, in forming an Axiom, a form of *Induction*, different from that hitherto in use, must be thought out; and this,
too, not only for testing and discovering principles (as they
call them), but also for lesser, then for intermediate, and
finally for all Axioms. For that Induction which proceeds by
simple enumeration is a puerile thing, and concludes uncertainly,
and is exposed to danger from any contradictory instance, and for
the most part pronounces from fewer instances than it ought, and
of these only from such as are at hand. But the Induction which
will be useful for the discovery and demonstrations of Sciences
and Arts, ought to separate Nature by due rejections and exclusions; and then, after a sufficient number of negatives, to conclude upon affirmatives; a thing which hitherto has not been
done, nor indeed attempted, save only by Plato, who for the formation of Definitions and Ideas certainly uses this form of
Induction up to a certain point. But for the good and legitimate
appointing of this Induction or Demonstration, very many things
are to be made use of which have as yet entered into the thoughts
of no man; so that more labour must be spent upon it than has
hitherto been spent upon the Syllogism. And the assistance of
this Induction must be had not only to discover Axioms, but to
limit conceptions also. And on this Induction depends our greatest Hope.

*   *   *   *   *

Aphorisms on
the Interpretation of Nature
or the Reign of Man.

Book The Second.

Upon a given body to generate and superinduce a new Nature
or new Natures is the work and aim of Human Power. To discover
the Form of a given Nature, or its true Difference, or its causal
Nature, or fount of its emanation (for these are the Terms in use
which most nearly indicate the thing we mean)--this is the work
and aim of Human Knowledge. And under these primary operations
must be put two others, secondary and of a lower stamp. Under
the former the transformation of concrete bodies from one into
another, within the limits of possibility: under the latter the

discovery in all generation and motion of the *Latent Process* which goes on without break from the manifest Efficient, and Matter, up to the inward Form; and in like manner, the discovery of the *Latent Conformation* of bodies in rest, not in motion.

The unhappy case of Human Knowledge, as it is now, is even manifested by what is ordinarily asserted. It is rightly laid down that "true knowledge is knowledge by causes." Also the establishment of four Causes is not bad: Material, Formal, Efficient, Final. Of these, however, the Final Cause is so far from profiting us, that it even corrupts Knowledge, except in Morals. The discovery of Form is held to be hopeless. And the Efficient and Material Causes (such as are now sought for and received, i.e. those remote from, and without *Latent Process* towards Form) are slovenly and superficial, and of scarcely any avail for true and active Knowledge. Nor have we forgotten how we above noticed and corrected the error of the human mind in assigning to Forms the first qualities of Essence. For although in Nature nothing really exists except individual bodies, which produce individual pure acts according to Law: yet in science, that Law itself and the investigation, discovery, and unfolding thereof are the foundation both of knowledge and of practice. This *Law*, then, *and its Paragraphs* we mean when we speak of Forms; especially as this word has grown into common use, and is of familiar occurrence.

His Knowledge is imperfect, who knows the cause of any Nature (Whiteness, for example, or Heat) only in certain subjects: His Power likewise is imperfect, who can induce the effect only upon certain materials (among those which are capable of it). And he who knows only the Efficient and Material Causes, (which are variable, and nothing more than vehicles, and causes conveying Form in some substances,) can arrive at new discoveries in such Matter as is to some extent of one kind and previously prepared: but he does not move the limits of things more deeply fixed. Whilst he who knows Forms embraces the Unity of Nature in most dissimilar materials; and so can disclose and produce things which as yet have not been done, such as neither the changes of Nature, nor industry in experiment, nor even chance itself would ever have brought into action, and such as would never have entered the thoughts of man. Wherefore from the discovery of Forms follow both true contemplation and free operation.

*   *   *   *   *

From the two kinds of Axioms laid down above, arises a true division of Philosophy, and of the Sciences; if those received Terms, which most nearly approach to our meaning, be transferred to our sense. Namely, let the inquiry into Forms, which are (in reason at any rate, and after their own Law) eternal and immoveable, constitute *Metaphysics*; let the inquiry after the Efficient and Material causes, after the *Latent Process* and *Structure*, all of which regard the common and ordinary course of Nature, not its fundamental and eternal Laws, constitute *Physics*: and to these in like manner let two practical divisions be subordinate; to

Physics Mechanics, to *Metaphysics Magic* (in a purified sense of the Term), because of its broad ways and wider dominion over Nature.

Thus the aim of our teaching having been laid down, we must go on to its precepts: and that too in an order as little deranged and disturbed as possible. And our hints for the *Interpretation of Nature* embrace two parts differing in kind; the first is on the eliciting or producing Axioms from experience: the second, on the deducing or deriving new experiments from Axioms. The former part is divided into three Ministrations; the Ministration to the Senses, the Ministration to the Memory, and the Ministration to the Mind or Reason.

For first, a *Natural and Experimental History* must be prepared, sufficient and good; for this is the basis of the whole thing: for we must not fancy nor think out, but must discover what Nature does or endures.

But *Natural and Experimental History* is so varied and scattered as to confound and distract the intellect, unless it be fixed and appear in due order. And so *Tables*, and *Coordinations of Instances* are to be formed in such a manner and with such arrangement, that the Intellect may be able to act upon them.

And even though this be done; yet the Intellect, if left to itself and acting spontaneously, is incompetent and unequal to the task of constructing Axioms, unless it be regulated and directed. And so, in the third place, legitimate and true *Induction*, the very key of Interpretation, is to be applied. And moreover we must begin at the end, and travel backwards to the rest.

The Investigation of Forms proceeds thus: in the case of a given Nature we must first make a *Presentation to the Intellect* of all known *Instances* which agree in having this same Nature in materials even the most unlike. And a collection of this kind must be made historically, and without too hasty contemplation, or any toogreat subtilty.E.g. take the Investigation of the Form of Heat.

Instances agreeing in having the Form of Heat.

i. The Sun's Rays, especially in Summer and at Noon.
ii. The Sun's Rays reflected and combined, as between mountains, or along walls of houses, and specially in burning-glasses.
iii. Ignited Meteors.
iv. Burning Lightning.
v. Eruptions of Flames from the Cavities of Mountains, &c.
vi. All Flame.
vii. Ignited Solids.
viii. Natural Hot Baths.
ix. Warm or heated Liquids.
x. Warm Vapours and Smoke, and the Air itself, which admits a most powerful and raging heat, if confined; as in Reverberatories.
xi. Some fine Weather, arising from the constitution of the Air itself, without respect to the time of year.

xii.   Confined and subterraneous Air in some caverns, especially in the Winter.

xiii.   All shaggy substances, as Wool, Hides, Plumage, have some warmth.

xiv.   All bodies, solid as well as liquid, dense as well as rare (like the Air itself), placed near fire for a time.

xv.   Sparks from Flint and Steel gotten by sharp percussion.

xvi.   All bodies rubbed violently, as Stone, Wood, Cloth, &c.; so that poles of carriages, and axles, sometimes catch fire: and the way the West Indians obtain fire is by attrition.

xvii. Green and moist vegetable matter confined and pressed together, as Roses. Peas in baskets; so that Hay if it be damp when stacked often catches fire.

xviii.   Quicklime, slaked with water.

xix.   Iron when it is first dissolved by aqua fortis in glass, and that too without putting it near fire: similarly with Tin, &c. but not so intensely.

xx.   Animals, especially and always internally; though in Insects the Heat is not detected by the touch in consequence of the smallness of their bodies.

xxi.   Horsedung, and like fresh excrement of Animals.

xxii.   Strong Oil of Sulphur and of Vitriol follows the operation of Heat in burning linen.

xxiii.   Oil of Marjoram, and of like substances, follow the operation of Heat in burning bones.

xxiv.   Strong and well-rectified Spirit of Wine follows the operation of Heat: so that if white of egg be cast into it, it grows hard and white, almost in the same way as when boiled; bread thrown into it becomes parched and crusted, like toast.

xxv.   Aromatic substances, and warm plants, as the Dracunculus, the old Nasturtium, &c., though to the hand they be not hot, neither when whole or powdered, yet to the tongue and palate, if chewed a little, they are felt to be hot, and almost burning.

xxvi.   Strong Vinegar, and all Acids, on any part of the body where there is no epidermis--as in the eye, on the tongue, or any wounded part, or where the skin is removed,--cause pain, not much unlike that produced by Heat.

xxvii.   Even severe and intense cold produces a kind of sensation of burning.

xxviii.   Other Instances.

This we are wont to call a *Table of Existence and Presence.*

Secondly; we must make a *Presentation to the Intellect of Instances* which are without the given Nature: because Form, (as we have said,) ought no less to be absent where the given Nature is absent, than to be present where it is present. But this would be an infinite task if we took every Instance.

And so we must class the *Negatives* under the *Affirmatives,* and the want of the given Nature must be investigated only in those subjects which are most cognate to those in which the given Nature is present and manifest. This we are wont to call a *Table of Declination,* or of *Absence in Proximate Instances.*

Proximate Instances, wanting the Nature of Heat.

First Negative Instance subjunctive to the First Affirmative.

i.   The Rays of the Moon, the Stars, and Comets, are not found hot to the touch: nay, rather, the severest cold is usually observed at Full Moon.

But the larger Fixed Stars, when the sun passes under them or approaches them, are thought to increase and intensify the warmth of the Sun; as is the case when the Sun is in the Sign of the Lion, and in the Dogdays.

First Negative subjunctive to the Second Affirmative.

ii.   The Sun's Rays in the middle region of the Air (as they call it) give no Heat; the commonly given reason for which is not bad, viz. that that region neither approaches near enough to the Body of Sun, whence the Rays emanate, nor on the other hand near enough to the Earth, whence they are reflected.   And this is man-ifested by the tops of mountains, (unless they are exceedingly high,) where the snow is perpetual. . . .

Second Negative to the Second.

iii.   The reflection of the Sun's Rays, in the regions near the Polar circles, is found to be very weak and lacking in power of producing Heat: so that the Dutch, who wintered in Nova Zembla, and expected the liberation and disentanglement of their ship from the mass of ice which had blocked it up, about the be-ginning of July were disappointed of their hope, and were com-pelled to take to boat.   And so the direct Rays of the Sun seem to have but little power even upon a level surface; nor even after reflection, unless they be multiplied and united, which takes place when the Sun approaches nearer to the Perpendicular; because then the incidence of the Rays makes acuter angles (with the reflection), so that the lines of the Rays are nearer to one another: while, on the other hand, when the Sun is in a very oblique position, its angles are very obtuse, and consequently the lines of the Rays farther apart. . . .

Third Negative to the Second.

iv.   Let an experiment of this kind be made.   Take a Lens made concave instead of convex like Burning Glasses; place it between the hand and the Sun's Rays; and observe whether it diminishes the Heat of the Sun, as the Burning Glass increases and intensifies it.   For it is manifest with regard to Visual Rays, that according as a Lens is made of unequal thickness in respect to its middle and its sides, so do images appear larger or smaller.   And so the same thing must be looked after in Heat.

Fourth Negative to the Second.

v.   Let diligent experiment be made, as to whether the Rays of the Moon can be caught and collected so as to produce any even the least degree of Heat, by means of Burning Glasses of the greatest strength and best make. . . .

Fifth Negative to the Second.

vi. Let also the Burning Glass be tried on warm substances which throw out no rays nor light; as, on Iron or Stone heated but not ignited; or on Hot Water, or the like; and let observation be taken as to whether there is any increase and intensity of Heat, as in the case of the Sun's Rays.

Sixth Negative to the Second.

vii. Also let the Burning Glass be tried upon common Flame.

Negative to the Third.

viii. The effect of Comets (if one may number them also among Meteors) is not found to be constant or manifest in increasing the Heat of a year, although droughts have been very often noticed as following them. Moreover, Beams, Columns of light, Aurora Borealis, and the like, appear more often in Winter than in Summer; and most of all in time of most intense cold, when it is joined with dry weather. And yet Lightning, Flashes, and Thunder rarely happen in Winter, but at the time of great Heat. While Falling Stars, as they are called, are thought by the vulgar to be composed of some bright and inflamed viscous substance, rather than to be of a stronger fiery Nature. But on this point let farther inquiry be made.

Negative to the Fourth.

ix. There are some Coruscations which afford Light, but do not burn: but these are always unaccompanied by Thunder.

*   *   *   *   *

To the Sixth.

xi. All flame is always hot, more or less; and so there is no *Negative* subjoined to this at all. And yet they say that the Ignis Fatuus, as they call it, which sometimes lights upon a wall, has no great Heat; perhaps it is like the flame of Spirits of Wine, which is gentle and mild. . . .

To the Seventh.

xii. Every thing ignited so as to be turned into a fiery redness, is always hot even without flame; nor is there a *Negative* subjoined to this *Affirmative*. But that which seems to be most like one is Rotten Wood, which shines by night, and yet is not found to be hot; and putrefying Fish scales, which also shine by night, and yet are not found to be hot to the touch; nor is the body of the Glowworm, nor of that fly they call *Lucciola* found hot to the touch.

*　　　*　　　*　　　*　　　*

First Negative to the Tenth.

xv. Similarly as *Negative* to hot Vapour is subjoined the
Nature of Vapour itself, as it is found among us. Farther,
exhalations from oily substances, though easily kindled, are not
found to be hot, unless they have been recently exhaled from a
hot body.

Second Negative to the Tenth.

xvi. Similarly as *Negative* to hot Air itself is subjoined
the Nature of Air itself. For Air is not found among us to be
hot, unless it be either confined or under friction, or clearly
heated by sun, fire, or any other hot body.

*　　　*　　　*　　　*　　　*

Negative to the Thirteenth.

xix. There is a similar doubt as to whether the warmth in
Wool, Skins, Feathers, &c. arises from some slight inherent Heat,
caused by their being the outward growth of animals, or from some
fatness and oiliness, which may be of a Nature agreeing with
warmth; or simply from the confinement and separation of Air of
which we spoke in the last Article. For all Air seems, if cut
off from the external Air, to have in it some warmth. And so let
experiment be made on fibrous substances which are made of Flax;
not on those made of Wool, Feathers, Silk, which are animal
products. Also it is to be noted that all powders, (in which Air
is clearly enclosed,) are less cold than the bodies before they
are pulverised; just, too, as we think that all froth (as containing Air) is less cold than the liquid it comes from.

*　　　*　　　*　　　*　　　*

To the Sixteenth.

xxii. We think that no *Negative* is subjoined to this
Instance. For no tangible body is found among men, which does
not clearly grow hot under friction; so much so that the Ancients
used to dream that the Heavenly bodies had in them no other power
or virtue of generating Heat, except through friction of the Air
by rapid and violent rotation. But in this kind we must make
farther inquiry as to whether bodies, cast forth from machines--
as balls from cannon--do not contract some degree of Heat from
the percussion itself; so that after they have fallen they are
found somewhat hot. But Air in motion cools rather than heats;
as in winds, bellows, and the blowing from the mouth when it is
contracted. But motion of this kind is not so rapid as to excite
Heat; and acts according to the whole; not through particles: so
that no wonder it does not generate Heat.

*　　　*　　　*　　　*　　　*

To the Eighteenth.

xxiv. About this Instance, too, more diligent inquiry must
be made. For Quicklime, if water be scattered over it, conceives
Heat; either because of the union of Heat, which before was scattered (as was before said of Herbs when confined) or because of
the irritation and exasperation of the fiery spirit by the water,
so as to cause a kind of conflict and struggle (Antiperistasis).
But whichever the cause may be, it will appear more readily if
instead of water oil be used. For oil will be as good as water
to collect the enclosed spirits, but not to irritate them. Also
the experiment must be made more widely both on ashes and calcined products of different bodies, and by use of different
liquids.

*   *   *   *   *

To the Twenty-second and Twenty-third.

xxviii. Liquids (whether they be called "Waters" or "Oils")
which have great and intense acridity, produce the effects of
Heat in rending bodies asunder, and after a while in burning
them--but yet to the touch of the hand they are not hot at first.
They work, however, according to affinity and the pores of the
body to which they are applied. For *Aqua Regis* dissolves Gold,
but Silver not at all: on the other hand, *Aqua Fortis* dissolves
Silver, but Gold not at all: neither of them dissolves Glass.
And so of the rest.

To the Twenty-fourth.

xxix. Let an experiment be made with Spirits of Wine on
Wood, also on Butter, Wax, Pitch; to see if perhaps by its own
Heat it liquifies them at all. Farthermore, the 24th Instance
shows its power of imitating Heat, by its Incrustations. And so
let experiment in like manner be made in liquefactions. Let experiment be also made by means of a graduated Glass or Thermometer, concave outwards at the top, by pouring into that outer
cavity Spirits of Wine well rectified, with a covering, so that
it may the better retain its Heat; and let note be taken as to
whether it makes the water descend by its own Heat.

To the Twenty-fifth.

xxx. Spices, and Herbs sharp to the Taste, especially if
taken internally, are perceived to be hot. And so we must see in
what other materials they produce the effects of Heat. And
sailors tell us, that when heaps and masses of Spices which have
been long shut up are opened suddenly, there is some danger to
those who first stir and take them out of fevers and inflamma-
tions. Similarly, experiment can be made, as to whether powders
of Spices and Herbs of this kind do not dry Bacon, and Meat hung
over them, just as smoke does.

*   *   *   *   *

Thirdly, we must make a *Presentation to the Intellect* of Instances in which the Nature we are investigating exists in greater or less degree; either by comparing increase and decrease in the same subject, or its degree in different subjects in turns. For since the Form of a thing is that thing's very essence; and since a thing differs from its Form no otherwise than as the apparent differs from the essential, or the external from the internal, or what is referred to man from what is referred to the Universe: it surely follows, that no Nature is to be received as true Form, unless it perpetually decreases, as that Nature itself decreases; and likewise perpetually increases, as that Nature itself increases. And this Table we are wont to call *a Table of Degrees*, or *of Comparatives*.

A Table of Degrees, or *Comparatives in Heat.*

And first, we will speak of those things which have no degree of Heat at all to the touch; but seem to have only some potential Heat, or disposition towards and preparation for Heat. Afterwards we shall descend to those things which are actually, or to the touch, hot, and to their strength and degrees.

i. Among solid and tangible bodies there is none found which in its own Nature is originally hot. For no stone, metal, sulphur, fossil, no wood, nor water, nor corpse of any animal, is found to be hot. Hot waters in baths seem to be heated by accident, or by flame or subterraneous fire, such as belches forth from Etna and many other mountains; or by conflict of bodies, as Heat arises in solution of Iron and Tin. And so there are no degrees of Heat in things inanimate, as far as man's touch discerns; and yet these differ in degree of Cold; for wood and metal are not equally cold. But this belongs to a Table of Degrees in Cold.

ii. But as regards potential Heat and preparations for flame, very many inanimate substances are found much disposed towards it, as Sulphur, Naphtha, Saltpetre.

iii. Things which before were hot, like horse-dung in animal substances, or lime, or perchance ashes, or soot of fire, retain some latent remnants of their former Heat. And so there arise certain distillations and separations of bodies, through burial in horse-dung; and Heat is caused in lime by scattering water on it; as was just now said.

iv. Among vegetables there is no plant or part of a plant (like exsudations or pith) which is found to be hot to man's touch. Yet (as has been said above), green herbs when confined grow hot; and to the inner sense of touch, as to the Palate or the Stomach, or even to the outward parts after some delay (as in plasters and ointments) some vegetables are found to be hot and others cold.

v. In the parts of Animals after death or separation, there

is not found to be any Heat to man's touch. For horse-dung itself does not retain Heat unless it be confined and buried. And
yet all dung seems to have potential Heat, as is shewn by its
fertilising fields. And likewise corpses of Animals have latent
and potential Heat of this kind; so that in Cemeteries, where
burials take place daily, the earth collects a kind of occult
Heat, which consumes any corpse newly laid there far more rapidly
than pure earth would. . . .

viii. And so the first degree of Heat among those things
which are perceived to be hot to the touch, seems to be the Heat
of Animals, which has a considerable extent of degrees: for the
lowest degree (as in insects) is scarcely perceptible to the
touch; while the highest degree scarcely equals the degree of
Heat of the Sun's Rays in the hottest regions and seasons; nor is
it so great as to be unbearable by the hand. . . .

ix. Animals increase in Heat by motion and exercise, wine
and feasting, love, burning fevers, and pain.

x. Animals in attacks of intermittent fevers are taken with
cold and shivering at first; but after a little grow much hotter:
this also takes place from the beginning in burning and pestilen-
tial fevers.

xi. Let farther inquiry be made as to the comparative Heat
in different Animals, as Fish, Quadrupeds, Serpents, Birds; and
in their Species also; as in the Lion, the Kite, or Man; for
according to popular opinion, Fishes are less hot internally,
Birds most hot; especially Doves, Hawks, Ostriches. . . .

xiv. The Heat of the Heavenly Bodies even in the hottest
region, and hottest periods of the year and day, does not reach
such a degree of Heat as to kindle and burn up either very dry
wood, straw, or even tinder, unless it be increased by means of
Burning Glasses; but yet it can draw out vapour from moist substances.

xv. According to the teaching of Astronomers, some Stars
are laid down to be more, some less hot. For among the Planets,
Mars is put next in Heat to the Sun: then Jupiter; then Venus;
the Moon is regarded as cold, and coldest of all Saturn. Moreover, among fixed Stars, Sirius is set down as hottest; then
Cor Leonis or Regulus: then Canicula; &c.

xvi. The Sun causes greater Heat, the nearer it approaches
a perpendicular position or the Zenith; and this too is to be
believed of the other Planets in their degree of Heat: e.g.
Jupiter gives out greater Heat when he is in Cancer or Leo, than
when in Capricorn or Aquarius.

xvii. One must believe that the Sun itself, and the other
Planets cause greater Heat in their Perigees, in consequence of
their nearness to the Earth, than in their Apogees. And if it

should so happen, that in any region the Sun is at the same time in Perigee, and nearer to the Perpendicular; it is necessary it should cause more Heat than in a region in which the Sun is also in Perigee, but more oblique. So that a comparison of the height of Planets ought to be marked down, as they are more perpendicular or oblique, according to the difference of regions.

xviii. The Sun, too, and the other Planets likewise are thought to cause greater Heat, when nearest the larger fixed Stars; as when the Sun is in Leo, he is nearer Cor Leonis, Cauda Leonis, Spica Virginis, Sirius, and Canicula, than when he is in Cancer, where however he is more perpendicular. And one must believe that the different parts of the sky pour down more Heat (though any thing but perceptible to the touch) according as they are more adorned with Stars, especially if they be large ones.

xix. On the whole, the Heat of Heavenly Bodies is increased in three ways; viz. (1) as they become perpendicular: (2) by nearness or Perigee; (3) by conjunction or consort of Stars.

*   *   *   *   *

xxi. Of Flame and ignited substances there are very many degrees in strength and weakness of Heat. But in this there has no diligent inquiry been made; so that it is necessary for us to pass lightly over it. Of all flames that of Spirits of Wine seems to be softest; unless perhaps the Ignis fatuus, or the flames or flashes of animal perspiration, be softer. We think the flame of light and porous vegetables, as straw, reeds, dry leaves, follows next; from which the flame of hair or feathers differs but little. Then perhaps follows flame of wood, especially of those kinds which have no great amount of rosin or pitch in them; that of small wood, such as is commonly gathered into fagots, is gentler than that of trunks of trees and roots. And this may be commonly tried in furnaces for melting Iron, in which the fire of fagots and boughs is not very useful. After this follow (as we think) the flames of oil, tallow, wax, and the like oily and fat substances, which have no great sharpness. But the most powerful Heat is found in Pitch and Rosin, and still more in Sulphur, Camphor, Naphtha, Saltpetre, Salts (after their crude matter has been discharged), and in their compounds, as in Gunpowder, Greek Fire (which men commonly call wildfire), and its different kinds, which have so obstinate a Heat, that they are not easily extinguished by water. . . .

xxiii. The flame of forked Lightning seems to exceed all these flames; so that sometimes it has melted wrought Iron into drops; a thing which those other kinds of flame cannot do.

*   *   *   *   *

xxvii. Motion increases Heat; as one can see in bellows and the blowpipe; so that the harder metals are not dissolved or melted by means of still quiet fire, unless it be quickened by the blowpipe.

xxviii. Let experiment be made by means of Burning Glasses, in which (as far as I remember) this follows, that if the Glass be put (say) a span distant from the combustible object, it does not kindle or burn so much as if it be placed (say) at half a span, and is then gradually and slowly drawn to a span's distance. Yet the cone and focus of rays are the same, but it is the motion that increases the operation of the Heat.

xxix. We think that those conflagrations which take place when a high wind is blowing make more progress against than with the wind; because flame leaps back with a swifter motion when the wind lulls, than it advances when the wind drives. . . .

xxxi. The Anvil under the Hammer becomes very hot: so much so that if the Anvil were of a somewhat thin plate, we think that by strong and continual blows of the Hammer it might grow redhot, like ignited Iron: but let the experiment be made.

xxxii. But in ignited porous substances, where space is allowed for exercise of the motion of fire, if that motion be restrained by violent compression, the fire is immediately extinguished; as when Tinder, or the burning wick of a candle or lamp, or even burning charcoal or coal, are squeezed by the snuffers, or stamped on by the foot, or the like, the operations of fire immediately cease.

xxxiii. Approximation to a hot body increases Heat, according to the degree of approximation; as is also the case with light: for the nearer an object is placed to the light the more visible it is.

xxxiv. Union of different Heats augments Heat, unless an actual combination of bodies takes place. For a great fire and a little fire in the same place augment somewhat one another's Heat; whereas warm water poured into boiling cools it. . . .

*   *   *   *   *

xxxviii. Of all bodies we know Air is the most ready to receive and lose Heat: and this is best seen in Heat-Glasses (Thermometers). Their construction is as follows: Take a glass with a hollow belly, and thin long neck; turn it upside down, and put it, mouth down, belly up, into another glass containing water, so that the mouth of the first vessel touches the bottom of the other; then let the neck of the first lean gently on the mouth of the second, so that it may be at rest; for greater ease in doing this, let a little wax be put on the mouth of the second vessel, not though so that its mouth is quite closed up, lest, by preventing the transit of Air, the motion, of which we are now going to speak, and which is very gentle and delicate, be hindered.

The first glass ought, before being placed in the second, to have its upper part (its belly) heated. After it is placed, the air (which had been expanded by the heating) will draw in and contract (after a sufficient time to allow for the extinction of the adventitious Heat) to the same extension or dimension as that of the ordinary outer Air at the moment of its insertion; and will draw the water up to a proportionate height. There ought too to be attached to it a long narrow slip of Paper, marked off with Degrees at pleasure. Then you will see, that as the temperature of the day grows colder or hotter, the air contracts from the Cold, expands from the Heat: and this will be exhibited by the ascent of the water when the air contracts, and its descent or depression, when the air expands. The sensibility of the Air, as to Heat and Cold, is so subtle and exquisite, that it far surpasses the human Touch: so that any ray of Sunlight, or Heat of breath, or, far more, Heat of the hand placed on the top of the Glass, directly and clearly depresses the water. . . .

xl. The less the mass of a body, the quicker it grows hot by approximation of a hot body. This shews that all Heat we know of is somehow averse to a tangible body.

xli. Heat, as far as regards human sense and touch, is a shifting and relative thing; so that warm water, if one's hand be cold, is felt to be hot; if one's hand be hot, is felt to be cold. . . .

After *Presentation* made, *Induction* itself is to be set to work. For there must be found, on *Presentation* of each and all Instances, such a Nature as may be always present or absent when the given Nature is so; which may increase and decrease with it; and which may be (as has been said above) a limitation of a more common Nature. Now if the mind tries to do this affirmatively from the beginning; (and when left to itself it is ever wont to do so;) there will rise up Phantoms, Matters of Opinion, Conceptions ill defined, Axioms needing daily emendation; unless one is allowed (as in the schools) to fight for what is false. And these will doubtless be better or worse according to the powers and strength of the Intellect which produces them. But it only belongs to God, the Bestower and Maker of Forms, or perhaps to Angels and Intelligences, to know Forms immediately and affirmatively, and from the beginning of contemplation. But certainly it is above man; to whom it is permitted only to proceed first by *Negatives*, and lastly to end with *Affirmatives* after every kind of exclusion.

16. And so there must be made an entire solution and separation of Nature; not by fire, indeed, but by the mind, as by a Divine Fire. And so the first duty of true *Induction* (with a view to discovery of Forms) is the *rejection* or *exclusion* of single Natures, which are not found in any Instance in which the given Nature is present; or which are found in any Instance from which the given Nature is absent; or are found to increase in any Instance, while the given Nature decreases; or to decrease, while the given Nature increases. Then after *Rejection* and *Exclusion*

made in the proper ways, there will remain (as a Residuum)--
volatile opinions having passed off like smoke--Form, affirmative,
solid, true, and well limited. And this is a short matter to
tell; though one arrives at it after many windings. . . .

18. Now must be set forth an Example of *Exclusion* or *Rejection* of Natures, which by the *Tables of Presentation* are found not to
be of the Form of Heat.
Meanwhile we must warn people, that not only is each Table
sufficient for the *Rejection* of any Nature, but even any one of
the single Instances contained in them. For it is manifest from
what has been said, that every *contradictory Instance* destroys
that hypothesis as to Form (which it contradicts). But nevertheless we sometimes, for clearness, and to shew more plainly the
use of Tables, double or repeat the *Exclusion*.

*An Example of an Exclusive Table, or Rejection of
Natures from the Form of Heat.*

i. By the Sun's Rays, *reject* Elementary Nature.
ii. By common Fire, and especially by subterraneous Fires
(which are most remote, and are most shut off from the rays of
the Heavenly Bodies) *reject* Heavenly Nature.
iii. By heating of every kind of Body (i.e. Minerals, Vegetables, exterior parts of Animals, Water, Oil, Air, and the rest),
by approximation only to fire or other hot body; *reject* all variety or more subtle texture of bodies.
iv. By Iron and ignited Metals, which heat other bodies,
and yet are not at all lessened in weight or substance; *reject*
the imparting or mixture of the substance of another hot body.
v. By boiling Water and Air, and even by Metals and other
solid bodies when heated, but not so as to ignite or become red-
hot; *reject* light and the being luminous.
vi. By the Rays of the Moon, and of other Stars (except the
Sun), *reject* light and the being luminous.
vii. By the *comparative* of ignited Iron, and of the flame
of Spirits of Wine (whereof ignited Iron has more Heat and less
Light; flame of Spirits of Wine more Light and less Heat), *reject*
also light and the being luminous.
viii. By Gold and other Metals when ignited, which are most
dense of body in their whole (*secundum totum*), *reject* rarity.
ix. By Air, which for the most part is found to be cold,
and yet remains rare, *reject* also rarity.
x. By ignited Iron, which does not expand in mass, but
remains within the same visible dimensions; *reject* local or
expansive motion in the whole (*secundum totum*).
xii. By the ready warming of all bodies, without any notable destruction or alteration; *reject* destructive Nature, or the
violent communication of any new Nature.
xiii. By consent and conformity of similar effects, produced by Heat and Cold; *reject* both expansive and contracting
motion in the whole (*secundum totum*).
xiv. By the kindling of Heat from rubbing bodies together;
reject Principal Nature, by which we mean that which is found

existing positively in Nature, and is not caused by any preceding Nature.

*   *   *   *   *

19.   In the *Exclusive Table* are laid the foundations of true *Induction*, which, however, is not completed till we rest in the Affirmative.   Nor is the *Exclusive Table* itself at all complete, nor can it be so at first.   For the *Exclusive Table* is clearly a *Rejection* of simple Natures.   But if we have not as yet good and true conceptions of simple Natures, how can the *Exclusive Table* be rectified?   Some of the above (as the conceptions of Elementary Nature, of Heavenly Nature, of Rarity) are vague and ill defined.   And so we, who are neither ignorant nor forgetful of the magnitude of the work we are attempting (viz. the rendering man's Intellect equal to things and Nature) do not in the least rest in what we have already taught; but carry on the matter farther, and contrive and administer stronger aids for the use of the Intellect.   These we will next subjoin. . . .

20.   Moreover, since Truth emerges more quickly from error than from confusion, we think it useful to grant permission to the Intellect, after having composed and weighed three such *Tables of First Presentation* as we have made, to gird itself up and attempt the *Interpretation of Nature* in the Affirmative, both from the Instances in the Tables, and from those which occur elsewhere.   And this kind of attempt we are wont to call *The Permission of the Intellect*, or *The Commencement of Interpretation*, or *The First Vintage*.

First Vintage of the Form of Heat.

It must be observed that the Form of a thing (as is clear from what has been said) subsists in each and all the Instances in which the thing itself subsists; for otherwise it would not be Form: and so clearly no contradictory Instance can be alleged. And yet the Form is found to be far more conspicuous and evident in some Instances than in others; in those, that is, in which the Nature of the Form is less restrained and hindered and reduced to order by other Natures.   Now we are wont to call Instances of this sort *Glaring* or *Ostensive Instances*.   But now we must proceed to this the *First Vintage of the Form of Heat*.

From the *Instances*, each and all, it appears that the Nature of which Heat is a Limitation, is Motion.   This is most clearly shewn in Flame, which moves perpetually; and in hot or boiling liquids, which also move perpetually.   And it is also shewn in the rousing or increasing of Heat by means of Motion; as by bellows and winds: for which see Table iii. Inst. 29.   Similarly in other manners of motion; for which see Table iii. Instt. 28,31. Again it is shewn in the extinction of Fire and Heat by all strong compression, which bridles and stops Motion: see Table iii. Instt. 30,32.   It is also shewn in this, that every body is destroyed, or, at least strikingly changed by all strong and vehement Fire and Heat.   Whence it is quite clear that through Heat tumult, perturbation, and violent motion arise in the inner parts of the body, which gradually tends towards dissolution.

Let what we have said about Motion (viz. that it is like a Genus to Heat) be understood not to mean that Heat generates Motion, or Motion Heat, (though this too may be true in some cases); but that essential Heat, or the "*quid ipsum*" of Heat, is Motion, and nothing else; limited however by *Differences*, which we will presently subjoin, after we have added some cautions for the avoiding of ambiguity.

*   *   *   *   *

Nor indeed ought the communication of Heat, or its transitive Nature, by which a body applied to a hot body grows hot, to be confounded with the Form Heat. For Heat is one thing, and Heating another. For Heat is induced by Motion of attrition without any preceding Heat: whence Heating is excluded from the Form of Heat. And even where Heat is produced by approximation of a hot body, this is not caused by the Form of Heat; but it entirely depends on a higher and more common Nature; viz. on a Nature of Assimilation or Self-Multiplication: on which separate inquiry must be made.

Farther; the conception of Fire is vulgar and of no worth: for it is compounded of the concourse of Heat and Light in any body; as in common flame and redhot bodies.

And so every ambiguity having been removed, now at length we must come to the true *Differences* which limit Motion, and fashion it into the Form of Heat.

i. Now the *First Difference* is this; that Heat is *expansive* Motion, by which a body strives to dilate itself, and to occupy a larger sphere or space than it did before. Now this *Difference* is most shewn in flame, where the smoke, or thick vapour, is manifestly dilated and bursts into flame.

*   *   *   *   *

This Motion is, however, best observed in Air, which forthwith and plainly expands under a small degree of Heat, as is seen in Table III. Inst. 38.

It is also shewn in the contrary Nature of Cold. For Cold contracts every body and forces it into a narrower space: so that through intense Cold nails fall out of walls; brass cracks; heated glass suddenly exposed to Cold cracks and breaks. Similarly, Air contracts under influence of slight cooling: as is seen Table iii. Inst. 38. But on this shall more be said in inquiry into Cold.

*   *   *   *   *

ii. The *Second Difference* is a modification of the foregoing; viz. that Heat is expansive Motion (or towards the exterior), but under this law, that the body is borne upwards with it. For without doubt there are very many kinds of mixed Motion. For example: an arrow or javelin acquires a rotary motion by progression, and a progressive one by rotation. Similarly the Motion of Heat is both expansive and tends upwards.

But this *Difference* is shewn by putting tongs or poker into the fire. For if put in perpendicularly, with the hand above, they quickly burn the hand; if sideways or from below, much more slowly.

*   *   *   *   *

iii. *The Third Difference* is this. Heat is Motion, not expansive uniformly in the whole, but expansive through the lesser particles of the body; and at the same time restrained, repelled, and reflected; so that it obtains an alternative Motion, ever hurrying, striving, struggling, and irritated by repercussion; whence the fury of fire and Heat has its origin.

This *Difference* is shewn most in flame and boiling liquids: for these are in perpetual excitement, swell in small portions, and subside again.

It is also shewn in those bodies, which are so tightly knit together, that when heated or ignited they do not swell or dilate in bulk; as in the case of ignited Iron, in which Heat is most violent.

It is also shewn in the fact that during the coldest weather the fire burns most brightly.

It is also shewn in this; that when air is expanded in the Thermometer without impediment or repulsion, (i.e. uniformly and equally,) Heat is not perceived. Also in confined winds, though they burst forth with the greatest violence, yet no remarkable Heat is perceived; because in that case Motion takes place in the whole, and without alternating Motion in particles. And let experiment also be tried as to whether flame does not burn more briskly at the sides than in the middle of the flame.

It is also shewn in the fact that any kind of burning proceeds through minute pores of the body burnt; so that burning undermines, penetrates, pierces, pricks, just as if it were an infinite number of needle-points. And so it comes, that all strong waters (if taken in due proportion to the body on which they act) exhibit the effects of Fire, through their corrosive and pungent Nature.

And this *Difference*, of which we are now speaking, is common with the Nature of Cold; in which the contracting Motion is restrained by the resistance of expansion; just as in Heat the expansive Motion is confined by the resistance of contraction.

And so whether parts of a body penetrate towards the interior or the exterior, the reason is the same; though the force in the two cases is very different, arising from the fact that we have nothing here upon the surface of the earth that is intensely cold. See Table i. Inst. 27.

iv. The *Fourth Difference* is a modification of the foregoing one: viz. this Motion of stimulation or penetration ought to be somewhat rapid, and not at all sluggish; and to take place through particles, which, though minute, are still not of extreme subtilty, but of rather larger dimensions.

This *Difference* is shewn in comparing the effects of Fire with the effects of Time or Age. For Age or Time dry up, consume, subvert, reduce to ashes, as well as Fire; nay far more subtly;

but because Motion in their case is very sluggish, and in particles of great minuteness, Heat is not perceived.

It is also shewn in comparison between the dissolving of Iron and Gold. For Gold is dissolved without excitement of Heat; but Iron with vehement excitement; though they take about the same time. This is because in Gold the entrance of the acid of separation is gentle and subtly insinuating, and the particles of Gold yield easily: whereas in Iron the entrance is rough and with conflict, and the parts of Iron are more obstinate.

It is also shewn (up to a certain point) in some gangrenes and mortifications of flesh; which, from the subtilty of the putrefaction, do not excite great Heat or pain.

And let this be the *First Vintage*, or *Commencement of Interpretation* of the Form of Heat, made by the *Permission of the Intellect*.

Now from this *First Vintage* the Form or true Definition of Heat (i.e. of Heat relative to the Universe, not merely to man's senses) is briefly this. *Heat is Motion, expansive, restrained, and struggling through the lesser parts (of a body).* Expansion is modified: *though expanding in every direction, yet it somewhat tends upwards.* And that struggling through the parts is also modified: *it may not be at all sluggish, but vigorous and of some impetuosity.*

But as regards the practical side, the thing is the same. For this is the account of it. *If in any natural body you can excite the Motion of self-dilation or expansion; and also can so repress that Motion, and turn it upon itself, that that dilation proceed unequally, partly taking place, partly being repressed, without doubt you will generate Heat:* and this without considering whether that body is elementary, (as they term it,) or imbued with celestial influence; whether luminous or opaque; rare or dense; locally expanded, or contained within bounds of its first dimensions; verging towards dissolution, or remaining in its condition; animal, vegetable, or mineral; water, oil, or air; or any other substance whatsoever that is susceptible of the aforesaid Motion. Sensible Heat, also, is the same thing; but under such relation as agrees with the Senses.

But now we must proceed to farther helps.

21. After the *Tables of First Presentation*, and *Rejection* or *Exclusion*, and also of the *First Vintage* made according to them; we must proceed to the remaining helps of the Intellect for *Interpretation of Nature* and true and perfect *Induction*. And in setting forth these we will proceed, where Tables are required, with Heat and Cold; but where there are only few examples required, we will proceed with all other subjects; so that inquiry be not confounded, and yet our teaching be within less narrow limits.

We will speak, then, (1) of *Prerogative Instances*; (2) of *the Supports of Induction*; (3) of *the Rectification of Induction*; (4) of *the Variation of Inquiry according to the Nature of the Subject*; (5) of *Prerogative Natures*, with a view to investigation; or of what is to be investigated first and what afterwards; (6) of *the Limits of Investigation*, or *the Synopsis of all Natures* in the Universe; (7) of *Deduction to Practice*, or of what is arranged relatively to man; (8) of *the Preparations for Investigation*; (9) of *the Ascending and Descending Ladder of Axioms*.

22. First among *Prerogative Instances* we will set forth *Solitary Instances*. Those are *Solitary* which (1) exhibit the Nature under Investigation, in those subjects which have nothing in common with other subjects except that Nature itself: or again, (2) those which do not exhibit the Nature under Investigation, in those subjects which are like in all points to other subjects, except in that Nature itself. For it is clear that instances of this kind remove doubt, and accelerate and strengthen the *Exclusive* part: so that a few of them are a host.

(1) For example: In Investigation into the Nature of *Colour; Solitary Instances* are Prisms, crystalline Gems, which produce Colours, not only in themselves, but when externally cast upon a wall, Dew, &c. For these have nothing in common with fixed Colours in Flowers, coloured Gems, Metals, Wood, &c. except Colour itself. Hence it is readily gathered that Colour is nothing but a modification of the image of Light incident and refracted; in the former kind by different degrees of Incidence; in the latter, by various textures and structures of body. And these are *Solitary Instances* of resemblance.

(2) Again, in the same Investigation, distinct veins of white and black in Marble, and variegations of Colour in flowers of the same species, are *Solitary Instances*. For white and black Marble, and white and purple spots in the Gillyflower, agree in almost every point except in Colour itself. Hence it is readily gathered that Colour has not much to do with the intrinsic Natures of any body, but only depends on the gross and as it were mechanical position of parts. And these *Instances* are *Solitary* in discrepant subjects. Both kinds we are wont to call *Solitary Instances*, or *Ferinæ*, to take a Term from Astronomers.

b.

René Descartes' Discourse on the Method of Rightly Conducting the Reason and Seeking for Truth in the Sciences, *published
in 1637, presented a method diametrically opposed to that advocated by Bacon. Because of its simplicity and apparent cogency,
it was eagerly accepted by a large number of natural philosophers
in the seventeenth century. And, although Descartes' physical
doctrines were to be progressively discarded in the eighteenth
century, his method still had the power to charm and seduce men
during the nineteenth century.*

By these considerations I was induced to seek some other
Method which would comprise the advantages of the three and be
exempt from their defects. And as a multitude of laws often only
hampers justice, so that a state is best governed when, with few
laws, these are rigidly administered; in like manner, instead of
the great number of precepts of which Logic is composed, I believed that the four following would prove perfectly sufficient
for me, provided I took the firm and unwavering resolution never
in a single instance to fail in observing them.

The *first* was never to accept anything for true which I did
not clearly know to be such; that is to say, carefully to avoid
precipitancy and prejudice, and to comprise nothing more in my
judgment than what was presented to my mind so clearly and distinctly as to exclude all ground of doubt.

The *second*, to divide each of the difficulties under examination into as many parts as possible, and as might be necessary
for its adequate solution.

The *third*, to conduct my thoughts in such order that, by
commencing with objects the simplest and easiest to know, I might
ascend by little and little, and, as it were, step by step, to
the knowledge of the more complex; assigning in thought a certain
order even to those objects which in their own nature do not
stand in a relation of antecedence and sequence.

And the *last*, in every case to make enumerations so complete,
and reviews so general, that I might be assured that nothing was
omitted.

The long chains of simple and easy reasonings by means of
which geometers are accustomed to reach the conclusions of their
most difficult demonstrations, had led me to imagine that all
things, to the knowledge of which man is competent, are mutually
connected in the same way, and that there is nothing so far removed from us as to be beyond our reach, or so hidden that we
cannot discover it, provided only we abstain from accepting the
false for the true, and always preserve in our thoughts the order
necessary for the deduction of one truth from another. And I had
little difficulty in determining the objects with which it was

---

*René Descartes, *Discourse on Method* . . . , translated by John
Veitch, 5th edition, William Blackwood and Sons, Edinburgh and
London, 1873. Pp. 60-4; 74-82; 88-96; 104-6.

necessary to commence, for I was already persuaded that it must
be with the simplest and easiest to know, and, considering that
of all those who have hitherto sought truth in the Sciences, the
mathematicians alone have been able to find any demonstrations,
that is, any certain and evident reasons, I did not doubt but that
such must have been the rule of their investigations. I resolved
to commence, therefore, with the examination of the simplest objects, not anticipating, however, from this any other advantage
than that to be found in accustoming my mind to the love and
nourishment of truth, and to a distaste for all such reasonings
as were unsound. But I had no intention on that account of
attempting to master all the particular Sciences commonly denominated Mathematics: but observing that, however different their
objects, they all agree in considering only the various relations
or proportions subsisting among those objects, I thought it best
for my purpose to consider these proportions in the most general
form possible, without referring them to any objects in particular, except such as would most facilitate the knowledge of them,
and without by any means restricting them to these, that afterwards I might thus be the better able to apply them to every
other class of objects to which they are legitimately applicable.
Perceiving further, that in order to understand these relations
I should sometimes have to consider them one by one, and sometimes only to bear them in mind, or embrace them in the aggregate,
I thought that, in order the better to consider them individually,
I should view them as subsisting between straight lines, than
which I could find no objects more simple, or capable of being
more distinctly represented to my imagination and senses; and on
the other hand, that in order to retain them in the memory, or
embrace an aggregate of many, I should express them by certain
characters the briefest possible. In this way I believed that I
could borrow all that was best both in Geometrical Analysis and
in Algebra, and correct all the defects of the one by help of the
other.

  And, in point of fact, the accurate observance of these few
precepts gave me, I take the liberty of saying, such ease in
unravelling all the questions embraced in these two sciences,
that in the two or three months I devoted to their examination,
not only did I reach solutions of questions I had formerly deemed
exceedingly difficult, but even as regards questions of the solution of which I continued ignorant, I was enabled, as it appeared
to me, to determine the means whereby, and the extent to which,
a solution was possible; results attributable to the circumstance
that I commenced with the simplest and most general truths, and
that thus each truth discovered was a rule available in the
discovery of subsequent ones. Nor in this perhaps shall I appear
too vain, if it be considered that, as the truth on any particular point is one, whoever apprehends the truth, knows all that on
that point can be known. The child, for example, who has been
instructed in the elements of Arithmetic, and has made a particular addition, according to rule, may be assured that he has
found, with respect to the sum of the numbers before him, all
that in this instance is within the reach of human genius. Now,
in conclusion, the Method which teaches adherence to the true

order, and an exact enumeration of all the conditions of the thing sought includes all that gives certitude to the rules of Arithmetic.

But the chief ground of my satisfaction with this Method, was the assurance I had of thereby exercising my reason in all matters,if not with absolute perfection, at least with the greatest attainable by me: besides, I was conscious that by its use my mind was becoming gradually habituated to clearer and more distinct conceptions of its objects; and I hoped also, from not having restricted this Method to any particular matter, to apply it to the difficulties of the other Sciences, with not less success than to those of Algebra. I should not, however, on this account have ventured at once on the examination of all the difficulties of the Sciences which presented themselves to me, for this would have been contrary to the order prescribed in the Method, but observing that the knowledge of such is dependent on principles borrowed from Philosophy, in which I found nothing certain, I thought it necessary first of all to endeavour to establish its principles. And because I observed, besides, that an inquiry of this kind was of all others of the greatest moment, and one in which precipitancy and anticipation in judgment were most to be dreaded, I thought that I ought not to approach it till I had reached a more mature age, (being at that time but twenty-three,) and had first of all employed much of my time in preparation for the work, as well by eradicating from my mind all the erroneous opinions I had up to that moment accepted, as by amassing variety of experience to afford materials for my reasonings, and by continually exercising myself in my chosen Method with a view to increased skill in its application.

*   *   *   *   *

I am in doubt as to the propriety of making my first meditations in the place above mentioned matter of discourse; for these are so metaphysical, and so uncommon, as not, perhaps, to be acceptable to every one. And yet, that it may be determined whether the foundations that I have laid are sufficiently secure, I find myself in a measure constrained to advert to them. I had long before remarked that, in relation to practice, it is sometimes necessary to adopt, as if above doubt, opinions which we discern to be highly uncertain, as has been already said; but as I then desired to give my attention solely to the search after truth, I thought that a procedure exactly the opposite was called for, and that I ought to reject as absolutely false all opinions in regard to which I could suppose the least ground for doubt, in order to ascertain whether after that there remained aught in my belief that was wholly indubitable. Accordingly, seeing that our senses sometimes deceive us, I was willing to suppose that there existed nothing really such as they presented to us; and because some men err in reasoning, and fall into paralogisms, even on the simplest matters of Geometry, I, convinced that I was as open to error as any other, rejected as false all the reasonings I had hitherto taken for demonstrations; and finally, when I considered that the very same thoughts (presentations) which we experience when awake may also be experienced when we are asleep, while there is at that time not one of them true, I supposed that all the objects (presentations) that had ever entered into my mind when awake, had in them no more truth than the illusions of my dreams. But immediately upon this I observed that, whilst I thus wished to think that all was false, it was absolutely necessary that I, who thus thought, should be somewhat; and as I observed that this truth, *I think, hence I am*, was so certain and of such evidence, that no ground of doubt, however extravagant, could be alleged by the Sceptics capable of shaking it, I concluded that I might, without scruple, accept it as the first principle of the Philosophy of which I was in search.

In the next place, I attentively examined what I was, and as I observed that I could suppose that I had no body, and that there was no world nor any place in which I might be; but that I could not therefore suppose that I was not; and that, on the contrary, from the very circumstance that I thought to doubt of the truth of other things, it most clearly and certainly followed that I was; while, on the other hand, if I had only ceased to think, although all the other objects which I had ever imagined had been in reality existent, I would have had no reason to believe that I existed; I thence concluded that I was a substance whose whole essence or nature consists only in thinking, and which, that it may exist, has need of no place, nor is dependent on any material thing; so that "I," that is to say, the mind by which I am what I am, is wholly distinct from the body, and is even more easily known than the latter, and is such, that although the latter were not, it would still continue to be all that it is.

After this I inquired in general into what is essential to the truth and certainty of a proposition; for since I had discovered one which I knew to be true, I thought that I must likewise be able to discover the ground of this certitude. And as I observed that in the words *I think, hence I am*, there is nothing at all which gives me assurance of their truth beyond this, that I see very clearly that in order to think it is necessary to exist, I concluded that I might take, as a general rule, the principle,that all the things which we very clearly and distinctly conceive are true, only observing, however, that there is some difficulty in rightly determining the objects which we distinctly conceive.

In the next place, from reflecting on the circumstance that I doubted, and that consequently my being was not wholly perfect, (for I clearly saw that it was a greater perfection to know than to doubt,) I was led to inquire whence I had learned to think of something more perfect than myself; and I clearly recognised that I must hold this notion from some Nature which in reality was more perfect. As for the thoughts of many other objects external to me, as of the sky, the earth, light, heat, and a thousand more, I was less at a loss to know whence these came; for since I remarked in them nothing which seemed to render them superior to myself, I could believe that, if these were true, they were dependencies on my own nature, in so far as it possessed a certain

perfection, and, if they were false, that I held them from nothing, that is to say, that they were in me because of a certain
imperfection of my nature. But this could not be the case with
the idea of a Nature more perfect than myself; for to receive it
from nothing was a thing manifestly impossible; and, because it
is not less repugnant that the more perfect should be an effect
of, and dependence on the less perfect, than that something
should proceed from nothing, it was equally impossible that I
could hold it from myself: accordingly, it but remained that it
had been placed in me by a Nature which was in reality more perfect than mine, and which even possessed within itself all the
perfections of which I could form any idea; that is to say, in
a single word, which was God. And to this I added that, since I
knew some perfections which I did not possess, I was not the only
being in existence, (I will here, with your permission, freely
use the terms of the schools); but, on the contrary, that there
was of necessity some other more perfect Being upon whom I was
dependent, and from whom I had received all that I possessed; for
if I had existed alone, and independently of every other being,
so as to have had from myself all the perfection, however little,
which I actually possessed, I should have been able, for the same
reason, to have had from myself the whole remainder of perfection,
of the want of which I was conscious, and thus could of myself
have become infinite, eternal, immutable, omniscient, all-
powerful, and, in fine, have possessed all the perfections which
I could recognise in God. For in order to know the nature of
God, (whose existence has been established by the preceding
reasonings,) as far as my own nature permitted, I had only to
consider in reference to all the properties of which I found in
my mind some idea, whether their possession was a mark of perfection; and I was assured that no one which indicated any imperfection was in him, and that none of the rest was awanting. Thus I
perceived that doubt, inconstancy, sadness, and such like, could
not be found in God, since I myself would have been happy to be
free from them. Besides, I had ideas of many sensible and corporeal things; for although I might suppose that I was dreaming,
and that all which I saw or imagined was false, I could not,
nevertheless, deny that the ideas were in reality in my thoughts.
But, because I had already very clearly recognised in myself that
the intelligent nature is distinct from the corporeal, and as I
observed that all composition is an evidence of dependency, and
that a state of dependency is manifestly a state of imperfection,
I therefore determined that it could not be a perfection in God
to be compounded of these two natures, and that consequently he
was not so compounded; but that if there were any bodies in the
world, or even any intelligences, or other natures that were not
wholly perfect, their existence depended on his power in such a
way that they could not subsist without him for a single moment.
     I was disposed straightway to search for other truths; and
when I had represented to myself the object of the geometers,
which I conceived to be a continuous body, or a space indefinitely extended in length, breadth, and height or depth, divisible
into divers parts which admit of different figures and sizes, and of
being moved or transposed in all manner of ways, (for all this

the geometers suppose to be in the object they contemplate,) I went over some of their simplest demonstrations. And, in the first place, I observed, that the great certitude which by common consent is accorded to these demonstrations, is founded solely upon this, that they are clearly conceived in accordance with the rules I have already laid down. In the next place, I perceived that there was nothing at all in these demonstrations which could assure me of the existence of their object: thus, for example, supposing a triangle to be given, I distinctly perceived that its three angles were necessarily equal to two right angles, but I did not on that account perceive anything which could assure me that any triangle existed: while, on the contrary, recurring to the examination of the idea of a Perfect Being, I found that the existence of the Being was comprised in the idea in the same way that the equality of its three angles to two right angles is comprised in the idea of a triangle, or as in the idea of a sphere, the equidistance of all points on its surface from the centre, or even still more clearly; and that consequently it is at least as certain that God, who is this Perfect Being, is, or exists, as any demonstration of Geometry can be.

But the reason which leads many to persuade themselves that there is a difficulty in knowing this truth, and even also in knowing what their mind really is, is that they never raise their thoughts above sensible objects, and are so accustomed to consider nothing except by way of imagination, which is a mode of thinking limited to material objects, that all that is not imaginable seems to them not intelligible. The truth of this is sufficiently manifest from the single circumstance, that the philosophers of the Schools accept as a maxim that there is nothing in the Understanding which was not previously in the Senses, in which however it is certain that the ideas of God and of the soul have never been; and it appears to me that they who make use of their imagination to comprehend these ideas do exactly the same thing as if, in order to hear sounds or smell odours, they strove to avail themselves of their eyes; unless indeed that there is this difference, that the sense of sight does not afford us an inferior assurance to those of smell or hearing; in place of which, neither our imagination nor our senses can give us assurance of anything unless our Understanding intervene.

Finally, if there be still persons who are not sufficiently persuaded of the existence of God and of the soul, by the reasons I have adduced, I am desirous that they should know that all the other propositions, of the truth of which they deem themselves perhaps more assured, as that we have a body, and that there exist stars and an earth, and such like, are less certain; for, although we have a moral assurance of these things, which is so strong that there is an appearance of extravagance in doubting of their existence, yet at the same time no one, unless his intellect is impaired, can deny, when the question relates to a metaphysical certitude, that there is sufficient reason to exclude entire assurance, in the observation that when asleep we can in the same way imagine ourselves possessed of another body and that we see other stars and another earth, when there is nothing of the kind. For how do we know that the thoughts which occur in dreaming are false rather than those other which we

experience when awake, since the former are often not less vivid
and distinct than the latter? And though men of the highest
genius study this question as long as they please, I do not
believe that they will be able to give any reason which can be
sufficient to remove this doubt, unless they presuppose the existence of God. For, in the first place, even the principle which
I have already taken as a rule, viz., that all the things which
we clearly and distinctly conceive are true, is certain only
because God is or exists, and because he is a Perfect Being, and
because all that we possess is derived from him: whence it follows that our ideas or notions, which to the extent of their
clearness and distinctness are real, and proceed from God, must
to that extent be true. Accordingly, whereas we not unfrequently
have ideas or notions in which some falsity is contained, this
can only be the case with such as are to some extent confused and
obscure, and in this proceed from nothing, (participate of
negation,) that is, exist in us thus confused because we are not
wholly perfect. And it is evident that it is not less repugnant
that falsity or imperfection, in so far as it is imperfection,
should proceed from God, than that truth or perfection should
proceed from nothing. But if we did not know that all which we
possess of real and true proceeds from a Perfect and Infinite
Being, however clear and distinct our ideas might be, we should
have no ground on that account for the assurance that they
possessed the perfection of being true.

But after the knowledge of God and of the soul has rendered
us certain of this rule, we can easily understand that the truth
of the thoughts we experience when awake, ought not in the
slightest degree to be called in question on account of the
illusions of our dreams. For if it happened that an individual,
even when asleep, had some very distinct idea, as, for example,
if a geometer should discover some new demonstration, the circumstance of his being asleep would not militate against its truth;
and as for the most ordinary error of our dreams, which consists
in their representing to us various objects in the same way as
our external senses, this is not prejudicial, since it leads us
very properly to suspect the truth of the ideas of sense; for we
are not unfrequently deceived in the same manner when awake; as
when persons in the jaundice see all objects yellow, or when the
stars or bodies at a great distance appear to us much smaller
than they are. For, in fine, whether awake or asleep, we ought
never to allow ourselves to be persuaded of the truth of anything
unless on the evidence of our Reason. And it must be noted that
I say of our *Reason*, and not of our imagination or of our senses:
thus, for example, although we very clearly see the sun, we ought
not therefore to determine that it is only of the size which our
sense of sight presents; and we may very distinctly imagine the
head of a lion joined to the body of a goat, without being therefore shut up to the conclusion that a chimera exists; for it is
not a dictate of Reason that what we thus see or imagine is in
reality existent; but it plainly tells us that all our ideas or
notions contain in them some truth; for otherwise it could not
be that God, who is wholly perfect and veracious, should have
placed them in us. And because our reasonings are never so clear

or so complete during sleep as when we are awake, although sometimes the acts of our imagination are then as lively and distinct, if not more so than in our waking moments, Reason further
dictates that, since all our thoughts cannot be true because of
our partial imperfection, those possessing truth must infallibly
be found in the experience of our waking moments rather than in
that of our dreams.

      *   *   *   *   *

But, in order to show how I there handled this matter, I
mean here to give the explication of the motion of the heart and
arteries, which, as the first and most general motion observed in
animals, will afford the means of readily determining what should
be thought of all the rest. And that there may be less difficulty in understanding what I am about to say on this subject, I
advise those who are not versed in Anatomy, before they commence
the perusal of these observations, to take the trouble of getting
dissected in their presence the heart of some large animal possessed of lungs, (for this is throughout sufficiently like the
human,) and to have shewn to them its two ventricles or cavities:
in the first place, that in the right side, with which correspond
two very ample tubes, viz., the hollow vein, (vena cava,) which
is the principal receptacle of the blood, and the trunk of the
tree, as it were, of which all the other veins in the body are
branches; and the arterial vein, (vena arteriosa,) inappropriately so denominated, since it is in truth only an artery, which,
taking its rise in the heart, is divided, after passing out from
it, into many branches which presently disperse themselves all
over the lungs; in the second place, the cavity in the left side,
with which correspond in the same manner two canals in size equal
to or larger than the preceding, viz., the venous artery, (arter-
ia venosa,) likewise inappropriately thus designated, because it
is simply a vein which comes from the lungs, where it is divided
into many branches, interlaced with those of the arterial vein,
and those of the tube called the windpipe, through which the air
we breathe enters; and the great artery which, issuing from the
heart, sends its branches all over the body. I should wish also
that such persons were carefully shewn the eleven pellicles
which, like so many small valves, open and shut the four orifices
that are in these two cavities, viz., three at the entrance of
the hollow vein, where they are disposed in such a manner as by
no means to prevent the blood which it contains from flowing into
the right ventricle of the heart, and yet exactly to prevent its
flowing out; three at the entrance to the arterial vein, which,
arranged in a manner exactly the opposite of the former, readily
permit the blood contained in this cavity to pass into the lungs,
but hinder that contained in the lungs from returning to this
cavity; and, in like manner, two others at the mouth of the
venous artery, which allow the blood from the lungs to flow into
the left cavity of the heart, but preclude its return; and three
at the mouth of the great artery, which suffer the blood to flow
from the heart, but prevent its reflux. Nor do we need to seek
any other reason for the number of these pellicles beyond this

that the orifice of the venous artery being of an oval shape from the nature of its situation, can be adequately closed with two, whereas the others being round are more conveniently closed with three. Besides, I wish such persons to observe that the grand artery and the arterial vein are of much harder and firmer texture than the venous artery and the hollow vein; and that the two last expand before entering the heart, and there form, as it were, two pouches denominated the auricles of the heart, which are composed of a substance similar to that of the heart itself; and that there is always more warmth in the heart than in any other part of the body; and, finally, that this heat is capable of causing any drop of blood that passes into the cavities rapidly to expand and dilate, just as all liquors do when allowed to fall drop by drop into a highly heated vessel.

For, after these things, it is not necessary for me to say anything more with a view to explain the motion of the heart, except that when its cavities are not full of blood, into these the blood of necessity flows,--from the hollow vein into the right, and from the venous artery into the left; because these two vessels are always full of blood, and their orifices, which are turned towards the heart, cannot then be closed. But as soon as two drops of blood have thus passed, one into each of the cavities, these drops which cannot but be very large, because the orifices through which they pass are wide, and the vessels from which they come full of blood, are immediately rarefied, and dilated by the heat they meet with. In this way they cause the whole heart to expand, and at the same time press home and shut the five small valves that are at the entrances of the two vessels from which they flow, and thus prevent any more blood from coming down into the heart, and becoming more and more rarefied, they push open the six small valves that are in the orifices of the other two vessels, through which they pass out, causing in this way all the branches of the arterial vein and of the grand artery to expand almost simultaneously with the heart-- which immediately thereafter begins to contract, as do also the arteries, because the blood that has entered them has cooled, and the six small valves close, and the five of the hollow vein and of the venous artery open anew and allow a passage to other two drops of blood, which cause the heart and the arteries again to expand as before. And, because the blood which thus enters into the heart passes through these two pouches called auricles, it thence happens that their motion is the contrary of that of the heart, and that when it expands they contract. But lest those who are ignorant of the force of mathematical demonstrations, and who are not accustomed to distinguish true reasons from mere verisimilitudes, should venture, without examination, to deny what has been said, I wish it to be considered that the motion which I have now explained follows as necessarily from the very arrangement of the parts, which may be observed in the heart by the eye alone, and from the heat which may be felt with the fingers, and from the nature of the blood as learned from experience, as does the motion of a clock from the power, the situation, and shape of its counterweights and wheels.

But if it be asked how it happens that the blood in the

veins, flowing in this way continually into the heart, is not
exhausted, and why the arteries do not become too full, since all
the blood which passes through the heart flows into them, I need
only mention in reply what has been written by a physician of
England, who has the honour of having broken the ice on this
subject, and of having been the first to teach that there are
many small passages at the extremities of the arteries, through
which the blood received by them from the heart passes into the
small branches of the veins, whence it again returns to the
heart; so that its course amounts precisely to a perpetual circulation. Of this we have abundant proof in the ordinary experience of surgeons, who, by binding the arm with a tie of moderate
straitness above the part where they open the vein, cause the
blood to flow more copiously than it would have done without any
ligature; whereas quite the contrary would happen were they to
bind it below; that is, between the hand and the opening, or were
to make the ligature above the opening very tight. For it is
manifest that the tie, moderately straitened, while adequate to
hinder the blood already in the arm from returning towards the
heart by the veins, cannot on that account prevent new blood from
coming forward through the arteries, because these are situated
below the veins, and their coverings, from their greater consistency, are more difficult to compress; and also that the blood
which comes from the heart tends to pass through them to the hand
with greater force than it does to return from the hand to the
heart through the veins. And since the latter current escapes
from the arm by the opening made in one of the veins, there must
of necessity be certain passages below the ligature, that is,
towards the extremities of the arm through which it can come
thither from the arteries. This physician likewise abundantly
establishes what he has advanced respecting the motion of the
blood, from the existence of certain pellicles, so disposed in
various places along the course of the veins, in the manner of
small valves, as not to permit the blood to pass from the middle
of the body towards the extremities, but only to return from the
extremities to the heart; and farther, from experience which
shows that all the blood which is in the body may flow out of it
in a very short time through a single artery that has been cut,
even although this had been closely tied in the immediate neighbourhood of the heart, and cut between the heart and the ligature, so as to prevent the supposition that the blood flowing out
of it could come from any other quarter than the heart.

But there are many other circumstances which evince that
what I have alleged is the true cause of the motion of the blood:
thus, in the first place, the difference that is observed between
the blood which flows from the veins, and that from the arteries,
can only arise from this, that being rarefied, and, as it were,
distilled by passing through the heart,it is thinner, and more
vivid, and warmer immediately after leaving the heart, in other
words, when in the arteries, than it was a short time before
passing into either, in other words, when it was in the veins;
and if attention be given, it will be found that this difference
is very marked only in the neighbourhood of the heart; and is not
so evident in parts more remote from it. In the next place, the
consistency of the coats of which the arterial vein and the great

artery are composed, sufficiently shows that the blood is impelled against them with more force than against the veins. And why should the left cavity of the heart and the great artery be wider and larger than the right cavity and the arterial vein, were it not that the blood of the venous artery, having only been in the lungs after it has passed through the heart, is thinner, and rarefies more readily, and in a higher degree, than the blood which proceeds immediately from the hollow vein? And what can physicians conjecture from feeling the pulse unless they know that according as the blood changes its nature it can be rarefied by the warmth of the heart, in a higher or lower degree, and more or less quickly than before? And if it be inquired how this heat is communicated to the other members, must it not be admitted that this is effected by means of the blood, which, passing through the heart, is there heated anew, and thence diffused over all the body? Whence it happens, that if the blood be withdrawn from any part, the heat is likewise withdrawn by the same means; and although the heart were as hot as glowing iron, it would not be capable of warming the feet and hands as at present, unless it continually sent thither new blood. We likewise perceive from this, that the true use of respiration is to bring sufficient fresh air into the lungs, to cause the blood which flows into them from the right ventricle of the heart, where it has been rarefied and, as it were, changed into vapours, to become thick, and to convert it anew into blood, before it flows into the left cavity, without which process it would be unfit for the nourishment of the fire that is there. This receives confirmation from the circumstance, that it is observed of animals destitute of lungs that they have also but one cavity in the heart, and that in children who cannot use them while in the womb, there is a hole through which the blood flows from the hollow vein into the left cavity of the heart, and a tube through which it passes from the arterial vein into the grand artery without passing through the lung. In the next place, how could digestion be carried on in the stomach unless the heart communicated heat to it through the arteries, and along with this certain of the more fluid parts of the blood, which assist in the dissolution of the food that has been taken in? Is not also the operation which converts the juice of food into blood easily comprehended, when it is considered that it is distilled by passing and repassing through the heart perhaps more than one or two hundred times in a day? And what more need be adduced to explain nutrition, and the production of the different humours of the body, beyond saying, that the force with which the blood, in being rarefied, passes from the heart towards the extremities of the arteries, causes certain of its parts to remain in the members at which they arrive, and there occupy the place of some others expelled by them; and that according to the situation, shape, or smallness of the pores with which they meet, some rather than others flow into certain parts, in the same way that some sieves are observed to act, which, by being variously perforated, serve to separate different species of grain? And, in the last place, what above all is here worthy of observation, is the generation of the animal spirits, which are like a very subtle wind, or rather a very pure and

vivid flame which, continually ascending in great abundance from
the heart to the brain, thence penetrates through the nerves into
the muscles, and gives motion to all the members; so that to
account for other parts of the blood which, as most agitated and
penetrating, are the fittest to compose these spirits, proceeding
towards the brain, it is not necessary to suppose any other
cause, than simply, that the arteries which carry them thither
proceed from the heart in the most direct lines, and that, according to the rules of Mechanics, which are the same with those of
Nature, when many objects tend at once to the same point where
there is not sufficient room for all, (as is the case with the
parts of the blood which flow forth from the left cavity of the
heart and tend towards the brain,) the weaker and less agitated
parts must necessarily be driven aside from that point by the
stronger which alone in this way reach it.

*   *   *   *   *

I remarked, moreover, with respect to experiments, that they
become always more necessary the more one is advanced in knowledge; for, at the commencement, it is better to make use only
of what is spontaneously presented to our senses, and of which we
cannot remain ignorant, provided we bestow on it any reflection,
however slight, than to concern ourselves about more uncommon and
recondite phænomena : the reason of which is, that the more uncommon often only mislead us so long as the causes of the more
ordinary are still unknown; and the circumstances upon which they
depend are almost always so special and minute as to be highly
difficult to detect. But in this I have adopted the following
order: first, I have essayed to find in general the principles,
or first causes of all that is or can be in the world, without
taking into consideration for this end anything but God himself
who has created it, and without educing them from any other
source than from certain germs of truths naturally existing in
our minds. In the second place, I examined what were the first
and most ordinary effects that could be deduced from these
causes; and it appears to me that, in this way, I have found
heavens, stars, an earth, and even on the earth, water, air,
fire, minerals, and some other things of this kind, which of all
others are the most common and simple, and hence the easiest to
know. Afterwards, when I wished to descend to the more particular, so many diverse objects presented themselves to me, that I
believed it to be impossible for the human mind to distinguish
the forms or species of bodies that are upon the earth, from an
infinity of others which might have been, if it had pleased God
to place them there, or consequently to apply them to our use,
unless we rise to causes through their effects, and avail ourselves of many particular experiments. Thereupon, turning over
in my mind all the objects that had ever been presented to my
senses, I freely venture to state that I have never observed any
which I could not satisfactorily explain by the principles I had
discovered. But it is necessary also to confess that the power
of nature is so ample and vast, and these principles so simple
and general, that I have hardly observed a single particular

effect which I cannot at once recognise as capable of being deduced in many different modes from the principles, and that my
greatest difficulty usually is to discover in which of these
modes the effect is dependent upon them; for out of this difficulty I cannot otherwise extricate myself than by again seeking
certain experiments, which may be such that their result is not
the same, if it is in the one of these modes that we must explain
it, as it would be if it were to be explained in the other. As
to what remains, I am now in a position to discern, as I think,
with sufficient clearness what course must be taken to make the
majority of those experiments which may conduce to this end: but
I perceive likewise that they are such and so numerous, that
neither my hands nor my income, though it were a thousand times
larger than it is, would be sufficient for them all; so that,
according as henceforward I shall have the means of making more
or fewer experiments, I shall in the same proportion make greater
or less progress in the knowledge of nature. This was what I had
hoped to make known by the Treatise I had written, and so clearly
to exhibit the advantage that would thence accrue to the public,
as to induce all who have the common good of man at heart, that
is, all who are virtuous in truth, and not merely in appearance,
or according to opinion, as well to communicate to me the experiments they had already made, as to assist me in those that
remain to be made.

C.

*Galileo Galilei wrote no specific treatise on method but he
did follow one that led to important results. In the selections
that follow, Galileo first shows how to go about attacking
Aristotelians; he then goes on to examine the claims of Scripture
as revelatory of physical truths. Finally he suggests how truth
might be approached.*

1. Galileo Galilei, *Letters on Sunspots**

*In 1609, Galileo constructed a telescope and immediately
turned it on the heavens. Among his discoveries was that of
spots on the Sun which appeared to contradict the Aristotelian
doctrine that the Heavens were perfect and incorruptible. In
his* Letters, *Galileo attacked the silly prejudice (as he saw it)
of preferring the authority of Aristotle to the evidence of the
senses.*

Neither the satellites of Jupiter nor any other stars are
spots or shadows, nor are the sunspots stars. It is indeed true
that I am quibbling over names, while I know that anyone may
impose them to suit himself. So long as a man does not think
that by names he can confer inherent and essential properties on
things, it would make little difference whether he calls these
"stars." Thus the novae of 1572 and 1604 were called "stars,"
and meteorologists call comets and meteors "stars," and for that
matter lovers and poets so refer to the eyes of their ladyloves:

> When Astolfo's successor is seen
> By the glance of those two smiling stars.

For reasons of this kind the sunspots may also be called stars;
but essentially they have properties that differ not a little
from the true stars, which are always of one shape and quite
regular, while the spots are of various shapes and most irregular; the former are consistent in size and shape, the latter
always instable and changing; the former are ever the same, and
permanent in a manner that transcends the memories of all past
ages, while the latter are capable of being produced and dissolved from one day to the next. Stars are never seen except
luminous; spots are always dark; the first are either motionless
or most regular in motion; the others have but a single common
motion though they are affected by myriads of irregularities; the
stars are arranged at varying distances from the sun; sunspots
are all contiguous to it or imperceptibly removed from its
surface; we see the former only if far to one side of the sun,
the latter only in line with the sun; the former are most probably made of dense and very opaque matter, the latter being
rarefied in the manner of clouds and smoke.
Now I fail to see any reason for placing the spots with
things differing from them in a hundred ways and having but a

---

*Galileo, *Letters on Sunspots*, in Stillman Drake, *Discoveries and
Opinions of Galileo*, Doubleday Anchor Books, New York, 1957.
Pp. 139-43.

single property in common, instead of with things that agree with
them in every way. I liken the sunspots to clouds or smokes.
Surely if anyone wished to imitate them by means of earthly
materials, no better model could be found than to put some drops
of incombustible bitumen on a red-hot iron plate. From the black
spot thus impressed on the iron, there will arise a black smoke
that will disperse in strange and changing shapes. And if anyone
were to insist that continual food and nourishment would have to
be supplied for the refueling of the immense light that our great
lamp, the sun, continually diffuses through the universe, then we
have countless experiences harmoniously agreeing in showing us
the conversion of burning materials first into something black or
dark in color. Thus we see wood, straw, paper, candlewicks, and
every burning thing to have its flame planted in and rising from
neighboring parts of the material that have first become black.
It might even be that if we more accurately observed the bright
spots on the sun that I have mentioned, we should find them
occurring in the very places where large dark spots had been a
short time before. But as to this I do not mean to assert anything positively, nor to oblige myself to defend the conjecture,
for I do not wish to mix dubious things with those which are
definite and certain.

I believe that there are not a few Peripatetics on this side
of the Alps who go about philosophizing without any desire to
learn the truth and the causes of things, for they deny these
new discoveries or jest about them, saying that they are illusions. It is about time for us to jest right back at these men
and say that they likewise have become invisible and inaudible.
They go about defending the inalterability of the sky, a view
which perhaps Aristotle himself would abandon in our age. Their
view of sunspots resembles that of Apelles, save that where he
puts a single star for each spot, these fellows make the spots a
congeries of many minute stars which gather together in greater
or smaller numbers to form spots of irregular and varying shapes.
Now though it is true in general that when many objects unite,
each in itself being too small or too distant to be visible, they
may form an aggregate which becomes perceptible to our sight.
Still, one may not conclude as these men do from such a generalization; one must come down to the particular things observed in
stars and in spots. A captain who has but a small number of
soldiers to defend a fortress must not dash with his whole force
to some point under attack, leaving all other positions open and
undefended. When trying to defend the inalterability of the
heavens, we must not forget the perils to which other positions
just as essential to the Peripatetic philosophy may be exposed.
To maintain the integrity and solidity of that philosophy, its
other propositions must be supported by saying that some stars
are fixed and others wandering; those are called "fixed" which
are all in one single sphere and which move with its motion while
remaining fixed with respect to each other, and "wandering" stars
are those of which each has its own special motion. These propositions being true, the "solar stars" cannot be said to be fixed,
for if they did not change with respect to one another it would
be impossible to see the continual mutations that are observed in

the spots, and the same patterns would always return. Hence anyone who wished to maintain that the spots were a congeries of
minute stars would have to introduce into the sky innumerable
movements, tumultuous,uneven, and without any regularity. But
this does not harmonize with any plausible philosophy. And to
what purpose would it be done? To keep the heavens free from
even the tiniest alteration of material. Well, if alteration
were annihilation, the Peripatetics would have some reason for
concern; but since it is nothing but mutation, there is no
reason for such bitter hostility to it. It seems to me unrea-
sonable to call "corruption" in an egg that which produces a
chicken. Besides, if "corruption" and "generation" are discovered in the moon, why deny them to the sky? If the earth's small
mutations do not threaten its existence (if, indeed, they are
ornaments rather than imperfections in it), why deprive the other
planets of them? Why fear so much for the dissolution of the sky
as a result of alterations no more inimical than these?

These men are forced into their strange fancies by attempting to measure the whole universe by means of their tiny scale.
Our special hatred of death need not render fragility odious.
Why should we want to become less mutable? We should thereby
suffer the fate caused by the Medusa's head, being converted to
marble and losing our senses and qualities which could not exist
in us without corporeal alterations. But I shall not go on; I
reserve to another time the examination of the Peripatetic arguments, merely remarking that it appears to me not entirely
philosophical to cling to conclusions once they have been discovered to be manifestly false. These men are persuaded that if
Aristotle were back on earth in our age, he would do the same--as
if it were a sign of more perfect judgment and a more noble consequence of deep learning to defend what is false than to learn
the truth! People like this, it seems to me, give us reason to
suspect that they have not so much plumbed the profundity of the
Peripatetic arguments as they have conserved the imperious
authority of Aristotle. It would be enough for them, and would
save them a great deal of trouble, if they were to avoid these
really dangerous arguments; for it is easier to consult indexes
and look up texts than to investigate conclusions and form new
and conclusive proofs. Besides, it seems to me that we abase our
own status too much and do this not without some offense to
Nature (and I might add to divine Providence), when we attempt to
learn from Aristotle that which he neither knew nor could find
out, rather than consult our own senses and reason. For she, in
order to aid our understanding of her great works, has given us
two thousand more years of observations, and sight twenty times
as acute as that which she gave Aristotle.

2. *In the Letter to the Grand Duchess Christina, Galileo
raised a question of fundamental importance for the nascent
Scientific Revolution. Was the Bible to be taken as a source
of physics? (or of any science). If the answer were yes, then
Galileo predicted a stormy career ahead for the Church. Men,
he insisted, would continue to desire to know physical truth
and if the truth they discovered conflicted with the teachings
of the Church, then ultimately the Church, not science, would
be discredited. Unfortunately for both the Church(es) and
science, Galileo was not listened to.*

To
Her most Serene
HIGHNES
The
Gran Duchess Mother.

Some years since, as Your most Serene Highness well knoweth,
I did discover many particulars in Heaven that had been unseen
and unheard of untill this our Age; which, as well for their
Novelty, as for certain consequences which depend upon them,
clashing with some Physical Propositions commonly received by
the Schools, did stir up against me no small number of such as
professed the vulgar Philosophy in the Universities; as if I
had with my own hand newly placed these things in Heaven to
obscure and disturb Nature and the Sciences: who forgetting
that the multitude of Truths contribute, and concur to the
investigation, augmentation, and establishment of the Arts,
and not to their diminution, and destruction; and at the same
time shewing themselves more affectionate to their own Opinions,
than to Truth, went about to deny, and to disprove those Novelties; of which their very sense, had they but pleased to have
intensly beheld them, would have rendered them thorowly assured.
And to this purpose they alledged sundry things, and published
certain Papers fraughted with vain discourses; and which was a
more gross errour, interwoven with the attestations of the
Sacred Scriptures, taken from places by them not rightly
understood, and which did not any thing concern the point for
which they were produced. Into which errour perhaps they would
not have run, if they had but been advertised of a most profitable Document which S. *Augustine* giveth us, concerning our proceeding warily, in making positive determinations in points that
are obscure and hard to be understood by the meer help of ratiocination; where treating (as we) of a certain natural conclusion concerning Celestial Bodies, he thus writes: (a) *But now
having evermore a respect to the moderation of pious Gravity,
we ought to believe nothing unadvisedly in a doubtful point;
lest we conceive a prejudice against that, in favour to our*

---

* Galileo Galilei, "Epistle to the Grand Dutchesse Mother, Concerning the Authority of Holy Scripture in Philosophical Controversies" in Thomas Salusbury, *Mathematical Collections and
Translations*, 2 vols., London, 1661. Pp. 427-436,442-443,456-459.

Errour, which Truth hereafter may discover to be no wise con-
trary to the Sacred Books either of the Old, or New Testament.
It hath since come to pass, that Time hath by degrees discovered to every one the truths before by me indicated: and together with the truth of the fact, a discovery hath been made
of the difference of humours between those who simply and without passion did refuse to admit such like *Phænomena* for true,
and those who to their incredulity had added some discomposed
affection: For as those who were better grounded in the Science of Astronomy, and Natural Philosophy, became satisfied
upon my first intimation of the news; so all those who stood
not in the Negative, or in doubt for any other reason, but
because it was an unlookt-for-Novelty, and because they had not
an occasion of seeing a sensible experiment thereof, did by
degrees come to satisfie themselves: But those, who besides
the love they bore to their first Errour, have I know not what
imaginary interests to render them disaffected; not so much
towards the things, as towards the Author of them, not being
able any longer to deny them, conceal themselves under an obstinate silence; and being exasperated more than ever by that
whereby those others were satisfied and convinced, they divert
their thoughts to other projects, and seek to prejudice me
some other wayes: of whom I profess that I would make no more
account than I have done of those who heretofore have contradicted me (at whom I alwaies laugh, as being assured of the
issue that the business is to have) but that I see that those
new Calumnies and Persecutions do not determine in our greater
or lesser Learning (in which I will scarce pretend to anything)
but extend so far as to attempt to asperse me with Crimes which
ought to be, and are more abhorred by me than Death it self:
Nor ought I to content my self that they are known to be unjust
by those onely who know me and them, but by all men whatsoever.
They persisting therefore in their first Resolution, Of ruining
me and whatsoever is mine, by all imaginable waies; and knowing
how that I in my Studies of Astronomy and Philosophy hold, as
to the Worlds Systeme, That the Sun, without changing place, is
situate in the Centre of the Conversion of the Celestial Orbes;
and that the Earth, convertible about its own Axis, moveth it
self about the Sun: And moreover understanding, that I proceed
to maintain this Position, not onely by refuting the Reasons of
Ptolomy and *Aristotle*, but by producing many on the contrary;
and in particular, some Physical pertaining to Natural Effects,
the causes of which perhaps can be by no other way assigned;
and others Astronomical depending upon many circumstances and
encounters of new Discoveries in Heaven, which manifestly
confute the Ptolomaick Systeme, and admirably agree with and
confirm this other Hypothesis: and possibly being ashamed to
see the known truth of other positions by me asserted, different from those that have been commonly received; and therefore
distrusting their defence so long as they should continue in
the Field of Philosophy: for these respects, I say, they have
resolved to try whether they could make a Shield for the fallacies of their Arguments of the Mantle of a feigned Religion,
and of the Authority of the Sacred Scriptures, applyed by them

with little judgment to the confutation of such Reasons of mine
as they had neither understood, nor so much as heard.

And first, they have indeavoured, as much as in them lay, to
divulge an opinion thorow the Universe, that those Propositions
are contrary to the Holy Letters, and consequently Damnable and
Heretical: And thereupon perceiving, that for the most part,
the inclination of Mans Nature is more prone to imbrace those
enterprizes, whereby his Neighbour may, although unjustly, be
oppressed, than those from whence he may receive just incour-
agement; it was no hard matter to find those Complices, who for
such (that is, for Damnable and Heretical) did from their Pul-
pits with unwonted confidence preach it, with but an unmerciful
and less considerate injury, not only to this Doctrine, and to
its followers, but to all Mathematicks and Mathematicians together. Hereupon assuming greater confidence, and vainly
hoping that that Seed which first took root in their unsound
mindes, might spread its branches, and ascend towards Heaven,
they went scattering rumours up and down among the People, That
it would, ere long be condemned by Supreme Authority: and
knowing that such a *Censure* would supplant not onely these two
Conclusions of the Worlds Systeme, but would make all other
Astronomical and Physical Observations that have correspondence
and necessary connection therewith to become damnable, to
facilitate the business they seek all they can to make this
opinion (at least among the vulgar) to seem new, and peculiar
to my self, not owing to know that *Nicholas Copernicus* was its
Authour, or rather Restorer and Confirmer: a person who was
not only a Catholick, but a Priest, Canonick, and so esteemed,
that there being a Dispute in the *Lateran Council*, under *Leo* X,
Touching the correction of the Ecclesiastick Calendar, he was
sent for to *Rome* from the remotest parts of *Germany*, for to
assist in this Reformation, which for that time was left imperfect, onely because as then the true measure of the Year and
Lunar Moneth was not exactly known: whereupon it was given him
in charge by the Bishop of *Sempronia*, at that time Super-
intendent in that Affair, to search with reiterated studies and
pains for greater light and certainty, touching those Cœlestial
Motions. Upon which, with a Labour truly *Atlantick* and with
his admirable Wit, setting himself again to that Study, he
made such a progress in these Sciences, and reduced the knowledge of the Cœlestial Motions to such exactnesse, that he
gained the title of an Excellent *Astronomer*. And, according
unto his Doctrine, not only the Calendar hath been since regulated, but the Tables of all the Motions of the Planets have
also been calculated: and having reduced the said Doctrine
into six Books, he published them to the World at the instance
of the Cardinal of *Capua*, and of the Bishop of *Culma*. And in
regard that he had re-assumed this so laborious an enterprize
by the order of The Pope; he dedicated his Book *De Revolutionibus Cœlestibus* to His Successour, namely *Paul* III. which,
being then also Printed, hath been received by The Holy Church,
and read and studied by all the World, without any the least
umbrage of scruple that hath ever been conceived at his Doctrine; The which, whilst it is now proved by manifest Experiments and necessary Demonstrations to have been well grounded,

there want not persons that, though they never saw that same
Book intercept the reward of those many Labours to its Authour,
by causing him to be censured and pronounced an Heretick; and
this, only to satisfie a particular displeasure conceived,
without any cause, against another man, that hath no other interest in *Copernicus* but only as he is an approver of his
Doctrine.

Now in regard of these false aspersions, which they so
unjustly seek to throw upon me, I have thought it necessary for
my justification before the World (of whose judgment in matters
of Religion and Reputation I ought to make great esteem) to
discourse concerning those Particulars, which these men produce
to scandalize and subvert this Opinion, and in a word, to condemn it, not only as false, but also as Heretical; continually
making an Hipocritical Zeal for Religion their Shield; going
about moreover to interest the Sacred Scriptures in the Dispute,
and to make them in a certain sense Ministers of their deceipt-
ful purposes: and farthermore desiring, if I mistake not,
contrary to the intention of them, and of the Holy Fathers to
extend (that I may not say abuse) their Authority, so as that
even in Conclusions meerly Natural, and not *de Fide*, they would
have us altogether leave Sense and Demonstrative Reasons, for
some place of Scripture which sometimes under the apparent
words may contain a different sense. Now I hope to shew with
how much greater Piety and Religious Zeal I proceed, than they
do, in that I propose not, that the Book of *Copernicus* is not
to be condemned, but that it is not to be condemned, as they
would have it; without understanding it, hearing it, or so
much as seeing it; and especially he being an Author that never
treateth of matters of Religion or Faith; nor by Reasons any
way depending on the Authority of Sacred Scriptures whereupon
he may have erroniously interpreted them; but alwaies insists
upon Natural Conclusions belonging to the Celestial Motions,
handled with Astronomical and Geometrical Demonstrations. Not
that he had not a respect to the places of the Sacred Leaves,
but because he knew very well that his said Doctrine being
demonstrated, it could not contradict the Scriptures, rightly,
and according to their true meaning understood. And therefore
in the end of his Epistle Dedicatory, speaking to The Pope, he
saith thus: *(b) If there should chance to be any Matæologists,
who though ignorant in all the Mathematicks, yet pretending a
skill in those Learnings, should dare, upon the authority of
some place of Scripture wrested to their purpose, to condemn
and censure this my Hypothesis, I value them not, but shall
slight their inconsiderate Judgement. For it is not unknown,
that* Lactantius *(otherwise a Famous Author, though mean Mathematician) writeth very childishly touching the Form of the
Earth, when he scoffs at those who affirm the Earth to be in
Form of a Globe. So that it ought not to seem strange to the
Ingenious, if any such should likewise now deride us. The
Mathematicks are written for Mathematitians, to whom (if I
deceive not my self) these Labours of mine shall seem to add
something, as also to the Common-weale of the Church, whose
Government is now in the hands of Your Holiness.*

And of this kinde do these appear to be who indeavour to perswade that *Copernicus* may be condemned before his Book is read; and to make the World believe that it is not onely lawfull but commendable so to do, produce certain Authorities of the Scripture, of Divines, and of Councils; which as they are by me had in reverence, and held of Supream Authority, insomuch that I should esteem it high temerity for any one to contradict them whilst they are used according to the Institutes of Holy Church, so I believe that it is no errour to speak, so long as one hath reason to suspect that a person hath a desire, for some concern of his own, to produce and alledge them, to purposes different from those that are in the most Sacred intention of The Holy Church. Therefore I not onely protest (and my sincerity shall manifest it self) that I intend to submit my self freely to renounce those errors, into which, through ignorance, I may run in this Discourse of matters pertaining to Religion; but I farther declare, that I desire not in these matters to engage dispute with any one, although it should be in points that are disputable: for my end endeth onely to this, That if in these considerations, besides my own profession, amongst the errours that may be in them, there be any thing apt to give others an hint of some Notion beneficial to the Holy Church, touching the determining about the *Copernican* Systeme, it may be taken and improved as shall seem best to my Superiours: If not, let my Book be torn and burnt; for that I do neither intend, nor pretend to gain to my self any fruit from my writings, that is not Pious and Catholick. And moreover, although that many of the things that I observe have been spoken in my own hearing, yet I shall freely admit and grant to those that spake them, that they never said them, if so they please, but confess that I might have been mistaken: And therefore what I say, let it be supposed to be spoken not by them, but by those which were of this opinion.

The motive therefore that they produce to condemn the Opinion of the Mobility of the Earth, and Stability of the Sun, is, that reading in the Sacred Leaves, in many places, that the Sun moveth, that the Earth standeth still; and the Scripture not being capable of lying, or erring, it followeth upon necessary consequence, that the Position of those is Erronious and Heretical, who maintain that the Sun of it self is immoveable, and the Earth moveable.

Touching this Reason I think it fit in the first place, to consider, That it is both piously spoken, and prudently affirmed, That the Sacred Scripture can never lye, when ever its true meaning is understood: Which I believe none will deny to be many times very abstruce, and very different from that which the bare sound of the words signifieth. Whence it cometh to pass, that if ever any one should constantly confine himself to the naked Grammatical Sence, he might, erring himself, make not only Contradictions and Propositions remote from Truth to appear in the Scriptures, but also gross Heresies and Blasphemies: For that we should be forced to assign to God feet, and hands, and eyes, yea more corporal and humane affections, as of Anger, of Repentance, of Hatred, nay, and sometimes the Forgetting of things past, and Ignorance of those to come: Which Propositions, like as (so the

Holy Ghost affirmeth) they were in that manner pronounced by the
Sacred Scriptures, that they might be accommodated to the Capacity of the Vulgar, who are very rude and unlearned; so likewise,
for the sakes of those that deserve to be distinguished from the
Vulgar, it is necessary that grave and skilful Expositors produce
the true senses of them, and shew the particular Reasons why
they are dictated under such and such words. And this is a Doctrine so true and common amongst Divines, that it would be superfluous to produce any attestation thereof.

*   *   *   *   *

This therefore being granted, methinks that in the Discussion of Natural Problemes, we ought not to begin at the authority
of places of Scripture; but at Sensible Experiments and Necessary
Demonstrations: For, from the Divine Word, the Sacred Scripture
and Nature did both alike proceed; the first, as the Holy Ghosts
Inspiration; the second, as the most observant Executrix of Gods
Commands: And moreover it being convenient in the Scriptures (by
way of condescension to the understanding of all men) to speak
many things different, in appearance; and so far as concernes the
naked signification of the words, from absolute truth: But on
the contrary, Nature being inexorable and immutable, and never
passing the bounds of the Laws assigned her, as one that nothing
careth whether her abstruse reasons and methods of operating be,
or be not exposed to the Capacity of Men; I conceive that that,
concerning Natural Effects, which either Sensible Experience
sets before our eyes, or Necessary Demonstrations do prove unto
us, ought not, upon any account, to be called into question, much
less condemned upon the testimony of Texts of Scripture, which
may, under their words, couch Senses seemingly contrary thereto;
In regard that every Expression of Scripture is not tied to so
strict conditions, as every Effect of Nature: Nor doth God less
admirably discover himself unto us in Nature's Actions, than in
the Scriptures Sacred Dictions. Which peradventure *Tertullian*
intended to express in those words: *(c) We conclude, God is
known; first, by Nature, and then again more particularly known
by Doctrine: by Nature, in his Works; by Doctrine, in his Word
preached.*

*   *   *   *   *

This maketh me to suppose, that the Authority of the Sacred
Volumes was intended principally to perswade men to the belief of
those Articles and Propositions, which, by reason they surpass
all humane discourse, could not by any other Science, or by any
other means be made credible, than by the Mouth of the Holy
Spirit it self. Besides that, even in those Propositions, which
are not *de Fide*, the Authority of the same Sacred Leaves ought to
be preferred to the Authority of all Humane Sciences that are not
written in a Demonstrative Method, but either with bare Narrations, or else with probable Reasons; and this I hold to be so
far convenient and necessary, by how far the said Divine Wisdome
surpasseth all humane Judgment and Conjecture. But that that

self same God who hath indued us with Senses, Discourse, and
Understanding hath intended, laying aside the use of these, to
give the knowledg of those things by other means, which we may
attain by these, so as that even in those Natural Conclusions,
which either by Sensible Experiments or Necessary Demonstrations
are set before our eyes, or our Understanding, we ought to deny
Sense and Reason, I do not conceive that I am bound to believe
it; and especially in those Sciences, of which but a small part,
and that divided into Conclusions is to be found in the Scripture: Such as, for instance, is that of *Astronomy*, of which
there is so small a part in Holy Writ, that it doth not so much
as name any of the Planets, except the Sun and the Moon, and once
or twice onely *Venus* under the name of *Lucifer*. For if the Holy
Writers had had any intention to perswade People to believe the
Dispositions and Motions of the Cœlestial Bodies; and that consequently we are still to derive that knowledge from the Sacred
Books they would not, in my opinion, have spoken so little
thereof, that it is as much as nothing, in comparison of the
infinite admirable Conclusions, which in that Science are comprized and demonstrated. Nay, that the Authours of the Holy
Volumes did not only not pretend to teach us the Constitutions
and Motions of the Heavens and Stars, their Figures, Magnitudes,
and Distances, but that intentionally (albeit that all these
things were very well known unto them) they forbore to speak of
them, is the opinion of the Most Holy & Most Learned Fathers:
and in S. *Augustine* we read the following words. *(c) It is
likewise commonly asked, of what Form and Figure we may believe
Heaven to be, according to the Scriptures: For many contend much
about those matters, which the greater prudence of our Authors
hath forborn to speak of, as nothing furthering their Learners in
relation to a blessed life; and, (which is the chiefest thing)
taking up much of that time which should be spent in holy exercises. For what is it to me whether Heaven, as a Sphere, doth on
all sides environ the Earth, a Mass ballanced in the middle of
the World; or whether like a Dish it doth onely cover or over-
cast the same? But because belief of Scripture is urged for that
cause, which we have oft mentioned, that is, That none through
ignorance of Divine Phrases, when they shall find any thing of
this nature in, or hear any thing cited out of our Bibles which
may seem to oppose manifest Conclusions, should be induced to
suspect their truth, when they admonish, relate, & deliver more
profitable matters. Briefly be it spoken, touching the Figure of
Heaven, that our Authors knew the truth: But the H. Spirit would
not, that men should learn what is profitable to none for
salvation.*
    And the same intentional silence of these sacred Penmen in
determining what is to be believed of these accidents of the Celestial Bodies, is again hinted to us by the same Father in the
ensuing 10. Chapter upon the Question, Whether we are to believe
that Heaven moveth, or standeth still, in these words: *(d) There
are some of the Brethren that start a question concerning the
motion of Heaven, Whether it be fixed, or moved: For if it be
moved (say they) how is it a Firmament? If it stand still, how
do these Stars which are held to be fixed go round from East to*

West, the more Northern performing shorter Circuits near the Pole; so that Heaven, if there be another Pole, to us unknown, may seem to revolve upon some other Axis; but if there be not another Pole, it may be thought to move as a Discus? To whom I reply, That these points require many subtil and profound Reasons, for the making out whether they be really so, or no; the undertakeing and discussing of which is neither consistent with my leasure, nor their duty, whom I desire to instruct in the necessary matters more directly conducing to their salvation, and to the benefit of The Holy Church.

From which (that we may come nearer to our particular case) it necessarily followeth, that the Holy Ghost not having intended to teach us, whether Heaven moveth or standeth still; nor whether its Figure be in Form of a Sphere, or of a Discus, or distended *in Planum*: Nor whether the Earth be contained in the Centre of it, or on one side; he hath much less had an intention to assure us of other Conclusions of the same kinde, and in such a manner, connected to these already named, that without the determination of them, one can neither affirm one or the other part; which are, The determining of the Motion and Rest of the said Earth, and of the Sun. And if the same Holy Spirit hath purposely pretermitted to teach us those Propositions, as nothing concerning his intention, that is, our salvation; how can it be affirmed, that the holding of one part rather than the other, should be so necessary, as that it is *de Fide*, and the other erronious? Can an Opinion be Heretical, and yet nothing concerning the salvation of souls? Or can it be said that the Holy Ghost purposed not to teach us a thing that concerned our salvation? I might here insert the Opinion of an Ecclesiastical Person, raised to the degree of *Eminentissimo*, to wit, *That the intention of the Holy Ghost, is to teach us how we shall go to Heaven, and not how Heaven goeth.*

But let us return to consider how much necessary Demonstrations, and sensible Experiments ought to be esteemed in Natural Conclusions; and of what Authority Holy and Learned Divines have accounted them, from whom amongst an hundred other attestations, we have these that follow: *(e) We must also carefully heed and altogether avoid in handling the Doctrine of* Moses, *to avouch or speak any thing affirmatively and confidently which contradicteth the manifest Experiments and Reasons of Philosophy, or other Sciences. For since all Truth is agreeable to Truth, the Truth of Holy Writ cannot be contrary to the solid Reasons and Experiments of Humane Learning.*

*   *   *   *   *

I would entreat these Wise and Prudent Fathers, that they would withal diligence consider the difference that is between Opinable and Demonstrative Doctrines: To the end, that well weighing in their minds with what force Necessary Illations oblige, they might the better ascertain themselves, that it is not in the Power of the Professors of Demonstrative Sciences to change their Opinions at pleasure, and apply themselves one while to one side, and another while to another; and that there is a great difference between commanding a Mathematitian or a Philosopher, and the disposing of a Lawyer or a Merchant; and that the demonstrated Conclusions touching the things of Nature and of the Heavens cannot be changed with the same facility, as the Opinions are touching what is lawful or not in a Contract, Bargain, or Bill of Exchange. This difference was well understood by the Learned and Holy Fathers, as their having been at great pains to confute many Arguments, or to say better, many Philosophical Fallacies, doth prove unto us; and as may expresly be read in some of them, and particularly we have in S. *Augustine* the following words: *This is to be held for an undoubted Truth, That we may be confident, that whatever the Sages of this World have demonstrated touching Natural Points, is no waies contrary to our Bibles: And in case they teach any thing in their Books that is contrary to the Holy Scriptures, we may without any scruple conclude it to be most false; And according to our ability let us make the same appear: And let us so keep the Faith of our Lord, in whom are hidden all the Treasures of Wisdom; that we be neither seduced with the Loquacity of false Philosophy, nor scared by the superstition of a counterfeit Religion.*

From which words, I conceive that I may collect this Doctrine, namely, That in the Books of the Wise of this World, there are contained some Natural truths that are solidly demonstrated, and others again that are barely taught; and that as to the first sort, it is the Office of wise Divines to shew that they are not contrary to the Sacred Scriptures; As to the rest, taught, but not necessarily demonstrated, if they shall contain anything contrary to the Sacred Leaves, it ought to be held undoubtedly false, and such it ought by all possible waies to be demonstrated.

If therefore Natural Conclusions veritably demonstrated, are not to be postposed to the Places of Scripture, but that it ought to be shewn how those Places do not interfer with the said Conclusions; then its necessary before a Physical Proposition be condemned, to shew that it is not necessarily demonstrated; and this is to be done not by them who hold it to be true, but by those who judge it to be false. And this seemeth very reasonable, and agreeable to Nature; that is to say, that they may much more easily find the fallacies in a Discourse, who believe it to be false, than those who account it true and concludent. Nay, in this particular it will come to passe, that the followers of this opinion, the more that they shall turn over Books, examine the Arguments, repeat the Observations, and compare the Experiments, the more shall they be confirmed in this belief. And your Highness knoweth what happened to the late Mathematick Professor in the University of *Pisa*, Who betook himself in his old age to look into the Doctrine of *Copernicus*, with hope that he might be able solidly to confute it (for that he held it so far to be false, as that he had never studied it) but it was his fortune, that as soon as he had understood the grounds, proceedings, and demonstrations of *Copernicus*, he found himself to be perswaded, and of an opposer became his most confident Defender. I might also nominate other Mathematicians, who being moved by my last Discoveries, have confessed it necessary to change the formerly received Constitution of the World, it not being able by any means to subsist any longer.

    *   *   *   *   *

It remaineth now, that we consider whether it be true, that
the Place in *Joshuah* may be taken without altering the pure signification of the words: and how it can be that the Sun, obeying
the command of *Joshuah*, which was, *That it should stand still*,
the day might thereupon be much lengthened. Which businesse, if
the Celestial Motions be taken according to the *Ptolomaick*
Systeme, can never any wayes happen, for that the Sun moving
thorow the Ecliptick, according to the order of the Signes, which
is from East to West (which is that which maketh Day and Night)
it is a thing manifest, that the Sun ceasing its true and proper
Motion, the day would become shorter and not longer; and that on
the contrary, the way to lengthen it would be to hasten and velo-
citate the Suns motion; insomuch that to cause the Sun to stay
above the Horizon for some time, in one and the same place, without declining towards the West, it would be necessary to accelerate its motion in such a manner as that it might seem equal to
that of the *Primum Mobile*, which would be an accelerating it
about three hundred and sixty times more than ordinary. If
therefore *Joshuah* had had an intention that his words should be
taken in their pure and proper signification, he would have bid
the Sun to have accelerated its Motion so, that the Rapture of
the *Primum Mobile* might not carry it to the West: but because
his words were heard by people which haply knew no other Celestial Motion, save this grand and common one, from East to West,
stooping to their Capacity, and having no intention to teach them
the Constitution of the Spheres, but only that they should perceive the greatness of the Miracle wrought, in the lengthening
of the Day, he spoke according to their apprehension. Possibly
this Consideration moved *Dionysius Areopagita* to say that in
this Miracle the *Primum Mobile* stood still, and this stopping,
all the Celestial Spheres did of consequence stay: of which
opinion is S. *Augustine* himself, and *Abulensis* at large confirm-
eth it. Yea, that *Joshua's* intention was, that the whole Systeme
of the Celestial Spheres should stand still, is collected from
the command he gave at the same time to t he Moon, although that
it had nothing to do in the lengthening of the day; and under the
injunction laid upon the Moon, we are to understand the Orbes of
all the other Planets; passed over in silence here, as also in
all other places of the Sacred Scriptures; the intention of
which, was not to teach us the Astronomical Sciences. I suppose
therefore, (if I be not deceived) that it is very plain, that if
we allow the *Ptolemaick* Systeme, we must of necessity interpret
the words to some sense different from their strict signification.
Which Interpretation (being admonished by the most usefull precepts of S. *Augustine*) I will not affirm to be of necessity this
above-mentioned, since that some other man may haply think of
some other more proper, and more agreeable Sense.

But now, if this same passage may be understood in the
Copernican Systeme, to agree better with what we read in *Joshuah*,
with the help of another Observation by me newly shewen in the
Body of the Sun; I will propound it to consideration, speaking
alwaies with those safe Reserves; That I am not so affectionate
to my own inventions, as to prefer them before those of other
men, and to believe that better and more agreeable to the inten-

tion of the Sacred Volumes cannot be produced.

Supposing therefore in the first place, that in the Miracle of *Joshuah*, the whole Systeme of the Celestial Revolutions stood still, according to the judgement of the afore-named Authors: And this is the rather to be admitted, to the end, that by the staying of one alone, all the Constitutions might not be confounded, and a great disorder needlesly introduced in the whole course of Nature: I come in the second place to consider how the Solar Body, although stable in one constant place, doth nevertheless revolve in it self, making an entire Conversion in the space of a Month, or thereabouts; as I conceive I have solidly demonstrated in my Letters on Sunspots: Which motion we sensibly see to be in the upper part of its Globe, inclined towards the South; and thence towards the lower part, to encline towards the North, just in the same manner as all the other Orbs of the Planets do. Thirdly, If we respect the Nobility of the Sun, and his being the Fountain of Light, by which, (as I necessarily demonstrate) not onely the Moon and Earth, but all the other Planets (all in the same manner dark of themselves) become illuminated; I conceive that it will be no unlogicall Illation to say, That it, as the Grand Minister of Nature, and in a certain sense the Soul and Heart of the world, infuseth into the other Bodies which environ it; not onely Light, but Motion also; by revolving in it self: So that in the same manner that the motion of the Heart of an Animal ceasing, all the other motions of its Members would cease; so, the Conversion of the Sun ceasing, the Conversions of all the Planets would stand still. And though I could produce the testimonies of many grave Writers to prove the admirable power and influence of the Sun, I will content my self with one sole place of Holy *Dionisius Areopagita* in his Book *de Divinis Nominibus*; who thus writes of the Sun: *His Light gathereth and converts all things to himself, which are seen, moved, illustrated, wax hot, and (in a word) those things which are preserved by his splendor: Wherefore the Sun is called Ἥλιος, for that he collecteth and gathereth together all things dispersed.* And a little after of the Sun again he adds; *If this Sun which we see, as touching the Essences and Qualities of those things which fall within our Sense, being very many and different; yet if he who is one, and equally bestowes his Light, doth renew, nourish, defend, perfect, divide, conjoyn, cherish, make fruitfull, encrease, change, fix, produce, move, and fashion all living creatures: And everything in this Universe at his Pleasure, is partaker of one and the same Sun; and the causes of many things which participate of him, are equally anticipated in him: Certainly by greater reason;* &c. The Sun therefore being the Fountain of Light and, Principle of Motion, God intending, that at the Command of *Joshuah*, all the Worlds Systeme, should continue many hours in the same state, it sufficeth to make the Sun stand still, upon whose stay (all the other Conversions ceasing) the Earth, the Moon, the Sun did abide in the same Constitution as before, as likewise all the other Planets: Nor in all that time did the Day decline towards Night, but it was miraculously prolonged: And in this manner, upon the standing still of the Sun, without altering, or in the least disturbing the other Aspects and mutual Positions of the Stars, the

Day might be lengthned on Earth; which exactly agreeth with the Litteral sense of the Sacred Text.

But that of which, if I be not mistaken, we are to make no small account, is, That by help of this *Copernican* Hypothesis, we have the Litteral, apert, and Natural Sense of another particular that we read of in the same Miracle; which is, That the Sun Stood still *in Medio Cœli*: Upon which passage grave Divines raise many questions, in regard it seemeth very probable, That when *Joshuah* desired the lengthning of the Day, the Sun was near setting, and not in the Meridian; for if it had been in the Meridian, it being then about the Summer *Solstice*, and consequently the dayes being at the longest, it doth not seem likely that it was necessary to pray for the lengthning of the day, to prosecute Victory in a Battail, the space of seven hours and more, which remained to Night, being sufficient for that purpose. Upon which Grave Divines have been induced to think that the Sun was near setting. And so the words themselves seem to sound, saying, *Ne movearis Sol, ne movearis*. For if it had been in the Meridian, either it had been needless to have asked a Miracle, or it would have been sufficient to have onely praid for some retardment. Of this opinion is *Cajetan*, to which subscribeth *Magaglianes*, confirming it by saying, that *Joshuah* had that very day done so many other things before his commanding the Sun, as were not possibly to be dispatch't in half a day. Whereupon they are forced to read the Words *in Medio Cœli* (to confess the truth) with a little harshness, saying that they import no more than this: *That the Sun stood still, being in our Hemisphere, that is, above the Horizon.* But (if I do not erre) we shall avoid that and all other harsh expositions, if according to the *Copernican* Systeme we place the Sun in the midst, that is, in the Centre of the Cœlestial Orbes, and of the Planetary Conversions, as it is most requisite to do. For supposing any hour of the day (either Noon, or any other, as you shall please neerer to the Evening) the Day was lengthened, and all the Cœlestial Revolutions stayed by the Suns standing still, *In the midst*, that is, *in the Centre of Heaven*, where it resides: A Sense so much the more accomodate to the Letter (besides what hath been said already) in that, if the Text had desired to have affirmed the Suns Rest to have been caused at Noon-day, the proper expression of it had been to say, *It stood still at Noon-day*, or *in the Meridian Circle*, and not *in the midst of Heaven*: In regard that the true and only *Middle* of a Spherical Body (as is Heaven) is the Centre.

3. *The* Dialogue on the Great World Systems* *is Galileo's master-piece. Written in the form of a dialogue, this work examines the rival claims of the Aristotelian (Ptolemaic) and the Copernican systems. There is no doubt where Galileo's allegiance lies. He is not only intent on discrediting the content of the older cosmology; he wishes, as well, to show that the method by which this system was constructed is faulty.*

SIMPL. I, for my part, have not made either so long, or so exact observations, as to enable me to boast my self Master of the *Quod est* of this matter: but I will more accurately consider the same, and make tryal my self for my own satisfaction, whether I can reconcile that which experience shews us, with that which *Aristotle* teacheth us; for it's a certain Maxim, that two Truths cannot be contrary to one another.

SALV. If you would reconcile that which sense sheweth you, with the solider Doctrines of *Aristotle*, you will find no great difficulty in the undertaking; and that so it is, doth not *Aristotle* say, that one cannot treat confidently of the things of Heaven, by reason of their great remoteness?

SIMPL. He expressly saith so.

SALV. And doth he not likewise affirm, that we ought to prefer that which sense demonstrates, before all Arguments, though in appearance never so well grounded? and saith he not this without the least doubt or hæsitation?

SIMPL. He doth so.

SALV. Why then, the second of these propositions, which are both the doctrine of *Aristotle*, that saith, that sense is to take place of Logick, is a doctrine much more solid and undoubted, than that other which holdeth the Heavens to be unalterable; and therefore you shall argue more *Aristotelically*, saying, the Heavens are alterable, for that so my sense telleth me, than if you should say, the Heavens are unalterable, for that Logick so perswaded *Aristotle*. Furthermore, we may discourse of Cœlestial matters much better than *Aristotle*; because, he confessing the knowledg thereof to be difficult to him, by reason of their remoteness from the senses, he thereby acknowledgeth, that one to whom the senses can better represent the same, may philosophate upon them with more certainty. Now we by help of the Telescope, are brought thirty or forty times nearer to the Heavens, than ever *Aristotle* came; so that we may discover in them an hundred things, which he could not see, and amongst the rest, these spots in the Sun, which were to him absolutely invisible; therefore we may discourse of the Heavens and Sun, with more certainty than *Aristotle*.

SAGR. I see into the heart of *Simplicius*, and know that he is much moved at the strength of these so convincing Arguments; but on the other side, when he considereth the great authority which *Aristotle* hath won with all men, and remembreth the great number of famous Interpreters, which have made it their business to explain his sense; and seeth other Sciences, so necessary and

---

*Thomas Salusbury, *Mathematical collections and translations*, 2 vols., London, 1661 and 1665. Galileus Galileus, his System of the world, pp. 42-45; 86-88.

profitable to the publick, to build a great part of their esteem
and reputation on the credit of *Aristotle* he is much puzzled and
perplexed: and methinks I hear him say, To whom then should we
repair for the decision of our controversies, if *Aristotle* were
removed from the chair? What other Author should we follow in
the Schools, Academies and Studies? What Philosopher hath writ
all the parts of Natural Philosophy, and that so methodically
without omitting so much as one single conclusion? Shall we then
overthrow that Fabrick under which so many passengers find shel-
ter? Shall we destroy that *Asylum*, that *Prytaneum*, wherein so
many Students meet with commodious harbour, where without expos-
ing themselves to the injuries of the air, with the onely turning
over of a few leaves, one may learn all the secrets of Nature?
Shall we dismantle that fort in which we are safe from all hos-
tile assaults? But I pitie him no more than I do that Gentleman
who with great expence of time and treasure, and the help of many
hundred artists, erects a very sumptuous Pallace, and afterwards
beholds it ready to fall, by reason of the bad foundation; but
being extremely unwilling to see the Walls stript which are
adorned with so many beautifull Pictures; or to suffer the columns
to fall, that uphold the stately Galleries; or the gilded roofs,
chimney-pieces, the freizes, the cornishes of marble, with so
much cost erected, to be ruined; goeth about with girders, props,
shoars, butterasses, to prevent their subversion.

      SALV. But alas, *Simplicius* as yet fears no such fall, and I
would undertake to secure him from that mischief at a far less
charge. There is no danger that so great a multitude of subtle
and wise Philosophers should suffer themselves to be *Hector'd*
by one or two, who make a little blustering; nay, they will
rather, without ever turning the points of their pens against
them, by their silence onely render them the object of universal
scorn and contempt. It is a fond conceit for any one to think to
introduce new Philosophy, by reproving this or that Author: it
will be first necessary to new-mold the brains of men, and make
them apt to distinguish truth from falshood. A thing which onely
God can do. But from one discourse to another whither are we
stray'd? your memory must help to guide me into the way again.

      SIMPL. I remember very well where we left. We were upon
the answer of *Anti-Tycho*, to the objections against the immutability of the Heavens, among which you inserted this of the Solar
spots, not spoke of by him; and I believe you intended to examine
his answer to the instance of the New Stars.

      SALV. Now I remember the rest, and to proceed, Methinks
there are some things in the answer of *Anti-Tycho*, worthy of
reprehension. And first, if the two New Stars, which he can do
no less than place in the uppermost parts of the Heavens, and
which were of a long duration, but finally vanished, give him no
obstruction in maintaining the inalterability of   Heaven,   in
that they were not certain parts thereof, nor mutations made in
the antient Stars, why doth he set himself so vigorously and
earnestly against the Comets, to banish them by all ways from the
Cœlestial Regions? Was it not enough that he could say of them
the same which he spoke of the New stars? to wit, that in regard
they were no certain parts of Heaven, nor mutations made in any

cf the Stars, they could no wise prejudice either Heaven, or the
Doctrine of *Aristotle*? Secondly, I am not very well satisfied of
his meaning; when he saith that the alterations that should be
granted to be made in the Stars, would be destructive to the prerogative of Heaven; namely, its incorruptibility, &c. and this,
because the Stars are Cœlestial substances, as is manifest by
the consent of every one; and yet is nothing troubled that the
same alterations should be made without the Stars in the rest of
the Cœlestial expansion. Doth he think that Heaven is no Cœlestial substance? I, for my part, did believe that the Stars were
called Cœlestial bodies, by reason that they were in Heaven, or
for that they were made of the substance of Heaven; and yet I
thought that Heaven was more Cœlestial than they; in like sort,
as nothing can be said to be more Terrestrial, or more fiery than
the Earth or Fire themselves. And again, in that he never made
any mention of the Solar spots, which have been evidently demonstrated to be produced, and dissolved, and to be neer the Sun,
and to turn either with, or about the same, I have reason to
think that this Author probably did write more for others pleasure, than for his own satisfaction; and this I affirm, forasmuch
as he having shewn himself to be skilful in the Mathematicks, it
is impossible but that he should have been convinced by Demonstrations, that those substances are of necessity contiguous with
the body of the Sun, and are so great generations and corruptions,
that none comparable to them, ever happen in the Earth: And if
such, so many, and so frequent be made in the very Globe of the
Sun, which may with reason be held one of the noblest parts of
Heaven, what should make us think that others may not happen in
the other Orbs?

SAGR. I cannot without great admiration, nay more, denial
of my understanding, hear it to be attributed to natural bodies,
for a great honour and perfection that they are impassible, immutable, inalterable, &c. And on the contrary, to hear it to be
esteemed a great imperfection to be alterable, generable, mutable, &c. It is my opinion that the Earth is very noble and admirable, by reason of so many and so different alterations, mutations, generations, &c. which are incessantly made therein; and
if without being subject to any alteration, it had been all one
vast heap of sand, or a masse of *Jasper*, or that in the time of
the Deluge, the waters freezing which covered it, it had continued an immense Globe of Christal, wherein nothing had ever grown,
altered, or changed, I should have esteemed it a lump of no benefit to the World, full of idlenesse, and in a word superfluous,
and as if it had never been in nature; and should make the same
difference in it, as between a living and dead creature: The
like I say of the *Moon, Jupiter*, and all the other Globes of the
World. But the more I dive into the consideration of the vanity
of popular discourses, the more empty and simple I find them.
And what greater folly can there be imagined, than to call Jems,
Silver and Gold pretious; and Earth and dirt vile? For do not
these persons consider, that if there should be as great a scarcity of Earth, as there is of Jewels and pretious metals, there
would be no Prince, but would gladly give a heap of Diamonds and
Rubies, and many Wedges of Gold, to purchase onely so much Earth

as should suffice to plant a Gessemine in a little pot, or to set
therein a *China Orange*, that he might see it sprout, grow up, and
bring forth so goodly leaves, so odiriferous flowers, and so delicate fruit? It is therefore scarcity and plenty that make
things esteemed and contemned by the vulgar; who will say that
same is a most beautiful Diamond, for that it resembleth a cleer
water, and yet will not part with it for ten Tun of water: These
men that so extol incorruptibility, inalterability, &c. speak
thus I believe out of the great desire they have to live long,
and for fear of death; not considering, that if men had been im-
mortal, they should have had nothing to do in the World. These
deserve to meet with a *Medusa's* head, that would transform them
into Statues of *Dimond* and *Jasper*, that so they might become more
perfect than they are.

SALV. And it may be such a *Metamorphosis* would not be altogether unprofitable to them; for I am of opinion that it is better not to discourse at all, than to argue erroniously.

        *   *   *   *   *

SALV. You argue very cunningly, but to reply to your objection I must have recourse to a Philosophical distinction, and say
that the understanding is to be taken too ways, that is *intensive*,
or *extensive*; and that *extensive*, that is, as to the multitude of
intelligibles, which are infinite, the understanding of man is as
nothing, though he should understand a thousand propositions; for
that a thousand, in respect of infinity is but as a cypher: but
taking the understanding *intensive*, (in as much as that term imports) intensively, that is, perfectly some propositions, I say,
that humane wisdom understandeth some propositions so perfectly,
and is as absolutely certain thereof, as Nature her self; and
such are the pure Mathematical sciences, to wit, Geometry and
Arithmetick: in which Divine Wisdom knows infinite more propositions, because it knows them all; but I believe that the knowledge of those few comprehended by humane understanding, equall-
eth the divine, as to the certainty *objective*, for that it
arriveth to comprehend the necessity thereof, than which there
can be no greater certainty.

SIMPL. This seemeth to me a very bold and rash expression.

SALV. These are common notions, and far from all umbrage of
temerity, or boldness, and detract not in the least from the Majesty of divine wisdom; as it nothing diminisheth the omnipotence
thereof to say, that God cannot make what is once done, to be un-
done: but I doubt, *Simplicius*, that your scruple ariseth from an
opinion you have, that my words are somewhat equivocal; therefore
the better to express my self I say, that as to the truth, of
which Mathematical demonstrations give us the knowledge, it is
the same, which the divine wisdom knoweth; but this I must grant
you, that the manner whereby God knoweth the infinite propositions, of which we understand some few, is highly more excellent
than ours, which proceedeth by ratiocination, and passeth from
conclusion to conclusion, whereas his is done at one single
thought or intuition; and whereas we, for example, to attain the
knowledg of some passion of the Circle, which hath infinite, be-

ginning from one of the most simple, and taking that for its
definition, do proceed with argumentation to another, and from
that to a third, and then to a fourth, &c. the Divine Wisdom, by
the apprehension of its essence comprehends, without temporary
raciocination, all these infinite passions; which notwithstanding, are in effect virtually comprised in the definitions of all
things; and, to conclude, as being infinite, perhaps are but one
alone in their nature, and in the Divine Mind; the which neither
is wholly unknown to humane understanding, but onely be-clouded
with thick and grosse mists; which come in part to be dissipated
and clarified, when we are made Masters of any conclusions, firmly demonstrated, and so perfectly made ours, as that we can
speedily run through them; for in sum, what other, is that proposition, that the square of the side subtending the right angle in
any triangle, is equal to the squares of the other two, which
include it, but onely the Paralellograms being upon common bases,
and between parallels equal amongst themselves? and this, lastly,
is it not the same, as to say that those two superficies are equal,
of which equal parts applyed to equal parts, possesse equal
place? Now these inferences, which our intellect apprehendeth
with time and a gradual motion, the Divine Wisdom, like light,
penetrateth in an instant, which is the same as to say, hath them
alwayes present: I conclude therefore, that our understanding,
both as to the manner and the multitude of the things comprehended by us, is infinitely surpast by the Divine Wisdom; but yet I
do not so vilifie it, as to repute it absolutely nothing; yea
rather, when I consider how many and how great misteries men have
understood, discovered, and contrived, I very plainly know and
understand the mind of man to be one of the works, yea one of the
most excellent works of God.

    SAGR. I have oft times considered with my self, in pursu-
ance of that which you speak of, how great the wit of man is; and
whil'st I run thorow such and so many admirable inventions found
out by him, as well in the Arts, as Sciences; and again reflecting upon my own wit, so far from promising me the discovery of
any thing new, that I despair of comprehending what is already
discovered, confounded with wonder, and surprised with despera-
tion, I account my self little lesse than miserable. If I behold
a Statue of some excellent Master, I say with my self; When wilt
thou know how to chizzle away the refuse of a piece of Marble,
and discover so lovely a figure, as lyeth hid therein? When wilt
thou mix and spread so many different colours upon a Cloth, or
Wall, and represent therewith all visible objects, like a *Michael
Angelo*, a *Raphaello*, or a *Tizvano*? If I behold what inventions
men have in comparting Musical intervals, in establishing Precepts and Rules for the management thereof with admirable delight
to the ear: When shall I cease my astonishment? What shall I
say of such and so various Instruments of that Art? The reading
of excellent Poets, with what admiration doth it swell any one
that attentively considereth the invention of conceits, and their
explanation? What shall we say of Architecture? What of Navigation? But, above all other stupendious inventions, what sublimi-
ty of mind was that in him, that imagined to himself to find out
a way to communicate his most secret thoughts to any other person,

though very far distant from him either in time, or place, speaking with those that are in the *India's*; speaking to those that are not yet born, nor shall be this thousand, or ten thousand years? and with how much facility? but by the various collocation of twenty little letters upon a paper? Let this be the Seal of all the admirable inventions of man, and the close of our Discourse for this day: For the warmer hours being past, I suppose that *Salviati* hath a desire to go and take the air in his Gondelo; but too morrow we will both wait upon you, to continue the Discourses we have begun, &c.

d.

William Harvey's Excercitatio Anatomica De Motu Cordis et Sanguinis Animalibus (Anatomical Exercises on the Motion of the Heart and Blood in Animals)** was published in 1628 and established the circulation of the blood. It is a landmark in the history of physiology. Just as important as its substance was its method. Harvey combined observations, experiments, measurements and hypotheses in extraordinary fashion to arrive at his doctrine. His work is a model of its kind.*

The Author's Reasons for Writing

When I first tried animal experimentation for the purpose of discovering the motions and functions of the heart by actual inspection and not by other people's books, I found it so truly difficult that I almost believed with Fracastorius, that the motion of the heart was to be understood by God alone. I could not really tell when systole or diastole took place, or when and where dilatation or constriction occurred, because of the quickness of the movement. In many animals this takes place in the twinkling of an eye, like a flash of lightning. Systole seemed at one time here, diastole there, then all reversed, varied and confused. So I could reach no decision, neither about what I might conclude myself nor believe from others. I did not marvel that Andreas Laurentius wrote that the motion of the heart was as perplexing as the flux and reflux of Euripus was to Aristotle.

The Motions of the Heart as Observed in Animal Experiments

In the first place, when the chest of a living animal is opened, and the capsule surrounding the heart is cut away, one may see that the heart alternates in movement and rest. There is a time when it moves, and a time when it is quiet.

This is more easily seen in the hearts of cold-blooded animals, as toads, snakes, frogs, snails, shell-fish, crustaceans and fish. It is also more apparent in other animals as the dog and pig, if one carefully observes the heart as it moves more slowly when about to die. The movements then become slower and weaker and the pauses longer, so that it is easy to see what the motion really is and how made. During a pause, the heart is soft, flaccid, exhausted, as in death.

Three significant features are to be noted in the motion and in the period of movement:

---

*William Harvey, Excercitatio Anatomica De Motu Cordis et Sanguinis Animalibus, trans. by Chauncey D. Leake, Charles C. Thomas, Publisher, Springfield, Illinois, 1928. Pp. 25; 28-33; 47-9; 53-5; 58-9; 69-71; 73-6; 97-101; 104.

1. The heart is lifted, and rises up to the apex, so that it strikes the chest at that moment, and the beat may be felt on the outside.

2. It contracts all over, but particularly to the sides, so that it looks narrower and longer. An isolated eel's heart placed on a table or in the hand shows this well, but it may also be seen in the hearts of fishes and of cold-blooded animals in which the heart is conical or lengthened.

3. Grasping the heart in the hand, it feels harder when it moves. This hardness is due to tension, as when one grasps the fore-arm and feels its tendons become knotty when the fingers are moved.

4. An additional point may be noted in fishes and cold-blooded animals, as serpents and frogs. When the heart moves it is paler in color, but when it pauses it is of a deeper blood color.

From these facts it seems clear to me that the motion of the heart consists of a tightening all over, both contraction along the fibers, and constriction everywhere. In its movement it becomes erect, hard, and smaller. The motion is just the same as that of muscles when contracting along their tendons and fibers. The muscles in action become tense and tough, and lose their softness in becoming hard, while they thicken and stand out. The heart acts similarly.

From these points it is reasonable to conclude that the heart at the moment it acts, becomes constricted all over, thicker in its walls and smaller in its ventricles, in order to expel its content of blood. This is clear from the fourth observation above in which it was noted that the heart becomes pale when it squeezes the blood out during contraction, but when quiet in relaxation the deep blood red color returns as the ventricle fills again with blood. But no one need doubt further, for if the cavity of the ventricle be cut into, the blood contained therein will be forcibly squirted out when the heart is tense with each movement or beat.

The following things take place, then, simultaneously: the contraction of the heart; the beat at the apex against the chest, which may be felt outside; the thickening of the walls; and the forcible ejection of the blood it contains by the constriction of the ventricles.

So the opposite of the commonly received opinion seems true. Instead of the heart opening its ventricles and filling with blood at the moment it strikes the chest and its beat is felt on the outside, the contrary takes place so that the heart while contracting empties. Therefore the motion commonly thought the diastole of the heart is really the systole, and the significant movement of the heart is not the diastole but the systole. The heart does not act in diastole but in systole for only when it contracts is it active.

*   *   *   *   *

Likewise, it is not true, as commonly believed, that the heart by its own action or distention draws blood into its ventricles. When it moves and contracts it expels blood, when it relaxes and is quiet it receives blood in the manner soon to be described.

The Actions and Functions of the Heart

From these and other observations I am convinced that the motion of the heart is as follows:

First, the auricle contracts, and this forces the abundant blood it contains as the cistern and reservoir of the veins, into the ventricle. This being filled, the heart raises itself, makes its fibers tense, contracts, and beats. By this beat it at once ejects into the arteries the blood received from the auricle; the right ventricle sending its blood to the lungs through the vessel called the *vena arteriosa*, but which in structure and function is an artery; the left ventricle sending its blood to the aorta, and to the rest of the body through the arteries.

These two motions, one of the auricles, the other of the ventricles, are consecutive, with a rhythm between them, so that only one movement may be apparent, especially in warm-blooded animals where it happens rapidly. This is like a piece of machinery in which one wheel moves another, though all seem to move simultaneously, or like the mechanism in fire-arms, where touching the trigger brings down the flint, lights a spark, which falls in the powder and explodes it, firing the ball, which reaches the mark. All these events because of their quickness seem to occur simultaneously in the twinking of an eye. Likewise in swallowing: lifting the tongue and pressing the mouth forces the food to the throat, the larynx and the epiglottis are closed by their own muscles, the gullet rises and opens its mouth like a sac, and receiving the bolus forces it down by its transverse and longitudinal muscles. All these diverse movements, carried out by different organs, are done so smoothly and regularly that they seem to be a single movement and action, which we call swallowing.

So it happens in the movement and action of the heart, which is sort of a deglutition or transference of blood from the veins to the arteries. If anyone with these points in mind will carefully watch the cardiac action in a living animal, he will see, not only what I have said, that the heart contracts in a continuous movement with the auricles, but also a peculiar side-wise turning toward the right ventricle as if it twists slightly on itself in performing its work. It is easy to see when a horse drinks that water is drawn in and passed to the stomach with each gulp, the movement making a sound, and the pulsation may be heard and felt. So it is with each movement of the heart when a portion of the blood is transferred from the veins to the arteries, that a pulse is made which may be heard in the chest.

The motion of the heart, then, is of this general type. The chief function of the heart is the transmission and pumping of the blood through the arteries to the extremities of the body. Thus the pulse which we feel in the arteries is nothing else than the impact of blood from the heart.

*   *   *   *   *

The Way by which the Blood Passes from the
Vena Cava to the Arteries, or from the
Right Ventricle of the Heart to the Left

Since the close contact of the heart and lungs in man has
probably been a source of error, as I have said, the common practice of anatomists, in dogmatizing on the general make-up of the
animal body, from the dissections of dead human subjects alone,
is objectionable. It is like devising a general system of
politics, from the study of a single state, or deigning to know
all agriculture from an examination of a single field. It is
fallacious to attempt to draw general conclusions from one particular proposition.

If only anatomists were as familiar with the dissection of
lower animals as with that of the human body, all these perplexing difficulties would, in my opinion, be cleared up.

The situation is first of all clear enough in fishes, where
there is a single ventricle in the heart, and no lungs. The sac
at the base of the heart, doubtless corresponding to the auricle,
pushes the blood into the heart, which plainly transmits it by a
tube analogous to an artery. This may be confirmed by inspection, or section of the artery, the blood spurting with each beat
of the heart.

It is not hard to see the same thing in other animals with
but a single ventricle, as toads, frogs, serpents and lizzards.
They have lungs of a sort, as a voice. I have made notes on the
excellent structure of their lungs, but they are not appropriate
here. It is obvious in opening these animals that the blood is
transferred from the veins to the arteries by the heart beat.
The way is wide open; there is no difficulty or hesitancy about
it; it is the same as it would be in man were the septum of the
heart perforated or removed, making one ventricle of the two.
Were this so, no one would doubt, I think, how blood passes from
veins to arteries.

Since there really are more animals without lungs than with
them, and also more with a single ventricle in the heart than
with two, it may be concluded that for the majority of animals,
an open way exists for blood to pass through the cavity of the
heart from the veins to the arteries.

I have perceived further that the same thing is very apparent in the embryos of animals possessing lungs.

It is well known by all anatomists that the four blood vessels belonging to the heart, the vena cava, pulmonary artery,
pulmonary vein, and aorta, are connected differently in the fetus
than in the adult. In a fetus a lateral anastomosis joins the
vena cava to the pulmonary vein. This is located before the vena
cava opens into the right ventricle of the heart, or gives off
the coronary vein, just above its exit from the liver. This is a
good-sized oval-shaped hole opening a passage from the vena cave
to the pulmonary vein, so that blood may freely flow from the one
to the other, then into the left auricle of the heart, and then
to the left ventricle. In this *foramen ovale*, there is a thin
tough membrane, larger than the opening, hanging like a cover
from the pulmonary vein side. In the adult this blocks the fora-

men, and adhering on all sides, finally closes and obliterates
it. In the fetus, however, this membrane hangs loosely, opening
an easy way to the lungs and heart for the blood flowing from
the vena cava, but at the same time blocking any passage back
into that vein. In the embryo, one may conclude then that blood
continually passes through this foramen from the vena cava to
the pulmonary vein, and then into the left ventricle of the
heart. After making this passage, it can not regurgitate.

$$*\qquad*\qquad*\qquad*\qquad*$$

So it seems obviously true in the fetus that the heart by
its beat transfers blood from the vena cava to the aorta by as
open a passage as if in the adult, as I have said, the two ventricles were united by removing the septum. Since these ways
for the passage of blood are so conspicuous in the majority of
animals,--indeed in all at certain times,--we must examine
another matter. Why may we not conclude that this passage is
made through the substance of the lungs in warm-blooded adult
animals as man? Nature made these ways in the embryo at a time
when the lungs were not used, apparently because of the lack of
a passage through them. Why is it better, for Nature always does
what is best, to close completely to the passage of blood in
adolescence those open ways which are used in the embryos of so
many animals, without opening any others for this transfer of
blood?

The situation is such that those who seek the ways in man
by which blood reaches the pulmonary vein and left ventricle
from the vena cava, will do best to proceed by animal experimentation. Here the reason may be found why Nature, in larger
adult animals, filters the blood through the lungs instead of
choosing a direct path. No other way seems possible. It may
be the larger, more perfect animals are warmer and when full
grown their greater heat is thus more easily damped. For this
reason the blood may go through the lungs, to be cooled by the
inspired air and saved from boiling and extinction. There may be
other reasons. To discuss and argue these points would be to
speculate on the function of the lungs. I have made many
observations on this matter, on ventilation, and on the necessity
and use of air, as well as on the various organs in animals concerned in these matters. Nevertheless I shall leave these things
to be more conveniently discussed in a separate tract lest I seem
to wander too far from the proposition of the motion and function
of the heart, and to confuse the question. Returning to our
present concern, I shall go on with my demonstration.

Amount of Blood Passing Through the Heart from the Veins
to the Arteries, and the Circular Motion of the Blood

So far we have considered the transfer of blood from the
veins to the arteries, and the ways by which it is transmitted
and distributed by the heart beat. There may be some who will
agree with me on these points because of the authority of Galen

or Columbus or the reasons of others. What remains to be said on the quantity and source of this transferred blood, is, even if carefully reflected upon, so strange and undreamed of, that not only do I fear danger to myself from the malice of a few, but I dread lest I have all men as enemies, so much does habit or doctrine once absorbed, driving deeply its roots, become second nature, and so much does reverence for antiquity influence all men. But now the die is cast; my hope is in the love of truth and in the integrity of intelligence.

First I seriously considered in many investigations how much blood might be lost from cutting the arteries in animal experiments. Then I reflected on the symmetry and size of the vessels entering and leaving the ventricles of the heart, for Nature, making nothing in vain, would not have given these vessels such relative greatness uselessly. Then I thought of the arrangement and structure of the valves and the rest of the heart. On these and other such matters I pondered often and deeply. For a long time I turned over in my mind such questions as, how much blood is transmitted, and how short a time does its passage take. Not deeming it possible for the digested food mass to furnish such an abundance of blood, without totally draining the veins or rupturing the arteries, unless it somehow got back to the veins from the arteries and returned to the right ventricle of the heart, I began to think there was a sort of motion as in a circle.

This I afterwards found true, that blood is pushed by the beat of the left ventricle and distributed through the arteries to the whole body, and back through the veins to the vena cava, and then returned to the right auricle, just as it is sent to the lungs through the pulmonary artery from the right ventricle and returned from the lungs through the pulmonary vein to the left ventricle, as previously described.

This motion may be called circular in the way that Aristotle says air and rain follow the circular motion of the stars. The moist earth warmed by the sun gives off vapors, which, rising, are condensed to fall again moistening the earth. By this means things grow. So also tempests and meteors originate by a circular approach and recession of the sun.

This it happens in the body by the movement of the blood, all parts are fed and warmed by the more perfect, more spiritous, hotter, and, I might say, more nutritive blood. But in these parts this blood is cooled, thickened, and loses its power, so that it returns to its source, the heart, the inner temple of the body, to recover its virtue.

Here it regains its natural heat and fluidity, its power and vitality, and filled with spirits, is distributed again. All this depends on the motion and beat of the heart.

So the heart is the center of life, the sun of the Microcosm, as the sun itself might be called the heart of the world. The blood is moved, invigorated, and kept from decaying by the power and pulse of the heart. It is that intimate shrine whose function is the nourishing and warming of the whole body, the basis and source of all life. But of these matters we may speculate more appropriately in considering the final causes of this motion.

*   *   *   *   *

The Circulation of the Blood is Proved by
a Prime Consideration

If anyone says these are empty words, broad assertions without basis, or innovations without just cause, there are three points coming for proof, from which I believe the truth will necessarily follow, and be clearly evident.

First, blood is constantly being transmitted from the vena cava to the arteries by the heart beat in such amounts that it cannot be furnished by the food consumed, and in such a way that the total quantity must pass through the heart in a short time.

Second, blood is forced by the pulse in the arteries continually and steadily to every part of the body in a much greater amount than is needed for nutrition or than the whole mass of food could supply.

And likewise third, the veins continually return this blood from every part of the body to the heart.

These proved, I think it will be clear that the blood circulates, passing away from the heart to the extremities and then returning back to the heart, thus moving in a circle.

Let us consider, arbitrarily or by experiment, that the left ventricle of the heart when filled in diastole, contains two or three ounces, or only an ounce and a half. In a cadaver I have found it holding more than three ounces. Likewise let us consider how much less the ventricle contains when the heart contracts or how much blood it forces into the aorta with each contraction, for, during systole, everyone will admit something is always forced out, and apparent from the structure of the valves. As a reasonable conjecture suppose a fourth, fifth, sixth, or even an eighth part is passed into the arteries. Then we may suppose in man that a single heart beat would force out either a half ounce, three drams, or even one dram of blood, which because of the valvular block could not flow back that way into the heart.

The heart makes more than a thousand beats in a half hour, in some two, three, or even four thousand. Multiplying by the drams, there will be in half an hour either 3,000 drams, 2,000 drams, five hundred ounces, or some other such proportionate amount of blood forced into the arteries by the heart, but always a greater quantity than is present in the whole body. Likewise in a sheep or dog, suppose one scruple goes out with each stroke of the heart, then in half an hour 1,000 scruples or about three and a half pounds of blood would be pumped out. But as I have determined in the sheep, the whole body does not contain more than four pounds of blood.

On this assumption of the passage of blood, made as a basis for argument, and from the estimation of the pulse rate, it is apparent that the entire quantity of blood passes from the veins to the arteries through the heart, and likewise through the lungs.

But suppose this would not occur in half an hour, but rather in an hour, or even in a day, it is still clear that more blood continually flows through the heart than can be supplied by the digested food or be held in the veins at any one time.

It cannot be said that the heart in contracting sometimes pumps and sometimes doesn't, or that it propels a mere nothing or something imaginary. This point has been settled previously, and besides, it is contrary to common sense. If the ventricles must be filled with blood in cardiac dilatation, something must always be pushed out in contraction, and not a little amount either, since the passages are not small nor the contractions few. This quantity expelled is some proportion of the contents of the ventricle, a third, a sixth, or an eighth, and an equivalent amount of blood must fill it up in diastole, so that there is a relation between the ventricular capacity in contraction and in dilatation. Since the ventricles in dilating do not become filled with nothing, or with something imaginary, so in contracting they never expel nothing or something imaginary, but always blood in an amount proportionate to the contraction.

So it may be inferred that if the heart in a single beat in man, sheep, or ox, pumps one dram, and there are 1,000 beats in half an hour, the total amount pumped in that time would be ten pounds five ounces; if two drams at a single stroke, then twenty pounds ten ounces; if half an ounce, then forty-one pounds eight ounces; and if one ounce, then a total of eighty-three pounds four ounces, all of which would be transferred from the veins to the arteries in half an hour.

The amount pumped at a single beat, and the factors involved in increasing or diminishing it, may perhaps be more carefully studied later from many observations of mine.

The Third Proposition is Proven, and the Circulation of the Blood is Demonstrated from it

So far we have considered the amount of blood flowing through the heart and lungs in the body cavity, and similarly from the arteries to the veins in the periphery. It remains for us to discuss how blood from the extremities gets back to the heart through the veins, and whether or not these are the only vessels serving this purpose. This done we may consider the three basic propositions proving the circulation of the blood so well established, so plain and obvious, as to force belief.

This proposition will be perfectly clear from a consideration of the valves found in the venous cavities, from their functions, and from experiments demonstrable with them.

The celebrated anatomist, Hieronymus Fabricius of Aquapendente, or, instead of him, Jacobus Sylvius, as Doctor Riolan wishes it, first described membranous valves in the veins, of sigmoid or semilunar shape, and being very delicate eminences on the inner lining of these vessels. They are placed differently in different individuals, but are attached to the sides of the veins, and they are directed upwards toward the main venous trunks. As there are usually two together, they face and touch each other, and their edges are so apt to join or close that they prevent anything from passing from the main trunks or larger veins to the smaller branches. They are so arranged that the horns of one set are opposite the hollow part of the preceding set, and so on alternately.

The discoverer of these valves and his followers did not

rightly appreciate their function. It is not to prevent blood from falling by its weight into areas lower down, for there are some in the jugular vein which are directed downwards, and which prevent blood from being carried upwards. They are thus not always looking upwards, but more correctly, always towards the main venous trunks and the heart. Others as well as myself have sometimes found them in the milky veins and in the venous branches of the mesentery directed towards the vena cava and portal vein. To this may be added that there are none in the arteries, and that one may note that dogs, oxen, and all such animals have valves at the branches of the crural veins at the top of the sacrum, and in branches from the haunches, in which no such weight effect of an erect stature is to be feared.

Nor, as some say, are the valves in the jugular veins to prevent apoplexy, since the head is more likely to be influenced by what flows into it through the carotid arteries. Nor are they present to keep blood in the smaller branches, not permitting it to flow entirely into the larger more open trunks, for they are placed where there are no branches at all, although I confess they are more frequently seen where there are branchings. Nor are they present for slowing the flow of blood from the center of the body, for it seems likely it would flow slowly enough anyway, as it would then be passed from larger to smaller branches, become separated from the source and mass, and be moved from warmer to cooler places.

The valves are present solely that blood may not move from the larger veins into the smaller ones lest it rupture or varicose them, and that it may not advance from the center of the body into the periphery through them, but rather from the extremities to the center. This latter movement is facilitated by these delicate valves, the contrary completely prevented. They are so situated that what may pass the horns of a set above is checked by those below, for whatever may slip past the edges of one set is caught on the convexity of those beyond, so it may not pass farther.

I have often noticed in dissecting veins, that no matter how much care I take, it is impossible to pass a probe from the main venous trunks very far into the smaller branches on account of the valvular obstructions. On the contrary it is very easy to push it in the opposite direction, from the branches toward the larger trunks. In many places a pair of valves are so placed that when raised they join in the middle of the vein, and their edges are so nicely united that one cannot perceive any crack along their junction. On the other hand, they yield to a probe introduced from without inwards and are easily released in the manner of flood-gates opposing a river flow. So they intercept, and when tightly closed, completely prevent in many places a flow of blood back from the heart and vena cava. They are so constituted that they can never permit blood to move in the veins from the heart upwards to the head, downwards toward the feet, or sidewise to the arms. They oppose any movement of blood from the larger veins toward the smaller ones, but they favor and facilitate a free and open route starting from the small veins and ending in the larger ones.

*   *   *   *   *

Conclusion of the Demonstration of the
Circulation of the Blood

Briefly let me now sum up and propose generally my idea of the circulation of the blood.

It has been shown by reason and experiment that blood by the beat of the ventricles flows through the lungs and heart and is pumped to the whole body. There it passes through pores in the flesh into the veins through which it returns from the periphery everywhere to the center, from the smaller veins into the larger ones, finally coming to the vena cava and right auricle. This occurs in such an amount, with such an outflow through the arteries, and such a reflux through the veins, that it cannot be supplied by the food consumed. It is also much more than is needed for nutrition. It must therefore be concluded that the blood in the animal body moves around in a circle continuously, and that the action or function of the heart is to accomplish this by pumping. This is the only reason for the motion and beat of the heart.

B. THE ACHIEVEMENT OF THE SCIENTIFIC REVOLUTION

1. The Birth of the New Physics

a. *Nicholas Copernicus'* De Revolutionibus Orbium Coelestium (On the Revolutions of the Heavenly Spheres),* *published in
1543, is considered to be the work that began the Scientific Revolution. There can be no doubt that Copernicus' suggestion that
the Earth was not at the center of the universe and that it must
move in a path around the Sun had revolutionary implications. It
is equally true that Copernicus was a most reluctant revolutionary, couching his new system in traditional terms and staying as
close to the Ptolemaic universe as he could.*

To the Most Holy Lord, Pope Paul III.

The Preface of Nicolaus Copernicus to the
Books of the Revolutions

I may well presume, most Holy Father, that certain people,
as soon as they hear that in this book *On the Revolutions of the
Spheres of the Universe* I ascribe movement to the earthly globe,
will cry out that, holding such views, I should at once be hissed
off the stage. For I am not so pleased with my own work that I
should fail duly to weigh the judgment which others may pass
thereon; and though I know that the speculations of a philosopher
are far removed from the judgment of the multitude--for his aim
is to seek truth in all things as far as God has permitted human
reason so to do--yet I hold that opinions which are quite erroneous should be avoided.
Thinking therefore within myself that to ascribe movement to
the Earth must indeed seem an absurd performance on my part to
those who know that many centuries have consented to the establishment of the contrary judgment, namely that the Earth is
placed immovably as the central point in the middle of the Universe, I hesitated long whether, on the one hand, I should give
to the light these my Commentaries written to prove the Earth's
motion, or whether, on the other hand, it were better to follow
the example of the Pythagoreans and others who were wont to im-
part their philosophic mysteries only to intimates and friends,
and then not in writing but by word of mouth, as the letter of
Lysis to Hipparchus witnesses. In my judgment they did so not,
as some would have it, through jealousy of sharing their doctrines, but as fearing lest these so noble and hardly won discoveries of the learned should be despised by such as either care
not to study aught save for gain, or--if by the encouragement and
example of others they are stimulated to philosophic liberal pur-
suits--yet by reason of the dulness of their wits are in the company of philosophers as drones among bees. Reflecting thus, the
thought of the scorn which I had to fear on account of the novel-

Nicholas Copernicus, *De Revolutionibus Orbium Coelestium, Libri
VI*, Book I, Translated by J. F. Dobson. *Occasional Notes of the
Royal Astronomical Society*, No. 10, May 1947. Pp. 3-6; 9-23.

ty and incongruity of my theory, well-nigh induced me to abandon
my project.

*   *   *   *   *

That I allow the publication of these my studies may surprise your Holiness the less in that, having been at such travail
to attain them, I had already not scrupled to commit to writing
my thoughts upon the motion of the Earth. How I came to dare to
conceive such motion of the Earth, contrary to the received
opinion of the Mathematicians and indeed contrary to the impression of the senses, is what your Holiness will rather expect to
hear. So I should like your Holiness to know that I was induced
to think of a method of computing the motions of the spheres by
nothing else than the knowledge that the Mathematicians are inconsistent in these investigations.

For, first, the mathematicians are so unsure of the movements of the Sun and Moon that they cannot even explain or observe the constant length of the seasonal year. Secondly, in
determining the motions of these and of the other five planets,
they do not even use the same principles and hypotheses as in
their proofs of seeming revolutions and motions. So some use
only concentric circles, while others eccentrics and epicycles.
Yet even by these means they do not completely attain their ends.
Those who have relied on concentrics, though they have proven
that some different motions can be compounded therefrom, have not
thereby been able fully to establish a system which agrees with
the phenomena. Those again who have devised eccentric systems,
though they appear to have well-nigh established the seeming
motions by calculations agreeable to their assumptions, have yet
made many admissions which seem to violate the first principle
of uniformity in motion. Nor have they been able thereby to discern or deduce the principal thing--namely the shape of the Universe and the unchangeable symmetry of its parts. With them it
is as though an artist were to gather the hands, feet, head and
other members for his images from divers models, each part ex-
cellently drawn, but not related to a single body, and since they
in no way match each other, the result would be monster rather
than man. So in the course of their exposition, which the mathematicians call their system we find that they have either omitted
some indispensable detail or introduced something foreign and
wholly irrelevant. This would of a surety not have been so had
they followed fixed principles; for if their hypotheses were not
misleading, all inferences based thereon might be surely verified.
Though my present assertions are obscure, they will be made clear
in due course.

I pondered long upon this uncertainty of mathematical tradition in establishing the motions of the system of the spheres.
At last I began to chafe that philosophers could by no means
agree on any one certain theory of the mechanism of the Universe,
wrought for us by a supremely good and orderly Creator, though in
other respects they investigated with meticulous care the minutest points relating to its orbits. I therefore took pains to
read again the works of all the philosophers on whom I could lay

hand to seek out whether any of them had ever supposed that the
motions of the spheres were other than those demanded by the
mathematical schools. I found first in Cicero that Hicetas had
realized that the Earth moved. Afterwards I found in Plutarch
that certain others had held the like opinion. I think fit here
to add Plutarch's own words, to make them accessible to all:--

> "The rest hold the Earth to be stationary, but Philolaus
> the Pythagorean says that she moves around the (central)
> fire on an oblique circle like the Sun and Moon.
> Heraclides of Pontus and Ecphantus the Pythagorean also
> make the Earth to move, not indeed through space but by
> rotating round her own centre as a wheel on an axle from
> West to East."

Taking advantage of this I too began to think of the mobility of the Earth; and though the opinion seemed absurd, yet knowing now that others before me had been granted freedom to imagine
such circles as they chose to explain the phenomena of the stars,
I considered that I also might easily be allowed to try whether,
by assuming some motion of the Earth, sounder explanations than
theirs for the revolution of the celestial spheres might so be
discovered.
Thus assuming motions, which in my work I ascribe to the
Earth, by long and frequent observations I have at last discovered that, if the motions of the rest of the planets be brought
into relation with the circulation of the Earth and be reckoned
in proportion to the orbit of each planet, not only do their
phenomena presently ensue, but the orders and magnitudes of all
stars and spheres, nay the heavens themselves, become so bound
together that nothing in any part thereof could be moved from its
place without producing confusion of all the other parts and of
the Universe as a whole.

      *   *   *   *   *

I doubt not that gifted and learned mathematicians will
agree with me if they are willing to comprehend and appreciate,
not superficially but thoroughly, according to the demands of
this science, such reasoning as I bring to bear in support of my
judgment. But that learned and unlearned alike may see that I
shrink not from any man's criticism, it is to your Holiness
rather than anyone else that I have chosen to dedicate these
studies of mine, since in this remote corner of Earth in which
I live you are regarded as the most eminent by virtue alike of
the dignity of your Office and of your love of letters and science. You by your influence and judgment can readily hold the
slanderers from biting, though the proverb hath it that there is
no remedy against a sycophant's tooth. It may fall out, too, that
idle babblers, ignorant of mathematics, may claim a right to
pronounce a judgment on my work, by reason of a certain passage
of Scripture basely twisted to suit their purpose. Should any
such venture to criticize and carp at my project, I make no
account of them; I consider their judgment rash, and utterly des-
pise it. I well know that even Lactantius, a writer in other
ways distinguished but in no sense a mathematician, discourses in

a most childish fashion touching the shape of the Earth, ridiculing even those who have stated the Earth to be a sphere. Thus my supporters need not be amazed if some people of like sort ridicule me too.

Mathematics are for mathematicians, and they, if I be not wholly deceived, will hold that these my labours contribute somewhat even to the Commonwealth of the Church, of which your Holiness is now Prince. For not long since, under Leo X, the question of correcting the ecclesiastical calendar was debated in the Council of the Lateran. It was left undecided for the sole cause that the lengths of the years and months and the motions of the Sun and Moon were not held to have been yet determined with sufficient exactness. From that time on I have given thought to their more accurate observation, by the advice of that eminent man Paul, Lord Bishop of Sempronia, sometime in charge of that business of the calendar. What results I have achieved therein, I leave to the judgment of learned mathematicians and of your Holiness in particular. And now, not to seem to promise your Holiness more than I can perform with regard to the usefulness of the work, I pass to my appointed task.

*   *   *   *   *

*That the Motion of the Heavenly Bodies is
Uniform, Circular, and Perpetual, or
Composed of Circular Motions.*

We now note that the motion of heavenly bodies is circular. Rotation is natural to a sphere and by that very act is its shape expressed. For here we deal with the simplest kind of body, wherein neither beginning nor end may be discerned nor, if it rotate ever in the same place, may the one be distinguished from the other.

Now in the multitude of heavenly bodies various motions occur. Most evident to sense is the diurnal rotation, marking day and night. By this motion the whole Universe, save Earth alone, is thought to glide from East to West. This is the common measure of all motions, since Time itself is numbered in days. Next we see other revolutions in contest, as it were, with this daily motion and opposing it from West to East. Such opposing motions are those of Sun and Moon and the five planets. Of these the Sun portions out the year, the Moon the month, the common measures of time. In like manner the five planets define each his own independent period.

But these bodies exhibit various differences in their motion. First their axes are not that of the diurnal rotation, but of the Zodiac, which is oblique thereto. Secondly, they do not move uniformly even in their own orbits; for are not Sun and Moon found now slower, now swifter in their courses? Further, at times the five planets become stationary at one point and another and even go backward. While the Sun ever goes forward unswerving on his own course, they wander in divers ways, straying now southward, now northward. For this reason they are named *Planets*. Furthermore, sometimes they approach Earth, being then in *Perigee*, while at other times receding they are in *Apogee*.

Nevertheless, despite these irregularities, we must conclude that the motions of these bodies are ever circular or compounded of circles. For the irregularities themselves are subject to a definite law and recur at stated times, and this could not happen if the motions were not circular, for a circle alone can thus restore the place of a body as it was. So with the Sun which, by a compounding of circular motions, brings ever again the changing days and nights and the four seasons of the year. Now therein it must be that divers motions are conjoined, since a simple celestial body cannot move irregularly in a single orbit. For such irregularity must come of unevenness either in the moving force (whether inherent or acquired) or in the form of the revolving body. Both these alike the mind abhors regarding the most perfectly disposed bodies.

It is then generally agreed that the motions of Sun, Moon and Planets do but seem irregular either by reason of the divers directions of their axes of revolution, or else by reason that Earth is not the centre of the circles in which they revolve, so that to us on Earth the displacements of these bodies when near seem greater than when they are more remote, as is shewn in the *Optics*. If then we consider equal arcs in the paths of the planets we find that they seem to describe differing distances in equal periods of time. It is therefore above all needful to observe carefully the relation of the Earth toward the Heavens, lest, searching out the things on high, we should pass by those nearer at hand, and mistakenly ascribe earthly qualities to heavenly bodies.

Whether Circular Motion belongs to the Earth; and concerning its position.

Since it has been shown that Earth is spherical, we now consider whether her motion is conformable to her shape and her position in the Universe. Without these we cannot construct a proper theory of the heavenly phenomena. Now authorities agree that Earth holds firm her place at the centre of the Universe, and they regard the contrary as unthinkable, nay as absurd. Yet if we examine more closely it will be seen that this question is not so settled, and needs wider consideration.

A seeming change of place may come of movement either of object or of observer, or again of unequal movements of the two (for between equal and parallel motions no movement is perceptible). Now it is Earth from which the rotation of the Heavens is seen. If then some motion of Earth be assumed it will be reproduced in external bodies, which will seem to move in the opposite direction.

Consider first the diurnal rotation. By it the whole Universe, save Earth alone and its contents, appears to move very swiftly. Yet grant that Earth revolves from West to East, and you will find, if you ponder it, that my conclusion is right. It is the vault of Heaven that contains all things, and why should not motion be attributed rather to the contained than to the container, to the located than the locater? The latter view was certainly that of Heraclides and Ecphantus the Pythagorean and

Hicetas of Syracuse (according to Cicero). All of them made the
Earth rotate in the midst of the Universe, believing that the
Stars set owing to the Earth coming in the way, and rise again
when it has passed on.

There is another difficulty, namely, the position of Earth.
Nearly all have hitherto held that Earth is at the centre of the
Universe. Now, grant that Earth is not at the exact centre but
at a distance from it which, while small compared to the starry
sphere, is yet considerable compared with the orbits of Sun and
the other planets. Then calculate the consequent variations in
their seeming motions, assuming these to be really uniform and
about some centre other than the Earth's. One may then perhaps
adduce a reasonable cause for these variable motions. And indeed
since the Planets are seen at varying distances from the Earth,
the centre of Earth is surely not the centre of their orbits.
Nor is it certain whether the Planets move toward and away from
Earth, or Earth toward and away from them. It is therefore justifiable to hold that the Earth has another motion in addition to
the diurnal rotation. That the Earth, besides rotating, wanders
with several motions and is indeed a Planet, is a view attributed
to Philolaus the Pythagorean, no mean mathematician, and one whom
Plato is said to have eagerly sought out in Italy.

Many, however, have thought that Earth could be shown by
geometry to be at the centre and like a mere point in the vast
Heavens. They have thought too that Earth, as centre, ever
remains unmoved, since if the whole system move the centre must
remain at rest, and the parts nearest the centre must move most
slowly.

Of the Vastness of the Heavens compared with the Size of the Earth.

That the size of Earth is insignificant in comparison with
the Heavens, may be inferred thus.

The bounding Circles (interpreting the Greek word *horizons*)
bisect the Celestial Sphere. This could not be if the size of the
Earth or its distance from the centre were considerable compared
with the Heavens--for a circle to bisect a sphere must pass
through its centre and be in fact a "great circle." Let the circle ABCD represent the celestial horizon, and E that point of the
Earth from which we observe. The "horizon" or boundary line between bodies visible and bodies invisible has its centre at this

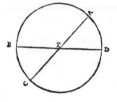

point. Suppose that from point E we observe with Dioptra or
Astrolabe or Chorobates the first point of the sign Cancer rising
at C and at the same moment the first point of Capricorn setting
at A. AEC, since it is observed as a straight line through the
Dioptra, is a diameter of the Ecliptic, for six Zodiacal Signs
form a semi-circle and its centre E coincides with that of the
horizon. Next, suppose that after some time the first point of
Capricorn rises at B; then Cancer will be seen setting at D, and
BED will be a straight line, again a diameter of the ecliptic.
Hence, it is clear that E, the point of intersection of the two
lines, is the centre of the horizon. Therefore the horizon always bisects the ecliptic, which is a great circle on the sphere.
But a circle that bisects a great circle must itself be a great
circle. Therefore the horizon is a great circle and its centre
is that of the ecliptic.

It is true that a line from the surface of Earth cannot
coincide with the one from its centre. Yet owing to their
immense length compared to the size of Earth these lines are
practically parallel. Moreover, owing to the great distance of
their meeting point they are practically one line--for the distance between them is immeasurably small in comparison with their
length--as is shewn in the *Optics*. It therefore follows that the
Heavens are immeasurable in comparison with the Earth. Thus the
Earth appears as a mere point compared to the Heavens, as a finite thing to the infinite.

Yet it does not follow that the Earth must be at rest at the
centre of the Universe. Should we not be more surprised if the
vast Universe revolved in twenty-four hours, than that little
Earth should do so? For the idea that the centre is at rest and
the parts nearest it move least does not imply that Earth remains
still. It is merely as one should say that the Heavens revolve,
but the poles are still, and the parts nearest them move least
(as *Cynosura* moves slower than *Aquila* or *Procyon* because, being
nearer the pole, it describes a smaller circle). These all belong to the same sphere, whose motion becomes zero at the axis.
Such motion does not admit that all the parts have the same rate
of motion, since the revolution of the whole brings back each
point to the original position in the same time, though the distances moved are unequal.

So too, it may be said, Earth, as part of the celestial
sphere, shares in the motion thereof, though being at the centre
she moves but little. Being herself a body and not a mere point,
she will therefore move through the same angle as the Heavens but
with a smaller radius in any given period of time. The falsity of
this is clear, for if true it would always be mid-day in one
place and midnight in another, and the daily phenomena of rising
and setting could not occur, for the motion of the whole and the
part are one and inseparable. A quite different theory is required to explain the various motions observed, namely that
bodies moving in smaller paths revolve more quickly than those
moving in larger paths. Thus Saturn, most distant of the Planets,
revolves in 30 years, and Moon, nearest the Earth, compasses her
circuit in a month. Lastly, then, the Earth must be taken to go
round in the course of a day and a night, and so doubt is again

cast on the diurnal rotation of the Heavens.

Besides we have not yet fixed the exact position of the Earth, which as shown above, is quite uncertain. For what was proved is only the vast size of the Heavens compared with the Earth, but how far this immensity extends is quite unknown.

      *   *   *   *   *

Now if one should say that the Earth *moves*, that is as much as to say that the motion is natural, not forced; and things which happen according to nature produce the opposite effects to those due to force. Things subjected to any force, gradual or sudden, must be disintegrated, and cannot long exist. But natural processes being adapted to their purpose work smoothly.

Idle therefore is the fear of Ptolemy that Earth and all thereon would be disintegrated by a natural rotation, a thing far different from an artificial act. Should he not fear even more for the Universe, whose motion must be as much more rapid as the Heavens are greater than the Earth? Have the Heavens become so vast because of the centrifugal force of their violent motion, and would they collapse if they stood still? If this were so the Heavens must be of infinite size. For the more they expand by the centrifugal force of their motion, the more rapid will become the motion because of the ever increasing distance to be traversed in 24 hours. And in turn, as the motion waxes, must the immensity of the Heavens wax. Thus velocity and size would increase each the other to infinity--and as the infinite can neither be traversed nor moved, the Heavens must stand still!

They say too that outside the Heavens is no body, no space, nay not even void, in fact absolutely nothing, and therefore no room for the Heavens to expand. Yet surely it is strange that something can be held by nothing. Perhaps indeed it will be easier to understand this nothingness outside the Heavens if we assume them to be infinite, and bounded internally only by their concavity, so that everything, however great, is contained in them, while the Heavens remain immovable. For the fact that it moves is the principal argument by which men have inferred that the Universe is finite.

Let us then leave to Physicists the question whether the Universe be finite or no, holding only to this that Earth is finite and spherical. Why then hesitate to grant Earth that power of motion natural to its shape, rather than suppose a gliding round of the whole Universe, whose limits are unknown and unknowable? And why not grant that the diurnal rotation is only apparent in the Heavens but real in the Earth? It is but as the saying of Aeneas in Virgil--"We sail forth from the harbour, and lands and cities retire." As the ship floats along in the calm, all external things seem to have the motion that is really that of the ship, while those within the ship feel that they and all its contents are at rest.

It may be asked what of the clouds and other objects suspended in the air, or sinking and rising in it? Surely not only the Earth, with the water on it, moves thus, but also a quantity of air and all things so associated with the Earth. Perhaps the contiguous air contains an admixture of earthy or watery matter

and so follows the same natural law as the Earth, or perhaps the
air acquires motion from the perpetually rotating Earth by pro-
pinquity and absence of resistance. So the Greeks thought that
the higher regions of the air follow the celestial motion, as
suggested by those swiftly moving bodies, the "Comets", or
"Pogoniae" as they called them, for whose origin they assign this
region, for these bodies rise and set just like other stars. We
observe that because of the great distance from the Earth that
part of the air is deprived of terrestrial motion, while the air
nearest Earth, with the objects suspended in it, will be stationary, unless disturbed by wind or other impulse which moves them
this way or that--for a wind in the air is as a current in the
sea.

We must admit the possibility of a double motion of objects
which fall and rise in the Universe, namely the resultant of
rectilinear and circular motion. Thus heavy falling objects,
being specially earthy, must doubtless retain the nature of the
whole to which they belong. So also there are objects which by
their fiery force are carried up into the higher regions. This
terrestrial fire is nourished particularly by earthy matter,
and flame is simply burning smoke. Now it is a property of fire
to expand that which it attacks, and this so violently that it
cannot in any wise be restrained from breaking its prison and
fulfilling its end. The motion is one of extension from the centre outward, and consequently any earthy parts set on fire are
carried to the upper region.

That the motion of a simple body must be simple is true then
primarily of circular motion, and only so long as the simple body
rests in its own natural place and state. In that state no
motion save circular is possible, for such motion is wholly self-
contained and similar to being at rest. But if objects move or
are moved from their natural place rectilinear motion supervenes.
Now it is inconsistent with the whole order and form of the
Universe that it should be outside its own place. Therefore
there is no rectilinear motion save of objects out of their
right place, nor is such motion natural to perfect objects, since
they would be separated from the whole to which they belong and
thus would destroy its unity. Moreover, even apart from circular
motion, things moving up and down do not move simply and uniformly; for they cannot avoid the influence of their lightness or
weight. Thus all things which fall begin by moving slowly, but
their speed is accelerated as they go. On the other hand earthly
fire (the only kind we can observe) when carried aloft loses
energy, owing to the influence of the earthy matter.

A circular motion must be uniform for it has a never failing
cause of motion; but other motions have always a retarding factor, so that bodies having reached their natural place cease to
be either heavy or light, and their motion too ceases.

Circular motion then is of things as a whole, parts may
possess rectilinear motion as well. Circular motion, therefore,
may be combined with the rectilinear--just as a creature may be
at once animal and horse. Aristotle's method of dividing simple
motion into three classes, from the centre, to the centre, and
round the centre, is thus merely abstract reasoning; just as we

form separate conceptions of a line, a point, and a surface, though one cannot exist without another, and none can exist without substance.

Further, we conceive immobility to be nobler and more divine than change and inconstancy, which latter is thus more appropriate to Earth than to the Universe. Would it not then seem absurd to ascribe motion to that which contains or locates, and not rather to that contained and located, namely the Earth?

Lastly, since the planets approach and recede from the Earth, both their motion round the centre, which is held to be the Earth, and also their motion outward and inward are the motion of one body. Therefore we must accept this motion round the centre in a more general sense, and must be satisfied provided that every motion has a proper centre. From all these considerations it is more probable that the Earth moves than that it remains at rest. This is especially the case with the diurnal rotation, as being particularly a property of the Earth.

> *Whether more than one Motion can be attributed*
> *to the Earth, and of the centre of the Universe.*

Since then there is no reason why the Earth should not possess the power of motion, we must consider whether in fact it has more motions than one, so as to be reckoned as a Planet.

That Earth is not the centre of all revolutions is proved by the apparently irregular motions of the planets and the variations in their distances from the Earth. These would be unintelligible if they moved in circles concentric with Earth. Since, therefore, there are more centres than one, we may discuss whether the centre of the Universe is or is not the Earth's centre of gravity.

Now it seems to me gravity is but a natural inclination, bestowed on the parts of bodies by the Creator so as to combine the parts in the form of a sphere and thus contribute to their unity and integrity. And we may believe this property present even in the Sun, Moon and Planets, so that thereby they retain their spherical form notwithstanding their various paths. If, therefore, the Earth also has other motions, these must necessarily resemble the many outside motions having a yearly period. For if we transfer the motion of the Sun to the Earth, taking the Sun to be at rest, then morning and evening risings and settings of Stars will be unaffected, while the stationary points, retrogressions, and progressions of the Planets are due not to their own proper motions, but to that of the Earth, which they reflect. Finally we shall place the Sun himself at the centre of the Universe. All this is suggested by the systematic procession of events and the harmony of the whole Universe, if only we face the facts, as they say, "with both eyes open."

> *Of the Order of the Heavenly Bodies.*

No one doubts that the Sphere of the Fixed Stars is the most distant of visible things. As for the planets, the early Philosophers were inclined to believe that they form a series in order of magnitude of their orbits. They adduce the fact that of objects moving with equal speed, those further distant seem to move more slowly (as is proved in Euclid's *Optics*). They think that the Moon describes her path in the shortest time because, being nearest to the Earth, she revolves in the smallest circle. Furthest they place Saturn, who in the longest time describes the greatest orbit. Nearer than his is Jupiter, and then Mars.

Opinions differ as to Venus and Mercury which, unlike the others, do not altogether leave the Sun. Some place them beyond the Sun, as Plato in his *Timaeus*; others nearer than the Sun, as Ptolemy and many of the moderns. Alpetragius makes Venus nearer and Mercury further than the Sun. If we agree with Plato in thinking that the planets are themselves dark bodies that do but reflect light from the Sun, it must follow, that if nearer than the Sun, on account of their proximity to him they would appear as half or partial circles; for they would generally reflect such light as they receive, upwards, that is toward the Sun, as with the waxing or waning Moon. Some think that since no eclipse even proportional to their size is ever caused by these planets they can never be between us and the Sun.

On the other hand, those who place Venus and Mercury nearer than the Sun adduce in support the great distance which they posit between Sun and Moon. For the maximum distance of Moon from Earth, namely 64 1/6 times Earth's radius, they calculate as about 1/18 of the minimum distance of the Sun from Earth, which is 1160 times Earth's radius. So the distance between the Sun and the Moon is 1096 such units. So vast a space must not remain empty. By calculating the widths of the paths of these planets from their greatest and least distances from the Earth they find that the sum of the widths is approximately the same as this whole distance. Thus the perigee of Mercury comes immediately beyond the apogee of the Moon and the apogee of Mercury is followed by the perigee of Venus, who, finally, at her apogee practically reaches the perigee of the Sun. For they estimate that the difference between the greatest and least distances of Mercury is nearly 177 1/2 of the aforesaid units, and that the remaining space is very nearly filled up by the difference between the maximum and minimum distances of Venus, reckoned at 910 units.

They therefore deny that the planets are opaque like the Moon, but think that they either shine by their own light or that their bodies are completely pervaded by the light of the Sun. They also claim that the Sun is not obstructed by them for they are very rarely interposed between our eyes and the Sun since they usually differ from him in latitude. They are small, too, compared with the Sun. According to Albategni Aratensis even Venus, which is greater than Mercury, can scarcely cover a hundredth part of the Sun. He estimates the Sun's diameter to be ten times that of Venus; and, therefore, so small a spot to be almost invisible in so powerful a light. Averroes indeed, in his Paraphrase of Ptolemy, records that he saw a kind of black spot when investigating the numerical relation between the Sun and Mercury. This is the evidence that these two planets are nearer than the Sun.

But this reasoning is weak and uncertain. Whereas the least

distance of the Moon is 38 times Earth's radius, according to
Ptolemy, but, according to a truer estimate, more than 52 (as
will be shown later) yet we are not aware of anything in all that
space except air, and, if you will, the so called "fiery element".
Besides, the diameter of the orbit of Venus, by which she passes
to a distance of 45 degrees more or less on either side of the
Sun, must be six times the distance from the Earth's centre to
her perigee, as will also be shown later. What then will they
say is contained in the whole of that space, which is so much
bigger than that which could contain the Earth, the Air, the
Aether, the Moon and Mercury, in addition to the space that the
huge epicycle of Venus would occupy if it revolved round the
resting Earth?

Unconvincing too is Ptolemy's proof that the Sun moves
between those bodies that do and those that do not recede from
him completely. Consideration of the case of the Moon, which
does so recede, exposes its falseness. Again, what cause can
be alleged, by those who place Venus nearer than the Sun, and
Mercury next, or in some other order? Why should not these
planets also follow separate paths, distinct from that of the
Sun, as do the other planets? and this might be said even if
their relative swiftness and slowness does not belie their
alleged order. Either then the Earth cannot be the centre to
which the order of the planets and their orbits is related, or
certainly their relative order is not observed, nor does it
appear why a higher position should be assigned to Saturn than
to Jupiter, or any other planet.

Therefore I think we must seriously consider the ingenious
view held by Martianus Capella the author of the *Encyclopaedia*
and certain other Latins, that Venus and Mercury do not go round
the Earth like the other planets but run their courses with the
Sun as centre, and so do not depart from him further than the
size of their orbits allows. What else can they mean than that
the centre of these orbits is near the Sun? So certainly the
orbit of Mercury must be within that of Venus, which, it is
agreed, is more than twice as great.

We may now extend this hypothesis to bring Saturn, Jupiter
and Mars also into relation with this centre, making their orbits
great enough to contain those of Venus and Mercury and the Earth;
and their proportional motions according to the Table demonstrate
this. These outer planets are always nearer to the Earth about
the time of their evening rising, that is, when they are in
opposition to the Sun, and the Earth between them and the Sun.
They are more distant from the Earth at the time of their evening
setting, when they are in conjunction with the Sun and the Sun
between them and the Earth. These indications prove that their
centre pertains rather to the Sun than to the Earth, and that
this is the same centre as that to which the revolutions of Venus
and Mercury are related.

But since all these have one centre it is necessary that
the space between the orbit Venus and the orbit of Mars must also
be viewed as a Sphere concentric with the others, capable of
receiving the Earth with her satellite the Moon and whatever is
contained within the Sphere of the Moon--for we must not separate

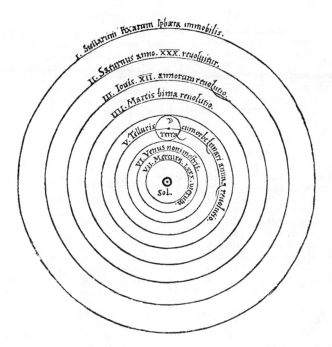

the Moon from the Earth, the former being beyond all doubt nearest to the latter, especially as in that space we find suitable
and ample room for the Moon.

We therefore assert that the centre of the Earth, carrying
the Moon's path, passes in a great orbit among the other planets
in an annual revolution round the Sun; that near the Sun is the
centre of the Universe; and that whereas the Sun is at rest, any
apparent motion of the Sun can be better explained by motion of
the Earth. Yet so great is the Universe that though the distance
of the Earth from the Sun is not insignificant compared with the
size of any other planetary path, in accordance with the ratios
of their sizes, it is insignificant compared with the distance of
the Sphere of the Fixed Stars.

I think it is easier to believe this than to confuse the
issue by assuming a vast number of Spheres, which those who keep
Earth at the centre must do. We thus rather follow Nature, who
producing nothing vain or superfluous often prefers to endow one
cause with many effects. Though these views are difficult, contrary to expectation, and certainly unusual, yet in the sequel
we shall, God willing, make them abundantly clear at least to
mathematicians.

Given the above view--and there is none more reasonable--

that the periodic times are proportional to the sizes of the orbits, then the order of the Spheres, beginning from the most distant, is as follows. Most distant of all is the Sphere of the Fixed Stars, containing all things, and being therefore itself immovable. It represents that to which the motion and position of all the other bodies must be referred. Some hold that it too changes in some way, but we shall assign another reason for this apparent change, as will appear in the account of the Earth's motion. Next is the planet Saturn, revolving in 30 years. Next comes Jupiter, moving in a 12 year circuit: then Mars, who goes round in 2 years. The fourth place is held by the annual revolution in which the Earth is contained, together with the orbit of the Moon as on an epicycle. Venus, whose period is 9 months, is in the fifth place, and sixth is Mercury, who goes round in the space of 80 days.

In the middle of all sits Sun enthroned. In this most beautiful temple could we place this luminary in any better position from which he can illuminate the whole at once? He is rightly called the Lamp, the Mind, the Ruler of the Universe; Hermes Trismegistus names him the Visible God, Sophocles' Electra calls him the All-seeing. So the Sun sits as upon a royal throne ruling his children the planets which circle round him. The Earth has the Moon at her service. As Aristotle says, in his *de Animalibus*, the Moon has the closest relationship with the Earth. Meanwhile the Earth conceives by the Sun, and becomes pregnant with an annual rebirth.

So we find underlying this ordination an admirable symmetry in the Universe, and a clear bond of harmony in the motion and magnitude of the orbits such as can be discovered in no other wise. For here we may observe why the progression and retrogression appear greater for Jupiter than Saturn, and less than for Mars, but again greater for Venus than for Mercury; and why such oscillation appears more frequently in Saturn than in Jupiter, but less frequently in Mars and Venus than in Mercury; moreover why Saturn, Jupiter and Mars are nearer to the Earth at opposition to the Sun than when they are lost in or emerge from the Sun's rays. Particularly Mars, when he shines all night, appears to rival Jupiter in magnitude, being only distinguishable by his ruddy colour; otherwise he is scarce equal to a star of the second magnitude, and can be recognised only when his movements are carefully followed. All these phenomena proceed from the same cause, namely Earth's motion.

That there are no such phenomena for the fixed stars proves their immeasurable distance, compared to which even the size of the Earth's orbit is negligible and the parallactic effect unnoticeable. For every visible object has a certain distance beyond which it can no more be seen (as is proved in the *Optics*). The twinkling of the stars, also, shows that there is still a vast distance between the furthest of the planets, Saturn, and the Sphere of the Fixed Stars, and it is chiefly by this indication that they are distinguished from the planets. Further, there must necessarily be a great difference between moving and non-moving bodies. So great is this divine work of the Great and Noble Creator!

Explanation of the Threefold Motion of the Earth

Since then planets agree in witnessing to the possibility that Earth moves, we shall now briefly discuss the motion itself, in so far as the phenomena can be explained by this hypothesis. This motion we must take to be threefold. The first defines the Greek *nychthēmerinon*, the cycle of night and day. It is produced by the rotation of the Earth on its axis from West to East, corresponding to the opposite motion by which the Universe appears to move round the equinoctial circle, that is the equator, which some call the "equidial" circle, translating the Greek expression *isēmerinos*. The second is the annual revolution of the centre of the Earth, together with all things on the Earth. This describes the ecliptic round the Sun, also from West to East, that is, backwards, between the orbits of Venus and Mars. So it comes about that the Sun himself seems to traverse the ecliptic with a similar motion. For instance, when the centre of the Earth passes over Capricorn, as seen from the Sun, the Sun appears to pass over Cancer as seen from the Earth; but seen from Aquarius, he would seem to pass over Leo, and so on. The equator and Earth's axis are variably inclined to this circle, which passes through the middle of the Zodiac, and to its plane, since if they were fixed and followed simply the motion of the Earth's centre there would be no inequality of days and nights. Then there is a third motion, of declination, which is also an annual revolution, but forwards, that is, tending in opposition to the motion of the Earth's centre; and thus, as they are nearly equal and opposite, it comes about that the axis of the Earth, and its greatest parallel, the equator, point in an almost constant direction, as if they were fixed. But meantime the Sun is seen to move along the oblique direction of the Ecliptic with that motion which is really due to the centre of the Earth (just as if the Earth were the centre of the Universe, remembering that we see the line joining Sun and Earth projected on the Sphere of the Fixed Stars).

To express it graphically, draw a circle ABCD to represent the annual path of Earth's centre in the plane of the Ecliptic. Let E near its centre be the Sun. Divide this circle into four equal parts by the diameters AEC and BED. Let the first point of Cancer be at A, of Libra at B, of Capricorn at C and Aries at D. Now let the centre of the Earth be first at A and round it draw the terrestrial Equator FGHI. This circle FGHI however is not in the same plane as the Ecliptic but its diameter GAI is the line of intersection with the ecliptic. Draw the diameter FAH, at right angles to GAI, and let F be the point of the greatest declination to the South, H to the North. This being so the inhabitants of the Earth will see the Sun near the centre E at its winter solstice in Capricorn, owing to the turning towards the Sun of the point of greatest Northern declination H. Hence in the diurnal rotation the inclination of the equator to AE makes the Sun move along the tropic of Capricorn, which is distant from the equator by an angle equal to EAH.

Now let the centre of the Earth travel forwards and let F, the point of greatest declination, move to the same extent back-

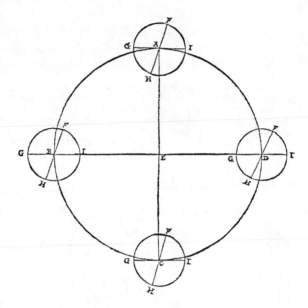

wards until both have completed quadrants of their circles at B. During this time the angle EAI remains always equal to the angle AEB, on account of the equality of the motions. The diameters FAH, FBH and GAI, GBI are also always parallel each to each, and the Equator remains parallel to itself. These parallel lines appear coincident in the immensity of the Heavens as has often been mentioned. Therefore, from the first point of Libra, E will appear to be in Aries, and the intersection of the planes will be the line GBIE, so that the diurnal rotation will give no declination, and all motion of the Sun will be lateral [in the plane of the Ecliptic]. The Sun is now at the vernal equinox. Further, suppose that the centre of the Earth continues its course. When it has completed a semi-circle at C, the Sun will appear to be entering Cancer. F, the point of greatest southern declination of the Equator, is now turned towards the Sun, and he will appear to be running along the Tropic of Cancer, distant from the Equator by an angle equal to ECF. Again, when F has turned through its third quadrant, the line of intersection GI will once more fall along the line ED, and from this position the Sun will be seen in Libra at the autumnal equinox. As the process continues and HF gradually turns towards the Sun, it will produce a return of the same phenomena as we observed at the starting-point.

We can explain it otherwise as follows. Take the diameter AEC in the plane of the paper. AEC is the line of intersection by this plane of a circle perpendicular to it. At points A and C, that is at Cancer and Capricorn respectively, describe in this

plane a circle of longitude of the Earth DFGI. Let DF be the
axis of the Earth, D the North Pole, F the South, and GI a diameter of the equator. Since then F turns towards the Sun at E,
and the northern inclination of the Equator is the angle IAE,
the rotation round the axis will describe a parallel south of the
equator with diameter KL and at a distance from the equator equal
to LI, the apparent distance from the equator of the Sun in Capricorn. Or better, by this rotation round the axis the line of
sight AE describes a conical surface, with vertex at Earth's
centre and as base a circle parallel to the equator. At the
opposite point C the same phenomena occur, but conversely. Thus
the contrary effects of the two motions, that of the centre and
that of declination, constrain the axis of the Earth to remain
in a constant direction, and produce all the phenomena of Solar
motions.

We were saying that the annual revolution of the centre and
of declination were *almost* equal. If they tallied exactly the
equinoctial and solstitial points and the whole obliquity of the
Ecliptic with reference to the Sphere of the Fixed Stars would be
unchangeable. There is, however, a slight discrepancy, which has
only become apparent as it accumulated in the course of ages.
Between Ptolemy's time and ours it has reached nearly 21°, the
amount by which the equinoxes have precessed. For this reason
some have thought that the Sphere of the Fixed Stars also moves,
and they have therefore postulated a ninth sphere. This being
found insufficient, modern authorities now add a tenth. Yet they
have still not attained the result which we hope to attain by the
motion of the Earth.

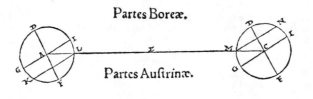

170

b.   In many ways, the first real "revolutionary" of the Scien-
     tific Revolution was Johann Kepler. It was Kepler's dis-
     covery that the orbits of the planets were ellipses that
     broke abruptly with the ancient tradition of circular
     planetary paths. This discovery, in turn, raised the funda-
     mental problem of accounting for such motion by a new
     physics.

     1.   *In the preface to his treatise on Optics,* Kepler cited
          Galileo's telescopic observations as examples of what
          was new in the new astronomy.*

"*The Sidereal Messenger*" of Galileo has been for a long time
in everybody's hands, also my "*Discussion*, such as it is, *with
this Messenger*," and my *Brief Narrative* in confirmation of
Galileo's *Sidereal Messenger*, so any reader may briefly weigh the
chief points of that *Messenger* and see the nature and the value
of the discoveries made by the aid of the telescope, the theory
of which I am intending to demonstrate in this treatise. Actual
sight testified that there is a certain bright heavenly body
which we call the Moon. It was demonstrated from the laws of
optics that this body is round; also Astronomy, by some arguments
founded upon optics, had built up the conclusion that its distance from the earth is about sixty semi-diameters of the earth.
Various spots showed themselves in that body; and the result was
a dubious opinion among a few philosophers, derived from
Hecatæus' account of the stories about the island of the Hyper-
boreans, that the reflected images of mountains and valleys, sea
and land, were seen there; but now the telescope places all these
matters before our eyes in such a way that he must be an intellectual coward who, while enjoying such a view, still thinks
that the matter is open to doubt. Nothing is more certain than
that the southern parts of the moon teem with mountains, very
many in number, and vast in size; and that the northern parts,
inasmuch as they are lower, receive in most extensive lakes the
water flowing down from the south. The conclusions which previously Pena published as disclosed by the aid of optics, started
indeed from certain slight supports, rather than foundations,
afforded by actual sight, but were proved by long arguments depending one upon another, so that they might be assigned to
human reason rather than to sight; but now our very eyes, as if
a new door of heaven had been opened, are led to the view of
matters once hidden from them. But if it should please any one
to exhaust the force of reasoning upon these new observations,
who does not see how far the contemplation of nature will extend
her boundaries, when we ask, "What is the use of the tracts of

*Johann Kepler, Preface to the *Dioptrics*, in *The Sidereal Messenger of Galileo Galilei and a part of the Preface to Kepler's
Dioptrics*, trans. by Edward Stafford Carlos, London, 1880. Pp.
79-83, 90-1.

mountains and valleys, and the very wide expanse of seas in the moon?" and "May not some creature less noble than man be imagined such as might inhabit those tracts?"

With no less certainty also do we decide by the use of this instrument even that famous question, which, coeval with philosophy itself, is disputed to this day by the noblest intellects--I mean, "Whether the earth can move (as the theory of the Planets greatly requires) without the overthrow of all bodies that have weight, or the confusion of the motion of the elements?" For if the earth were banished from the centre of the universe, some fear lest the water should leave the orb of the earth and flow to the centre of the universe; and yet we see that in the moon, as well as in the earth, there is a quantity of moisture occupying the sunken hollows of that globe; and although this orb revolves actually in the ether, and outside the centres not merely of the universe, but even of our earth, yet the mass of water in the moon is not at all hindered from cleaving invariably to the orb of the moon, and tending to the centre of the body to which it belongs. So, by this instance of the phenomena of the moon, the science of optics amends the received theory of mechanics, and confirms on this point my introduction to my *Commentaries upon the Motions of the Planet Mars*.

The followers of the Samian philosophy (for I may use this epithet to designate the philosophy originated by the Samians, Pythagoras and Aristarchus) have a strong argument against the apparent immobility of the earth provided in the phenomena of the moon. For we are taught by optics that if any one of us was in the moon, to him the moon, his abode, would seem quite immovable, but our earth and sun and all the rest of the heavenly bodies movable; for the conclusions of sight are thus related.

Pena has noticed how astronomers, using the principles of optics, have by most laborious reasoning removed the Milky Way from the elementary universe, where Aristotle had placed it, into the highest region of the ether; but now, by the aid of the telescope lately invented, the very eyes of astronomers are conducted straight to a thorough survey of the substance of the Milky Way; and whoever enjoys this sight is compelled to confess that the Milky Way is nothing else but a mass of extremely small stars.

Again, up to this time the nature of nebulous stars had been entirely unknown; but if the telescope be directed to one of such nebulous balls, as Ptolemy calls them, it again shows, as in the case of the Milky Way, three or four very bright stars clustered very close together.

Again, who without this instrument would have believed that the number of fixed stars was ten times, or perhaps twenty times, more than that which is given in Ptolemy's description of the fixed stars? And whence, pray, should we seek for conclusive evidence about the end or boundary of this visible universe, proving that it is actually the sphere of the fixed stars, and that there is nothing beyond, except from this very discovery by the telescope of this multitude of fixed stars, which is, as it were, the vaulting of the mobile universe? Again, how greatly an astronomer would go wrong in determining the magnitude of the fixed stars, except he should survey the stars all over again with a

telescope, also may be seen in Galileo's treatise, and we will
also hereafter produce in proof a letter from a German astronomer.
But no words can express my admiration of that chapter of
the *Sidereal Messenger* where the story is told of the discovery,
by the aid of a very highly finished telescope, of another world,
as it were, in the planet Jupiter. The mind of the philosopher
almost reels as he considers that there is a vast orb, which is
equal in mass to fourteen orbs like the earth (unless on this
point the telescope of Galileo shall shortly reveal something
more exact than the measurements of Tycho Brahe) round which circle four moons, not unlike this moon of ours; the slowest revolving in the space of fourteen of our days, as Galileo has published; the next to this, by far the brightest of the four, in
the space of eight days, as I detected in last April and May;
the other two in still shorter periods. And here the reasoning
of my *Commentaries about the Planet Mars*, applied to a similar
case, induces me to conclude also that the actual orb of Jupiter
rotates with very great rapidity, most certainly faster than once
in the space of one of our days; so that this rotation of the
mighty orb upon its own axis is accompanied wherever it goes by
the perpetual circuits of those four moons. Moreover, this sun
of ours, the common source of heat and light for this terrestrial world as well as for that world of Jupiter, which we consider to be of the angular magnitude of 30' at most, there
scarcely subtends more than 6' or 7', and is found again in the
same position among the fixed stars, having completed the zodiac
in the interval, after a period of twelve of our years. Accordingly, the creatures which live on that orb of Jupiter, while
they contemplate the very swift courses of those four moons among
the fixed stars, while they behold them and the sun rising and
setting day by day, would swear by Jupiter-in-stone, like the
Romans (for I have lately returned from those parts), that their
orb of Jupiter remains immovable in one spot, and that the fixed
stars and the sun, which are the bodies really at rest, no less
than those four moons of theirs, revolve round that abode of
theirs with manifold variety of motions. And from this instance
now, much more than before from the instance of the moon, any
follower of the Samian philosophy will learn what reply may be
made to any one objecting to the theory of the motion of the
earth as absurd, and alleging the evidence of our sight. O
telescope, instrument of much knowledge, more precious than any
sceptre! Is not he who holds thee in his hand made king and lord
of the works of God? Truly

> "All that is overhead, the mighty orbs
> With all their motions, thou dost subjugate
> To man's intelligence."

If there is any one in some degree friendly to Copernicus and the
lights of the Samian philosophy, who finds this difficulty only,
that he doubts how it can happen, supposing the earth to perform
again and again her course among the planets through the ethereal
plains, that the moon should keep so constantly by her side, like
an inseparable companion, and at the same time fly round and
round the actual orb of the earth, just like a faithful dog which

goes round and round his master on some journey, now running in front, now deviating to this side or that, in ever-varying mazes, let him look at the planet Jupiter, which, as this telescope shows, certainly carries in its train not one such companion only, like the earth, as Copernicus showed, but actually four, that never leave it, though all the time hastening each in its own orbit.

But enough has been said about these matters in my *Discussion with the Sidereal Messenger*. It is time that I should turn to those discoveries which have been made since the publication of Galileo's *Sidereal Messenger*, and since my *Discussion* with it, by means of this telescope.

It is now just a year since Galileo wrote to Prague, and gave full notice that he had detected something new in the heavens beyond his former discoveries; and that there might not be any one who, with the intention of detracting from his credit, should try to pass himself off as an earlier observer of the phenomenon, Galileo gave a certain space of time for the publication of the new phenomena which any one had seen; he himself meanwhile described his discovery in letters transposed in this manner: *s m a i s m r m i l m e p o e t a l e u m i b u n e n u g t t a u i r a s*. Out of these letters I made an uncouth verse which I inserted in my *Short Account* in the month of September of last year:--

> Salve umbistineum geminatum Martia proles.
> Hail, twin companionship, children of Mars.

But I was a very long way from the meaning of the letters; it contained nothing to do with Mars; and, not to detain you, reader, here is the solution of the riddle in the words of Galileo himself, the author of it:--"But to come now to my second topic. Since Kepler has published in that recent *'Narrative'* of his the letters which I sent as an anagram to your illustrious Lordship, and since an intimation has been given me that his Majesty desires to be taught the meaning of those letters, I send it to your illustrious Lordship, that your Lordship may communicate it to his Majesty, to Kepler, and to any one your Lordship may wish.

"The letters when joined together as they ought to be, say this,

> 'Altissimum planetam tergeminum observavi,'
> 'I have observed the most distant of the planets to have a triple form.'

"For in truth I have found out with the most intense surprise that the planet Saturn is not merely one single star, but three stars very close together, so much so that they are all but in contact one with another. They are quite immovable with regard to each other, and are arranged in this manner, oOo. The middle star of the three is by far greater than the two on either side. They are situated one towards the east, the other towards the west, in one straight line to a hair's-breadth; not, however, exactly in the direction of the Zodiac, for the star furthest to the west rises somewhat towards the north, perhaps they are parallel to the equator. If you look at them through a glass that does not multiply much, the stars will not appear

clearly separate from one another, but Saturn's orb will appear
somewhat elongated, of the shape of an olive, thus, ⬯.   But
if you should use a glass which multiplies a surface more than a
thousand times, there will appear very distinctly three orbs,
almost touching one another; and they will be thought to be not
further apart than the breadth of a very fine and scarcely
visible thread.   So you see a guard of satellites has been found
for Jupiter, and for the decrepit little old man two servants to
help his steps and never leave his side.   Concerning the rest of
the planets I have found nothing new."

2.   *In his* Epitome of Copernican Astronomy,* *Kepler came to grips with the physical problem of accounting for the revolution of the earth around the sun, as well as justifying the Copernican view of the universe.*

What are the hypotheses or principles wherewith Copernican astronomy saves the appearances in the proper movements of the planets?

They are principally: (1) that the sun is located at the centre of the sphere of the fixed stars--or approximately at the centre--and is immovable in place; (2) that the single planets move really around the sun in their single systems, which are compounded of many perfect circles revolved in an absolutely uniform movement; (3) that the Earth is one of the planets, so that by its mean annual movement around the sun it describes its orbital circle between the orbital circles of Mars and of Venus; (4) that the ratio of its orbital circle to the diameter of the sphere of the fixed stars is imperceptible to sense and therefore, as it were, exceeds measurements; (5) that the sphere of the moon is arranged around the Earth as its centre, so that the annual movement around the sun--and so the movement from place to place-- is common to the whole sphere of the moon and to the Earth.

Do you judge that these principles should be held to in this Epitome?

Since astronomy has two ends, to save the appearances and to contemplate the true form of the edifice of the world--of which I have treated in BOOK I, folia 4 and 5--there is no need of all these principles in order to attain the first end: but some can be changed and others can be omitted; however, the second principle must necessarily be corrected: and even though most of these principles are necessary for the second end, nevertheless they are not yet sufficient.

Which of these principles can be changed or omitted and the appearances still be saved?

Tycho Brahe demonstrates the appearances with the first and third principles changed: for he, like the ancients, places the Earth immobile, at the centre of the world; but the sun--which even for him is the centre of the orbital circles of the five planets--and the system of all the spheres he makes to go around the Earth in the common annual movement, while at the same time

*Johann Kepler, *Epitome of Copernican Astronomy*, trans. by Charles Glenn Wallis. In Great Books. Pp. 852-856, 859-860, 888, 894-895, 905-907. Reprinted with the permission of the Encyclopaedia Brittanica, Inc.

in this common system any planet completes its proper movements. Moreover, he omits the fourth principle altogether and exhibits the sphere of the fixed stars as not much greater than the sphere of Saturn.

What in turn do you substitute for the second principle and what else do you add to the true form of the dwelling of the world or to what belongs to the nature of the heavens?

Even though the true movements are to be left singly to the single planets, nevertheless these movements do not move by themselves nor by the revolutions of spheres--for there are no solid spheres--but the sun in the centre of the world, revolving around the centre of its body and around its axis, by this revolution becomes the cause of the single planets going around.

Further, even though the planets are really eccentric to the centre of the sun: nevertheless there are no other smaller circles called epicycles, which by their revolution vary the intervals between the planet and the sun; but the bodies themselves of the planets, by an inborn force [*vi insite*], furnish the occasion for this variation.

*   *   *   *   *

PART I

1. On the Principal Parts of the World

What do you judge to be the lay-out of the principal parts of the world?

The Philosophy of Copernicus reckons up the principal parts of the world by dividing the figure of the world into regions. For in the sphere, which is the image of God the Creator and the Archetype of the world--as was proved in Book I--there are three regions, symbols of the three persons of the Holy Trinity--the centre, a symbol of the Father; the surface, of the Son; and the intermediate space, of the Holy Ghost. So, too, just as many principal parts of the world have been made--the different parts in the different regions of the sphere: the sun in the centre, the sphere of the fixed stars on the surface, and lastly the planetary system in the region intermediate between the sun and the fixed stars.

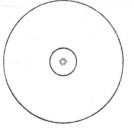

I thought the principal parts of the world are reckoned to be the heavens and the earth?

Of course, our uncultivated eyesight from the Earth cannot show us any other more notable parts--as was said in Book I, folia 8, 9, 10--since we tread upon the one with our feet and are roofed over by the other, and since both parts seem to be commingled and cemented together in the common limbo of the horizon-- like a globe in which stars, clouds, birds, man, and the various kinds of terrestrial animals are enclosed.

But we are practised in the discipline which discloses the causes of things, shakes off the deceptions of eyesight, and carries the mind higher and farther, outside of the boundaries of eyesight. Hence it should not be surprising to anyone that eyesight should learn from reason, that the pupil should learn something new from his master which he did not know before--namely, that the Earth, considered alone and by itself, should not be reckoned among the primary parts of the great world but should be added to one of the primary parts, i.e., to the planetary region, the movable world, and that the Earth has the proportionality of a beginning in that part; and that the sun in turn should be separated from the number of stars and set up as one of the principal parts of the whole universe. But I am speaking now of the Earth in so far as it is a part of the edifice of the world, and not of the dignity of the governing creatures which inhabit it.

By what properties do you distinguish these members of the great world from one another?

The perfection of the world consists in light, heat, movement, and the harmony of movements. These are analogous to the faculties of the soul: light, to the sensitive; heat, to the vital and the natural; movement, to the animal; harmony, to the rational. And indeed the adornment [*ornatus*] of the world consists in light; its life and growth, in heat; and, so to speak, its action, in movement; and its contemplation--wherein Aristotle places blessedness--in harmonies. Now since three things necessarily come together for every affection, namely, the cause *a qua*, the subject *in quo*, and the form *sub qua*--therefore, in respect to all the aforesaid affections of the world, the sun exercises the function of the efficient cause; the region of the fixed stars that of the thing forming, containing, and terminating; and the intermediate space, that of the subject--in accordance with the nature of each affection. Accordingly, in all these ways the sun is the principal body of the whole world.

For as regards light: since the sun is very beautiful with light and is as if the eye of the world, like a source of light or very brilliant torch, the sun illuminates, paints, and adorns the bodies of the rest of the world; the intermediate space is not itself light-giving, but light-filled and transparent and the channel through which light is conducted from its source, and there exist in this region the globes and the creatures upon which the light of the sun is poured and which make use of this light. The sphere of the fixed stars plays the role of the river-bed in which this river of light runs, and is as it were an opaque and illuminated wall, reflecting and doubling the light of the sun: you have very properly likened it to a lantern, which shuts out the winds.

Thus in animals the cerebrum, the seat of the sensitive faculty imparts to the whole animal all its senses, and by the act of common sense causes the presence of all those senses as if arousing them and ordering them to keep watch. And in another way, in this simile, the sun is the image of common sense; the globes in the intermediate space of the sense-organs; and the sphere of the fixed stars of the sensible objects.

As regards heat: the sun is the fireplace [*focus*] of the world; the globes in the intermediate space warm themselves at this fireplace, and the sphere of the fixed stars keeps the heat from flowing out, like a wall of the world, or a skin or garment--to use the metaphor of the Psalm of David. The sun is fire, as the Pythagoreans said, or a red-hot stone or mass, as Democritus said--and the sphere of the fixed stars is ice, or a crystalline sphere, comparatively speaking. But if there is a certain vegetative faculty not only in terrestrial creatures but also in the whole ether throughout the universal amplitude of the world--and both the manifest energy of the sun in warming and physical considerations concerning the origin of comets lead us to draw this inference--it is believable that this faculty is rooted in the sun as in the heart of the world, and that thence by the orange of light and heat it spreads out into this most wide space of the world--in the way that in animals the seat of heat and of the vital faculty is in the heart and the seat of the vegetative faculty in the liver, whence these faculties by the intermingling of the spirits spread out into the remaining members of the body. The sphere of the fixed stars, situated diametrically opposite on every side, helps this vegetative faculty by· concentrating heat, as they say; as it were a kind of skin of the world.

As regards movement: the sun is the first cause of the movement of the planets and the first mover of the universe, even by reason of its own body. In the intermediate space the movables, i.e., the globes of the planets, are laid out. The region of the fixed stars supplies the movables with a place and a base upon which the movables are, as it were, supported; and movement is understood as taking place relative to its absolute immobility. So in animals the cerebellum is the seat of the motor faculty, and the body and its members are that which is moved. The Earth is the base of an animal body; the body, the base of the arm or head; and the arm, the base of the finger. And the movement of each part takes place upon this base as upon something immovable.

Finally, as regards the harmony of the movements: the sun occupies that place in which alone the movements of the planets give the appearance of magnitudes harmonically proportioned [*contemperatarum*]. The planets themselves, moving in the intermediate space, exhibit the subject or terms, wherein the harmonies are found; the sphere of the fixed stars, or the circle of the zodiac, exhibits the measures whereby the magnitude of the apparent movements is known. So too in man there is the intel-

lect, which abstracts universals and forms numbers and proportions, as things which are not outside of intellect; but individuals [*individua*], received inwardly through the senses are the
foundation of universals; and indivisible [*individuae*] and discrete unities, of numbers; and real terms of proportions.
Finally, memory, divided as it were into compartments of quantities and times, like the sphere of the fixed stars, is the store-
house and repository of sensations. And further, there is never
judgment of sensations except in the cerebrum; and the effect of
joy never arises from a sense-perception except in the heart.

    Accordingly, the aforesaid vegetating corresponds to the
nutritive faculty of animals and plants; heating corresponds to
the vital faculty; movement, to the animal faculty; light, to
the sensitive; and harmony, to the rational. Wherefore most
rightly is the sun held to be the heart of the world and the seat
of reason and life, and the principal one among three primary
members of the world; and these praises are true in the philosophic sense, since the poets honour the sun as the king of the
stars, but the Sidonians, Chaldees, and Persians--by an idiom of
language observed in German too--as the queen of the heavens, and
the Platonists, as the king of intellectual fire.

*   *   *   *   *

*Prove by means of the office of the sun that the centre is due
to it.*

    That has already been partly done in rebutting the Aristo-
telian refutation. For (1) if the whole world, which is spherical, is equally in need of the light of the sun and its heat,
then it would be best for the sun to be at the midpart, whence
light and heat may be distributed to all the regions of the
world. And that takes place more uniformly and rightly, with the
sun resting at the centre than with the sun moving around the
centre. For if the sun approached certain regions for the sake
of warming them, it would draw away from the opposite regions and
would cause alternations while it itself remained perfectly simple. And it is surprising that some people use jokingly the
similitude of light at the centre of the lamp, as it is a very
apt similitude, least fitted to satirize this opinion but suited
rather to painting the power of this argument.

    (2) But a special argument is woven together concerning
light, which presupposes fitness, not necessity. Imagine the
sphere of the fixed stars as a concave mirror: you know that the
eye placed at the centre of such a mirror gazes upon itself
everywhere: and if there is a light at the centre, it is everywhere reflected at right angles from the concave surface and the
reflected rays come together again at the centre. And in fact
that can occur at no other point in the concave mirror except at
the centre. Therefore, since the sun is the source of light and
eye of the world, the centre is due to it in order that the sun--
as the Father in the divine symbolizing--may contemplate itself
in the whole concave surface--which is the symbol of God the
Son--and take pleasure in the image of itself, and illuminate itself by shining and inflame itself by warming. These melodious

little verses apply to the sun:

*Thou who dost gaze at thy face
and dost everywhere leap back
from the navel of the upper air
O gushing up of the gleams flowing
through the glass emptiness, Sun,
who dost again swallow thy reflections.*

       *   *   *   *   *

*How is the ratio of the periodic times, which you have assigned
to the mobile bodies, related to the aforesaid ratio of the
spheres wherein those bodies are borne?*

The ratio of the times is not equal to the ratio of the
spheres, but greater than it, and in the primary planets exactly
the ratio of the 3/2th powers. That is to say, if you take the
cube roots of the 30 years of Saturn and the 12 years of Jupiter
and square them, the true ratio of the spheres of Saturn and
Jupiter will exist in these squares. This is the case even if
you compare spheres which are not next to one another. For
example, Saturn takes 30 years; the Earth takes one year. The
cube root of 30 is approximately 3.11. But the cube root of 1
is 1. The squares of these roots are 9.672 and 1. Therefore the
sphere of Saturn is to the sphere of the Earth as 9.672 is to
1.000. And a more accurate number will be produced, if you take
the times more accurately.

What is gathered from this?

Not all the planets are borne with the same speed, as Aristotle wished, otherwise their times would be as their spheres,
and as their diameters; but according as each planet is higher
and farther away from the sun, so it traverses less space in one
hour by its mean movement: Saturn--according to the magnitude of
the solar sphere believed in by the ancients--traverses 240 German miles (in one hour), Jupiter 320 German miles, Mars 600, the
centre of the Earth 740, Venus 800, and Mercury 1,200. And if
this is to be according to the solar interval proved by me in
the above, the number of miles must everywhere be tripled.

       *   *   *   *   *

*Why do you say that a celestial body, which is unchanging with
respect to its matter, cannot be moved by assent alone? For if
the celestial bodies are neither heavy nor light, but most suited
for circular movement, then do they resist the motor mind?*

Even if a celestial globe is not heavy in the way in which a
stone on the earth is said to be heavy, and is not light in the
way in which among us fire is said to be light: nevertheless by
reason of its matter it has a natural ἀδυναμια or powerlessness
of crossing from place to place, and it has a natural inertia or
rest whereby it rests in every place where it is placed alone.

And hence in order that it may be moved out of its position and its rest, it has need of some power which should be stronger than its matter and its naked body, and which should overcome its natural inertia. For such a faculty is above the capacity of nature and is a sprout of form, or a sign of life.

Whence do you prove that the matter of the celestial bodies resists its movers, and is overcome by them, as in a balance the weights are overcome by the motor faculty?

This is proved in the first place from the periodic times of the rotation of the single globes around their axes, as the terrestrial time of one day and the solar time of approximately twenty-five days. For if there were no inertia in the matter of the celestial globe--and this inertia is as it were a weight in the globe--there would be no need of a virtue [*virtute*] in order to move the globe; and if the least virtue for moving the globe were postulated, then there would be no reason why the globe should not revolve in an instant. But the revolutions of the globes take place in a fixed time, which is longer for one planet and shorter for another: hence it is apparent that the inertia of matter is not to the motor virtue in the ratio in which nothing is to something. Therefore the inertia is not nil, and thus there is some resistance of celestial matter.

Secondly, this same thing is proved by the revolution of the globes around the sun--considering them generally. For one mover by one revolution of its own globe moves six globes, as we shall hear below. Wherefore if the globes did not have a natural resistance of a fixed proportion, there would be no reason why they should not follow exactly the whirling movement of their mover, and thus they would revolve with it in one and the same time. Now indeed all the globes go in the same direction as the mover with its whirling movement, nevertheless no globe fully attains the speed of its mover, and one follows another more slowly. Therefore they mingle the inertia of matter with the speed of the mover in a fixed proportion.

The ratio of the periodic times seems to be the work of a mind and not of material necessity.

The most accurately harmonic attunement of the extreme movements--the slowest and the fastest movement in any given planet--is the work of the highest and most adored creator Mind or Wisdom. But if the lengths of the periodic times were the work of a mind, they would have something of beauty, like the rational ratios, duplicate, triplicate, and so on. But the ratios of the periodic times are irrational [*ineffabiles, irrationales vulgo*] and thus partake of infinity, wherein there is no beauty for the mind, as there is no definiteness [*finitio*].

Secondly, these times cannot be the work of a mind--I am not speaking of the Creator but of the nature of the mover; because the unequal delays in different parts of the circle add up to the times of one period. But the unequal delays arise from material necessity, as will be said below, and as if by reason of the balance [*ex ratione staterae*].

Therefore by what force do you suspend your material globes and the Earth in especial, so that each remains within the boundaries of its region, though it is destitute of the bonds of the solid spheres?

Since it is certain that there are no solid spheres, it is necessary that we should take refuge in this inertia of matter, whereby any globe, placed in any place on the world beyond the motor virtues, naturally rests in that place, because matter, as such, has no faculty of transporting its body from place to place.

Then what is it which makes the planets move around the sun, each planet within the boundaries of its own region, if there are not any solid spheres, and if the globes themselves cannot be fastened to anything else and made to stick there, and if without solid spheres they cannot be moved from place to place by any soul?

Even if things are very far removed from us and which are without a real exemplification are difficult to explain and give rise to quite uncertain judgements, as Ptolemy truly warns; nevertheless if we follow probability [*verisimilitudinem*] and take care not to postulate anything which is contrary to us, it will of necessity be clear that no mind is to be introduced which should turn the planets by the dictation of reason and so to speak by a nod, and that no soul is to be put in charge of this revolution, in order that it should impress something into the globes by the balanced contest of the forces, as takes place in the revolution around the axis; but that there is one only solar body, which is situated at the centre of the whole universe, and to which this movement of the primary planets around the body of the sun can be ascribed.

3. On the Revolution of the Solar Body Around its Axis and its Effect in the Movement of the Planets

By what reasons are you led to make the sun the moving cause or the source of movement for the planets?

1. Because it is apparent that in so far as any planet is more distant from the sun than the rest, it moves the more slowly--so that the ratio of the periodic times is the ratio of the 3/2th powers of the distances from the sun. Therefore we reason from this that the sun is the source of movement.
2. Below we shall hear the same thing come into use in the case of the single planets--so that the closer any one planet approaches the sun during any time, it is borne with an increase of velocity in exactly the ratio of the square.
3. Nor is the dignity or the fitness of the solar body opposed to this, because it is very beautiful and of a perfect roundness and is very great and is the source of light and heat, whence all life flows out into the vegetables: to such an extent that heat and light can be judged to be as it were certain in-

struments fitted to the sun for causing movement in the planets.

4. But in especial, all the estimates of probability are fulfilled by the sun's rotation in its own space around its immobile axis, in the same direction in which all the planets proceed: and in a shorter period than Mercury, the nearest to the sun and fastest of all the planets.

*   *   *   *   *

4. On the Causes of the Ratio of the Periodic Times

In the beginning of this consideration of movement you said that the periodic times of the planets are found to be quite exactly in the ratio of the 3/2th powers of their orbits or circles. I ask what the cause of this thing is.

Four causes come together in establishing the length of the periodic time. The first is the length of the route; the second is the weight or the amount [*copia*] of matter to be transported; the third is the strength of the motor virtue; the fourth is the bulk [*moles*] or space in which the matter to be transported is unrolled. For as is the case in a mill, where the wheel is turned by the force of the stream, so that, the wider and longer the wings, planks, or oars which you fasten to the wheel, the greater the force of the stream pouring through the width and depth which you will divert into the machine; so too that is the case in this celestial vortex of the solar form moving rapidly in a gyro--and this form causes the movement. Consequently

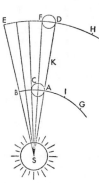

the more space the body--A or D in this case--occupies, the more widely and deeply it occupies the motor virtue, as in this case BCA understood according to its width; and the more swiftly, other things being equal, is it borne forward; and the more quickly does it complete its periodic journey.

But the circular journeys of the planets are in the simple ratio of the intervals. For as SA is to SD, so too is the whole circle BA to the whole circle ED. But the weight, or the amount of matter in the different planets, is in the ratio of the 1/2th powers of the intervals, as was proved above, so that always the higher planet has more matter and is moved the more slowly and piles up the more time in its period, since even before now by reason of its journey it would have wanted more time. For with SK taken as a mean proportional between SA and SD the intervals of the two planets; as SK is to the greater distance SD, so the amount of matter in the planet A is to the amount

in the planet D. But the third and fourth causes balance one
another in the comparison of the different planets. But the simple ratio of the intervals plus the ratio of the 1/2th powers
constitute the ratio of the 3/2th powers of the same. Therefore
the periodic times are in the ratio of the 3/2th powers of the
intervals. Consequently if SD, SK, SA, and SL are continued
[mean] proportionals, then SL will be to SD as the time period
of planet A is to the time period of planet D.

*Prove, in comparing two planets, that the weakening of the motor
virtue is exactly balanced by the amplitude wherewith the movable
planetary bodies occupy the virtue.*

The bulks or expanses of the bodies are in the simple and
direct ratio of the intervals, as was demonstrated above. That
is, as SA is to SD, so is the bulk of the planetary body at A to
the bulk of the other planet at D. But too the motor virtue is
dense and strong, in the simple ratio of the intervals but inversely; for as the same interval SA is to SD, so the strength
of the form CA is to the strength of the form FD. Therefore the
virtue is in turn occupied in the same ratio in which it is
weakened; for example, Saturn is borne by a power ten times
feebler than the virtue by which the Earth is; but conversely,
it occupies with its body ten times more of the virtue of its
region than the Earth with its body occupies of the virtue of
its region. And let the total virtue which Saturn occupies by
its bulk be divided into ten parts which are equal in expanse
(*spatio*) to the total virtue which the Earth occupies. Any one
of these parts or expanses of virtue has only one tenth of the
strength which that one part which is occupied by the Earth has,
wherefore those ten parts added together into one are equal in
power [*potestate*] to that one part by which the Earth is borne.
And so if in the amplitude of the more rarefied globe of Saturn
there were not more matter than in the narrowness of the denser
terrestrial body, the globe of Saturn in one year would be borne
along as great a distance of its orbit as is the length of the
whole orbit of the Earth; and thus in ten years it would complete
its proper orbit. But in fact it has approximately thrice as
much matter and weight as the Earth does; wherefore it requires
thrice as long a time, namely thirty years.

*What need was there to teach of this balancing? Would it not
have been enough for establishing a demonstration to set down
that there is absolutely no cause for such an irregular movement
as this either in the different grades of the motor virtue or in
the different amplitudes of the planetary globes?*

Now for the demonstration that the ratio of the different
periods of the planets is the ratio of the 3/2th power of the
intervals, it would have made no difference whether this or that
were set down. But if we had progressed to the different delays
of one and the same planet at different intervals, we could not
have established from the same genus of things the reason why
the delays in arcs which are exactly equal should follow the
ratio of the intervals.

Then what is the reason why the farther distant from the sun any
equal arc of the eccentric circle is, the longer delays does the
planet make in that arc, and in the ratio of the intervals?

The reason is indeed the weakening of the motor virtue:
just as light is SD the longer interval from the sun is diffused
more thinly along the length FD than is the diffusion of the same
in the shorter interval SA. And so what of the virtue was at
that time occupied by the body of the planet, as FD, is more weak
than what of the denser virtue is occupied by the same CA which
is nearer.
    For here the three remaining causes are missing. For the
arc or route is assumed in both cases to be of the same length,
as DH, AI: the density of the body remains the same, and the
magnitude of the figure likewise; because FD and CA are in this
case one and the same planet. The strength of the virtue alone
is left. But more on this in the following.

In this case we seem to meet a greater difficulty than above.
For when the planet is nearer to the sun, it occupies not only
longer arcs of the circles of the motor virtue but also denser
arcs: wherefore should it not extend its delays in the ratio of
the squares rather than in the simple ratio of the intervals?

Now the same thing is said as above, and the same answer is
made. For even if Saturn at that time did not come down into
the sphere of the Earth: nevertheless we were comparing the expanse of power occupied by Saturn not merely with that which the
Earth would have occupied in the sphere of Saturn but also with
that which the Earth would occupy in its own sphere. Therefore,
as before, the fact that the circles are denser (*confertiores*) is
to be assigned to the form from the body; and this form is something distinct from the inhering motor virtue, which extends in
longitude alone and gets no advantage from the condensation of
its subject in latitude--unless a thin line without width (*lati-*
tudine carens) has no natural force in length (*in longum*): where
the width (*latitudo*) of such a line is judged not by the density
but by the expanse, namely on account of the width of the bodies
to be moved, as I taught above.

C. Galileo Galilei, *Dialogue on the Great World Systems**

    Both Copernicus and Kepler sensed that the establishing of
the new astronomy involved the creation of a new physics as well.
It was Galileo, however, who realized that a new physics was
essential if the Copernican system were to be taken seriously.
In his Dialogue on the Great World Systems *(1632), he dealt with*
those problems that were peculiarly bound up with the problem of
the Earth's motion. In the later Dialogues Concerning Two New
Sciences *(1638), he spelled out the laws of (terrestrial) motion*
which were later to form the cornerstone of the Newtonian syn-
thesis.

    SAGR. I would, in favour of *Simplicius*, defend *Aristotle* if
it were possible, or at least better satisfie my self concerning
the strength of your illation. You say, that the seeing the
stone rake along the Tower, is not sufficient to assure us, that
its motion is perpendicular (which is the middle term of the
Syllogism) unless it be presupposed, that the Earth standeth
still, which is the conclusion to be proved: For that if the
Tower did move together with the Earth, and the stone did slide
along the same, the motion of the stone would be transverse, and
not perpendicular. But I shall answer, that should the Tower
move, it would be impossible that the stone should fall gliding
along the side of it; and therefore from its falling in that manner the stability of the Earth is inferred.
    SIMPL. It is so; for if you would have the stone in des-
cending to grate upon the Tower, though it were carried round by
the Earth, you must allow the stone two natural motions, to wit,
the straight motion towards the Centre, and the circular about
the Centre, the which is impossible.
    SALV. *Aristotles* defense then consisteth in the impossibil-
itie, or at least in his esteeming it an impossibility, that the
stone should move with a motion mixt of right and circular: for
if he did not hold it impossible that the stone could move to the
Centre, and about the Centre at once, he must have understood,
that it might come to pass that the cadent stone might in its
descent, race the Tower as well when it moved as when it stood
still; and consequently he must have perceived, that from this
grating nothing could be inferred touching the mobility or
immobility of the Earth. But this doth not any way excuse
Aristotle; aswell because he ought to have exprest it, if he had
had such a conceit, it being so material a part of his Argument;
as also because it can neither be said that such an effect is
impossible, nor that *Aristotle* did esteem it so. The first cannot be affirmed, for that by and by I shall shew that it is not

---

*Galileus Galileus, his System of the world (Salusbury edition,
op. cit.). Pp. 122-130; 159-167; 331-334. Also found in Galileo
Galilei, *Dialogue on the Great World Systems* (Santillana edition,
op. cit.). Pp. 155-63; 193-200; 376-9.

onely possible, but necessary: nor much less can the second be averred, for that *Aristotle* himself granteth fire to move natur- ally upwards in a right line, and to move about with the diurnal motion, imparted by Heaven to the whole Element of Fire, and the greater part of the Air: If therefore he held it not impossible to mix the right motion upwards, with the circular communicated to the Fire and Air from the concave of the Moon, much less ought he to account impossible the mixture of the right motion down- wards of the stone, with the circular which we presuppose natural to the whole Terrestrial Globe, of which the stone is a part.

SIMPL. I see no such thing: for if the element of Fire revolve round together with the Air, it is a very easie, yea a necessary thing, that a spark of fire which from the Earth mounts upwards, in passing thorow the moving air, should receive the same motion, being a body so thin, light, and easie to be moved: but that a very heavy stone, or a Canon bullet, that descendeth from on high, and that is at liberty to move whither it will, should suffer it self to be transported either by the air or any other thing, is altogether incredible. Besides that, we have the Experiment, which is so proper to our purpose, of the stone let fall from the round top of the Mast of a ship, which when the ship lyeth still, falleth at the Partners of the Mast; but when the ship saileth, falls so far distant from that place, by how far the ship in the time of the stones falling had run forward; which will not be a few fathoms, when the ships course is swift.

SALV. There is a great disparity between the case of the Ship and that of the Earth, if the Terrestrial Globe be supposed to have a diurnal motion. For it is a thing very manifest, that the motion of the Ship, as it is not natural to it, so the motion of all those things that are in it is accidental, whence it is no wonder that the stone which was retained in the round top, being left at liberty, descendeth downwards without any obligation to follow the motion of the Ship. But the diurnal conversion is ascribed to the Terrestrial Globe for its proper and natural motion, and consequently, it is so to all the parts of the said Globe; and, as being impress'd by nature, is indelible in them; and therefore that stone that is on the top of the Tower hath an intrinsick inclination of revolving about the Centre of its *Whole* in twenty four hours, and this same natural instinct it exerci- seth eternally, be it placed in any state whatsoever. And to be assured of the truth of this, you have no more to do but to alter an antiquated impression made in your mind; and to say, Like as in that I hitherto holding it to be the property of the Terres- trial Globe to rest immoveable about its Centre, did never doubt or question but that all whatsoever particles thereof do also naturally remain in the same state of rest: So it is reason, in case the Terrestrial Globe did move round by natural instinct in twenty four hours, that the intrinsick and natural inclination of all its parts should also be, not to stand still, but to follow the same revolution. And thus without running into any incon- venience, one may conclude, that in regard the motion conferred by the force of Oars on the Ship, and by it on all the things that are contained within her, is not natural but forreign,it is very reasonable that that stone, it being separated from the ship, do reduce its self to its natural disposure, and return to exercise its pure simple instinct given it by nature. To this I add, that it's necessary, that at least that part of the Air which is beneath the greater heights of mountains, should be transported and carried round by the roughness of the Earths surface; or that, as being mixt with many Vapours, and terrene Exhalations, it do naturally follow the diurnal motion, which occurreth not in the Air about the ship rowed by Oars: So that your arguing from the ship to the Tower hath not the force of an illation; because that stone which falls from the round top of the Mast, entereth into a *medium*, which is unconcern'd in the motion of the ship: but that which departeth from the top of the Tower, finds a *medium* that hath a motion in common with the whole Terrestrial Globe; so that without being hindred, rather being assisted by the motion of the air, it may follow the universal course of the Earth.

SIMPL. I cannot conceive that the air can imprint in a very great stone, or in a gross Globe of Wood or Ball of Lead, as suppose of two hundred weight, the motion wherewith its self is moved, and which it doth perhaps communicate to feathers, snow, and other very light things: nay, I see that a weight of that nature, being exposed to any the most impetuous wind, is not thereby removed an inch from its place; now consider with your self whether the air will carry it along therewith.

SALV. There is great difference between your experiment and our case. You introduce the wind blowing against that stone, supposed in a state of rest, and we expose to the air, which already moveth, the stone which doth also move with the same velocity; so that the air is not to conferr a new motion upon it, but onely to maintain, or to speak better, not to hinder the motion already acquired: you would drive the stone with a strange and preternatural motion, and we desire to conserve it in its natural. If you would produce a more pertinent experiment, you should say, that it is observed, if not with the eye of the forehead, yet with that of the mind, what would evene, if an eagle that is carried by the course of the wind, should let a stone fall from its talons; which, in regard that at its being let go, it went along with the wind, and after it was let fall it entered into a *medium* that moved with equal velocity, I am very confident that it would not be seen to descend in its fall perpendicularly, but that following the course of the wind, and adding thereto that of its particular gravity, it would move with a transverse motion.

SIMPL. But it would first be known how such an experiment may be made; and then one might judg according to the event. In the meantime the effect of the ship doth hitherto incline to favour our opinion.

SALV. Well said you *hitherto*, for perhaps it may anon change countenance. And that I may no longer hold you in suspense, tell me, *Simplicius*, do you really believe, that the Experiment of the ship squares so very well with our purpose, as that it ought to be believed, that that which we see happen in it, ought also to evene in the Terrestrial Globe?

SIMPL. As yet I am of that opinion; and though you have alledged some small disparities, I do not think them of so great moment, as that they should make me change my judgment.

SALV. I rather desire that you would continue therein, and hold for certain, that the effect of the Earth would exactly answer that of the ship: provided, that when it shall appear prejudicial to your cause, you would not be humorous and alter your thoughts. You may haply say, Forasmuch as when the ship stands still, the stone falls at the foot of the Mast, and when she is under sail, it lights far from thence, that therefore by conversion, from the stones falling at the foot is argued the ships standing still, and from its falling far from thence is argued her moving; and because that which occurreth to the ship, ought likewise to befall the Earth: that therefore from the falling of the stone at the foot of the Tower is necessarily inferred the immobility of the Terrestrial Globe. Is not this your argumentation?

SIMPL. It is; and reduced into that conciseness, as that it is become most easie to be apprehended.

SALV. Now tell me; if the stone let fall from the Roundtop, when the ship is in a swift course, should fall exactly in the same place of the ship, in which it falleth when the ship is at anchor, what service would these experiments do you, in order to the ascertaining whether the vessel doth stand still or move?

SIMPL. Just none: Like as, for exemple, from the beating of the pulse one cannot know whether a person be asleep or awake, seeing that the pulse beateth after the same manner in sleeping as in waking.

SALV. Very well. Have you ever tryed the experiment of the ship?

SIMPL. I have not; but yet I believe that those Authors which alledg the same, have accurately observed it; besides that the cause of the disparity is so manifestly known, that it admits of no question.

SALV. That it is possible that those Authors instance in it, without having made tryal of it, you your self are a good testimony, that without having examined it, alledg it as certain, and in a credulous way remit it to their authority; as it is now not onely possible, but very probable that they likewise did; I mean, did remit the same to their Predecessors, without ever arriving at one that had made the experiment: for whoever shall examine the same, shall find the event succeed quite contrary to what hath been written of it: that is, he shall see the stone fall at all times in the same place of the Ship, whether it stand still, or move with any whatsoever velocity. So that the same holding true in the Earth, as in the Ship, one cannot from the stones falling perpendicularly at the foot of the Tower, conclude any thing touching the motion or rest of the Earth.

SIMPL. If you should refer me to any other means than to experience, I verily believe our Disputations would not come to an end in haste; for this seemeth to me a thing so remote from all humane reason, as that it leaveth not the least place for credulity or probability.

SALV. And yet it hath left place in me for both.

SIMPL. How is this? You have not made an hundred, no nor one proof thereof, and do you so confidently affirm it for true?

I for my part will return to my incredulity, and to the confidence I had that the Experiment hath been tried by the principal Authors who made use thereof, and that the event succeeded as they affirm.

SALV. I am assured that the effect will ensue as I tell you; for so it is necessary that it should: and I farther add, that you know your self that it cannot fall out otherwise, however you feign or seem to feign that you know it not. Yet I am so good at taming of wits, that I will make you confess the same whether you will or no. But *Sagredus* stands very mute, and yet, if I mistake not, I saw him make an offer to speak somewhat.

SAGR. I had an intent to say something, but to tell you true, I know not what it was; for the curiosity that you have moved in me, by promising that you would force *Simplicius* to discover the knowledg which he would conceal from us, hath made me to depose all other thoughts: therefore I pray you to make good your vaunt.

SALV. Provided that *Simplicius* do consent to reply to what I shall ask him, I will not fail to do it.

SIMPL. I will answer what I know, assured that I shall not be much put to it, for that of those things which I hold to be false, I think nothing can be known, in regard that Science respecteth truths and not falshoods.

SALV. I desire not that you should say or reply, that you know any thing, save that which you most assuredly know. Therefore tell me; If you had here a flat superficies as polite as a Lookingglass, and of a substance as hard as steel, and that it were not paralel to the Horizon, but somewhat inclining, and that upon it you did put a Ball perfectly spherical, and of a substance grave and hard, as suppose of brass; what think you it would do being let go? do not you believe (as for my part I do) that it would lie still?

SIMPL. If that superficies were inclining?

SALV. Yes; for so I have already supposed.

SIMPL. I cannot conceive how it should lie still: nay, I am confident that it would move towards the declivity with much propensness.

SALV. Take good heed what you say, *Simplicius*, for I am confident that it would lie still in what ever place you should lay it.

SIMPL. So long as you make use of such suppositions, *Salviatus*, I shall cease to wonder if you inferr most absurd conclusions.

SALV. Are you assured, then, that it would freely move towards the declivity?

SIMPL. Who doubts it?

SALV. And this you verily believe, not because I told you so, (for I endeavoured to perswade you to think the contrary) but of your self, and upon your natural judgment.

SIMPL. Now I see what you would be at; you spoke not this as really believing the same; but to try me, and to wrest matter out of my own mouth wherewith to condemn me.

SALV. You are in the right. And how long would that Ball move, and with what velocity? But take notice that I instanced in a Ball exactly round, and a plain exquisitely polished, that all external and accidental impediments might be taken away. And so would I have you remove all obstructions caused by the Airs resistance to division, and all other casual obstacles, if any other there can be.

SIMPL. I very well understand your meaning, and as to your demand, I answer, that the Ball would continue to move *in infinitum*, if the inclination of the plain should so long last, and continually with an accelerating motion; for such is the nature of ponderous moveables, that *vires acquirant eundo*: and the greater the declivity was, the greater the velocity would be.

SALV. But if one should require that that Ball should move upwards on that same superficies, do you believe that it would so do?

SIMPL. Not spontaneously; but being drawn, or violently thrown, it may.

SALV. And in case it were thrust forward by the impression of some violent *impetus* from without, what and how great would its motion be?

SIMPL. The motion would go continually decreasing and retarding, as being contrary to nature; and would be longer or shorter, according to the greater or less impulse, and according to the greater or less acclivity.

SALV. It seems, then, that hitherto you have explained to me the accidents of a moveable upon two different Planes; and that in the inclining plane, the grave moveable doth spontaneously descend, and goeth continually accelerating, and that to retain it in rest, force must be used therein: but that on the ascending plane, there is required a force to thrust it forward, and also to stay it in rest, and that the motion impressed goeth continually diminishing, till that in the end it cometh to nothing. You say yet farther, that in both the one and the other case, there do arise differences from the planes having a greater or less declivity or acclivity; so that the greater inclination is attended with the greater velocity; and contrariwise, upon the ascending plane, the same moveable thrown with the same force, moveth a greater distance, by how much the elevation is less. Now tell me, what would befall the same moveable upon a superficies that had neither acclivity nor declivity?

SIMPL. Here you must give me a little time to consider of an answer. There being no declivity, there can be no natural inclination to motion: and there being no acclivity, there can be no resistance to being moved; so that there would arise an indifference between propension and resistance of motion; therefore, methinks it ought naturally to stand still. But I had forgot my self: it was but even now that *Sagredus* gave me to understand that it would so do.

SALV. So I think, provided one did lay it down gently: but if it had an *impetus* given it towards any part, what would follow?

SIMP. There would follow, that it should move towards that part.

SALV. But with what kind of motion? with the continually accelerated, as in declining planes; or with the successively retarded, as in those ascending.

SIMP. I cannot tell how to discover any cause of acceleration, or retardation, there being no declivity or acclivity.

SALV. Well: but if there be no cause of retardation, much less ought there to be any cause of rest. How long therefore would you have the moveable to move?

SIMP. As long as that superficies, neither inclined nor declined shall last.

SALV. Therefore if such a space were interminate, the motion upon the same would likewise have no termination, that is, would be perpetual.

SIMP. I think so, if so be the moveable be of a matter durable.

SALV. That hath been already supposed, when it was said, that all external and accidental impediments were removed, and the brittlenesse of the moveable in this our case, is one of those impediments accidental. Tell me now, what do you think is the cause that that same Ball moveth spontaneously upon the inclining plane, and not without violence upon the erected?

SIMP. Because the inclination of grave bodies is to move towards the centre of the Earth, and onely by violence upwards towards the circumference; and the inclining superficies is that which acquireth vicinity to the centre, and the ascending one, remotenesse.

SALV. Therefore a superficies, which should be neither declining nor ascending, ought in all its parts to be equally distant from the centre. But is there any such superficies in the World?

SIMP. There is no want thereof: Such is our Terrestrial Globe, if it were more even, and not as it is rough and montainous; but you have that of the Water, at such time as it is calm and still.

SALV. Then a ship which moveth in a calm at Sea, is one of those moveables, which run along one of those superficies that are neither declining nor ascending, and therefore disposed, in case all obstacles external and accidental were removed, to move with the impulse once imparted incessantly and uniformly.

SIMPL. It should seem to be so.

SALV. And that stone which is on the round top, doth not it move, as being together with the ship carried about by the circumference of a Circle about the Centre; and therefore consequently by a motion in it indelible, if all extern obstacles be removed? And is not this motion as swift as that of the ship.

SIMPL. Hitherto all is well. But what followeth?

SALV. Then in good time recant, I pray you, that your last conclusion, if you are satisfied with the truth of all the premises.

SIMPL. By my last conclusion, you mean, That that same stone moving with a motion indelibly impressed upon it, is not to leave, nay rather is to follow the ship, and in the end to light in the self same place, where it falleth when the ship lyeth still; and so I also grant it would do, in case there were no outward impediments that might disturb the stones motion, after its being let go, the which impediments are two, the one is the moveables inability to break through the air with its meer *impetus* onely, it being deprived of that of the strength of Oars, of which it had been partaker, as part of the ship, at the time that it was upon the Mast; the other is the new motion of descent, which also must needs be an hinderance of that other progressive motion.

SALV. As to the impediment of the Air, I do not deny it you; and if the thing falling were a light matter, as a feather, or a lock of wool, the retardation would be very great, but in an heavy stone is very exceeding small. And you your self but even now did say, that the force of the most impetuous wind sufficeth not to stir a great stone from its place; now do but consider what the calmer air is able to do, being encountred by a stone no more swift than the whole ship. Neverthelesse, as I said before, I do allow you this small effect, that may depend upon such an impediment; like as I know, that you will grant to me, that if the air should move with the same velocity that the ship and stone hath, then the impediment would be nothing at all. As to the other of the additional motion downwards; in the first place it is manifest, that these two, I mean the circular, about the centre, and the streight, towards the centre, are not contraries, or destructive to one another, or incompatible. Because that as to the moveable, it hath no repugnance at all to such motions, for you your self have already confest the repugnance to be against the motion which removeth from the centre, and the inclination to be towards the motion which approacheth to the centre. Whence it doth of necessity follow, that the moveable hath neither repugnance, nor propension to the motion which neither approacheth, nor goeth from the centre, nor consequently is there any cause for the diminishing in it the faculty impressed. And forasmuch as the moving cause is not one alone, which it hath attained by the new operation of retardation; but that they are two, distinct from each other, of which, the gravity attends only to the drawing of the moveable towards the centre, and the vertue impress't to the conducting it about the centre, there remaineth no occasion of impediment.

*   *   *   *   *

SALV. See how far the winged wit of *Sagredus* anticipateth, and out-goeth the dulness of mine; which perhaps would have light upon these disparities, but not without long studie. Now turning to the matter in hand, there do remain to be considered by us the shots at point blank, towards the East and towards the West; the first of which, if the Earth did move, would always happen to be too high above the mark, and the second too low; forasmuch as the parts of the Earth Eastward, by reason of the diurnal motion, do continually descend beneath the tangent paralel to the Horizon, whereupon the Eastern stars to us appear to ascend; and on the contrary, the parts Westward do more and more ascend, whereupon the Western stars do in our seeming descend: and therefore the ranges which are leveled according to the said tangent at the Oriental mark, (which whilst the ball passeth along by the tangent descendeth) should prove too high, and the Occidental too low by means of the elevation of the mark, whilst the ball pas-

seth along the tangent. The answer is like to the rest: for as
the Eastern mark goeth continually descending, by reason of the
Earths motion, under a tangent that continueth immoveable; so
likewise the piece for the same reason goeth continually inclining, and with its mounture pursuing the said mark: by which
means the shot proveth true.

But here I think it a convenient opportunity to give notice
of certain concessions, which are granted perhaps over liberally
by the followers of *Copernicus* unto their Adversaries: I mean of
yielding to them certain experiments for sure and certain, which
yet the Adversaries themselves had never made tryal of: as for
example, that of things falling from the round-top of a ship
whilst it is in motion, and many others; amongst which I verily
believe, that this of experimenting whether the shot made by a
Canon towards the East proveth too high, and the Western shot too
low, is one: and because I believe that they have never made
tryal thereof, I desire that they would tell me what difference
they think ought to happen between the said shots, supposing the
Earth moveable, or supposing it moveable; and let *Simplicius* for
this time answer for them.

SIMP. I will not undertake to answer so confidently as
another more intelligent perhaps might do; but shall speak what
thus upon the sudden I think they would reply; which is in effect
the same with that which hath been said already, namely, that in
case the Earth should move, the shots made Eastward would prove
too high, &c. the ball, as it is probable, being to move along
the tangent.

SALV. But if I should say, that so it falleth out upon
triall, how would you censure me?

SIMP. It is necessary to proceed to experiments for the
proving of it.

SALV. But do you think, that there is to be found a Gunner
so skilful, as to hit the mark at every shoot, in a distance of
v.g. five hundred paces?

SIMP. No Sir; nay I believe that there is no one, how good
a marks-man soever that would promise to come within a pace of
the mark,

SALV. How can we then, with shots so uncertain, assure our
selves of that which is in dispute?

SIMP. We may be assured thereof two wayes; one, by making
many shots; the other, because in respect of the great velocity
of the Earths motion, the deviation from the mark would in my
opinion be very great.

SALV. Very great, that is more than one pace; in regard
that the varying so much, yea and more, is granted to happen
ordinarily even in the Earths mobility.

SIMP. I verily believe the variation from the mark would be
more than so.

SALV. Now I desire that for our satisfaction we do make
thus in grosse a slight calculation, if you consent thereto,
which will stand us in stead likewise (if the computation succeed
as I expect) for a warning how we do in other occurrences suffer
our selves, as the saying is, to be taken with the enemies
shouts, and surrender up our belief to what ever first presents
it self to our fancy. And now to give all advantages to the

Peripateticks and *Tychonicks*, let us suppose our selves to be under the Equinoctial, there to shoot a piece of Ordinance point blank Eastwards at a mark five hundred paces off. First, let us see thus (as I said) in a level, what time the shot after it is gone out of the Piece taketh to arrive at the mark; which we know to be very little, and is certainly no more than that wherein a travailer walketh two steps, which also is less than the second of a minute of an hour; for supposing that the travailer walketh three miles in an hour, which are nine thousand paces, being that an hour containes three thousand, six hundred second minutes, the travailer walketh two steps and an half in a second, a second therefore is more than the time of the balls motion. And for that the diurnal revolution is twenty four hours, the Western horizon riseth fifteen degrees in an hour, that is, fifteen first minutes of a degree, in one first minute of an hour; that is, fifteen seconds of a degree, in one second of an hour; and because one second is the time of the shot, therefore in this time the Western horizon riseth fifteen seconds of a degree, and so much likewise the mark; and therefore fifteen seconds of that circle, whose semidiameter is five hundred paces (for so much the distance of the mark from the Piece was supposed.) Now let us look in the table of Arches and Chords (see here is *Copernicus* his book) what part is the chord of fifteen seconds of the semi-diameter, that is, five hundred paces. Here you see the chord (or subtense) of a first minute to be less than thirty of those parts, of which the semidiameter is an hundred thousand. There-fore the chord of a second minute shall be less then half of one of those parts, that is less than one of those parts, of which the semidiameter is two hundred thousand; and therefore the chord of fifteen conds shall be less than fifteen of those same two hundred thousand parts; but that which is less than (a) fif-teen parts of two hundred thousand, is also more than that which is four centesmes of five hundred; therefore the ascent of the mark in the time of the balls motion is lesse than four cen-tesmes, that is, than one twenty fifth part of a pace; it shall be therefore (b) about two inches: And so much consequently shall be the variation of each Western shot, the Earth being supposed to have a diurnal motion. Now if I shall tell you, that this variation (I mean of falling two inches short of what they would do in case the Earth did not move) upon triall doth happen in all shots, how will you convince me *Simplicius*, shewing me by an experiment that it is not so? Do you not see that it is impossible to confute me, unless you first find out a way to shoot at a mark with so much exactnesse, as never to misse an hairs bredth? For whilst the ranges of great shot consist of different numbers of paces, as *de facto* they do, I will affirm that in each of those variations there is contained that of two inches caused by the motion of the Earth.

    SAGR. Pardon me, *Salviatus*, you are too liberal. For I would tell the *Peripateticks*, that though every shot should hit the very centre of the mark, that should not in the least dis-prove the motion of the Earth. For the Gunners are so constantly imployed in levelling the sight and gun to the mark, as that they can hit the same, notwithstanding the motion of the Earth. And I say, that if the Earth should stand still, the shots would not prove true; but the Occidental would be too low, and the Oriental too high: now let *Simplicius* disprove me if he can.

SALV. This is a subtilty worthy of *Sagredus*: But whether this variation be to be observed in the motion, or in the rest of the Earth, it must needs be very small, it must needs be swallowed up in those very great ones which sundry accidents continually produce. And all this hath been spoken and granted on good grounds to *Simplicius*, and only with an intent to advertise him how much it importeth to be cautious in granting many experiments for true to those who never had tried them, but only eagerly alledged them just as they ought to be for the serving their purpose: This is spoken, I say, by way of surplussage and Corollary to *Simplicius*, for the real truth is, that as concerning these shots, the same ought exactly to befall aswell in the motion as in the rest of the Terrestrial Globe; as likewise it will happen in all the other experiments that either have been or can be produced, which have at first blush so much semblance of truth, as the antiquated opinion of the Earths motion hath of equivocation.

SAGR. As for my part I am fully satisfied, and very well understand that who so shall imprint in his fancy this general community of the diurnal conversion amongst all things Terrestrial, to all which it naturally agreeth, aswell as in the old conceit of its rest about the centre, shall doubtlesse discern the fallacy and equivoke which made the arguments produced seem concluding. There yet remains in me some haesitancy (as I have hinted before) touching the flight of birds; the which having as it were an animate faculty of moving at their pleasure with a thousand motions, and to stay long in the Air separated from the Earth, and therein with most irregular windings to go fluttering to and again, I cannot conceive how amongst so great a confusion of motions, they should be able to retain the first commune motion; and in what manner, having once made any stay behind, they can get it up again, and overtake the same with flying, and keep pace with the Towers and trees which hurry with so precipitant a course towards the East; I say so precipitant, for in the great circle of the Globe it is little lesse than a thousand miles an hour, whereof the flight of the swallow I believe makes not fifty.

SALV. If the birds were to keep pace with the course of the trees by help of their wings, they would of necessity flie very fast; and if they were deprived of the universal conversion, they would lag as far behind; and their flight would seem as furious towards the West, and to him that could discern the same, it would much exceed the flight of an arrow; but I think we could not be able to perceive it, no more than we see a Canon bullet, whil'st driven by the fury of the fire, it flieth through the Air: But the truth is that the proper motion of birds, I mean of their flight, hath nothing to do with the universal motion, to which it is neither an help, nor an hinderance; and that which maintaineth the said motion unaltered in the birds, is the Air it self, thorough which they flie, which naturally following the *Vertigo* of the Earth, like as it carrieth

the clouds along with it, so it transporteth birds and every
thing else which is pendent in the same; in so much that as to
the businesse of keeping pace with the Earth, the birds need take
no care thereof, but for that work might sleep perpetually.

SAGR. That the Air can carry the clouds along with it, as
being matters easie for their lightnesse to be moved and deprived
of all other contrary inclination, yea more, as being matters
that partake also of the conditions and properties of the Earth;
I comprehend without any difficulty;but that birds, which as
having life, may move with a motion quite contrary to the diurnal, once having surceased the said motion, the Air should
restore them to it, seems to me a little strange, and the rather
for that they are solid and weighty bodies; and withal, we see;
as hath been said, stones and other grave bodies to lie unmoved
against the *impetus* of the air; and when they suffer themselves
to be overcome thereby, they never acquire so much velocity as
the wind which carrieth them.

SALV. We ascribe not so little force, *Sagredus*, to the
moved Air, which is able to move and bear before it ships full
fraught, to tear up trees by the roots, and overthrow Towers
when it moveth swiftly; and yet we cannot say that the motion of
the Air in these violent operations is neer so violent, as that
of the diurnal revolution.

SIMP. You see then that the moved Air may also continue
the motion of projects, according to the Doctrine of *Aristotle*;
and it seemed to me very strange that he should have erred in
this particular.

SALV. It may without doubt, in case it could continue it
self, but lik as when the wind ceasing neither ships go on, nor
trees are blown down, so the motion in the Air not continuing
after the stone is gone out of the hand, and the Air ceasing to
move, it followeth that it must be something else besides the
Air that maketh the projects to move.

SIMP. But how upon the winds being laid, doth the ship
cease to move? Nay you may see that when the wind is down, and
the sails furl'd, the vessel continueth to run whole miles.

SALV. But this maketh against your self *Simplicius*, for
that the wind being laid that filling the sails drove on the
ship, yet neverthelesse doth it without help of the *medium* continue its course.

SIMP. It might be said that the water was the *medium* which
carried forward the ship, and maintain'd it in motion.

SALV. It might indeed be so affirmed, if you would speak
quite contrary to truth; for the truth is, that the water, by
reason of its great resistance to the division made by the hull
of the ship, doth with great noise resist the same; nor doth it
permit it of a great while to acquire that velocity which the
wind would confer upon it, were the obstacle of the water removed.
Perhaps *Simplicius* you have never considered with what fury the
water besets a bark, whil'st it forceth its way through a standing water by help of Oars or Sails: for if you had ever minded
that effect, you would not now have produced such an absurdity.
And I am thinking that you have hitherto been one of those who
to find out how such things succeed, and to come to the knowledg

of natural effects, do not betake themselves to a Ship, a Crosse-
bow, or a piece of Ordinance, but retire into their studies, and
turn over Indexes and Tables to see whether *Aristotle* hath spoken
any thing thereof, and being assured of the true sense of the
Text, neither desire nor care for knowing any more.

SAGR.   This is a great felicity, and they are to be much en-
vied for it.   For if knowledg be desired by all, and if to be
wise, be to think ones self so, they enjoy a very great happi-
nesse, for that they may perswade themselves that they know and
understand all things, in scorn of those who knowing, that they
understand not what these think they understand, and consequently
seeking that they know not the very least particle of what is
knowable, kill themselves with waking and studying, and consume
their days in experiments and observations.   But pray you let us
return to our birds; touching which you have said, that the Air
being moved with great velocity, might restore unto them that
part of the diurnal motion which amongst the windings of their
flight they might have lost; to which I reply, that the agitated
Air seemeth unable to confer on a solid and grave body, so great
a velocity as its own: And because that of the Air is as great
as that of the Earth, I cannot think that the Air is able to
make good the losse of the birds retardation in flight.

SALV.   Your discourse hath in it much of probability, and
to stick at trivial doubts is not for an acute wit; yet neverthelesse the probability being removed, I believed that it hath not
a jot more force than the others already considered and resolved.

SAGR.   It is most certain that if it be not necessarily
concludent, its efficacy must needs be just nothing at all, for
it is onely when the conclusion is necessary that the opponent
hath nothing to alledg on the contrary.

SALV.   Your making a greater scruple of this than of the
other instances dependeth, if I mistake not, upon the birds being
animated, and thereby enabled to use their strength at pleasure
against the primary motion in-bred in terrene bodies: like as
for example, we see them whil'st they are alive to fly upwards, a
thing altogether impossible for them to do as they are grave
bodies; whereas being dead they can onely fall downwards; and
therefore you hold that the reasons that are of force in all the
kinds of projects above named, cannot take place in birds: Now
this is very true; and because it is so, *Sagredus*, that doth not
appear to be done in those projects, which we see the birds to
do.   For if from the top of a Tower you let fall a dead bird and
a live one, the dead bird shall do the same that a stone doth,
that is, it shall first follow the general motion diurnal, and
then the motion of descent, as grave; but if the bird let fall,
be a live, what shall hinder it, (there ever remaining in it the
diurnal motion) from soaring by help of its wings to what place
of the Horizon it shall please? and this new motion, as being
peculiar to the bird, and not participated by us, must of necessity be visible to us; and if it be moved by help of its wings
towards the West, what shall hinder it from returning with a like
help of its wings unto the Tower.   And, because, in the last
place, the birds wending its flight towards the West was no other
than a withdrawing from the diurnal motion, (which hath, suppose

ten degrees of velocity) one degree onely, there did thereupon
remain to the bird whil'st. it was in its flight nine degrees of
velocity, and so soon as it did alight upon the Earth, the ten
common degrees returned to it, to which, by flying towards the
East it might adde one, and with those eleven overtake the Tower.
And in short, if we well consider, and more narrowly examine the
effects of the flight of birds, they differ from the projects
shot or thrown to any part of the World in nothing, save onely
that the projects are moved by an external projicient, and the
birds by an internal principle. And here for a final proof of
the nullity of all the experiments before alledged, I conceive
it now a time and place convenient to demonstrate a way how to
make an exact trial of them all. Shut your self up with some
friend in the grand Cabbin between the decks of some large ship,
and there procure gnats, flies, and such other small winged
creatures: get also a great tub (or other vessel) full of water,
and within it put certain fishes; let also a certain bottle be
hung up, which drop by drop letteth forth its water into another
bottle placed underneath, having a narrow neck: and, the Ship
lying still, observe diligently how those small winged animals
fly with like velocity towards all parts of the Cabin; how the
fishes swim indifferently towards all sides; and how the distil-
ling drops all fall into the bottle placed underneath. And
casting any thing towards your friend, you need not throw it with
more force one way then another, provided the distances be equal:
and leaping, as the saying is, with your feet closed, you will
reach as far one way as another. Having observed all these
particulars, though no man doubteth that so long as the vessel
stands still, they ought to succeed in this manner; make the Ship
to move with what velocity you please; for (so long as the motion
is uniforme, and not fluctuating this way and that way) you shall
not discern any the least alteration in all the forenamed effects;
nor can you gather by any of them whether the Ship doth move or
stand still. In leaping you shall reach as far upon the floor,
as before; nor for that the Ship moveth shall you make a greater
leap towards the poop than towards the prow; howbeit in the time
that you staid in the Air, the floor under your feet shall have
run the contrary way to that of your jump; and throwing any thing
to your companion you shall not need to cast it with more
strength that it may reach him, if he shall be towards the prow,
and you towards the poop, then if you stood in a contrary situation; the drops shall all distill as before into the inferiour
bottle and not so much as one shall fall towards the poop, albeit
whil'st the drop is in the Air, the Ship shall have run many
feet; the Fishes in their water shall not swim with more trouble
towards the fore-part, than towards the hinder part of the tub;
but shall with equal velocity make to the bait placed on any side
of the tub; and lastly, the flies and gnats shall continue their
flight indifferently towards all parts: nor shall they ever happen to be driven together towards the side of the Cabbin next the
prow, as if they were wearied with following the swift course of
the Ship, from which through their suspension in the Air, they
had been long separated; and if burning a few graines of incense
you make a little smoke, you shall see it ascend on high, and

there in manner of a cloud suspend itself, and move indifferently, not inclining more to one side than another: and of this correspondence of effects the cause is for that the Ships motion is common to all the things contained in it, and to the Air also; I mean if those things be shut up in the Cabbin: but in case those things were above deck in the open Air, and not obliged to follow the course of the Ship, differences more or lesse notable would be observed in some of the fore-named effects, and there is no doubt but that the smoke would stay behind as much as the Air itself; the flies also, and the gnats being hindered by the Air would not be able to follow the motion of the Ship, if they were separated at any distance from it. But keeping neer thereto, because the Ship itself as being an unfractuous Fabrick, carrieth along with it part of its neerest Air, they would follow the said Ship without any pains or difficulty. And for the like reason we see sometimes in riding post, that the troublesome flies and hornets do follow the horses flying sometimes to one, sometimes to another part of the body, but in the falling drops the difference would be very small; and in the salts, and projections of grave bodies altogether imperceptible.

SAGR. Though it came not into my thoughts to make triall of these observations, when I was at Sea, yet am I confident that they will succeed in the same manner, as you have related; in confirmation of which I remember that being in my Cabbin I have asked an hundred times whether the Ship moved or stood still; and sometimes I have imagined that it moved one way, when it steered quite another way. I am therefore as hitherto satisfied and convinced of the nullity of all those experiments that have been produced in proof of the negative part. There now remains the objection founded upon that which experience shews us, namely, that a swift *Vertigo* or whirling about hath a faculty to extrude and disperse the matters adherent to the machine that turns round; whereupon many were of opinion, and *Ptolomy* amongst the rest, that if the Earth should turn round with so great velocity, the stones and creatures upon it should be tost into the Skie, and that there could not be a morter strong enough to fasten buildings so to their foundations, but that they would likewise suffer a like extrusion.

SALV. Before I come to answer this objection, I cannot but take notice of that which I have an hundred times observed, and not without laughter, to come into the minds of most men so soon as ever they hear mention made of this motion of the Earth, which is believed by them so fixt and immoveable, that they not only never doubted of that rest, but have ever strongly believed that all other men as well as they, have held it to be created immoveable, and so to have continued through all succeeding ages: and being setled in this perswasion, they stand amazed to hear that any one should grant it motion, as if, after that he had held it to be immoveable, he had fondly thought it to commence its motion then (and not till then) when *Pythagoras* (or whoever else was the first hinter of its mobility) said that it did move. Now that such a foolish conceit (I mean of thinking that those who admit the motion of the Earth, have first thought it to stand still from its creation, untill the time of *Pythagoras*, and have

onely made it moveable after that *Pythagoras* esteemed it so)
findeth a place in the mindes of the vulgar, and men of shallow
capacities, I do not much wonder; but that such persons as
Aristotle and *Ptolomy* should also run into this childish mistake, is to my thinking a more admirable and unpardonable
folly.

       *   *   *   *   *

    SALV. You might very well so conclude, *Simplicius*, if we
had nothing else to say in behalf of *Copernicus*: but we have
many things to alledge that yet have not been mentioned; and as
to that your reply, nothing hindereth, but that we may suppose
the distance of the fixed Stars to be yet much greater than
that which hath been allowed them, and you your self, and whoever
else will not derogate from the propositions admitted by
Ptolomy's sectators, must needs grant it as a thing most requisite to suppose the Starry sphere to be very much bigger yet
than that which even now we said it ought to be esteemed.
For all Astronomers agreeing in this, that the cause of the
greater tardity of the Revolutions of the Planets is, the majority of their Spheres, and that therefore *Saturn* is more slow
than *Jupiter*, and *Jupiter* than the Sun, for that the first is to
describe a greater circle than the second, and that than this
later, &c. considering that *Saturn v.g.* the altitude of whose
Orb is nine times higher than that of the Sun, and that for
that cause the time of one Revolution of *Saturn*, is thirty times
longer than that of a conversion of the Sun, in regard that according to the Doctrine of *Ptolomy*, one conversion of the
starry Sphere is finished in 36000. years, whereas that of
Saturn is consummate in thirty, and that of the Sun in one,
arguing with a like proportion, and saying, if the Orb of
Saturn, by reason it is nine times bigger than that of the Sun,
revolves in a time thirty times longer, by conversion, how great
ought that Orb to be, which revolves 36000. times more slowly?
it shall be found that the distance of the starry Sphere ought
to be 10800 semidiameters of the grand Orb, which should be full
five times bigger than that, which even now we computed it to be,
in case that a fixed Star of the sixth magnitude were equal to
the Sun. Now see how much lesser yet, upon this account, the
variation occasioned in the said Stars, by the annual motion of
the Earth, ought to appear. And if at the same rate we would
argue the distance of the starry Sphere from *Jupiter*, and from
Mars, that would give it us to be 15000. and this 27000 semidiameters of the grand Orb, to wit, the first seven, and the second
twelve times bigger than what the magnitude of the fixed Star,
supposed equal to the Sun, did make it.

SIMP. Methinks that to this might be answered, that the motion of the starry Sphere hath, since *Ptolomy*, been observed not to be so slow as he accounted it; yea, if I mistake not, I have heard that *Copernicus* himself made the Observation.

SALV. You say very well; but you alledge nothing in that which may favour the cause of the *Ptolomæans* in the least, who did never yet reject the motion of 36000 years in the starry Sphere, for that the said tardity would make it too vast and immense. For if that the said immensity was not to be supposed in Nature, they ought before now to have denied a conversion so slow as that it could not with good proportion adapt it self, save onely to a Sphere of monstrous magnitude.

SAGR. Pray you, *Salviatus*, let us lose no more time in proceeding, by the way of these proportions with people that are apt to admit things most dis-proportionate; so that its impossible to win any thing upon them this way: and what more disproportionate proportion can be imagined than that which these men swallow down, and admit, in that writing, that there cannot be a more convenient way to dispose the Cœlestial Spheres, in order, than to regulate them by the differences of the times of their periods, placing from one degree to another the more slow above the more swift, when they have constituted the Starry Sphere higher than the rest, as being the slowest, they frame another higher still than that, and consequently greater, and make it revolve in twenty four hours, whilst the next below, it moves not round under 36000. years?

SALV. I could wish, *Simplicius*, that suspending for a time the affection that you bear to the followers of your opinion, you would sincerely tell me, whether you think that they do in their minds comprehend that magnitude, which they reject afterwards as uncapable for its immensity to be ascribed to the Universe. For I, as to my own part, think that they do not; But believe, that like as in the apprehension of numbers, when once a man begins to passe those millions of millions, the imagination is confounded, and can no longer form a conceipt of the same, so it happens also in comprehending immense magnitudes and distances; so that there intervenes to the comprehension an effect like to that which befalleth the sense; For whilest that in a serene night I look towards the Stars, I judge, according to sense, that their distance is but a few miles, and that the fixed Stars are not a jot more remote than *Jupiter* or *Saturn*, nay than the Moon. But without more ado, consider the controversies that have past between the Astronomers and Peripatetick Philosophers, upon occasion of the New Stars of *Cassiopeia* and of *Sagittary*, the Astronomers placing them amongst the fixed Stars, and the Philosophers believing them to be below the Moon. So unable is our sense to distinguish great distances from the greatest, though these be in reality many thousand times greater than those. In a word, I ask of thee, O foolish man! Doth thy imagination comprehend that vast magnitude of the Universe, which thou afterwards judg-

estto be too immense? If thou comprehendest it; wilt thou hold
that thy apprehension extendeth it self farther than the Divine
Power? wilt thou say, that thou canst imagine greater things than
those which God can bring to passe? But if thou apprehendest it not,
why wilt thou passe thy verdict upon things beyond thy comprehension?

SIMP. All this is very well, nor can it be denied, but that
Heaven may in greatnesse surpasse our imagination, as also that
God might have created it thousands of times vaster than now it
is; but we ought not to grant any thing to have been made in
vain, and to be idle in the Universe. Now, in that we see this
admirable order of the Planets, disposed about the Earth in distances proportionate for producing their effects for our advantage, to what purpose is it to interpose afterwards between the
sublime Orb of *Saturn* and the starry Sphere, a vast vacancy,
without any star that is superfluous, and to no purpose? To what
end? For whose profit and advantage?

SALV. Methinks we arrogate too much to our selves, *Simplicius*, whilst we will have it, that the onely care of us, is the
adequate work, and bound, beyond which the Divine Wisdome and
Power doth, or disposeth of nothing. But I will not consent,
that we should so much shorten its hand, but desire that we may
content ourselves with an assurance that God and Nature are so
imployed in the governing of humane affairs, that they could not
more apply themselves thereto, although they had no other care
than onely that of mankind; and this, I think, I am able to make
out by a most pertinent and most noble example, taken from the
operation of the Suns light, which whilest it attracteth these
vapours, or scorcheth that plant, it attracteth, it scorcheth
them, as if it had no more to do; yea, in ripening that bunch of
grapes, nay that one single grape, it doth apply it self so, that
it could not be more intense if the sum of all its business had
been the only maturation of that grape. Now if this grape
receiveth all that it is possible for it to receive from the Sun,
not suffering the least injury by the Suns production of a thous-
and other effects at the same time; it would be either envy or
folly to blame that grape, if it should think or wish that the
Sun would onely appropriate its rayes to its advantage. I am
confident that nothing is omitted by the Divine Providence, of
what concernes the government of humane affairs; but that there
may not be other things in the Universe, that depend upon the
same infinite Wisdome, I cannot, of my self, by what my reason
holds forth to me, bring my self to believe. However, if it were
not so, yet should I not forbear to believe the reasons laid
before me by some more sublime intelligence. In the mean time,
if one should tell me, that an immense space interposed between
the Orbs of the Planets and the Starry Sphere, deprived of stars
and idle, would be vain and uselesse, as likewise that so great
an immensity for receipt of the fixed stars, as exceeds our utmost comprehension would be superfluous, I would reply, that it
is rashnesse to go about to make our shallow reason judg of the
Works of God, and to call vain and superfluous, whatsoever thing
in the Universe is not subservient to us.

SAGR. Say rather, and I believe you would say better, that

we know not what is subservient to us; and I hold it one of the
greatest vanities, yea follies, that can be in the World, to say,
because I know not of what use *Jupiter* or *Saturn* are to me, that
therefore these Planets are superfluous, yea more, that there
are no such things *in rerum natura*; when as, oh foolish man! I
know not so much as to what purpose the arteries, the gristles,
the spleen, the gall do serve; nay I should not know that I have
a gall, spleen, or kidneys, if in many desected Corps, they were
not shewn unto me; and then onely shall I be able to know what
the spleen worketh in me, when it comes to be taken from me.   To
be able to know what this or that Cœlestial body worketh in me
(seeing you will have it that all their influences direct themselves to us) it would be requisite to remove that body for some
time; and then whatsoever effect I should find wanting in me, I
would say that it depended on that star.   Moreover, who will
presume to say that the space which they call too vast and uselesse between *Saturn* and the fixed stars, is void of other mundane bodies?   Must it be so, because we do not see them?   Then
the four Medicean Planets, and the companions of *Saturn* came
first into Heaven, when we began to see them, and not before?
And by this rule the innumerable other fixed stars had no
existence before that men did look on them? and the cloudy con-
stellations called *Nebulosæ* were at first only white flakes, but
afterwards with the Telescope we made them to become constella-
tions of many lucid and bright stars.   Oh presumptious, rather
oh rash ignorance of man!

d. Galileo Galilei, *Dialogues Concerning Two New Sciences**

THIRD DAY

Change of Position. [*De Motu Locali*]

My purpose is to set forth a very new science dealing with a very ancient subject. There is, in nature, perhaps nothing older than motion, concerning which the books written by philosophers are neither few nor small; nevertheless I have discovered by experiment some properties of it which are worth knowing and which have not hitherto been either observed or demonstrated. Some superficial observations have been made, as, for instance, that the free motion [*naturalem motum*] of a heavy falling body is continuously accelerated; but to just what extent this acceleration occurs has not yet been announced; for so far as I know, no one has yet pointed out that the distances traversed, during equal intervals of time, by a body falling from rest, stand to one another in the same ratio as the odd numbers beginning with unity.

It has been observed that missiles and projectiles describe a curved path of some sort; however no one has pointed out the fact that this path is a parabola. But this and other facts, not few in number or less worth knowing, I have succeeded in proving; and what I consider more important, there have been opened up to this vast and most excellent science, of which my work is merely the beginning, ways and means by which other minds more acute than mine will explore its remote corners.

This discussion is divided into three parts; the first part deals with motion which is steady or uniform; the second treats of motion as we find it accelerated in nature; the third deals with the so-called violent motions and with projectiles.

Uniform Motion

In dealing with steady or uniform motion, we need a single definition which I give as follows:

Definition

By steady or uniform motion, I mean one in which the distances traversed by the moving particle during any equal intervals of time, are themselves equal.

Caution

We must add to the old definition (which defined steady motion simply as one in which equal distances are traversed in equal times) the word "any," meaning by this, all equal intervals

---

*Galileo Galilei, *Dialogues Concerning Two New Sciences*, Translated by Henry Crew and Alfonso de Salvio, Dover Publications, N.Y., n.d. Original copyright, Macmillan, 1914. Pp. 153-5; 160-5; 167-70; 173-6; 178-9; 244-6; 248-50.

of time; for it may happen that the moving body will traverse
equal distances during some equal intervals of time and yet the
distances traversed during some small portion of these time-
intervals may not be equal, even though the time-intervals be
equal.

From the above definition, four axioms follow, namely:

Axiom I

In the case of one and the same uniform motion, the distance
traversed during a longer interval of time is greater than the
distance traversed during a shorter interval of time.

Axiom II

In the case of one and the same uniform motion, the time
required to traverse a greater distance is longer than the time
required for a less distance.

Axiom III

In one and the same interval of time, the distance traversed
at a greater speed is larger than the distance traversed at a
less speed.

Axiom IV

The speed required to traverse a longer distance is greater
than that required to traverse a shorter distance during the
same time-interval.

*　　　　*　　　　*　　　　*　　　　*

Naturally Accelerated Motion

The properties belonging to uniform motion have been discussed in the preceding section; but accelerated motion remains
to be considered.

And first of all it seems desirable to find and explain a
definition best fitting natural phenomena. For anyone may
invent an arbitrary type of motion and discuss its properties;
thus, for instance, some have imagined helices and conchoids as
described by certain motions which are not met with in nature,
and have very commendably established the properties which these
curves possess in virtue of their definitions; but we have
decided to consider the phenomena of bodies falling with an
acceleration such as actually occurs in nature and to make this
definition of accelerated motion exhibit the essential features
of observed accelerated motions. And this, at last, after
repeated efforts we trust we have succeeded in doing. In this
belief we are confirmed mainly by the consideration that experimental results are seen to agree with and exactly correspond
with those properties which have been, one after another, demonstrated by us. Finally, in the investigation of naturally
accelerated motion we were led, by hand as it were, in following
the habit and custom nature herself, in all her various other

processes, to employ only those means which are most common, simple and easy.

For I think no one believes that swimming or flying can be accomplished in a manner simpler or easier than that instinctively employed by fishes and birds.

When, therefore, I observe a stone initially at rest falling from an elevated position and continually acquiring new increments of speed, why should I not believe that such increases take place in a manner which is exceedingly simple and rather obvious to everybody? If now we examine the matter carefully we find no addition or increment more simple than that which repeats itself always in the same manner. This we readily understand when we consider the intimate relationship between time and motion; for just as uniformity of motion is defined by and conceived through equal times and equal spaces (thus we call a motion uniform when equal distances are traversed during equal time-intervals), so also we may, in a similar manner, through equal time-intervals, conceive additions of speed as taking place without complication; thus we may picture to our mind a motion as uniformly and continuously accelerated when, during any equal intervals of time whatever, equal increments of speed are given to it. Thus if any equal intervals of time whatever have elapsed, counting from the time at which the moving body left its position of rest and began to descend, the amount of speed acquired during the first two time-intervals will be double that acquired during the first time-interval alone; so the amount added during three of these time-intervals will be treble; and that in four, quadruple that of the first time-interval. To put the matter more clearly, if a body were to continue its motion with the same speed which it had acquired during the first time-interval and were to retain this same uniform speed, then its motion would be twice as slow as that which it would have if its velocity had been acquired during *two* time-intervals.

And thus, it seems, we shall not be far wrong if we put the increment of speed as proportional to the increment of time; hence the definition of motion which we are about to discuss may be stated as follows: A motion is said to be uniformly accelerated, when starting from rest, it acquires, during equal time-intervals, equal increments of speed.

SAGR. Although I can offer no rational objection to this or indeed to any other definition, devised by any author whomsoever, since all definitions are arbitrary, I may nevertheless without offense be allowed to doubt whether such a definition as the above, established in an abstract manner, corresponds to and describes that kind of accelerated motion which we meet in nature in the case of freely falling bodies. And since the Author apparently maintains that the motion described in his definition is that of freely falling bodies, I would like to clear my mind of certain difficulties in order that I may later apply myself more earnestly to the propositions and their demonstrations.

SALV. It is well that you and Simplicio raise these difficulties. They are, I imagine, the same which occurred to me

when I first saw this treatise, and which were removed either by
discussion with the Author himself, or by turning the matter
over in my own mind.

SAGR. When I think of a heavy body falling from rest, that
is, starting with zero speed and gaining speed in proportion to
the time from the beginning of the motion; such a motion as
would, for instance, in eight beats of the pulse acquire eight
degrees of speed; having at the end of the fourth beat acquired
four degrees; at the end of the second, two; at the end of the
first, one; and since time is divisible without limit, it follows from all these considerations that if the earlier speed of
a body is less than its present speed in a constant ratio, then
there is no degree of speed however small (or, one may say, no
degree of slowness however great) with which we may not find
this body travelling after starting from infinite slowness, i.e.,
from rest. So that if that speed which it had at the end of the
fourth beat was such that, if kept uniform, the body would traverse two miles in an hour, and if keeping the speed which it had
at the end of the second beat, it would traverse one mile an
hour, we must infer that, as the instant of starting is more and
more nearly approached, the body moves so slowly that, if it
kept on moving at this rate, it would not traverse a mile in an
hour, or in a day, or in a year or in a thousand years; indeed,
it would not traverse a span in an even greater time; a phenomenon which baffles the imagination, while our senses show us
that a heavy falling body suddenly acquires great speed.

SALV. This is one of the difficulties which I also at the
beginning, experienced, but which I shortly afterwards removed,
and the removal was effected by the very experiment which creates the difficulty for you. You say the experiment appears to
show that immediately after a heavy body starts from rest it
acquires a very considerable speed: and I say that the same
experiment makes clear the fact that the initial motions of a
falling body, no matter how heavy, are very slow and gentle.
Place a heavy body upon a yielding material, and leave it there
without any pressure except that owing to its own weight; it is
clear that if one lifts this body a cubit or two and allows it
to fall upon the same material, it will, with this impulse,
exert a new and greater pressure than that caused by its mere
weight; and this effect is brought about by the [weight of the]
falling body together with the velocity acquired during the fall,
an effect which will be greater and greater according to the
height of the fall, that is according as the velocity of the
falling body becomes greater. From the quality and intensity
of the blow we are thus enabled to accurately estimate the speed
of a falling body. But tell me, gentlemen, is it not true that
if a block be allowed to fall upon a stake from a height of four
cubits and drives it into the earth, say, four finger-breadths,
that coming from a height of two cubits it will drive the stake
a much less distance, and from the height of one cubit a still
less distance; and finally if the block be lifted only one
finger-breadth how much more will it accomplish than if merely
laid on top of the stake without percussion? Certainly very
little. If it be lifted only the thickness of a leaf, the

effect will be altogether imperceptible. And since the effect
of the blow depends upon the velocity of this striking body,
can any one doubt the motion is very slow and the speed more
than small whenever the effect [of the blow] is imperceptible?
See now the power of truth; the same experiment which at first
glance seemed to show one thing, when more carefully examined,
assures us of the contrary.

But without depending upon the above experiment, which is
doubtless very conclusive, it seems to me that it ought not to
be difficult to establish such a fact by reasoning alone.
Imagine a heavy stone held in the air at rest; the support is
removed and the stone set free; then since it is heavier than
the air it begins to fall, and not with uniform motion but slowly at the beginning and with a continuously accelerated motion.
Now since velocity can be increased and diminished without
limit, what reason is there to believe that such a moving body
starting with infinite slowness, that is, from rest, immediately
acquires a speed of ten degrees rather than one of four, or of
two, or of one, or of a half, or of a hundredth; or, indeed, of
any of the infinite number of small values [of speed]? Pray
listen. I hardly think you will refuse to grant that the gain
of speed of the stone falling from rest follows the same sequence as the diminution and loss of this same speed when, by
some impelling force, the stone is thrown to its former elevation: but even if you do not grant this, I do not see how you
can doubt that the ascending stone, diminishing in speed, must
before coming to rest pass through every possible degree of
slowness.

SIMP. But if the number of degrees of greater and greater
slowness is limitless, they will never be all exhausted, therefore such an ascending heavy body will never reach rest, but
will continue to move without limit always at a slower rate; but
this is not the observed fact.

SALV. This would happen, Simplicio, if the moving body were
to maintain its speed for any length of time at each degree of
velocity; but it merely passes each point without delaying more
than an instant: and since each time-interval however small may
be divided into an infinite number of instants, these will always be sufficient [in number] to correspond to the infinite
degrees of diminished velocity.

*   *   *   *   *

SAGR. From these considerations it appears to me that we
may obtain a proper solution   of the problem discussed by philosophers, namely, what causes the acceleration in the natural motion of heavy bodies? Since, as it seems
to me, the force [*virtù*] impressed by the agent projecting the
body upwards diminishes continuously, this force, so long as it
was greater than the contrary force of gravitation, impelled the
body upwards; when the two are in equilibrium the body ceases to
rise and passes through the state of rest in which the impressed
impetus [*impeto*] is not destroyed, but only its excess over the
weight of the body has been consumed--the excess which caused

the body to rise. Then as the diminution of the outside impetus [*impeto*] continues, and gravitation gains the upper hand, the fall begins, but slowly at first on account of the opposing impetus [*virtù impressa*], a large portion of which still remains in the body; but as this continues to diminish it also continues to be more and more overcome by gravity, hence the continuous acceleration of motion.

*   *   *   *   *

SAGR. So far as I see at present, the definition might have been put a little more clearly perhaps without changing the fundamental idea, namely, uniformly accelerated motion is such that its speed increases in proportion to the space traversed; so that, for example, the speed acquired by a body falling four cubits would be double that acquired in falling two cubits and this latter speed would be double that acquired in the first cubit. Because there is no doubt but that a heavy body falling from the height of six cubits has, and strikes with, a momentum [*impeto*] double that it had at the end of three cubits, triple that which it had at the end of one.

SALV. It is very comforting to me to have had such a companion in error; and moreover let me tell you that your proposition seems so highly probable that our Author himself admitted, when I advanced this opinion to him, that he had for some time shared the same fallacy. But what most surprised me was to see two propositions so inherently probable that they commanded the assent of everyone to whom they were presented, proven in a few simple words to be not only false, but impossible.

SIMP. I am one of those who accept the proposition, and believe that a falling body acquires force [*vires*] in its descent, its velocity increasing in proportion to the space, and that the momentum [*momento*] of the falling body is doubled when it falls from a doubled height; these propositions, it appears to me, ought to be conceded without hesitation or controversy.

SALV. And yet they are as false and impossible as that motion should be completed instantaneously; and here is a very clear demonstration of it. If the velocities are in proportion to the spaces traversed, or to be traversed, then these spaces are traversed in equal intervals of time; if, therefore, the velocity with which the falling body traverses a space of eight feet were double that with which it covered the first four feet (just as the one distance is double the other) then the time-intervals required for these passages would be equal. But for one and the same body to fall eight feet and four feet in the same time is possible only in the case of instantaneous [discontinuous] motion; but observation shows us that the motion of a falling body occupies time, and less of it in covering a distance of four feet than of eight feet; therefore it is not true that its velocity increases in proportion to the space.

The falsity of the other proposition may be shown with equal clearness. For if we consider a single striking body the difference of momentum in its blows can depend only upon the difference of velocity; for if the striking body falling from a double height were to deliver a blow of double momentum, it would be necessary for this body to strike with a doubled velocity; but with this doubled speed it would traverse a doubled space in the same time-interval; observation however shows that the time required for fall from the greater height is longer.

*   *   *   *   *

But now, it would seem that up to the present we have established the definition of uniformly accelerated motion which is expressed as follows:

A motion is said to be equally or uniformly accelerated when, starting from rest, its momentum (*celeritatis momenta*) receives equal increments in equal times.

SALV. This definition established, the Author makes a single assumption, namely,

The speeds acquired by one and the same body moving down planes of different inclinations are equal when the heights of these planes are equal.

By the height of an inclined plane we mean the perpendicular let fall from the upper end of the plane upon the horizontal line drawn through the lower end of the same plane. Thus, to illustrate, let the line AB be horizontal, and let the planes CA and CD be inclined to it; then the Author calls the perpendicular CB the "height" of the planes CA and CD; he supposes that the speeds acquired by one and the same body, descending along the planes CA and CD to the terminal points A and D are equal since the heights of these planes are the same, CB; and also it must be understood that this speed is that which would be acquired by the same body falling from C to B.

SAGR. Your assumption appears to me so reasonable that it ought to be conceded without question, provided of course there are no chance or outside resistances, and that the planes are hard and smooth, and that the figure of the moving body is perfectly round, so that neither plane nor moving body is rough.

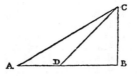

All resistance and opposition having been removed, my reason tells me at once that a heavy and perfectly round ball descending along the lines CA, CD, CB would reach the terminal points A, D, B, with equal momenta [*impeti eguali*].

*   *   *   *   *

Theorem I, Proposition I

The time in which any space is traversed by a body
starting from rest and uniformly accelerated is equal to
the time in which that same space would be traversed by
the same body moving at a uniform speed whose value is
the mean of the highest speed and the speed just before
acceleration began.

Let us represent by the line AB the time in which the space
CD is traversed by a body which starts from rest at C and is uniformly accelerated; let the final and highest value of the speed
gained during the interval AB be represented by the line EB drawn
at right angles to AB; draw the line AE, then all lines drawn
from equidistant points on AB and parallel to BE will represent
the increasing values of the speed, beginning with the instant A.
Let the point F bisect the line EB; draw FG parallel to BA, and
GA parallel to FB, thus forming a parallelogram AGFB which will
be equal in area to the triangle AEB, since the side GF bisects
the side AE at the point I; for if the parallel lines in the
triangle AEB are extended to GI, then the sum of all the parallels contained in the quadrilateral is equal to the sum of those

contained in the triangle AEB; for those in the triangle IEF are
equal to those contained in the triangle GIA, while those included in the trapezium AIFB are common. Since each and every
instant of time in the time-interval AB has its corresponding
point on the line AB, from which points parallels drawn in and
limited by the triangle AEB represent the increasing values of
the growing velocity, and since parallels contained within the
rectangle represent the values of a speed which is not increasing,
but constant, it appears, in like manner, that the momenta
[*momenta*] assumed by the moving body may also be represented, in
the case of the accelerated motion, by the increasing parallels
of the triangle AEB, and, in the case of the uniform motion, by
the parallels of the rectangle GB. For, what the momenta may
lack in the first part of the accelerated motion (the deficiency
of the momenta being represented by the parallels of the triangle
AGI) is made up by the momenta represented by the parallels of the
triangle IEF.

Hence it is clear that equal spaces will be traversed in
equal times by two bodies, one of which, starting from rest,

moves with a uniform acceleration, while the momentum of the other, moving with uniform speed, is one-half its maximum momentum under accelerated motion.   Q.E.D.

Theorem II, Proposition II

The spaces described by a body falling from rest with a uniformly accelerated motion are to each other as the squares of the time-intervals employed in traversing these distances.

Let the time beginning with any instant A be represented by the straight line AB in which are taken any two time-intervals AD and AE. Let HI represent the distance through which the body, starting from rest at H, falls with uniform acceleration. If HL

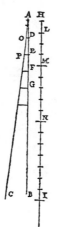

represents the space traversed during the time-interval AD, and HM that covered during the interval AE, then the space MH stands to the space LH in a ratio which is the square of the ratio of the time AE to the time AD; or we may say simply that the distances HM and HL are related as the squares of AE and AD.

Draw the line AC making any angle whatever with the line AB; and from the points D and E, draw the parallel lines DO and EP; of these two lines, DO represents the greatest velocity attained during the interval AD, while EP represents the maximum velocity acquired during the interval AE. But it has just been proved that so far as distances traversed are concerned it is precisely the same whether a body falls from rest with a uniform acceleration or whether it falls during an equal time-interval with a constant speed which is one-half the maximum speed attained during the accelerated motion. It follows therefore that the distances HM and HL are the same as would be traversed, during the time-intervals AE and AD, by uniform velocities equal to one-half those represented by DO and EP respectively. If, therefore,

one can show that the distances HM and HL are in the same ratio
as the squares of the time-intervals AE and AD, our proposition
will be proven.

But in the fourth proposition of the first book it has been
shown that the spaces traversed by two particles in uniform motion bear to one another a ratio which is equal to the product of
the ratio of the velocities by the ratio of the times. But in
this case the ratio of the velocities is the same as the ratio of
the time-intervals (for the ratio of AE to AD is the same as that
of 1/2 EP to 1/2 DO or of EP to DO). Hence the ratio of the
spaces traversed is the same as the squared ratio of the time-
intervals.   Q.E.D.

Evidently then the ratio of the distances is the square of
the ratio of the final velocities, that is, of the lines EP and
DO, since these are to each other as AE to AD.

Corollary I

Hence it is clear that if we take any equal intervals of
time whatever, counting from the beginning of the motion, such as
AD, DE, EF, FG, in which the spaces HL, LM, MN, NI are traversed,
these spaces will bear to one another the same ratio as the series of odd numbers, 1, 3, 5, 7; for this is the ratio of the
differences of the squares of the lines [which represent time],
differences which exceed one another by equal amounts, this excess being equal to the smallest line [viz. the one representing
a single time-interval]: or we may say [that this is the ratio]
of the differences of the squares of the natural numbers beginning with unity.

While, therefore, during equal intervals of time the velocities increase as the natural numbers, the increments in the
distances traversed during these equal time-intervals are to one
another as the odd numbers beginning with unity.

       *   *   *   *   *

SIMP. In truth, I find more pleasure in this simple and
clear argument of Sagredo than in the Author's demonstration
which to me appears rather obscure; so that I am convinced that
matters are as described, once having accepted the definition of
uniformly accelerated motion. But as to whether this acceleration is that which one meets in nature in the case of falling
bodies, I am still doubtful; and it seems to me, not only for my
own sake but also for all those who think as I do, that this
would be the proper moment to introduce one of those experi-
ments--and there are many of them, I understand--which illustrate
in several ways the conclusions reached.

SALV. The request which you, as a man of science, make, is
a very reasonable one; for this is the custom--and properly so--
in those sciences where mathematical demonstrations are applied
to natural phenomena, as is seen in the case of perspective,
astronomy, mechanics, music, and others where the principles,
once established by well-chosen experiments, become the foundations of the entire superstructure. I hope therefore it will not

appear to be a waste of time if we discuss at considerable length
this first and most fundamental question upon which hinge numerous consequences of which we have in this book only a small number, placed there by the Author, who has done so much to open a
pathway hitherto closed to minds of speculative turn. So far as
experiments go they have not been neglected by the Author; and
often, in his company, I have attempted in the following manner
to assure myself that the acceleration actually experienced by
falling bodies is that above described.

A piece of wooden moulding or scantling, about 12 cubits
long, half a cubit wide, and three finger-breadths thick, was
taken; on its edge was cut a channel a little more than one finger in breadth; having made this groove very straight, smooth,
and polished, and having lined it with parchment, also as smooth
and polished as possible, we rolled along it a hard, smooth, and
very round bronze ball. Having placed this board in a sloping
position, by lifting one end some one or two cubits above the
other, we rolled the ball, as I was just saying, along the channel, noting, in a manner presently to be described, the time
required to make the descent. We repeated this experiment more
than once in order to measure the time with an accuracy such that
the deviation between two observations never exceeded one-tenth
of a pulse-beat. Having performed this operation and having
assured ourselves of its reliability, we now rolled the ball only
one-quarter the length of the channel; and having measured the
time of its descent, we found it precisely one-half of the former.
Next we tried other distances, comparing the time for the whole
length with that for the half, or with that for two-thirds, or
three-fourths, or indeed for any fraction; in such experiments,
repeated a full hundred times, we always found that the spaces
traversed were to each other as the squares of the times, and
this was true for all inclinations of the plane, i.e., of the
channel, along which we rolled the ball. We also observed that
the times of descent, for various inclinations of the plane, bore
to one another precisely that ratio which, as we shall see later,
the Author had predicted and demonstrated for them.

For the measurement of time, we employed a large vessel of
water placed in an elevated position; to the bottom of this vessel was soldered a pipe of small diameter giving a thin jet of
water, which we collected in a small glass during the time of
each descent, whether for the whole length of the channel or for
a part of its length; the water thus collected was weighed, after
each descent, on a very accurate balance; the differences and
ratios of these weights gave us the differences and ratios of
the times, and this with such accuracy that although the operation was repeated many, many times, there was no appreciable
discrepancy in the results.

SIMP. I would like to have been present at these experiments; but feeling confidence in the care with which you performed them, and in the fidelity with which you relate them, I am
satisfied and accept them as true and valid.

       *   *   *   *   *

FOURTH DAY

SALVIATI. Once more, Simplicio is here on time; so let us
without delay take up the question of motion. The text of our
Author is as follows:

The Motion of Projectiles

In the preceding pages we have discussed the properties of
uniform motion and of motion naturally accelerated along planes
of all inclinations. I now propose to set forth those properties
which belong to a body whose motion is compounded of two other
motions, namely, one uniform and one naturally accelerated; these
properties, well worth knowing, I propose to demonstrate in a
rigid manner. This is the kind of motion seen in a moving projectile; its origin I conceive to be as follows:
Imagine any particle projected along a horizontal plane
without friction; then we know, from what has been more fully
explained in the preceding pages, that this particle will move
along this same plane with a motion which is uniform and perpetual, provided the plane has no limits. But if the plane is limited and elevated, then the moving particle, which we imagine to
be a heavy one, will on passing over the edge of the plane acquire, in addition to its previous uniform and perpetual motion,
a downward propensity due to its own weight; so that the resulting motion which I call projection [*projectio*], is compounded of
one which is uniform and horizontal and of another which is vertical and naturally accelerated. We now proceed to demonstrate
some of its properties, the first of which is as follows:

Theorem I, Proposition I

A projectile which is carried by a uniform horizontal
motion compounded with a naturally accelerated vertical
motion describes a path which is a semi-parabola.
SAGR. Here, Salviati, it will be necessary to stop a little
while for my sake and, I believe, also for the benefit of Simplicio; for it so happens that I have not gone very far in my
study of Apollonius and am merely aware of the fact that he
treats of the parabola and other conic sections, without an
understanding of which I hardly think one will be able to follow
the proof of other propositions depending upon them. Since even
in this first beautiful theorem the author finds it necessary
to prove that the path of a projectile is a parabola, and since,
as I imagine, we shall have to deal with only this kind of curves,
it will be absolutely necessary to have a thorough acquaintance,
if not with all the properties which Apollonius has demonstrated
for these figures, at least with those which are needed for the
present treatment.
SALV. You are quite too modest, pretending ignorance of
facts which not long ago you acknowledged as well known--I mean
at the time when we were discussing the strength of materials and
needed to use a certain theorem of Apollonius which gave you no
trouble.

SAGR. I may have chanced to know it or may possibly have
assumed it, so long as needed, for that discussion; but now when
we have to follow all these demonstrations about such curves we
ought not, as they say, to swallow it whole, and thus waste time
and energy.

SIMP. Now even though Sagredo is, as I believe, well
equipped for all his needs, I do not understand even the elementary terms; for although our philosophers have treated the motion
of projectiles, I do not recall their having described the path
of a projectile except to state in a general way that it is
always a curved line, unless the projection be vertically upwards.
But if the little Euclid which I have learned since our previous
discussion does not enable me to understand the demonstrations
which are to follow, then I shall be obliged to accept the
theorems on faith without fully comprehending them.

*   *   *   *   *

SALV. Indeed, all real mathematicians assume on the part of
the reader perfect familiarity with at least the elements of
Euclid; and here it is necessary in your case only to recall a
proposition of the Second Book in which he proves that when a
line is cut into equal and also into two unequal parts, the rectangle formed on the unequal parts is less than that formed on
the equal (i.e., less than the square on half the line), by an
amount which is the square of the difference between the equal
and unequal segments. From this it is clear that the square of
the whole line which is equal to four times the square of the
half is greater than four times the rectangle of the unequal
parts. In order to understand the following portions of this
treatise it will be necessary to keep in mind the two elemental
theorems from conic sections which we have just demonstrated; and
these two theorems are indeed the only ones which the Author
uses. We can now resume the text and see how he demonstrates his
first proposition in which he shows that a body falling with a
motion compounded of a uniform horizontal and a naturally
accelerated [*naturale descendente*] one describes a semi-parabola.

Let us imagine an elevated horizontal line or plane ab along
which a body moves with uniform speed from a to b. Suppose this
plane to end abruptly at b; then at this point the body will, on
account of its weight, acquire also a natural motion downwards
along the perpendicular bn. Draw the line be along the plane ba
to represent the flow, or measure, of time; divide this line into
a number of segments, bc, cd, de, representing equal intervals of
time; from the points b, c, d, e, let fall lines which are parallel to the perpendicular bn. On the first of these lay off any
distance ci, on the second a distance four times as long, df; on
the third, one nine times as long, eh; and so on, in proportion
to the squares of cb, db, eb, or, we may say, in the squared
ratio of these same lines. Accordingly we see that while the
body moves from b to c with uniform speed, it also falls perpendicularly through the distance ci, and at the end of the time-
interval bc finds itself at the point i. In like manner at the
end of the time-interval bd, which is the double of bc, the ver-

tical fall will be four times the first distance ci; for it has
been shown in a previous discussion that the distance traversed
by a freely falling body varies as the square of the time; in
like manner the space eh traversed during the time be will be
nine times ci; thus it is evident that the distances eh, df, ci
will be to one another as the squares of the lines be, bd, bc.
Now from the points i, f, h draw the straight lines io, fg, hl
parallel to be; these lines hl, fg, io are equal to eb, db and
cb, respectively; so also are the lines bo, bg, bl respectively
equal to ci, df, and eh. The square of hl is to that of fg as
the line lb is to bg; and the square of fg is to that of io as gb
is to bo; therefore the points i, f, h, lie on one and the same
parabola. In like manner it may be shown that, if we take equal
time-intervals of any size whatever, and if we imagine the particle to be carried by a similar compound motion, the positions
of this particle, at the ends of these time-intervals, will lie
on one and the same parabola.   Q.E.D.

    SALV. This conclusion follows from the converse of the
first of the two propositions given above. For, having drawn a
parabola through the points b and h, any other two points, f and
i, not falling on the parabola must lie either within or without;
consequently the line fg is either longer or shorter than the
line which terminates on the parabola. Therefore the square of
hl will not bear to the square of fg the same ratio as the line
lb to bg, but a greater or smaller; the fact is, however, that
the square of hl does bear this same ratio to the square of fg.
Hence the point f does lie on the parabola, and so do all the
others.

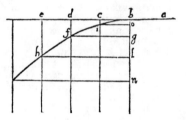

e.   *The man who put it all together was Isaac Newton.** His debt
     *to Galileo is obvious; that to Kepler is less clear but
     still present.   And, of course, the most immediate stimulus
     came from René Descartes whose* Principia Philosophiae,
     Newton was convinced, was a tissue of errors.   In the Phil-
     osophiae Naturalis Principia Mathematica (Mathematical
     Principles of Natural Philosophy) *Newton followed the form
     laid out by Galileo in the* Two New Sciences *but went far
     beyond that work in content.   This was the work which served
     as the solid foundation for the new physics.*

The Mathematical Principles
of Natural Philosophy.

Definitions

Definition I.

*The quantity of matter is the measure of the same, arising from
its density and bulk conjunctly.*

Thus air of a double density, in a double space, is quadruple in quantity; in a triple space, sextuple in quantity.   The
same thing is to be understood of snow, and fine dust or powders,
that are condensed by compression or liquefaction; and of all
bodies that are by any causes whatever differently condensed.   I
have no regard in this place to a medium, if any such there is,
that freely pervades the interstices between the parts of bodies.
It is this quantity that I mean hereafter every where under the
name of Body or Mass.   And the same is known by the weight of
each body: for it is proportional to the weight, as I have
found by experiments on pendulums, very accurately made, which
shall be shewn hereafter.

Definition II.

*The quantity of motion is the measure of the same, arising from
the velocity and quantity of matter conjunctly.*

The motion of the whole is the sum of the motions of all the
parts; and therefore in a body double in quantity, with equal
velocity, the motion is double; with twice the velocity, it is
quadruple.

---

*The Mathematical Principles of Natural Philosophy by Sir Isaac
Newton.   Translated into English by Andrew Motte: to which are
added Newton's System of the World; 3 Volumes (London: Sherwood,
Neely and Jones, 1819).   Vol I: pp. 1-8; 14-15; 40-42; 52-54;
174-176; 178-179. Vol II: pp. 157-159; 172-176; 183-185;
309-314.

Definition III.

The vis insita, *or innate force of matter, is a power of resisting, by which every body, as much as in it lies, endeavours to persevere in its present state, whether it be of rest, or of moving uniformly forward in a right line.*

This force is ever proportional to the body whose force it is; and differs nothing from the inactivity of the mass, but in our manner of conceiving it. A body from the inactivity of matter is not without difficulty put out of its state of rest or motion. Upon which account, this *vis insita* may, by a most significant name, be called *vis inertiæ* , or force of inactivity. But a body exerts this force only, when another force, impressed upon it, endeavours to change its condition; and the exercise of this force may be considered both as resistance and impulse: it is resistance, in so far as the body, for maintaining its present state, withstands the force impressed; it is impulse, in so far as the body, by not easily giving way to the impressed force of another, endeavours to change the state of that other. Resistance is usually ascribed to bodies at rest, and impulse to those in motion: but motion and rest, as commonly conceived, are only relatively distinguished; nor are those bodies always truly at rest, which commonly are taken to be so.

Definition IV.

An impressed force is an action exerted upon a body, in order to change its state, either of rest, or of moving uniformly forward in a right line.

This force consists in the action only; and remains no longer in the body, when the action is over. For a body maintains every new state it acquires, by its *vis inertiæ* only. Impressed forces are of different origins; as from percussion, from pressure, from centripetal force.

Definition V.

A centripetal force is that by which bodies are drawn or impelled, or any way tend, towards a point as to a centre.

Of this sort is gravity, by which bodies tend to the centre of the earth; magnetism, by which iron tends to the loadstone; and that force, whatever it is, by which the planets are perpetually drawn aside from the rectilinear motions, which otherwise they would pursue, and made to revolve in curvilinear orbits. A stone, whirled about in a sling, endeavours to recede from the hand that turns it; and by that endeavour, distends the sling, and that with so much the greater force, as it is revolved with the greater velocity, and as soon as ever it is let go, flies away. That force which opposes itself to this endeavour, and by which the sling perpetually draws back the stone towards the hand, and retains it in its orbit, because it is directed to the

hand as the centre of the orbit, I call the centripetal force.
And the same thing is to be understood of all bodies, revolved
in any orbits. They all endeavour to recede from the centres of
their orbits; and were it not for the opposition of a contrary
force which restrains them to, and detains them in their orbits,
which I therefore call centripetal, would fly off in right lines,
with an uniform motion. A projectile, if it was not for the
force of gravity, would not deviate towards the earth, but would
go off from it in a right line, and that with an uniform motion,
if the resistance of the air was taken away. It is by its gravity that it is drawn aside perpetually from its rectilinear
course, and made to deviate towards the earth, more or less,
according to the force of its gravity, and the velocity of its
motion. The less its gravity is, for the quantity of its matter,
or the greater the velocity with which it is projected, the less
will it deviate from a rectilinear course, and the farther it
will go. If a leaden ball, projected from the top of a mountain
by the force of gun-powder with a given velocity, and in a direction parallel to the horizon, is carried in a curve line to the
distance of two miles before it falls to the ground; the same, if
the resistance of the air was took away, with a double or decuple
velocity, would fly twice or ten times as far. And by increasing
the velocity, we may at pleasure increase the distance to which
it might be projected, and diminish the curvature of the line,
which it might describe, till at last it should fall at the distance of 10, 30, or 90 degrees, or even might go quite round the
whole earth before it falls; or lastly, so that it might never
fall to the earth, but go forwards into the celestial spaces, and
proceed in its motion *in infinitum*. And after the same manner
that a projectile, by the force of gravity, may be made to revolve in an orbit, and go round the whole earth, the moon also,
either by the force of gravity, if it is endued with gravity, or
by any other force that impels it towards the earth, may be perpetually drawn aside towards the earth, out of the rectilinear
way, which by its innate force it would pursue; and be made to
revolve in the orbit which it now describes: nor could the moon,
without some such force, be retained in its orbit. If this force
was too small, it would not sufficiently turn the moon out of a
rectilinear course: if it was too great, it would turn it too
much, and draw down the moon from its orbit towards the earth.
It is necessary, that the force be of a just quantity, and it belongs to the mathematicians to find the force, that may serve
exactly to retain a body in a given orbit, with a given velocity;
and *vice versa*, to determine the curvilinear way, into which a
body projected from a given place, with a given velocity, may be
made to deviate from its natural rectilinear way, by means of a
given force.
   The quantity of any centripetal force may be considered as
of three kinds; absolute, accelerative, and motive.

Definition VI.

*The absolute quantity of a centripetal force is the measure of
the same, proportional to the efficacy of the cause that propa-*

gates it from the centre, through the spaces round about.

Thus the magnetic force is greater in one load-stone and less in another, according to their sizes and strength.

Definition VII.

The accelerative quantity of a centripetal force is the measure of the same, proportional to the velocity which it generates in a given time.

Thus the force of the same load-stone is greater at a less distance, and less at a greater: also the force of gravity is greater in valleys, less on tops of exceeding high mountains; and yet less (as shall be hereafter shewn) at greater distances from the body of the earth; but at equal distances, it is the same every where; because (taking away, or allowing for, the resistance of the air) it equally accelerates all falling bodies, whether heavy or light, great or small.

Definition VIII.

The motive quantity of a centripetal force is the measure of the same, proportional to the motion which it generates in a given time.

Thus the weight is greater in a greater body, less in a less body; it is greater near to the earth, and less at remoter distances. This sort of quantity is the centripetency, or propension of the whole body towards the centre, or, as I may say, its weight; and it is ever known by the quantity of a force equal and contrary to it, that is just sufficient to hinder the descent of the body.
These quantities of forces we may, for brevity's sake, call by the names of motive, accelerative, and absolute forces; and for distinction's sake consider them, with respect to the bodies that tend to the centre; to the places of those bodies; and to the centre of force towards which they tend: that is to say, I refer the motive force to the body, as an endeavour and propensity of the whole towards a centre, arising from the propensities of the several parts taken together; the accelerative force to the place of the body, as a certain power or energy diffused from the centre to all places around to move the bodies that are in them; and the absolute force to the centre, as endued with some cause, without which those motive forces would not be propagated through the spaces round about; whether that cause is some central body (such as is the load-stone, in the centre of the force of magnetism, or the earth in the centre of the gravitating force), or anything else that does not yet appear. For I here design only to give a mathematical notion of those forces, without considering their physical causes and feats.
Wherefore the accelerative force will stand in the same relation to the motive, as celerity does to motion. For the quantity of motion arises from the celerity drawn into the quantity

of matter; and the motive force arises from the accelerative force drawn into the same quantity of matter. For the sum of the actions of the accelerative force, upon the several particles of the body, is the motive force of the whole. Hence it is, that near the surface of the earth, where the accelerative gravity, or force productive of gravity, in all bodies is the same, the motive gravity or the weight is as the body: but if we should ascend to higher regions, where the accelerative gravity is less, the weight would be likewise diminished, and would always be as the product of the body, by the accelerative gravity. So in those regions, where the accelerative gravity is diminished into one half, the Weight of a body two or three times less, will be four or six times less.

I likewise call attractions and impulses, in the same sense, accelerative, and motive; and use the words attraction, impulse, or propensity of any sort towards a centre, promiscuously, and indifferently, one for another; considering those forces not physically, but mathematically: wherefore, the reader is not to imagine, that, by those words, I any where take upon me to define the kind, or the manner of any action, the causes or the physical reason thereof, or that I attribute forces, in a true and physical sense, to certain centres (which are only mathematical points); when at any time I happen to speak of centres as attracting, or as endued with attractive powers.

Scholium.

Hitherto I have laid down the definitions of such words as are less known, and explained the sense in which I would have them to be understood in the following discourse. I do not define time, space, place and motion, as being well known to all. Only I must observe, that the vulgar conceive those quantities under no other notions but from the relation they bear to sensible objects. And thence arise certain prejudices, for the removing of which, it will be convenient to distinguish them into absolute and relative, true and apparent, mathematical and common.

I. Absolute, true, and mathematical time, of itself, and from its own nature, flows equably without regard to any thing external, and by another name is called duration: relative, apparent, and common time, is some sensible and external (whether accurate or unequable) measure of duration by the means of motion, which is commonly used instead of true time; such as an hour, a day, a month, a year.

II. Absolute space, in its own nature, without regard to any thing external, remains always similar and immoveable. Relative space is some moveable dimension or measure of the absolute spaces; which our senses determine by its position to bodies, and which is vulgarly taken for immoveable space; such is the dimension of a subterraneous, an aerial, or celestial space, determined by its position in respect of the earth. Absolute and relative space are the same in figure and magnitude; but they do not remain always numerically the same. For if the earth, for instance, moves, a space of our air, which relatively and in respect of the earth remains always the same, it will at one time be one part of the absolute space into which the air passes; at another time it will be another part of the same, and so, absolutely understood, it will be perpetually mutable.

III. Place is part of space which a body takes up, and is according to the space, either absolute or relative. I say, a part of space; not the situation, nor the external surface of the body. For the places of equal solids are always equal; but their superficies, by reason of their dissimilar figures, are often unequal. Positions properly have no quantity, nor are they so much the places themselves, as the properties of places. The motion of the whole is the same thing with the sum of the motions of the parts; that is, the translation of the whole, out of its place, is the same thing with the sum of the translations of the parts out of their places; and therefore the place of the whole is the same thing with the sum of the places of the parts, and for that reason, it is internal, and in the whole body.

IV. Absolute motion is the translation of a body from one absolute place into another; and relative motion, the translation from one relative place into another. Thus in a ship under sail, the relative place of a body is that part of the ship which the body possesses; or that part of its cavity which the body fills, and which therefore moves together with the ship: and relative rest, is the continuance of the body in the same part of the ship, or of its cavity. But real, absolute rest, is the continuance of the body in the same part of that immoveable space, in which the ship itself, its cavity, and all that it contains, is moved. Wherefore, if the earth is really at rest, the body, which relatively rests in the ship, will really and absolutely move with the same velocity which the ship has on the earth. But if the earth also moves, the true and absolute motion of the body will arise, partly from the true motion of the earth, in immoveable space; partly from the relative motion of the ship on the earth: and if the body moves also relatively in the ship, its true motion will arise, partly from the true motion of the earth, in immoveable space, and partly from the relative motions as well of the ship on the earth, as of the body in the ship; and from these relative motions will arise the relative motion of the body on the earth. As if that part of the earth where the ship is, was truly moved toward the east, with a velocity of 10010 parts; while the ship itself with a fresh gale, and full sails, is carried towards the west, with a velocity expressed by 10 of those parts; but a sailor walks in the ship towards the east, with 1 part of the said velocity: then the sailor will be moved truly and absolutely in immoveable space towards the east with a velocity of 10001 parts, and relatively on the earth towards the west, with a velocity of 9 of those parts.

Absolute time, in astronomy, is distinguished from relative, by the equation or correction of the vulgar time. For the natural days are truly unequal, though they are commonly considered as equal, and used for a measure of time: astronomers correct this inequality for their more accurate deducing of the celestial motions. It may be, that there is no such thing as an equable motion, whereby time may be accurately measured. All motions may

be accelerated and retarded, but the true, or equable, progress
of absolute time is liable to no change. The duration or per-
severance of the existence of things remains the same, whether
the motions are swift or slow, or none at all: and therefore it
ought to be distinguished from what are only sensible measures
thereof; and out of which we collect it, by means of the astronomical equation. The necessity of which equation, for determining the times of the phænomenon, is evinced as well from the
experiments of the pendulum clock, as by eclipses of the satellites of *Jupiter.*

As the order of the parts of time is immutable, so also is
the order of the parts of space. Suppose those parts to be moved
out of their places, and they will be moved (if the expression
may be allowed) out of themselves. For times and spaces are, as
it were, the places as well of themselves as of all other things.
All things are placed in time as to order of succession; and in
space as to order of situation. It is from their essence or
nature that they are places; and that the primary places of
things should be moveable, is absurd. These are, therefore,
the absolute places; and translations out of those places are
the only absolute motions.

But because the parts of space cannot be seen, or distinguished from one another by our senses, therefore in their stead
we use sensible measures of them. For from the positions and
distances of things from any body considered as immoveable, we
define all places: and then with respect to such places, we
estimate all motions, considering bodies as transferred from some
of those places into others. And so instead of absolute places
and motions we use relative ones; and that without any inconveni-
ence in common affairs: but in philosophical disquisitions, we
ought to abstract from our senses, and consider things themselves, distinct from what are only sensible measures of them.
For it may be that there is no body really at rest, to which the
places and motions of others may be referred.

*   *   *   *   *

Axioms; or, Laws of Motion.

Law I

*Every body perseveres in its state of rest, or of uniform motion
in a right line, unless it is compelled to change that state by
forces impressed thereon.*

Projectiles persevere in their motions, so far as they are
not retarded by the resistance of the air, or impelled downwards
by the force of gravity. A top, whose parts by their cohesion
are perpetually drawn aside from rectilinear motions, does not
cease its rotation, otherwise than as it is retarded by the air.
The greater bodies of the planets and comets, meeting with less
resistance in more free spaces, preserve their motions both progressive and circular for a much longer time.

Law II.

The alteration of motion is ever proportional to the motive force impressed, and is made in the direction of the right line in which that force is impressed.

If any force generates a motion, a double force will generate double the motion, a triple force triple the motion, whether that force be impressed altogether and at once, or gradually and successively. And this motion (being always directed the same way with the generating force), if the body moved before, is added to or subducted from the former motion, according as they directly conspire with or are directly contrary to each other; or obliquely joined, when they are oblique, so as to produce a new motion compounded from the determination of both.

Law III.

To every action there is always opposed an equal reaction: or the mutual actions of two bodies upon each other are always equal; and directed to contrary parts.

Whatever draws or presses another is as much drawn or pressed by that other. If you press a stone with your finger, the finger is also pressed by the stone. If a horse draws a stone tied to a rope, the horse (if I may so say) will be equally drawn back towards the stone: for the distended rope, by the same endeavour to relax or unbend itself, will draw the horse as much towards the stone, as it does the stone towards the horse, and will obstruct the progress of the one as much as it advances that of the other. If a body impinge upon another, and by its force change the motion of the other, that body also (because of the equality of the mutual pressure) will undergo an equal change, in its own motion, towards the contrary part. The changes made by these actions are equal, not in the velocities, but in the motions of bodies; that is to say, if the bodies are not hindered by any other impediments. For, because the motions are equally changed, the changes of the velocities made towards contrary parts are reciprocally proportional to the bodies. This law takes place also in attractions, as will be proved in the next scholium.

*   *   *   *   *

Section II.
Of the Invention of Centripetal Forces.

Proposition I.   Theorem I.

The areas, which revolving bodies describe by radii drawn to an immoveable centre of force do lie in the same immoveable planes, and are proportional to the times in which they are described.

For suppose the time to be divided into equal parts, and in the first part of that time let the body by its innate force

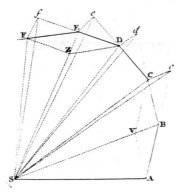

describe the right line AB. In the second part of that time, the
same would (by law 1.), if not hindered, proceed directly to c,
along the line Bc equal to AB; so that by the radii AS, BS, cS,
drawn to the centre, the equal areas ABS, BSc, would be described.
But when the body is arrived at B, suppose that a centripetal
force acts at once with a great impulse, and, turning aside the
body from the right line Bc, compels it afterwards to continue
its motion along the right line BC. Draw cC parallel to BS meeting BC in C; and at the end of the second part of the time, the
body (by cor. 1. of the laws) will be found in C, in the same
plane with the triangle ASB. Join SC, and, because SB and Cc are
parallel, the triangle SBC will be equal to the triangle SBc,
and therefore also to the triangle SAB. By the like argument, if
the centripetal force acts successively in C, D, E, &c. and makes
the body, in each single particle of time, to describe the right
lines CD, DE, EF, &c. they will all lie in the same plane; and
the triangle SCD will be equal to the triangle SBC, and SDE to
SCD, and SEF to SDE. And therefore, in equal times, equal areas
are described in one immoveable plane: and, by composition, any
sums SADS, SAFS, of those areas, are one to the other as the
times in which they are described. Now let the number of those
triangles be augmented, and their breadth diminished *in infinitum*;
and (by cor. 4, lem. 3.) their ultimate perimeter ADF will be a
curve line: and therefore the centripetal force, by which the
body is perpetually drawn back from the tangent of this curve,
will act continually; and any described areas SADS, SAFS, which
are always proportional to the times of description, will, in
this case also, be proportional to those times.   Q.E.D.
    COR. 1. The velocity of a body attracted towards an immove-
able centre, in spaces void of resistance, is reciprocally as
the perpendicular let fall from that centre on the right line
that touches the orbit. For the velocities in those places A, B,
C, D, E, are the bases AB, BC, CD, DE, EF, of equal triangles;

and these bases are reciprocally as the perpendiculars let fall
upon them.

COR. 2. If the chords AB, BC of two arcs, successively
described in equal times by the same body, in spaces void of resistance, are completed into a parallelogram ABCV, and the diag-
onal BV of this parallelogram , in the position which it ultimately acquires when those arcs are diminished *in infinitum*, is
produced both ways, it will pass through the centre of force.

COR. 3. If the chords AB, BC, and DE, EF, of arcs described
in equal times, in spaces void of resistance, are completed into
the parallelograms ABCV, DEFZ; the forces in B and E are one to
the other in the ultimate ratio of the diagonals BV, EZ, when
those arcs are diminished *in infinitum*. For the motions BC and
EF of the body (by cor. 1 of the laws) are compounded of the
motions Bc, BV, and Ff, EZ: but BV and EZ, which are equal to
Cc and Ff, in the demonstration of this proposition, were generated by the impulses of the centripetal force in B and E, and are
therefore proportional to those impulses.

COR. 4. The forces by which bodies, in spaces void of resistance, are drawn back from rectilinear motions, and turned
into curvilinear orbits, are one to another as the versed sines
of arcs described in equal times; which versed sines tend to the
centre of force, and bisect the chords when those arcs are
diminished to infinity. For such versed sines are the halves of
the diagonals mentioned in cor. 3.

COR. 5. And therefore those forces are to the force of
gravity as the said versed sines to the versed sines perpendicular to the horizon of those parabolic arcs which projectiles
describe in the same time.

COR. 6. And the same things do all hold good (by cor. 5 of
the laws), when theplanes in which the bodies are moved, together
with the centres of force which are placed in those planes, are
not at rest, but move uniformly forward in right lines.

*   *   *   *   *

Proposition X.   Problem V.

*If a body revolves in an ellipsis; it is proposed to find the law
of the centripetal force tending to the centre of the ellipsis.*

Suppose CA, CB to be semi-axes of the ellipsis GP, DK, con-
jugate diameters; PF, QT perpendiculars to those diameters; Qv
an ordinate to the diameter GP; and if the parallelogram QvPR be
completed, then (by the properties of the conic sections) the
rectangle PvG will be to Qv^2 as PC^2 to CD^2; and (because of the
similar triangles QvT, PCF) Qv^2 to QT^2 as PC^2 to PF^2; and, by
composition, the ratio of PvG to QT^2 is compounded of the ratio
of PC^2 to CD^2, and of the ratio of PC^2 to PF^2, that is, vG to
$\frac{QT^2}{Pv}$ as PC^2 to $\frac{CD^2 \times PF^2}{PC^2}$. Put QR for Pv, and (by lem. 12) BC × CA
for CD × PF; also (the points P and Q coinciding) 2PC for vG; and
multiplying the extremes and means together, we shall have

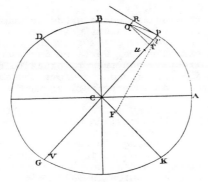

$\dfrac{QT^2 \times PC^2}{QR}$ equal to $\dfrac{2BC^2 \times CA^2}{PC}$. Therefore (by cor. 5, prop. 6) the centripetal force is reciprocally as $\dfrac{2BC^2 \times CA^2}{PC}$; that is (because $2BC^2 \times CA^2$ is given), reciprocally as $\dfrac{1}{PC}$; that is, directly as the distance PC.   Q.E.I.

The same otherwise.

In the right line PG on the other side of the point T, take the point u so that Tu may be equal to Tv; then take nV, such as shall be to vG as DC^2 to PC^2. And because Qv^2 is to PvG as DC^2 to PC^2 (by the conic sections), we shall have $Qv^2 = Pv \times uV$. Add the rectangle uPv to both sides, and the square of the chord of the arc PQ will be equal to the rectangle VPv; and therefore a circle which touches the conic section in P, and passes through the point Q, will pass also through the points V. Now let the points P and Q meet, and the ratio of uV to vG, which is the same with the ratio of DC^2 to PC^2, will become the ratio of PV to PG, or PV to 2PC; and therefore PV will be equal to $\dfrac{2DC^2}{PC}$. And therefore the force by which the body P revolves in the ellipsis will be reciprocally as $\dfrac{2DC^2}{PC} \times PF^2$ (by cor. 3, prop. 6); that is (because $2DC^2 \times PF^2$ is given), directly as PC.   Q.E.I.

COR. 1. And therefore the force is as the distance of the body from the centre of the ellipsis; and, vice versa, if the force is as the distance, the body will move in an ellipsis whose centre coincides with the centre of force, or perhaps in a circle into which the ellipsis may degenerate.

COR. 2. And the periodic times of the revolutions made in all ellipses whatsoever about the same centre will be equal. For those times in similar ellipses will be equal (by corol. 3 and 8, prop. 4); but in ellipses that have their greater axis common,

they are one to another as the whole areas of the ellipses
directly, and the parts of the areas described in the same time
inversely; that is, as the lesser axes directly, and the velocities
of the bodies in their principal vertices inversely; that is, as
those lesser axes directly, and the ordinates to the same point
of the common axis inversely; and therefore (because of the
equality of the direct and inverse ratios) in the ratio of
equality.

Scholium.

If the ellipsis, by having its centre removed to an infinite
distance, degenerates into a parabola, the body will move in this
parabola; and the force, now tending to a centre infinitely remote, will become equable. Which is *Galileo's* theorem. And if
the parabolic section of the cone (by changing the inclination of
the cutting plane to the cone) degenerates into an hyperbola, the
body will move in the perimeter of this hyperbola, having its
centripetal force changed into a centrifugal force. And in like
manner as in the circle, or in the ellipsis, if the forces are
directed to the centre of the figure placed in the abscissa,
those forces, by increasing or diminishing the ordinates in any
given ratio, or even by changing the angle of the inclination of
the ordinates to the abscissa, are always augmented or diminished
in the ratio of the distances from the centre; provided the
periodic times remain equal: so also in all figures whatsoever,
if the ordinates are augmented or diminished in any given ratio,
or their inclination is any way changed, the periodic time
remaining the same, the forces directed to any centre placed in
the abscissa are in the several ordinates augmented or diminished
in the ratio of the distances from the centre.

SECTION XII
Of the attractive forces of sphærical bodies.

Proposition LXX.   Theorem XXX.

*If to every point of a sphærical surface there tend equal cen-
tripetal forces, decreasing in the duplicate ratio of the
distances from those points; I say, that a corpuscle placed
within that superficies will not be attracted by those forces
any way.*

Let HIKL be that sphærical superficies, and P a corpuscle
placed within. Through P let there be drawn to this superficies
the two lines HK, IL, intercepting very small arcs HI, KL; and
because (by cor. 3, lem. 7) the triangles HPI, LPK, are alike,
those arcs will be proportional to the distances HP, LP; and any
particles at HI and KL of the sphærical superficies, terminated
by right lines passing through P, will be in the duplicate ratio
of those distances. Therefore the forces of these particles
exerted upon the body P are equal between themselves. For the
forces are as the particles directly, and the squares of the
distances inversely. And these two ratios compose the ratio of

equality. The attractions, therefore, being made equally towards
contrary parts, destroy each other. And, by a like reasoning,
all the attractions through the whole sphærical superficies are
destroyed by contrary attractions. Therefore the body P will not
be any way impelled by those attractions.   Q.E.D.

Proposition LXXI. Theorem XXXI.

*The same things supposed as above, I say, that a corpuscle placed
without the sphærical superficies is attracted towards the centre of the sphere with a force reciprocally proportional to the
square of its distance from that centre.*

Let AHKB, ahkb, be two equal sphærical superficies described about the centres S, s; their diameters AB, ab; and let P
and p be two corpuscles situate without the spheres in those
diameters produced. Let there be drawn from the corpuscles the
lines PHK, PIL, phk, pil, cutting off from the great circles AHB,

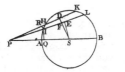
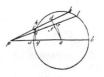

ahb, the equal arcs HK, hk, IL, il; and to those lines let fall
the perpendiculars SD, sd, SE, se, IR, ir; of which let SD, sd.
cut PL, pl, in F and f. Let fall also to the diameters the
perpendiculars IQ, iq. Let now the angles DPE, dpe, vanish;
and because DS and ds, ES and es, are equal, the lines PE, PF,
and pe, pf, and the lineolæ DF, df, may be taken for equal; because their last ratio, when the angles DPE, dpe, vanish together,
is the ratio of equality. These things then supposed, it will
be, as PI to PF so is RI to DF, and as pf to pi so is df or DF
to ri; and, *ex æquo*, as PI × pf to PF × pi so is RI to ri, that
is (by cor. 3, lem. 7), so is the arc IH to the arc ih. Again,
PI is to PS as IQ to SE, and ps to pi as se or SE to iq; and,
ex æquo, PI × ps to PS × pi as IQ to iq. And compounding the
ratios PI^2 × pf × ps, is to pi^2 × PF × PS, as IH × IQ to ih × iq;
that is, as the circular superficies which is described by the
arc IH, as the semicircle AKB revolves about the diameter AB, is
to the circular superficies described by the arc ih as the semi-
circle akb revolves about the diameter ab. And the forces with

with which these superficies attract the corpuscles P and p in
the direction of lines tending to those superficies, are, by the
hypothesis, as the superficies themselves directly, and the
squares of the distances of the superficies from those corpuscles
inversely; that is, as pf × ps to PF × PS. And these forces
again are to the oblique parts of them which (by the resolution
of forces, as in cor. 2, of the laws) tend to the centres in the
directions of the lines PS, ps, as PI to PQ, and pi to pq; that
is (because of the like triangles PIQ and PSF, piq and psf), as
PS to PF and ps to pf. Thence, *ex æquo*, the attraction of the
corpuscle P towards S is to the attraction of the corpuscle p
towards s as $\dfrac{PF \times pf \times ps}{PS}$ is to $\dfrac{pf \times PF \times PS}{ps}$, that is, as ps^2 to
PS^2. And, by a like reasoning, the forces which which the super-
ficies described by the revolution of the arcs KL, kl, attract
those corpuscles, will be as ps^2 to PS^2. And in the same ratio
will be the forces of all the circular superficies into which
each of the sphærical superficies may be divided by taking sd
always equal to SD, and se equal to SE. And therefore, by
composition, the forces of the entire sphærical superficies
exerted upon those corpuscles will be in the same ratio.   Q.E.D.

Proposition LXXII.   Theorem XXXIL.

*If to the several points of a sphere there tend equal centripetal
forces, decreasing in a duplicate ratio of the distances from
those points; and there be given both the density of the sphere
and the ratio of the diameter of the sphere to the distance of
the corpuscle from its centre; I say, that the force with which
the corpuscle is attracted is proportional to the semidiameter
of the sphere.*

For conceive two corpuscles to be severally attracted by
two spheres, one by one, the other by the other, and their distances from the centres of the spheres to be proportional to the
diameters of the spheres respectively; and the spheres to be resolved into like particles, disposed in a like situation to the
corpuscles. Then the attractions of one corpuscle towards the
several particles of one sphere will be to the attractions of the
other towards as many analogous particles of the other sphere in
a ratio compounded of the ratio of the particles directly, and
the duplicate ratio of the distances inversely. But the particles are as the spheres, that is, in a triplicate ratio of the
diameters, and the distances are as the diameters; and the first
ratio directly with the last ratio, taken twice inversely,
becomes the ratio of diameter to diameter.   Q.E.D.

COR. 1. Hence if corpuscles revolve in circles about
spheres composed of matter equally attracting, and the distances
from the centres of the spheres be proportional to their diameters, the periodic times will be equal.

COR. 2. And, *vice versa*, if the periodic times are equal,
the distances will be proportional to the diameters. These two
corollaries appear from cor. 3, prop. 4.

COR. 3. If to the several points of any two solids whatever, of like figure and equal density, there tend equal centripetal forces decreasing in a duplicate ratio of the distances from those points, the forces with which corpuscles placed in a like situation to those two solids will be attracted by them will be to each other as the diameters of the solids.

Proposition LXXIII. Theorem XXXIII.

If to the several points of a given sphere there tend equal centripetal forces decreasing in a duplicate ratio of the distances from the points; I say, that a corpuscle placed within the sphere is attracted by a force proportional to its distance from the centre.

In the sphere ABCD, described about the centre S, let there be placed the corpuscle P; and about the same centre S, with the interval SP, conceive described an interior sphere PEQF. It is

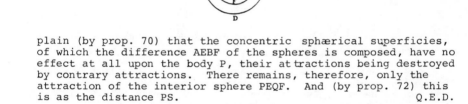

plain (by prop. 70) that the concentric sphærical superficies, of which the difference AEBF of the spheres is composed, have no effect at all upon the body P, their attractions being destroyed by contrary attractions. There remains, therefore, only the attraction of the interior sphere PEQF. And (by prop. 72) this is as the distance PS.   Q.E.D.

Scholium.

By the superficies of which I here imagine the solids composed, I do not mean superficies purely mathematical, but orbs so extremely thin, that their thickness is as nothing; that is, the evanescent orbs of which the sphere will at last consist, when the number of the orbs is increased, and their thickness diminished without end. In like manner, by the points of which lines, surfaces, and solids are said to be composed, are to be understood equal particles, whose magnitude is perfectly inconsiderable.

Proposition LXXIV. Theorem XXXIV.

The same things supposed, I say, that a corpuscle situate without the sphere is attracted with a force reciprocally proportional to the square of its distance from the centre.

For suppose the sphere to be divided into innumerable concentric sphærical superficies, and the attractions of the corpuscle arising from the several superficies will be reciprocally proportional to the square of the distance of the corpuscle from the centre of the sphere (by prop. 71). And, by composition, the sum of those attractions, that is, the attraction of the corpuscle towards the entire sphere, will be in the same ratio. Q.E.D.

COR. 1. Hence the attractions of homogeneous spheres at equal distances from the centres will be as the spheres themselves. For (by prop. 72), if the distances be proportional to the diameters of the spheres, the forces will be as the diameters. Let the greater distance be diminished in that ratio; and the distances now being equal, the attraction will be increased in the duplicate of that ratio; and therefore will be to the other attraction in the triplicate of that ratio; that is, in the ratio of the spheres.

COR. 2. At any distances whatever the attractions are as the spheres applied to the squares of the distances.

COR. 3. If a corpuscle placed without an homogeneous sphere is attracted by a force reciprocally proportional to the square of its distance from the centre, and the sphere consists of attractive particles, the force of every particle will decrease in a duplicate ratio of the distance from each particle.

*   *   *   *   *

Proposition LIII.   Theorem XLI.

Bodies carried about in a vortex, and returning in the same orb, are of the same density with the vortex, and are moved according to the same law with the parts of the vortex, as to velocity and direction of motion.

For if any small part of the vortex, whose particles or physical points preserve a given situation among each other, be supposed to be congealed, this particle will move according to the same law as before, since no change is made either in its density, *vis insita*, or figure. And again; if a congealed or solid part of the vortex be of the same density with the rest of the vortex, and be resolved into a fluid, this will move according to the same law as before, except in so far as its particles, now become fluid, may be moved among themselves. Neglect, therefore, the motion of the particles among themselves as not at all concerning the progressive motion of the whole, and the motion of the whole will be the same as before. But this motion will be the same with the motion of other parts of the vortex at equal distances from the centre; because the solid, now resolved into a fluid, is become perfectly like to the other parts of the vortex. Therefore a solid, if it be of the same density with the matter of the vortex, will move with the same motion as the parts thereof, being relatively at rest in the matter that surrounds it. If it be more dense, it will endeavour more than before to recede from the centre; and therefore overcoming that force of the vortex, by which, being, as it were, kept in equilibrio, it was retained in its orbit, it will recede from the centre, and in its revolution describe a spiral, returning no longer into the same orbit. And, by the same argument, if it be more rare, it will approach to the centre. Therefore it can never continually go round in the same orbit, unless it be of the same density with the fluid. But we have shewn in that case that it would revolve according to the same law with those parts of the fluid that are at the same or equal distances from the centre of the vortex.

COR. 1. Therefore a solid revolving in a vortex, and continually going round in the same orbit, is relatively quiescent in the fluid that carries it.

COR. 2. And if the vortex be of an uniform density, the same body may revolve at any distance from the centre of the vortex.

Scholium.

Hence it is manifest that the planets are not carried round in corporeal vortices; for, according to the *Copernican* hypothesis, the planets going round the sun revolve in ellipses, having the sun in their common focus; and by radii drawn to the sun describe areas proportional to the times. But now the parts of a vortex can never revolve with such a motion. Let AD, BE, CF, represent

three orbits described about the sun S, of which let the utmost circle CF be concentric to the sun; and let the aphelia of the two innermost be A, B; and their perihelia D, E. Therefore a body revolving in the orb CF, describing, by a radius drawn to the sun, areas proportional to the times, will move with an uniform motion. And, according to the laws of astronomy, the body revolving in the orb BE will move slower in its aphelion B, and swifter in its perihelion E; whereas, according to the laws of mechanics, the matter of the vortex ought to move more swiftly in the narrow space between A and C than in the wide space between D and F; that is, more swiftly in the aphelion than in the perihelion. Now these two conclusions contradict each other. So at the beginning of the sign of Virgo, where the aphelion of Mars is at present, the distance between the orbits of Mars and Venus is to the distance between the same orbits, at the beginning of the sign of Pisces, as about 3 to 2; and therefore the matter of the vortex between those orbits ought to be swifter at the beginning of Pisces than at the beginning of Virgo in the ratio of 3 to 2; for the narrower the space is through which the same quantity of matter passes in the same time of one revolution, the greater will be the velocity with which it passes through it. Therefore if the earth being relatively at rest in this celestial matter should be

carried round by it, and revolve together with it about the sun,
the velocity of the earth at the beginning of Pisces would be to
its velocity at the beginning of Virgo in a sesquialteral ratio.
Therefore the sun's apparent diurnal motion at the beginning of
Virgo ought to be above 70 minutes, and at the beginning of
Pisces less than 48 minutes; whereas, on the contrary, that
apparent motion of the sun is really greater at the beginning of
Pisces than at the beginning of Virgo, as experience testifies;
and therefore the earth is swifter at the beginning of Virgo than
at the beginning of Pisces; so that the hypothesis of vortices is
utterly irreconcileable with astronomical phænomena, and rather
serves to perplex than explain the heavenly motions. How these
motions are performed in free spaces without vortices, may be
understood by the first book; and I shall now more fully treat of
it in the following book.

*   *   *   *   *

Proposition VI.   Theorem VI.

*That all bodies gravitate towards every planet; and that the
weights of bodies towards any the same planet, at equal distances
from the centre of the planet, are proportional to the quantities
of matter which they severally contain.*

It has been, now of a long time, observed by others, that
all sorts of heavy bodies (allowance being made for the inequality
of retardation which they suffer from a small power of resistance
in the air) descend to the earth *from equal heights* in equal times;
and that equality of times we may distinguish to a great accuracy,
by the help of pendulums. I tried the thing in gold, silver,
lead, glass, sand, common salt, wood, water, and wheat. I provided two wooden boxes, round and equal: I filled the one with
wood, and suspended an equal weight of gold (as exactly as I
could) in the centre of oscillation of the other. The boxes
hanging by equal threads of 11 feet made a couple of pendulums
perfectly equal in weight and figure, and equally receiving the
resistance of the air. And, placing the one by the other, I
observed them to play together forwards and backwards, for a long
time, with equal vibrations. And therefore the quantity of matter in the gold (by cor. 1 and 6, prop. 24, book 2) was to the
quantity of matter in the wood as the action of the motive force
(or *vis motrix*) upon all the gold to the action of the same upon
all the wood; that is, as the weight of the one to the weight of
the other: and the like happened in the other bodies. By these
experiments, in bodies of the same weight, I could manifestly have
discovered a difference of matter less than the thousandth part
of the whole, had any such been. But, without all doubt, the
nature of gravity towards the planets is the same as towards the
earth. For, should we imagine our terrestrial bodies removed to
the orb of the moon, and there, together with the moon, deprived
of all motion, to be let go, so as to fall together towards the
earth, it is certain, from what we have demonstrated before, that,
in equal times, they would describe equal spaces with the moon,

and of consequence are to the moon, in quantity of matter, as
their weights to its weight. Moreover, since the satellites of
Jupiter perform their revolutions in times which observe the
sesquiplicate proportion of their distances from Jupiter's
centre, their accelerative gravities towards Jupiter will be
reciprocally as the squares of their distances from Jupiter's
centre; that is, equal, at equal distances. And, therefore, these
satellites, if supposed to fall *towards Jupiter* from equal heights,
would describe equal spaces in equal times, in like manner as
heavy bodies do on our earth. And, by the same argument, if the
circumsolar planets were supposed to be let fall at equal distances from the sun, they would, in their descent towards the
sun, describe equal spaces in equal times. But forces which
equally accelerate unequal bodies must be as those bodies; that is
to say, the weights of the planets *towards the sun* must be as
their quantities of matter. Further, that the weights of Jupiter
and of his satellites towards the sun are proportional to the
several quantities of their matter, appears from the exceedingly
regular motions of the satellites (by cor. 3, prop. 65, book 1).
For if some of those bodies were more strongly attracted to the
sun in proportion to their quantity of matter than others, the
motions of the satellites would be disturbed by that inequality
of attraction (by cor. 2, prop. 65, book 1). If, at equal distances from the sun, any satellite, in proportion to the quantity
of its matter, did gravitate towards the sun with a force greater
than Jupiter in proportion to his, according to any given proportion, suppose of d to e; then the distance between the centres of
the sun and of the satellite's orbit would be always greater than
the distance between the centres of the sun and of Jupiter nearly
in the subduplicate of that proportion; as by some computations I
have found. And if the satellite did gravitate towards the sun
with a force, lesser in the proportion of e to d, the distance of
the centre of the satellite's orb from the sun would be less than
the distance of the centre of Jupiter from the sun in the subduplicate of the same proportion. Therefore if, at equal distances
from the sun, the accelerative gravity of any satellite towards
the sun were greater or less than the accelerative gravity of
Jupiter towards the sun but by one $\frac{1}{1000}$ part of the whole gravity,
the distance of the centre of the satellite's orbit from the sun
would be greater or less than the distance of Jupiter from the sun
by one $\frac{1}{2000}$ part of the whole distance; that is, by a fifth part
of the distance of the utmost satellite from the centre of Jupiter;
an eccentricity of the orbit which would be very sensible. But
the orbits of the satellites are concentric to Jupiter, and therefore the accelerative gravities of Jupiter, and of all its
satellites towards the sun, are equal among themselves. And by
the same argument, the weights of Saturn and of his satellites
towards the sun, at equal distances from the sun, are as their
several quantities of matter; and the weights of the moon and of
the earth towards the sun are either none, or accurately proportional to the masses of matter which they contain. But some they
are, by cor. 1 and 3, prop. 5.

But further; the weights of all the parts of every planet towards any other planet are one to another as the matter in the several parts; for if some parts did gravitate more, others less, than for the quantity of their matter, then the whole planet, according to the sort of parts with which it most abounds, would gravitate more or less than in proportion to the quantity of matter in the whole. Nor is it of any moment whether these parts are external or internal; for if, for example, we should imagine the terrestrial bodies with us to be raised up to the orb of the moon, to be there compared with its body; if the weights of such bodies were to the weights of the external parts of the moon as the quantities of matter in the one and in the other respectively, but to the weights of the internal parts in a greater or less proportion, then likewise the weights of those bodies would be to the weight of the whole moon in a greater or less proportion; against what we have shewed above.

COR. 1. Hence the weights of bodies do not depend upon their forms and textures; for if the weights could be altered with the forms, they would be greater or less, according to the variety of forms, in equal matter; altogether against experience.

COR. 2. Universally, all bodies about the earth gravitate towards the earth; and the weights of all, at equal distances from the earth's centre, are as the quantities of matter which they severally contain. This is the quality of all bodies within the reach of our experiments; and therefore (by rule 3) to be affirmed of all bodies whatsoever. If the *æther*, or any other body, were either altogether void of gravity, or were to gravitate less in proportion to its quantity of matter, then, because (according to *Aristotle, Des Cartes*, and others) there is no difference betwixt that and other bodies but in *mere* form of matter, by a successive change from form to form, it might be changed at last into a body of the same condition with those which gravitate most in proportion to their quantity of matter; and, on the other hand, the heaviest bodies, acquiring the first form of that body, might by degrees quite lose their gravity. And therefore the weights would depend upon the forms of bodies, and with those forms might be changed: contrary to what was proved in the preceding corollary.

COR. 3. All spaces are not equally full; for if all spaces were equally full, then the specific gravity of the fluid which fills the region of the air, on account of the extreme density of the matter, would fall nothing short of the specific gravity of quicksilver, or gold, or any other the most dense body; and, therefore, neither gold, nor any other body, could descend in air; for bodies do not descend in fluids, unless they are specifically heavier than the fluids. And if the quantity of matter in a given space can, by any rarefaction, be diminished, what should hinder a diminution to infinity?

COR. 4. If all the solid particles of all bodies are of the same density, nor can be rarefied without pores, a void, space, or vacuum, must be granted. By bodies of the same density, I mean those whose *vires inertiæ* are in the proportion of their bulks.

COR. 5. The power of gravity is of a different nature from the power of magnetism; for the magnetic attraction is not as the matter attracted. Some bodies are attracted more by the magnet;

others less; most bodies not at all. The power of magnetism in
one and the same body may be increased and diminished; and is
sometimes far stronger, for the quantity of matter, than the
power of gravity; and in receding from the magnet decreases not in
the duplicate but almost in the triplicate proportion of the distance, as nearly as I could judge from some rude observations.

$$* \qquad * \qquad * \qquad * \qquad *$$

Proposition XIII.   Theorem XIII.

*The planets move in ellipses which have their common focus in the
centre of the sun; and, by radii drawn to that centre, they describe areas proportional to the times of description.*

We have discoursed above of these motions from the phænomena. Now that we know the principles on which they depend, from
those principles we deduce the motions of the heavens *à priori*.
Because the weights of the planets towards the sun are reciprocally as the squares of their distances from the sun's centre, if
the sun was at rest, and the other planets did not mutually act
one upon another, their orbits would be ellipses, having the sun
in their common focus; and they would describe areas proportional
to the times *of description*, by prop. 1 and 11, and cor. 1,
prop. 13, book 1. But the mutual actions of the planets one upon
another are so very small, that they may be neglected; and, by
prop. 66, book 1, they less disturb the motions of the planets
around the sun in motion than if those motions were performed
about the sun at rest.
It is true, that the action of Jupiter upon Saturn is not to
be neglected; for the force of gravity towards Jupiter is to the
force of gravity towards the sun as 1 to 1067; and therefore in
the conjunction of Jupiter and Saturn, because the distance of
Saturn from Jupiter is to the distance of Saturn from the sun
almost as 4 to 9, the gravity of Saturn towards Jupiter will be
to the gravity of Saturn towards the sun as 81 to 16 × 1067; or,
as 1 to about 211. And hence arises a perturbation of the orb of
Saturn in every conjunction of this planet with Jupiter, so sensible, that astronomers are puzzled with it. As the planet is
differently situated in these conjunctions, its eccentricity is
sometimes augmented, sometimes diminished; its aphelion is sometimes carried forwards, sometimes backwards, and its mean motion
is by turns accelerated and retarded; yet the whole error in its
motion about the sun, though arising from so great a force, may
be almost avoided (except in the mean motion) by placing the lower
focus of its orbit in the common centre of gravity of Jupiter and
the sun (according to the prop. 67, book 1), and therefore that
error, when it is greatest, scarcely exceeds two minutes; and the
greatest error in the mean motion scarcely exceeds two minutes
yearly. But in the conjunction of Jupiter and Saturn, the accelerative forces of gravity of the sun towards Saturn, of Jupiter
towards Saturn, and of Jupiter towards the sun, are almost as 16,
81, and $\frac{16 \times 81 \times 3021}{25}$, or 156609; and therefore the difference of the

forces of gravity of the sun towards Saturn, and of Jupiter towards Saturn, is to the force of gravity of Jupiter towards the sun as 65 to 156609, or as 1 to 2409. But the greatest power of Saturn to disturb the motion of Jupiter is proportional to this difference; and therefore the perturbation of the orbit of Jupiter is much less than that of Saturn's. The perturbations of the other orbits are yet far less, except that the orbit of the earth is sensibly disturbed by the moon. The common centre of gravity of the earth and moon moves in an ellipsis about the sun in the focus thereof, and, by a radius drawn to the sun, describes areas proportional to the times of description. But the earth in the mean time by a menstrual motion is revolved about this common centre.

Proposition XIV. Theorem XIV.

The aphelions and nodes of the orbits of the planets are fixed.

The aphelions are immovable, by prop. 11, book 1; and so are the planes of the orbits, by prop. 1 of the same book. And if the planes are fixed, the nodes must be so too. It is true, that some inequalities may arise from the mutual actions of the planets and comets in their revolutions; but these will be so small, that they may be here passed by.

COR. 1. The fixed stars are immovable, seeing they keep the same position to the aphelions and nodes of the planets.

COR. 2. And since these stars are liable to no sensible parallax from the annual motion of the earth, they can have no force, because of their immense distance, to produce any sensible effect in our system. Not to mention that the fixed stars, every where promiscuously dispersed in the heavens, by their contrary attractions destroy their mutual actions, by prop. 70, book 1.

Scholium.

Since the planets near the sun (viz. Mercury, Venus, the Earth, and Mars) are so small that they can act but with little force upon each other, therefore their aphelions and nodes must be fixed, excepting in so far as they are disturbed by the actions of Jupiter and Saturn, and other higher bodies. And hence we may find, by the theory of gravity, that their aphelions move a little *in consequentia*, in respect of the fixed stars, and that in the sesquiplicate proportion of their several distances from the sun. So that if the aphelion of Mars, in the space of an hundred years, is carried 33' 20" *in consequentia*, in respect of the fixed stars, the aphelions of the Earth, of Venus, and of Mercury, will in an hundred years be carried forwards 17' 40", 10' 53", and 4' 16", respectively. But these motions are so inconsiderable, that we have neglected them in this proposition.

*   *   *   *   *

General Scholium.

The hypothesis of vortices is pressed with many difficulties. That every planet by a radius drawn to the sun may describe areas proportional to the times of description, the periodic times of the several parts of the vortices should observe the duplicate proportion of their distances from the sun; but that the periodic times of the planets may obtain the sesquiplicate proportion of their distances from the sun, the periodic times of the parts of the vortex ought to be in the sesquiplicate proportion of their distances. That the smaller vortices may maintain their lesser revolutions about *Saturn, Jupiter*, and other planets, and swim quietly and undisturbed in the greater vortex of the sun, the periodic times of the parts of the sun's vortex should be equal; but the rotation of the sun and planets about their axes, which ought to correspond with the motions of their vortices, recede far from all these proportions. The motions of the comets are exceedingly regular, are governed by the same laws with the motions of the planets, and can by no means be accounted for by the hypothesis of vortices; for comets are carried with very eccentric motions through all parts of the heavens indifferently, with a freedom that is incompatible with the notion of a vortex.

Bodies projected in our air suffer no resistance but from the air. Withdraw the air, as is done in Mr. *Boyle*'s vacuum, and the resistance ceases; for in this void a bit of fine down and a piece of solid gold descend with equal velocity. And the parity of reason must take place in the celestial spaces above the earth's atmosphere; in which spaces, where there is no air to resist their motions, all bodies will move with the greatest freedom; and the planets and comets will constantly pursue their revolutions in orbits given in kind and position, according to the laws above explained; but though these bodies may, indeed, persevere in their orbits by the mere laws of gravity, yet they could by no means have at first derived the regular position of the orbits themselves from those laws.

The six primary planets are revolved about the sun in circles concentric with the sun, and with motions directed towards the same parts, and almost in the same plane. Ten moons are revolved about the earth, Jupiter and Saturn, in circles concentric with them, with the same direction of motion, and nearly in the planes of the orbits of those planets: but it is not to be conceived that mere mechanical causes could give birth to so many regular motions, since the comets range over all parts of the heavens in very eccentric orbits; for by that kind of motion they pass easily through the orbs of the planets, and with great rapidity; and in their aphelions, where they move the slowest, and are detained the longest, they recede to the greatest distances from each other, and thence suffer the least disturbance from their mutual attractions. This most beautiful system of the sun, planets, and comets, could only proceed from the counsel and dominion of an intelligent and powerful BEING. And if the fixed stars are the centres of other like systems, these, being formed by the like wise counsel, must be all subject to the dominion of ONE; especially since the light of the fixed stars is of the same

nature with the light of the sun, and from every system light
passes into all the other systems: and lest the systems of the
fixed stars should, by their gravity, fall on each other mutually,
he hath placed those systems at immense distances one from
another.

　　This BEING governs all things, not as the soul of the world,
but as Lord over all; and on account of his dominion he is wont
to be called Lord God παντοκράτωρ, or *Universal Ruler*; for *God* is
a relative word, and has a respect to servants; and *Deity* is the
dominion of GOD not over his own body, as those imagine who fancy
GOD to be the soul of the world, but over servants. The SUPREME
GOD is a Being eternal, infinite, absolutely perfect; but a
being, however perfect, without dominion, cannot be said to be
Lord God; for we say, my God, your God, the God of *Israel*, the
God of gods, and Lord of lords; but we do not say, my Eternal,
your Eternal, the Eternal of *Israel*, the Eternal of gods; we do
not say, my Infinite, or my Perfect: these are titles which have
no respect to servants. The word *God** usually signifies Lord;
but every lord is not a God. It is the dominion of a spiritual
being which constitutes a God: a true, supreme, or imaginary
dominion makes a true, supreme, or imaginary God. And from his
true dominion it follows that the true GOD is a living, intelligent, and powerful Being; and, from his other perfections, that
he is supreme, or most perfect. He is eternal and infinite, omni-
potent and omniscient; that is, his duration reaches from eternity
to eternity; his presence from infinity to infinity; he governs
all things, and knows all things that are to can be done. He is
not eternity or infinity, but eternal and infinite; he is not
duration or space, but he endures and is present. He endures for
ever, and is every where present; and by existing always and
everywhere, he constitutes duration and space. Since every particle of space is *always*, and every indivisible moment of duration is *every where*, certainly the Maker and Lord of all things
cannot be *never* and *no where*. Every soul that has perception is,
though in different times and in different organs of sense and
motion, still the same indivisible person. There are given
successive parts in duration, co-existent parts in space, but
neither the one nor the other in the person of a man, or his
thinking principle; and much less can they be found in the thinking substance of GOD. Every man, so far as he is a thing that
has perception, is one and the same man during his whole life, in
all and each of his organs of sense. GOD is the same GOD, always
and every where. He is omnipresent not *virtually* only, but also
substantially; for virtue cannot subsist without substance. In
him** are all things contained and moved; yet neither affects the

---

*Dr. Pocock derives the Latin word *Deus* from the *Arabic du* (in
the oblique case *di*), which signifies *Lord*. And in this sense
princes are called *gods*, *Psal.* lxxxii, ver. 6; and *John* x, ver.
35. And *Moses* is called a *god* to his brother *Aaron*, and a *god* to
Pharaoh (*Exod.* iv, ver. 16; and vii, ver. 8). And in the same
sense the souls of dead princes were formerly, by the Heathens,
called *gods*, but falsely, because of their want of dominion.

**This was the opinion of the Antients. So *Pythagoras*, in *Cicer.*
de Nat. Deor. llb. i. *Thales, Anaxagoras, Virgil*, Georg. lib. iv,

other: GOD suffers nothing from the motion of bodies; bodies find no resistance from the omnipresence of GOD. It is allowed by all that the SUPREME GOD exists necessarily; and by the same necessity he exists *always* and *every where*. Whence also he is all similar, all eye, all ear, all brain, all arm, all power to perceive, to understand, and to act; but in a manner not at all human, in a manner not at all corporeal, in a manner utterly unknown to us. As a blind man has no idea of colours, so have we no idea of the manner by which the all-wise GOD perceives and understands all things. He is utterly void of all body and bodily figure, and can therefore neither be seen, nor heard, nor touched; nor ought he to be worshipped under the representation of any corporeal thing. We have ideas of his attributes, but what the real substance of any thing is we know not. In bodies, we see only their figures and colours, we hear only the sounds, we touch only their outward surfaces, we smell only the odours, and taste the savours; but their inward substances are not to be known either by our senses, or by any reflex act of our minds: much less, then, have we any idea of the substance of GOD. We know him only by his most wise and excellent contrivances of things, and final causes; we admire him for his perfections; but we reverence and adore him on account of his dominion: for we adore him as his servants; and a god without dominion, providence, and final causes, is nothing else but Fate and Nature. Blind metaphysical necessity, which is certainly the same always and every where, could produce no variety of things. All that diversity of natural things which we find suited to different times and places could arise from nothing but the ideas and will of a Being necessarily existing. But, by way of allegory, GOD is said to see, to speak, to laugh, to love, to hate, to desire, to give, to receive, to rejoice, to be angry, to fight, to frame, to work, to build; for all our notions of GOD are taken from the ways of mankind by a certain similitude, which, though not perfect, has some likeness, however. And thus much concerning GOD; to discourse of whom from the appearances of things does certainly belong to Natural Philosophy.

Hitherto we have explained the phænomena of the heavens and of our sea by the power of gravity, but have not yet assigned the cause of this power. This is certain, that it must proceed from a cause that penetrates to the very centres of the sun and planets, without suffering the least diminution of its force; that operates not according to the quantity of the surfaces of the particles upon which it acts (as mechanical causes use to do), but according to the quantity of the solid matter which they con-

---

ver. 220; and Æneid, lib. vi, ver. 721. *Philo Allegor.* at the beginning of lib. i. *Aratus*, in his Phenom. at the beginning. So also the sacred writers; as St. *Paul*, *Acts* xvii, ver. 27, 28. St. *John's* Gosp. chap. xiv, ver. 2. *Moses*, in *Deut.* iv, ver. 39, and x, ver. 14. *David*, *Psal.* cxxxix, ver. 7,8,9. *Solomon*, 1 *Kings*, viii, ver. 27. *Job* xxii, ver. 12,13,14. *Jeremiah* xxiii, ver. 23, 24. The Idolaters supposed the sun, moon, and stars, the souls of men, and other parts of the world, to be parts of the SUPREME GOD, and therefore to be worshipped; but erroneously.

tain, and propagates its virtue on all sides to immense distances, decreasing always in the duplicate proportion of the distances. Gravitation towards the sun is made up out of the gravitations towards the several particles of which the body of the sun is composed; and in receding from the sun decreases accurately in the duplicate proportion of the distances as far as the orb of Saturn, as evidently appears from the quiescence of the aphelions of the planets; nay, and even to the remotest aphelions of the comets, if those aphelions are also quiescent. But hitherto I have not been able to discover the cause of those properties of gravity from phænomena, and I frame no hypothesis; for whatever is not deduced from the phænomena is to be called an hypothesis; and hypotheses, whether metaphysical or physical, whether of occult qualities or mechanical, have no place in experimental philosophy. In this philosophy particular propositions are inferred from the phænomena, and afterwards rendered general by induction. Thus it was that the impenetrability, the mobility, and the impulsive force of bodies, and the laws of motion and of gravitation, were discovered. And to us it is enough that gravity does really exist, and act according to the laws which we have explained, and abundantly serves to account for all the motions of the celestial bodies, and of our sea.

And now we might add something concerning a certain most subtle Spirit which pervades and lies hid in all gross bodies; by the force and action of which Spirit the particles of bodies mutually attract one another at near distances, and cohere, if contiguous; and electric bodies operate to greater distances, as well repelling as attracting the neighbouring corpuscles; and light is emitted, reflected, refracted, inflected, and heats bodies; and all sensation is excited, and the members of animal bodies move at the command of the will, namely, by the vibrations of this Spirit, mutually propagated along the solid filaments of the nerves, from the outward organs of sense to the brain, and from the brain into the muscles. But these are things that cannot be explained in few words, nor are we furnished with that sufficiency of experiments which is required to an accurate determination and demonstration of the laws by which this electric and elastic Spirit operates.

2. The Mechanical Philosophy

a. Galileo Galilei, *The Assayer**

*The Copernican Revolution did more than call men's attention
to the problems of astronomy. It forced them to rethink the very
bases of their knowledge of the physical world. Out of this re-
thinking was to come the mechanical philosophy--a way of looking
at the physical universe which was to be of great importance in
the development of physics in the seventeenth and eighteenth
centuries. One of the earlier proponents of some, at least, of
the tenets of the mechanical philosophy was Galileo who, in* The
Assayer, *discussed some of the problems raised by his new way of
looking at the world.*

It now remains for me to tell Your Excellency, as I promised,
some thoughts of mine about the proposition "motion is the cause
of heat," and to show in what sense this may be true. But first
I must consider what it is that we call heat, as I suspect that
people in general have a concept of this which is very remote
from the truth. For they believe that heat is a real phenomenon,
or property, or quality, which actually resides in the material
by which we feel ourselves warmed. Now I say that whenever I
conceive any material or corporeal substance, I immediately feel
the need to think of it as bounded, and as having this or that
shape; as being large or small in relation to other things, and
in some specific place at any given time; as being in motion or
at rest; as touching or not touching some other body; and as
being one in number, or few, or many. From these conditions I
cannot separate such a substance by any stretch of my imagination.
But that it must be white or red, bitter or sweet, noisy or silent, and of sweet or foul odor, my mind does not feel compelled
to bring in as necessary accompaniments. Without the senses as
our guides, reason or imagination unaided would probably never
arrive at qualities like these. Hence I think that tastes,
odors, colors, and so on are no more than mere names so far as
the object in which we place them is concerned, and that they
reside only in the consciousness. Hence if the living creature
were removed, all these qualities would be wiped away and anni-
hilated. But since we have imposed upon them special names,
distinct from those of the other and real qualities mentioned
previously, we wish to believe that they really exist as actually
different from those.
I may be able to make my notion clearer by means of some
examples. I move my hand first over a marble statue and then

* Galileo Galilei, *The Assayer* in Stillman Drake, *op. cit.*,
pp. 273-8.

over a living man. As to the effect flowing from my hand, this
is the same with regard to both objects and my hand; it consists
of the primary phenomena of motion and touch, for which we have
no further names. But the live body which receives these
operations feels different sensations according to the various
places touched. When touched upon the soles of the feet, for
example, or under the knee or armpit, it feels in addition to the
common sensation of touch a sensation on which we have imposed a
special name, "tickling." This sensation belongs to us and not
to the hand. Anyone would make a serious error if he said that
the hand, in addition to the properties of moving and touching,
possessed another faculty of "tickling," as if tickling were a
phenomenon that resided in the hand that tickled. A piece of
paper or a feather drawn lightly over any part of our bodies
performs intrinsically the same operations of moving and touching,
but by touching the eye, the nose, or the upper lip it excites
in us an almost intolerable titillation, even though elsewhere
it is scarcely felt. This titillation belongs entirely to us
and not to the feather; if the live and sensitive body were removed it would remain no more than a mere word. I believe that
no more solid an existence belongs to many qualities which we
have come to attribute to physical bodies--tastes, odors,
colors, and many more.

A body which is solid and, so to speak, quite material, when
moved in contact with any part of my person produces in me the
sensation we call touch. This, though it exists over my entire
body, seems to reside principally in the palms of the hands and
in the finger tips, by whose means we sense the most minute differences in texture that are not easily distinguished by other
parts of our bodies. Some of these sensations are more pleasant
to us than others. . . . The sense of touch is more material
than the other sense; and, as it arises from the solidity of
matter, it seems to be related to the earthly element.

Perhaps the origin of two other senses lies in the fact
that there are bodies which constantly dissolve into minute particles, some of which are heavier than air and descend, while
others are lighter and rise up. The former may strike upon a
certain part of our bodies that is much more sensitive than the
skin, which does not feel the invasion of such subtle matter.
This is the upper surface of the tongue; here the tiny particles
are received, and mixing with and penetrating its moisture, they
give rise to tastes, which are sweet or unsavory according to
the various shapes, numbers, and speeds of the particles. And
those minute particles which rise up may enter by our nostrils
and strike upon some small protuberances which are the instrument
of smelling; here likewise their touch and passage is received to
our like or dislike according as they have this or that shape,
are fast or slow, and are numerous or few. The tongue and nasal
passages are providently arranged for these things, as the one
extends from below to receive descending particles, and the other
is adapted to those which ascend. Perhaps the excitation of
tastes may be given a certain analogy to fluids, which descend
through air, and odors to fires, which ascend.

Then there remains the air itself, an element available for
sounds, which come to us indifferently from below, above, and

all sides--for we reside in the air and its movements displace it
equally in all directions. The location of the ear is most
fittingly accommodated to all positions in space. Sounds are
made and heard by us when the air--without any special property
of "sonority" or "transonority"--is ruffled by a rapid tremor
into very minute waves and moves certain cartilages of a tympanum in our ear. External means capable of thus ruffling the
air are very numerous, but for the most part they may be reduced
to the trembling of some body which pushes the air and disturbs
it. Waves are propagated very rapidly in this way, and high
tones are produced by frequent waves and low tones by sparse
ones.

To excite in us tastes, odors, and sounds I believe that
nothing is required in external bodies except shapes, numbers,
and slow or rapid movements. I think that if ears, tongues and
noses were removed, shapes and numbers and motions would remain,
but not odors or tastes or sounds. The latter, I believe, are
nothing more than names when separated from living beings, just
as tickling and titillation are nothing but names in the absence
of such things as noses and armpits. And as these four senses
are related to the four elements, so I believe that vision, the
sense eminent above all others in the proportion of the finite
to the infinite, the temporal to the instantaneous, the quantitative to the indivisible, the illuminated to the obscure--that
vision, I say, is related to light itself. But of this sensation
and the things pertaining to it I pretend to understand but
little; and since even a long time would not suffice to explain
that trifle, or even to hint at an explanation, I pass this over
in silence.

Having shown that many sensations which are supposed to be
qualities residing in external objects have no real existence
save in us, and outside ourselves are mere names, I now say that
I am inclined to believe heat to be of this character. Those
materials which produce heat in us and make us feel warmth, which
are known by the general name of "fire," would then be a multitude of minute particles having certain shapes and moving with
certain velocities. Meeting with our bodies, they penetrate by
means of their extreme subtlety, and their touch as felt by us
when they pass through our substance is the sensation we call
"heat." This is pleasant or unpleasant according to the greater
or smaller speed of these particles as they go pricking and
penetrating; pleasant when this assists our necessary transpira-
tion, and obnoxious when it causes too great a separation and
dissolution of our substance. The operation of fire by means of
its particles is merely that in moving it penetrates all bodies,
causing their speedy or slow dissolution in proportion to the
number and velocity of the fire-corpuscles and the density or
tenuity of the bodies. Many materials are such that in their
decomposition the greater part of them passes over into additional tiny corpuscles, and this dissolution continues so long as
these continue to meet with further matter capable of being so
resolved. I do not believe that in addition to shape, number,
motion, penetration, and touch there is any other quality in
fire corresponding to "heat"; this belongs so intimately to us

that when the live body is taken away, heat becomes no more than a simple name. . . .

Since the presence of fire-corpuscles alone does not suffice to excite heat, but their motion is needed also, it seems to me that one may very reasonably say that motion is the cause of heat. . . . But I hold it to be silly to accept that proposition in the ordinary way, as if a stone or piece of iron or a stick must heat up when moved. The rubbing together and friction of two hard bodies, either by resolving their parts into very subtle flying particles or by opening an exit for the tiny fire-corpuscles within, ultimately sets these in motion; and when they meet our bodies and penetrate them, our conscious mind feels those pleasant or unpleasant sensations which we have named heat, burning, and scalding. And perhaps when such attrition stops at or is confined to the smallest quanta, their motion is temporal and their action calorific only; but when their ultimate and highest resolution into truly indivisible atoms is arrived at, light is created. This may have an instantaneous motion, or rather an instantaneous expansion and diffusion, rendering it capable of occupying immense spaces by its—I know not whether to say its subtlety, its rarity, its immateriality, or some other property which differs from all these and is nameless.

b. René Descartes, *Principia Philosophiae**

*It was René Descartes who systematically built his philoso-
phy upon mechanical principles. In his* Principia Philosophiae,*
*Descartes laid out the necessary axioms upon which the mechanical
philosophy (in his opinion) must rest.*

Part II
Of the Principles of Material Things.

I. The grounds on which the existence of material things
may be known with certainty.

Although we are all sufficiently persuaded of the existence
of material things, yet, since this was before called in question
by us, and since we reckoned the persuasion of their existence as
among the prejudices of our childhood, it is now necessary for
us to investigate the grounds on which this truth may be known
with certainty. In the first place, then, it cannot be doubted
that every perception we have comes to us from some object different from our mind; for it is not in our power to cause ourselves to experience one perception rather than another, the perception being entirely dependent on the object which affects our
senses. It may, indeed, be matter of inquiry whether that object
be God, or something different from God; but because we perceive,
or rather, stimulated by sense, clearly and distinctly apprehend,
certain matter extended in length, breadth, and thickness, the
various parts of which have different figures and motions, and
give rise to the sensations we have of colours, smells, pain,
etc., God would, without question, deserve to be regarded as a
deceiver, if he directly and of himself presented to our mind the
idea of this extended matter, or merely caused it to be presented
to us by some object which possessed neither extension, figure,
nor motion. For we clearly conceive this matter as entirely distinct from God, and from ourselves, or our mind; and appear even
clearly to discern that the idea of it is formed in us on occasion of objects existing out of our minds, to which it is in
every respect similar. But since God cannot deceive us, for this
is repugnant to his nature, as has been already remarked, we must
unhesitatingly conclude that there exists a certain object extended in length, breadth, and thickness, and possessing all those
properties which we clearly apprehend to belong to what is extended. And this extended substance is what we call body or matter.

II. How we likewise know that the human body is closely
connected with the mind.

We ought also to conclude that a certain body is more closely united to our mind than any other, because we clearly observe

---

*René Descartes, *The Principles of Philosophy* in *Discourse on the
Method*. . . translated by John Veitch, 5th edition, William
Blackwood and Sons, Edinburgh and London, 1873, pp. 152-185.
Also, Marie Boas Hall, *Nature and Nature's Laws*, Harper & Row,
1970.

that pain and other sensations affect us without our foreseeing
them; and these, the mind is conscious, do not arise from itself
alone, nor pertain to it, in so far as it is a thing which
thinks, but only in so far as it is united to another thing extended and moveable, which is called the human body. But this is
not the place to treat in detail of this matter.

III.   That the perceptions of the senses do not teach us
what is in reality in things, but what is beneficial or hurtful
to the composite whole of mind and body.

It will be sufficient to remark that the perceptions of the
senses are merely to be referred to this intimate union of the
human body and mind, and that they usually make us aware of what,
in external objects, may be useful or adverse to this union, but
do not present to us these objects as they are in themselves,
unless occasionally and by accident. For, after this observation, we will without difficulty lay aside the prejudices of the
senses, and will have recourse to our understanding alone on this
question, by reflecting carefully on the ideas implanted in it by
nature.

IV.   That the nature of body consists not in weight, hardness, colour, and the like, but in extension alone.

In this way we will discern that the nature of matter or
body, considered in general, does not consist in its being hard,
or ponderous, or coloured, or that which affects our senses in
any other way, but simply in its being a substance extended in
length, breadth, and depth. For, with respect to hardness, we
know nothing of it by sense farther than that the parts of hard
bodies resist the motion of our hands on coming into contact with
them; but if every time our hands moved towards any part, all the
bodies in that place receded as quickly as our hands approached,
we should never feel hardness; and yet we have no reason to believe that bodies which might thus recede would on this account
lose that which makes them bodies. The nature of body does not,
therefore, consist in hardness. In the same way, it may be
shown that weight, colour, and all the other qualities of this
sort, which are perceived in corporeal matter, may be taken from
it, itself meanwhile remaining entire: it thus follows that the
nature of body depends on none of these.

V.   That the truth regarding the nature of body is obscured
by the opinions respecting rarefaction and a vacuum with which we
are pre-occupied.

There still remain two causes to prevent its being fully admitted that the true nature of body consists in extension alone.
The first is the prevalent opinion, that most bodies admit of
being so rarefied and condensed that, when rarefied, they have
greater extension than when condensed; and some even have sub-
tilized to such a degree as to make a distinction between the
substance of body and its quantity, and between quantity itself
and extension. The second cause is this, that where we conceive
only extension in length, breadth, and depth, we are not in the
habit of saying that body is there, but only space and further
void space, which the generality believe to be a mere negation.

VI.   In what way rarefaction takes place.

But with regard to rarefaction and condensation, whoever

gives his attention to his own thoughts, and admits nothing of
which he is not clearly conscious, will not suppose that there is
anything in those processes further than a change of figure in
the body rarefied or condensed: so that, in other words, rare
bodies are those between the parts of which there are numerous
distances filled with other bodies; and dense bodies, on the
other hand, those whose parts approaching each other, either
diminish these distances or take them wholly away, in the latter
of which cases the body is rendered absolutely dense. The body,
however, when condensed, has not, therefore, less extension than
when the parts embrace a greater space, owing to their removal
from each other, and their dispersion into branches. For we
ought not to attribute to it the extension of the pores or distances which its parts do not occupy when it is rarefied, but to
the other bodies that fill these interstices; just as when we see
a sponge full of water or any other liquid, we do not suppose
that each part of the sponge has on this account greater extension than when compressed and dry, but only that its pores are
wider, and therefore that the body is diffused over a larger
space.

VII.   That rarefaction cannot be intelligibly explained
unless in the way here proposed.

And indeed I am unable to discover the force of the reasons
which have induced some to say that rarefaction is the result of
the augmentation of the quantity of body, rather than to explain
it on the principle exemplified in the case of a sponge. For
although when air or water are rarefied we do not see any of the
pores that are rendered large, or the new body that is added to
occupy them, it is yet less agreeable to reason to suppose
something that is unintelligible for the purpose of giving a
verbal and merely apparent explanation of the rarefaction of
bodies, than to conclude, because of their rarefaction, that
there are pores or distances between the parts which are increased in size, and filled with some new body. Nor ought we to
refrain from assenting to this explanation, because we perceive
this new body by none of our senses, for there is no reason which
obliges us to believe that we should perceive by our senses all
the bodies in existence. And we see that it is very easy to
explain rarefaction in this manner, but impossible in any other;
for, in fine, there would be, as appears to me, a manifest contradiction in supposing that any body was increased by a quantity
or extension which it had not before, without the addition to it
of a new extended substance, in other words, of another body,
because it is impossible to conceive any addition of extension or
quantity to a thing without supposing the addition of a substance
having quantity or extension, as will more clearly appear from
what follows.

VIII.   That quantity and number differ only in thought
(*ratione*) from that which has quantity and is numbered.

For quantity differs from extended substance, and number
from what is numbered, not in reality but merely in our thought;
so that, for example, we may consider the whole nature of a corporeal substance which is comprised in a space of ten feet, although we do not attend to this measure of ten feet, for the

obvious reason that the thing conceived is of the same nature in
any part of that space as in the whole; and, on the other hand,
we can conceive the number ten, as also a continuous quantity of
ten feet, without thinking of this determinate substance, because
the concept of the number ten is manifestly the same whether we
consider a number of ten feet or ten of anything else; and we can
conceive a continuous quantity of ten feet without thinking of
this or that determinate substance, although we cannot conceive it
without some extended substance of which it is the quantity. It
is in reality, however, impossible that any, even the least part,
of such quantity or extension, can be taken away, without the
retrenchment at the same time of as much of the substance, nor,
on the other hand, can we lessen the substance, without at the
same time taking as much from the quantity or extension.

IX.   That corporeal substance, when distinguished from its
quantity, is confusedly conceived as something incorporeal.

Although perhaps some express themselves otherwise on this
matter, I am nevertheless convinced that they do not think differently from what I have now said: for when they distinguish
(corporeal) substance from extension or quantity, they either
mean nothing by the word (corporeal) substance, or they form in
their minds merely a confused idea of incorporeal substance,
which they falsely attribute to corporeal, and leave to extension
the true idea of this corporeal substance; which extension they
call an accident, but with such impropriety as to make it easy
to discover that their words are not in harmony with their
thoughts.

X.   What space or internal place is.

Space or internal place, and the corporeal substance which
is comprised in it, are not different in reality, but merely in
the mode in which they are wont to be conceived by us. For, in
truth, the same extension in length, breadth, and depth, which
constitutes space, constitutes body; and the difference between
them lies only in this, that in body we consider extension as
particular, and conceive it to change with the body; whereas in
space we attribute to extension a generic unity, so that after
taking from a certain space the body which occupied it, we do not
suppose that we have at the same time removed the extension of
the space, because it appears to us that the same extension
remains there so long as it is of the same magnitude and figure,
and preserves the same situation in respect to certain bodies
around it, by means of which we determine this space.

XI.   How space is not in reality different from corporeal
substance.

And indeed it will be easy to discern that it is the same
extension which constitutes the nature of body as of space, and
that these two things are mutually diverse only as the nature
of the genus and species differs from that of the individual,
provided we reflect on the idea we have of any body, taking a
stone for example, and reject all that is not essential to the
nature of body. In the first place, then, hardness may be rejected, because if the stone were liquefied or reduced to powder, it
would no longer possess hardness, and yet would not cease to be a
body; colour also may be thrown out of account, because we have

frequently seen stones so transparent as to have no colour;
again, we may reject weight, because we have the case of fire,
which, though very light, is still a body; and, finally, we may
reject cold, heat, and all the other qualities of this sort,
either because they are not considered as in the stone, or
because, with the change of these qualities, the stone is not
supposed to have lost the nature of body. After this examination
we will find that nothing remains in the idea of body, except
that it is something extended in length, breadth, and depth; and
this something is comprised in our idea of space, not only of
that which is full of body, but even of what is called void
space.

XII. How space differs from body in our mode of conceiving
it.

There is, however, some difference between them in the mode
of conception; for if we remove a stone from the space or place
in which it was, we conceive that its extension also is taken
away, because we regard this as particular, and inseparable from
the stone itself: but meanwhile we suppose that the same extension of place in which this stone was remains, although the
place of the stone be occupied by wood, water, air, or by any
other body, or be even supposed vacant, because we now consider
extension in general, and think that the same is common to
stones, wood, water, air, and other bodies, and even to a vacuum
itself, if there is any such thing, provided it be of the same
magnitude and figure as before, and preserve the same situation
among the external bodies which determine this space.

XIII. What external place is.

The reason of which is, that the words place and space signify nothing really different from body which is said to be in
place, but merely designate its magnitude, figure, and situation
among other bodies. For it is necessary, in order to determine
this situation, to regard certain other bodies which we consider
as immoveable; and, according as we look to different bodies, we
may see that the same thing at the same time does and does not
change place. For example, when a vessel is being carried out to
sea, a person sitting at the stern may be said to remain always
in one place, if we look to the parts of the vessel, since with
respect to these he preserves the same situation; and on the
other hand, if regard be had to the neighbouring shores, the
same person will seem to be perpetually changing place, seeing he
is constantly receding from one shore and approaching another.
And besides, if we suppose that the earth moves, and that it
makes precisely as much way from west to east as the vessel from
east to west, we will again say that the person at the stern does
not change his place, because this place will be determined by
certain immoveable points which we imagine to be in the heavens.
But if at length we are persuaded that there are no points really
immoveable in the universe, as will hereafter be shown to be
probable, we will thence conclude that nothing has a permanent
place unless in so far as it is fixed by our thought.

XIV. Wherein place and space differ.

The terms place and space, however, differ in signification,
because place more expressly designates situation than magnitude

or figure, while, on the other hand, we think of the latter when
we speak of space. For we frequently say that a thing succeeds
to the place of another, although it be not exactly of the same
magnitude or figure; but we do not therefore admit that it
occupies the same space as the other; and when the situation is
changed we say that the place also is changed, although there are
the same magnitude and figure as before: so that when we say
that a thing is in a particular place, we mean merely that it is
situated in a determinate way in respect of certain other objects; and when we add that it occupies such a space or place,
we understand besides that it is of such determinate magnitude
and figure as exactly to fill this space.

XV. How external place is rightly taken for the superficies
of the surrounding body.

And thus we never indeed distinguish space from extension in
length, breadth, and depth; we sometimes, however, consider place
as in the thing placed, and at other times as out of it.   Internal place indeed differs in no way from space; but external place
may be taken for the superficies that immediately surrounds the
thing placed. It ought to be remarked that by superficies we do
not here understand any part of the surrounding body, but only
the boundary between the surrounding and surrounded bodies, which
is nothing more than a mode; or at least that we speak of superficies in general which is no part of one body rather than
another, but is always considered the same, provided it retain
the same magnitude and figure. For although the whole surrounding
body with its superficies were changed, it would not be supposed
that the body which was surrounded by it had therefore changed
its place, if it meanwhile preserved the same situation with
respect to the other bodies that are regarded as immoveable.
Thus, if we suppose that a boat is carried in one direction by
the current of a stream, and impelled by the wind in the opposite
with an equal force, so that its situation with respect to the
banks is not changed, we will readily admit that it remains in
the same place, although the whole superficies which surrounds
it is incessantly changing.

XVI. That a vacuum or space in which there is absolutely
no body is repugnant to reason.

With regard to a vacuum, in the philosophical sense of the
term, that is, a space in which there is no substance, it is evident that such does not exist, seeing the extension of space or
internal place is not different from that of body. For since
from this alone, that a body has extension in length, breadth,
and depth, we have reason to conclude that it is a substance, it
being absolutely contradictory that nothing should possess extension, we ought to form a similar inference regarding the space
which is supposed void, viz., that since there is extension in it
there is necessarily also substance.

XVII. That a vacuum in the ordinary use of the term does
not exclude all body.

And, in truth, by the term vacuum in its common use, we do
not mean a place or space in which there is absolutely nothing,
but only a place in which there is none of those things we presume ought to be there. Thus, because a pitcher is made to hold

water, it is said to be empty when it is merely filled with air;
or if there are no fish in a fish-pond, we say there is nothing
in it, although it be full of water; thus a vessel is said to be
empty, when, in place of the merchandise which it was designed to
carry, it is loaded with sand only, to enable it to resist the
violence of the wind; and, finally, it is in the same sense that
we say space is void when it contains nothing sensible, although
it contain created and self-subsisting matter; for we are not in
the habit of considering the bodies near us, unless in so far as
they cause in our organs of sense impressions strong enough to
enable us to perceive them. And if, in place of keeping in mind
what ought to be understood by these terms a vacuum and nothing,
we afterwards suppose that in the space we called a vacuum,
there is not only no sensible object, but no object at all, we
will fall into the same error as if, because a pitcher in which
there is nothing but air, is, in common speech, said to be empty,
we were therefore to judge that the air contained in it is not a
substance (*res subsistens*).

XVIII. How the prejudice of an absolute vacuum is to be
corrected.

We have almost all fallen into this error from the earliest
age, for, observing that there is no necessary connection between
a vessel and the body it contains, we thought that God at least
could take from a vessel the body which occupied it, without it
being necessary that any other should be put in the place of the
one removed. But that we may be able now to correct this false
opinion, it is necessary to remark that there is in truth no
connection between the vessel and the particular body which it
contains, but that there is an absolutely necessary connection
between the concave figure of the vessel and the extension considered generally which must be comprised in this cavity; so that
it is not more contradictory to conceive a mountain without a
valley than such a cavity without the extension it contains, or
this extension apart from an extended substance, for, as we have
often said, of nothing there can be no extension. And accordingly, if it be asked what would happen were God to remove from a
vessel all the body contained in it, without permitting another
body to occupy its place, the answer must be that the sides of
the vessel would thus come into proximity with each other. For
two bodies must touch each other when there is nothing between
them, and it is manifestly contradictory for two bodies to be
apart, in other words, that there should be a distance between
them, and this distance yet be nothing; for all distance is a
mode of extension, and cannot therefore exist without an extended
substance.

XIX. That this confirms what was said of rarefaction.

After we have thus remarked that the nature of corporeal
substance consists only in its being an extended thing, and that
its extension is not different from that which we attribute to
space, however empty, it is easy to discover the impossibility of
any one of its parts in any way whatsoever occupying more space
at one time than at another, and thus of being otherwise rarefied
than in the way explained above; and it is easy to perceive also

that there cannot be more matter or body in a vessel when it is
filled with lead or gold, or any other body however heavy and
hard, than when it but contains air and is supposed to be empty:
for the quantity of the parts of which a body is composed does
not depend on their weight or hardness, but only on the extension, which is always equal in the same vase.

XX. That from this the non-existence of atoms may likewise
be demonstrated.

We likewise discover that there cannot exist any atoms or
parts of matter that are of their own nature indivisible. For
however small we suppose these parts to be, yet because they are
necessarily extended, we are always able in thought to divide
any one of them into two or more smaller parts, and may accordingly admit their divisibility. For there is nothing we can
divide in thought which we do not thereby recognise to be
divisible; and, therefore, were we to judge it indivisible our
judgment would not be in harmony with the knowledge we have of
the thing; and although we should even suppose that God had
reduced any particle of matter to a smallness so extreme that it
did not admit of being further divided, it would nevertheless be
improperly styled indivisible, for though God had rendered the
particle so small that it was not in the power of any creature to
divide it, he could not however deprive himself of the ability
to do so, since it is absolutely impossible for him to lessen his
own omnipotence, as was before observed. Wherefore, absolutely
speaking, the smallest extended particle is always divisible,
since it is such of its very nature.

XXI. It is thus also demonstrated that the extension of
the world is indefinite.

We further discover that this world or the whole (*universi-*
tas) of corporeal substance, is extended without limit, for wherever we fix a limit, we still not only imagine beyond it spaces
indefinitely extended, but perceive these to be truly imaginable,
in other words, to be in reality such as we imagine them; so that
they contain in them corporeal substance indefinitely extended,
for, as has been already shown at length, the idea of extension
which we conceive in any space whatever is plainly identical with
the idea of corporeal substance.

XXII. It also follows that the matter of the heavens and
earth is the same, and that there cannot be a plurality of
worlds.

And it may also be easily inferred from all this that the
earth and heavens are made of the same matter; and that even
although there were an infinity of worlds, they would all be
composed of this matter; from which it follows that a plurality
of worlds is impossible, because we clearly conceive that the
matter whose nature consists only in its being an extended substance, already wholly occupies all the imaginable spaces where
these other worlds could alone be, and we cannot find in ourselves the idea of any other matter.

XXIII. That all the variety of matter, or the diversity of
its forms, depends on motion.

There is therefore but one kind of matter in the whole universe, and this we know only by its being extended. All the

properties we distinctly perceive to belong to it are reducible
to its capacity of being divided and moved according to its
parts; and accordingly it is capable of all those affections
which we perceive can arise from the motion of its parts. For
the partition of matter in thought makes no change in it; but
all variation of it, or diversity of form, depends on motion.
The philosophers even seem universally to have observed this, for
they said that nature was the principle of motion and rest, and
by nature they understood that by which all corporeal things
become such as they are found in experience.

    XXIV. What motion is, taking the term in its common use.

    But motion (viz., local, for I can conceive no other kind
of motion, and therefore I do not think we ought to suppose there
is any other in nature), in the ordinary sense of the term, is
nothing more than the *action by which a body passes from one
place to another*. And just as we have remarked above that the
same thing may be said to change and not to change place at the
same time, so also we may say that the same thing is at the same
time moved and not moved. Thus, for example, a person seated in
a vessel which is setting sail, thinks he is in motion if he look
to the shore that he has left, and consider it as fixed; but not
if he regard the ship itself, among the parts of which he preserves always the same situation. Moreover, because we are
accustomed to suppose that there is no motion without action, and
that in rest there is the cessation of action, the person thus
seated is more properly said to be at rest than in motion, seeing
he is not conscious of being in action.

    XXV. What motion is properly so called.

    But if, instead of occupying ourselves with that which has
no foundation, unless in ordinary usage, we desire to know what
ought to be understood by motion according to the truth of the
thing, we may say, in order to give it a determinate nature, that
it is *the transporting of one part of matter or of one body from
the vicinity of those bodies that are in immediate contact with it,
or which we regard as at rest, to the vicinity of other bodies*.
By a body as a part of matter, I understand all that which is
transferred together, although it be perhaps composed of several
parts, which in themselves have other motions; and I say that it
is the transporting and not the force or action which transports,
with the view of showing that motion is always in the moveable
thing, not in that which moves; for it seems to me that we are
not accustomed to distinguish these two things with sufficient
accuracy. Farther,I understand that it is a mode of the moveable
thing, and not a substance, just as figure is a property of the
thing figured, and repose of that which is at rest.

    LIV. To determine the nature of solid and fluid bodies, we
must first take into account the evidence of our senses, since
these are sensible qualities, and this teaches us that it consists only in the fact that the particles of fluid bodies so
easily give up their place that they offer no resistance to our
hands in an encounter, and that on the contrary the particles of
solid bodies are so closely united that they cannot be separated
without force, which then breaks their union. If we inquire further into the reason why some bodies yield their place without

resistance and why others do not do so, we can only find that
bodies already prepared for motion in no way prevent the places
they are about to leave themselves from being occupied by other
bodies. But those at rest cannot be chased out of their places
without an external force to cause this change. Whence it follows that a body is fluid when it is divided into many particles,
each of which moves individually and in its own way, and that it
is solid when all its particles touch one another and are in no
state to move away from each other.

LV. And I can imagine no cement fitter to unite the particles of solid bodies than *rest*. For what kind of a thing is it?
It cannot be more material, for since all these particles are
bodies, there is no more reason why they should be united by
another body than by themselves. It cannot be a property which
is not rest, because there is no quality which differs more from
the motion that can separate these particles than the rest which
belongs to them. And apart from bodies and their properties what
other things are there?

LVI. As for fluid bodies, although we do not observe the
motion of their particles, because they are too small, we can yet
know of its existence by several effects. The chief effect
arises from the fact that air and water corrupt many other substances and that the particles of which these fluids are composed
can produce no corporeal action such as corruption without real
motion. I shall later explain what causes there are for the
motion of these parts. . . .

LXI. It is easy to understand by the previous discussion
that a solid body at rest between the particles of a fluid body
which surrounds it on all sides is so balanced that the slightest
force can push it from side to side, even if it is thought to be
large, and this whether the force is external or arises because
the surrounding fluid body is moving in a certain direction. So
rivers flow to the sea and air towards the sunset when the east
wind blows. For in such a case the solid body surrounded by a
fluid on all sides is carried with it. . . .

LXII. And even if we pay strict attention to the true
nature of motion--which is, properly speaking, the transference
of the moving body from the neighbourhood of other bodies with
which it is in contact, while this transference is equally applicable to all the contiguous bodies--although we do not normally say that both bodies move, we yet know that it is not correct
to say that only the solid body moves when, being surrounded on
all sides by a fluid, it follows the fluid's path; or that if
it had sufficient force to resist it could prevent itself from
being moved, for it stays much closer to the surrounding particles if it follows the path of the fluid than if it does not
do so. So one must not say that a solid body moves when it is
thus carried along by a fluid body.

LXIII. Whence it comes about that there are bodies so solid
that they cannot be divided by our hands, although they are
smaller than these. If it is true that the particles of solid
bodies are not united by any cement and that there is absolutely
nothing preventing their separation except the relative rest between them, as stated above, and if it is also true that a body

in motion, however slow, always possesses sufficient force to
move another smaller body which is at rest . . . then one may ask
why we cannot break with our bare hands a nail or any other piece
of iron smaller than they are, when each half of the nail may be
considered as a body at rest relative to the other half and thus
it seems the nail ought to be capable of division by our hands
which are larger than it, since motion consists in the moving
body's being separated from its contiguous bodies. It must be
noted that our hands are very soft and thus share the nature of
fluids more than of solids, which is why their particles are not
sufficiently agitated against the body we wish to divide. For
as the half of a nail can be taken for a body, since it can be
separated from its other half, so the part of our hand which
touches that half of the nail, and which is much smaller than the
whole hand, can be taken as another body, since it can be separated from the other parts of the hand. And as it can be separated from the rest of the hand more easily than a part of the
nail from the rest of the nail, and as we feel pain at such an
act, we cannot break a nail with our hands. But if we take a
hammer or file or shears or some other similar instrument and if
we so employ it as to apply the force of our hand against the
part of the body we wish to divide, which must be smaller than
the part of the instrument applied against it, we can overcome
the solidity even of a large body.

Part III.

Of the Visible World.

I.   That we cannot think too highly of the works of God.
Having now ascertained certain principles of material
things, which were sought, not by the prejudices of the senses,
but by the light of reason, and which thus possess so great evidence that we cannot doubt of their truth, it remains for us to
consider whether from these alone we can deduce the explication
of all the phenomena of nature. We will commence with those
phenomena that are of the greatest generality, and upon which the
others depend, as, for example, with the general structure of
this whole visible world. But in order to our philosophising
aright regarding this, two things are first of all to be observed.
The first is, that we should ever bear in mind the infinity of
the power and goodness of God, that we may not fear falling into
error by imagining his works to be too great, beautiful, and
perfect, but that we may, on the contrary, take care lest, by
supposing limits to them of which we have no certain knowledge,
we appear to think less highly than we ought of the power of God.
II.   That we ought to beware lest, in our presumption, we
imagine that the ends which God proposed to himself in the creation of the world are understood by us.
The second is, that we should beware of presuming too highly
of ourselves, as it seems we should do if we supposed certain
limits to the world, without being assured of their existence
either by natural reasons or by divine revelation, as if the
power of our thought extended beyond what God has in reality

made; but likewise still more if we persuaded ourselves that all things were created by God for us only, or if we merely supposed that we could comprehend by the power of our intellect the ends which God proposed to himself in creating the universe.

III.   In what sense it may be said that all things were created for the sake of man.

For although, as far as regards morals, it may be a pious thought to believe that God made all things for us; seeing we may thus be incited to greater gratitude and love toward him; and although it is even in some sense true, because there is no created thing of which we cannot make some use, if it be only that of exercising our mind in considering it, and honouring God on account of it, it is yet by no means probable that all things were created for us in this way that God had no other end in their creation; and this supposition would be plainly ridiculous and inept in physical reasoning, for we do not doubt but that many things exist, or formerly existed and have now ceased to be, which were never seen or known by man, and were never of use to him.

XLVIII.   These things having been considered, let us, in order to begin to see what effects can be deduced from the laws of nature, reflect that all the matter of which the world is composed was at the beginning divided into many equal particles, but these particles could not at first have been all round, because many balls joined together could not make up a solid and continuous body like this universe in which, as I have shown, there can be no vacuum.   But whatever shape these particles had before, they must have become round in the course of their various circular motions.   And since the force with which they were moved at the beginning was large enough to separate one from another, this force still continuing afterwards was, without doubt, great enough to smooth off all their angles successively whenever they met, for it would require less for this effect than it did for the other.   And from this one fact, that all the angles of a body are thus smoothed off, it is easy to conceive that it is round.

XLIX.   Now as there can be no empty space in any part of the universe and as the particles of matter, being round, are prevented from joining together so tightly as to leave no little intervals or recesses between them, it necessarily follows that these recesses are filled with some other particles of matter, which must be extremely flexible so as to change their shape at any moment to conform to that of the places they enter into. Hence we must believe that what comes off the angles of material particles as they are rounded off by striking one against another is so flexible and acquires such a great speed that the impetuousness of its motion can divide it into innumerable particles which, having no predetermined size or shape, easily fill up all the little angles or recesses through which the other particles of matter cannot pass.

L.   It must be noted that, inasmuch as what comes off as shavings of the material particles when they are rounded off is more flexible, it can also be more easily set in motion and, as a result, whittled down or divided into yet smaller particles than before.   This follows because the smaller a body, the larger the surface in proportion to the quantity of matter, and the large surface makes for more numerous encounters with other bodies, which in turn make an effort to move it or divide it, at the same time that its small amount of matter makes it less resistant to their force.

LI.   It must also be noted that although what thus derives from the whittling away of the particles as they are rounded off has no motion except what comes from these particles, it nevertheless must move much more quickly, because while these particles travel by straight and open ways, they constrain these shavings or dust which lies between them to travel by other, narrower and more twisted ways.   In the same way, in compressing a bellows pretty slowly the air is made to go out quite quickly because the hole by which the air makes its escape is straight.   And I have already proved that there is necessarily a part of matter which moves quickly and divides into an infinity of little particles, so that all the circular and nonuniform motions in the world can take place without rarefaction or any vacuum, and I do not believe that anything more suitable for this purpose can be imagined than what I have just described.

LII.   Thus we can say that we have already found two different forms of matter which may be taken to be the forms of the two first elements of the visible world.   The first is that of those shavings which must have been separated from the other particles of matter when they were made round and which move with such speed that the force of their motion alone is sufficient to ensure that, meeting with other bodies, they will be crushed and divided by them into an infinite number of little particles whose shape is such as always exactly to fill up all the recesses which they find about other bodies.   The other is that of all the remainder of matter whose particles are round and very small in comparison with the bodies we see on earth, but nevertheless possess a determinate quantity, insomuch as they can be divided into other much smaller particles.   And we shall find hereafter yet a third form of some parts of matter--that is, of those which because of their size and shape cannot be so easily set in motion as the ones discussed above.   I shall try to show that all the bodies of this visible world are composed of these three forms to be found in matter, as if of three different elements.   Thus the sun and the fixed stars have the form of the first of these elements; the heavens that of the second; and the earth with the planets and comets that of the third. . . .

Part IV

Of the Earth

I.   Although I do not at all wish everyone to be convinced that the bodies of which the visible world is made up were ever produced in the way I have described above, as I have already warned the reader, yet I must here retain the same hypothesis to explain terrestrial objects, so that I may clearly show (as I hope) that by this means easily intelligible and exact causes for all the things observed there may be   deduced.   Further, since the same cannot be done by any other hypothesis that may be devised, we may reasonably conclude that, although the world was not made initially in this way but was directly created by God, yet everything in it does not fail to be *now* of the same nature as it would have been had it been so made.

II. Let us therefore now conceive that this earth of ours was formerly composed of the matter of the first element only, which occupied the center of one of the four vortices contained in the space which we call the first heaven, so that it did not differ in any way from the sun except in being smaller. But little by little (as we conceive) the less subtle particles of this matter, attaching themselves together, assembled on the surface and made the clouds and other thicker and darker bodies (like the spots which are seen constantly to be produced and soon dissipated on the surface of the sun), and these dark bodies were also dissipated a little after their production, so that the remaining particles, being heavier than those of the first two elements and having the form of the third, were piled in confusion around this earth and, surrounding it on all sides, made a substance very like the air we breath. Then when that air became thicker and much heavier, the dark bodies which continued to form on the surface of the earth could not be so easily destroyed as before, so that they slowly covered and obscured it completely. And perhaps several layers of such bodies were piled upon one another, all of which so decreased the force of the containing vortex that it was entirely destroyed, and the earth, with the air and the dark bodies surrounding it, descended towards the sun to the place where it now it. . . .

XIV. Now when the earth, then composed of three distinct regions, descended toward the sun, this could not cause much change to the two lower, central regions, but did so much to the outermost that it was obliged to divide into two different bodies, then into three, four, and more.

XV. I shall try to explain here how these bodies must have been produced. But first I must say something about three or four of the chief actions which contributed to this production. The first consists of the motion of the particles of the celestial matter taken in general; the second, of what is called weight; the third, of light; and the fourth, of heat. By "the motion of the particles of celestial matter taken in general," I understand their continual agitation, which is so great that it not only suffices to cause them to make a complete rotation about the sun each year and another each day around the earth, but also to move them in several other ways. And since once they have set out in some direction they always continue in a straight line as far as possible, it follows that, as they are intermingled with the particles of the third element which compose all the bodies of this outermost region of the earth, they produce various effects, of which I shall mention here the three chief.

XVI. The first is, that they render transparent all those fluid bodies composed of particles of the third element sufficiently small and so little crowded together that the particles of the second element can go around them on all sides. For in thus going between the particles of these bodies and having enough power to make them move, they do not fail to make passages which are quite straight in all directions, or at least passages equally suitable for transmitting the action of light and so making the body transparent. Thus we learn by experience that every fluid on earth which is both pure and composed of sufficiently small particles is transparent. . . . And all solid bodies are transparent that have been made from some transparent fluid whose particles have come to rest little by little one against another without anything being mixed with them that could change their order. Conversely, all bodies are opaque or dark whose particles have been united by some outside force not subject to the motion of the celestial matter. For though there may remain in such bodies many pores through which the particles of the second element can pass, at the same time since these pores are stopped up or interrupted in various places they cannot transmit the action of light. . . .

XVIII. The second effect produced by the agitation of the subtle matter in terrestrial bodies, chiefly in fluid ones, is that when two or more kinds of particles in these bodies are mingled in confusion, either it separates them or it sorts them out and distributes them equally in all parts of the body and so purifies it and makes every drop exactly like every other. The reason for this is, that sliding on all sides between unequal terrestrial particles it continually pushes those which by their size or shape or position get more in the way than the others, until it has so changed their position that they are uniformly spread through the body, and so fitted in with the others that it no longer impedes the motion of the subtle matter; or, if it cannot arrange them in this way, it separates them completely and makes a different body of them. . . .

XIX. The third effect of this celestial matter is to make all drops of fluid quite round whenever they are entirely surrounded by air or any other fluid whose nature is sufficiently different to prevent their mixing up together. . . .

XX. The second action of which I have undertaken to speak here is that which makes bodies heavy, which has a close connection with what makes drops of water round. For it is the same subtle matter which, by the mere fact of moving equally on all sides around a drop of water, pushes all the particles of the surface toward the center of the drop that, by the mere fact of moving around the earth, also pushes toward the earth all the bodies we call heavy, among which are the particles. . . .

XXII. Since there is no empty space around the earth and since it does not itself possess the power of turning every twenty-four hours about its axis, but   is carried around by the celestial matter which surrounds it and which penetrates through all its pores, it should be regarded as a body without motion. Similarly, the celestial matter would not be thought either heavy or light if it had no other motion than that which makes it rotate in twenty-four hours with the earth, but as it has many more motions not required to produce this effect, its other motions are employed either to turn more quickly than the earth in the same direction, or to make other motions in other directions. And these cannot be in such straight lines as if the earth were

not in the way, not only does the subtle matter [ether] try to
make the earth round or spherical, as with a drop of water but
also has more power of rising away from the center about which it
turns than the particles of the earth do, which makes it light
compared to them. . . .
XXIII. And it must be noted that the power the celestial
matter possesses of getting farther from the center of the earth
can have its effect only if the particles which rise take the
place of some terrestrial particles which fall at the same
time. . . . Thus each heavy body is not pushed toward the center
of the earth by all the celestial matter which surrounds it, but
only by those particles of this matter which rise into its
place at the same time that it falls and which consequently are
exactly as large as it is. . . .
CLXXXIX. What perception (*sensus*) is, and how we perceive.
We must know, therefore, that although the human soul is
united to the whole body, it has, nevertheless, its principal
seat in the brain, where alone it not only understands and imag-
ines, but also perceives; and this by the medium of the nerves,
which are extended like threads from the brain to all the other
members, with which they are so connected that we can hardly
touch any one of them without moving the extremities of some of
the nerves spread over it; and this motion passes to the other
extremities of those nerves which are collected in the brain
round the seat of the soul, as I have already explained with
sufficient minuteness in the fourth chapter of the Dioptrics.
But the movements which are thus excited in the brain by the
nerves, variously affect the soul or mind, which is intimately
conjoined with the brain, according to the diversity of the
motions themselves. And the diverse affections of the mind or
thoughts that immediately arise from these motions, are called
perceptions of the senses (*sensuum perceptiones*), or, as we
commonly speak, sensations (*sensus*).
CXC. Of the distinction of the senses; and, first, of the
internal, that is, of the affections of the mind (passions), and
the natural appetites.
The varieties of these sensations depend, firstly, on the
diversity of the nerves themselves, and, secondly, of the movements that are made in each nerve. We have not, however, as many
different senses as there are nerves. We can distinguish but
seven principal classes of nerves, of which two belong to the
internal, and the other five to the external senses. The nerves
which extend to the stomach, the œsophagus, the fauces, and the
other internal parts that are subservient to our natural wants,
constitute one of our internal senses. This is called the natural appetite (*appetitus naturalis*). The other internal sense,
which embraces all the emotions (*commotiones*) of the mind or
passions, and affections, as joy, sadness, love, hate, and the
like, depends upon the nerves which extend to the heart and the
parts about the heart, and are exceedingly small; for, by way of
example, when the blood happens to be pure and well tempered,
so that it dilates in the heart more readily and strongly than
usual, this so enlarges and moves the small nerves scattered
around the orifices, that there is thence a corresponding move-

ment in the brain, which affects the mind with a certain natural feeling of joy; and as often as these same nerves are moved in the same way, although this is by other causes, they excite in our mind the same feeling (*sensus, sentiment*). Thus, the imagination of the enjoyment of a good does not contain in itself the feeling of joy, but it causes the animal spirits to pass from the brain to the muscles in which these nerves are inserted; and thus dilating the orifices of the heart, it also causes these small nerves to move in the way appointed by nature to afford the sensation of joy. Thus, when we receive news, the mind first of all judges of it, and if the news be good, it rejoices with that intellectual joy (*gaudium intellectuale*) which is independent of any emotion (*commotio*) of the body, and which the Stoics did not deny to their wise man [although they supposed him exempt from all passion]. But as soon as this joy passes from the understanding to the imagination, the spirits flow from the brain to the muscles that are about the heart, and there excite the motion of the small nerves, by means of which another motion is caused in the brain, which affects the mind with the sensation of animal joy (*laetitia animalis*). On the same principle, when the blood is so thick that it flows but sparingly into the ventricles of the heart, and is not there sufficiently dilated, it excites in the same nerves a motion quite different from the preceding, which, communicated to the brain, gives to the mind the sensation of sadness, although the mind itself is perhaps ignorant of the cause of its sadness. And all the other causes which move these nerves in the same way may also give to the mind the same sensation. But the other movements of the same nerves produce other effects, as the feelings of love, hate, fear, anger, etc., as far as they are merely affections or passions of the mind; in other words, as far as they are confused thoughts which the mind has not from itself alone, but from its being closely joined to the body, from which it receives impressions; for there is the widest difference between these passions and the distinct thoughts which we have of what ought to be loved, or chosen, or shunned, etc., [although these are often enough found together]. The natural appetites, as hunger, thirst, and the others, are likewise sensations excited in the mind by means of the nerves of the stomach, fauces, and other parts, and are entirely different from the will which we have to eat, drink, [and to do all that which we think proper for the conservation of our body]; but, because this will or appetition almost always accompanies them, they are therefore named appetites.

CXCI. Of the external senses; and first of touch.

We commonly reckon the external senses five in number, because there are as many different kinds of objects which move the nerves and their organs, and an equal number of kinds of confused thoughts excited in the soul by these motions. In the first place, the nerves terminating in the skin of the whole body can be touched through this medium by any terrene objects whatever, and moved by these wholes, in one way by their hardness, in another by their gravity, in a third by their heat, in a fourth by their humidity, etc.—and in as many diverse modes as they are either moved or hindered from their ordinary motion, to

that extent are diverse sensations excited in the mind, from
which a corresponding number of tactile qualities derive their
appellations. Besides this, when these nerves are moved a little
more powerfully than usual, but not nevertheless to the degree
by which our body is in any way hurt, there thus arises a sensation of titillation, which is naturally agreeable to the mind,
because it testifies to it of the powers of the body with which
it is joined, [in that the latter can suffer the action causing
this titillation, without being hurt]. But if this action be
strong enough to hurt our body in any way, this gives to our mind
the sensation of pain. And we thus see why corporeal pleasure
and pain, although sensations of quite an opposite character,
arise nevertheless from causes nearly alike.

CXCII. Of taste.

In the second place, the other nerves scattered over the
tongue and the parts in its vicinity are diversely moved by the
particles of the same bodies, separated from each other and
floating in the saliva in the mouth, and thus cause sensations
of diverse tastes according to the diversity of figure in these
particles.

CXCIII. Of smell.

Thirdly, two nerves also or appendages of the brain, for
they do not go beyond the limits of the skull, are moved by the
particles of terrestrial bodies, separated and flying in the air,
not indeed by all particles indifferently, but by those only that
are sufficiently subtle and penetrating to enter the pores of the
bone we call the spongy, when drawn into the nostrils, and thus
to reach the nerves. From the different motions of these particles arise the sensations of the different smells.

CXCIV. Of hearing.

Fourthly, there are two nerves within the ears, so attached
to three small bones that are mutually sustaining, and the first
of which rests on the small membrane that covers the cavity we
call the tympanum of the ear, that all the diverse vibrations
which the surrounding air communicates to this membrane, are
transmitted to the mind by these nerves, and these vibrations
give rise, according to their diversity, to the sensations of
the different sounds.

CXCV. Of sight.

Finally, the extremities of the optic nerves, composing the
coat in the eyes called the retina, are not moved by the air nor
by any terrestrial object, but only by the globules of the second
element, whence we have the sense of light and colours: as I
have already at sufficient length explained in the Dioptrics
and treatise of Meteors.

CXCVI. That the soul perceives only in so far as it is in
the brain.

It is clearly established, however, that the soul does not
perceive in so far as it is in each member of the body, but only
in so far as it is in the brain, where the nerves by their movements convey to it the diverse actions of the external objects
that touch the parts of the body in which they are inserted.
For, in the first place, there are various maladies, which,
though they affect the brain alone, yet bring disorder upon, or
deprive us altogether of the use of, our senses, just as sleep,

which affects the brain only, and yet takes from us daily during a great part of our time the faculty of perception, which afterwards in our waking state is restored to us. The second proof is, that though there be no disease in the brain, [or in the members in which the organs of the external senses are], it is nevertheless sufficient to take away sensation from the part of the body where the nerves terminate, if only the movement of one of the nerves that extend from the brain to these members be obstructed in any part of the distance that is between the two. And the last proof is, that we sometimes feel pain as if in certain of our members, the cause of which, however, is not in these members where it is felt, but somewhere nearer the brain, through which the nerves pass that give to the mind the sensation of it. I could establish this fact by innumerable experiments; I will here, however, merely refer to one of them. A girl suffering from a bad ulcer in the hand, had her eyes bandaged whenever the surgeon came to visit her, not being able to bear the sight of the dressing of the sore; and, the gangrene having spread, after the expiry of a few days the arm was amputated from the elbow [without the girl's knowledge]; linen cloths tied one above the other were substituted in place of the part amputated, so that she remained for some time without knowing that the operation had been performed, and meanwhile she complained of feeling various pains, sometimes in one finger of the hand that was cut off, and sometimes in another. The only explanation of this is, that the nerves which before stretched downwards from the brain to the hand, and then terminated in the arm close to the elbow, were there moved in the same way as they required to be moved before in the hand for the purpose of impressing on the mind residing in the brain the sensation of pain in this or that finger. [And this clearly shows that the pain of the hand is not felt by the mind in so far as it is in the hand, but in so far as it is in the brain].

CXCVII. That the nature of the mind is such that from the motion alone of body the various sensations can be excited in it.

In the next place, it can be proved that our mind is of such a nature that the motions of the body alone are sufficient to excite in it all sorts of thoughts, without it being necessary that these should in any way resemble the motions which give rise to them, and especially that these motions can excite in it those confused thoughts called sensations (*sensus, sensationes*). For we see that words, whether uttered by the voice or merely written, excite in our minds all kinds of thoughts and emotions. On the same paper, with the same pen and ink, by merely moving the point of the pen over the paper in a particular way, we can trace letters that will raise in the minds of our readers the thoughts of combats, tempests, or the furies, and the passions of indignation and sorrow; in place of which, if the pen be moved in another way hardly different from the former, this slight change will cause thoughts widely different from the above, such as those of repose, peace, pleasantness, and the quite opposite passions of love and joy. Some one will perhaps object that writing and speech do not immediately excite in the mind any passions, or imaginations of things different from the letters and sounds, but afford simply the knowledge of these, on occasion of which the

mind, understanding the signification of the words, afterwards
excites in itself the imaginations and passions that correspond
to the words. But what will be said of the sensations of pain
and titillation? The motion merely of a sword cutting a part of
our skin causes pain, [but does not on that account make us aware
of the motion or figure of the sword]. And it is certain that
this sensation of pain is not less different from the motion that
causes it, or from that of the part of our body which the sword
cuts, than are the sensations we have of colour, sound, odour,
or taste. On this ground we may conclude that our mind is of
such a nature that the motions alone of certain bodies can also
easily excite in it all the other sensations, as the motion of
a sword excites in it the sensation of pain.

    CXCVIII. That by our senses we know nothing of external
objects beyond their figure [or situation], magnitude, and motion.

    Besides, we observe no such difference between the nerves
as to lead us to judge that one set of them convey to the brain
from the organs of the external senses anything different from
another, or that anything at all reaches the brain besides the
local motion of the nerves themselves. And we see that local
motion alone causes in us not only the sensation of titillation
and of pain, but also of light and sounds. For if we receive a
blow on the eye of sufficient force to cause the vibration of the
stroke to reach the retina, we see numerous sparks of fire,
which, nevertheless, are not out of our eye; and when we stop our
ear with our finger, we hear a humming sound, the cause of which
can only proceed from the agitation of the air that is shut up
within it. Finally, we frequently observe that heat [hardness,
weight], and the other sensible qualities, as far as they are in
objects, and also the forms of those bodies that are purely
material, as, for example, the forms of fire, are produced in
them by the motion of certain other bodies, and that these in
their turn likewise produce other motions in other bodies. And
we can easily conceive how the motion of one body may be caused
by that of another, and diversified by the size, figure, and
situation of its parts, but we are wholly unable to conceive how
these same things (viz., size, figure, and motion), can produce
something else of a nature entirely different from themselves,
as, for example, those substantial forms and real qualities which
many philosophers suppose to be in bodies; nor likewise can we
conceive how these qualities or forms possess force to cause motions in other bodies. But since we know, from the nature of our
soul, that the diverse motions of body are sufficient to produce
in it all the sensations which it has, and since we learn from
experience that several of its sensations are in reality caused
by such motions, while we do not discover that anything besides
these motions ever passes from the organs of the external senses
to the brain, we have reason to conclude that we in no way likewise apprehend that in external objects, which we call light,
colour, smell, taste, sound, heat or cold, and the other tactile
qualities, or that which we call their substantial forms, unless
as the various dispositions of these objects which have the power
of moving our nerves in various ways.

    CXCIX. That there is no phenomenon of nature whose explana-
tion has been omitted in this treatise.

And thus it may be gathered, from an enumeration that is
easily made, that there is no phenomenon of nature whose explanation has been omitted in this treatise; for beyond what is perceived by the senses, there is nothing that can be considered a
phenomenon of nature. But leaving out of account motion, magnitude, figure, [and the situation of the parts of each body],
which I have explained as they exist in body, we perceive
nothing out of us by our senses except light, colours, smells,
tastes, sounds, and the tactile qualities; and these I have
recently shown to be nothing more, at least so far as they are
known to us, than certain dispositions of the objects, consisting
in magnitude, figure, and motion.

CC. That this treatise contains no principles which are not
universally received; and that this philosophy is not new, but of
all others the most ancient and common.

But I am desirous also that it should be observed that,
though I have here endeavoured to give an explanation of the
whole nature of material things, I have nevertheless made use of
no principle which was not received and approved by Aristotle, and
by the other philosophers of all ages; so that this philosophy, so
far from being new, is of all others the most ancient and common:
for I have in truth merely considered the figure, motion, and
magnitude of bodies, and examined what must follow from their
mutual concourse on the principles of mechanics, which are confirmed by certain and daily experience. But no one ever doubted
that bodies are moved, and that they are of various sizes and
figures, according to the diversity of which their motions also
vary, and that from mutual collision those somewhat greater than
others are divided into many smaller, and thus change figure. We
have experience of the truth of this, not merely by a single
sense, but by several, as touch, sight, and hearing: we also
distinctly imagine and understand it. This cannot be said of any
of the other things that fall under our senses, as colours,
sounds, and the like; for each of these affects but one of our
senses, and merely impresses upon our imagination a confused
image of itself, affording our understanding no distinct knowledge of what it is.

CCI. That sensible bodies are composed of insensible
particles.

But I allow many particles in each body that are perceived
by none of our senses, and this will not perhaps be approved of
by those who take the senses for the measure of the knowable.
[We greatly wrong human reason, however, as appears to me, if
we suppose that it does not go beyond the eye-sight]; for no one
can doubt that there are bodies so small as not to be perceptible
by any of our senses, provided he only consider what is each
moment added to those bodies that are being increased little by
little, and what is taken from those that are diminished in
the same way. A tree increases daily, and it is impossible to
conceive how it becomes greater than it was before, unless we at
the same time conceive that some body is added to it. But who
ever observed by the senses those small bodies that are in one
day added to a tree while growing? Among the philosophers at
least, those who hold that quantity is indefinitely divisible,
ought to admit that in the division the parts may become so small
as to be wholly imperceptible. And indeed it ought not to be a

matter of surprise, that we are unable to perceive very minute
bodies; for the nerves that must be moved by objects to cause
perception are not themselves very minute, but are like small
cords, being composed of a quantity of smaller fibres, and thus
the most minute bodies are not capable of moving them. Nor do I
think that any one who makes use of his reason will deny that we
philosophize with much greater truth when we judge of what takes
place in those small bodies which are imperceptible from their
minuteness only, after the analogy of what we see occurring in
those we do perceive, [and in this way explain all that is in
nature, as I have essayed to do in this treatise], than when we
give an explanation of the same things by inventing I know not
what novelties, that have no relation to the things we actually
perceive, [as first matter, substantial forms, and all that grand
array of qualities which many are in the habit of supposing, each
of which it is more difficult to comprehend than all that is professed to be explained by means of them].

    CCII.   That the philosophy of Democritus is not less differ-
ent from ours than from the common.

    But it may be said that Democritus also supposed certain
corpuscles that were of various figures, sizes, and motions, from
the heaping together and mutual concourse of which all sensible
bodies arose; and, nevertheless, his mode of philosophizing is
commonly rejected by all. To this I reply that the philosophy of
Democritus was never rejected by any one, because he allowed the
existence of bodies smaller than those we perceive, and attributed to them diverse sizes, figures, and motions, for no one can
doubt that there are in reality such, as we have already shown;
but it was rejected, in the first place, because he supposed
that these corpuscles were indivisible, on which ground I also
reject it; in the second place, because he imagined there was a
vacuum about them, which I show to be impossible; thirdly, because he attributed gravity to these bodies, of which I deny the
existence in any body, in so far as a body is considered by itself, because it is a quality that depends on the relations of
situation and motion which several bodies bear to each other; and,
finally, because he has not explained in particular how all things
arose from the concourse of corpuscles alone, or, if he gave
this explanation with regard to a few of them, his whole reasoning was far from being coherent, [or such as would warrant us in
extending the same explanation to the whole of nature]. This, at
least, is the verdict we must give regarding his philosophy, if
we may judge of his opinions from what has been handed down to us
in writing. I leave it to others to determine whether the philosophy I profess possesses a valid coherency, [and whether on its
principles we can make the requisite number of deductions; and,
inasmuch as the consideration of figure, magnitude, and motion
has been admitted by Aristotle and by all the others, as well as
by Democritus, and since I reject all that the latter has supposed, with this single exception, while I reject generally all
that has been supposed by the others, it is plain that this mode
of philosophizing has no more affinity with that of Democritus
than of any other particular sect].

    CCIII.   How we may arrive at the knowledge of the figures, [magnitudes], and motions of the insensible particles of bodies.

But, since I assign determinate figures, magnitudes, and motions to the insensible particles of bodies, as if I had seen them, whereas I admit that they do not fall under the senses, some one will perhaps demand how I have come by my knowledge of them. [To this I reply, that I first considered in general all the clear and distinct notions of material things that are to be found in our understanding, and that, finding no others except those of figures, magnitudes, and motions, and of the rules according to which these three things can be diversified by each other, which rules are the principles of geometry and mechanics, I judged that all the knowledge man can have of nature must of necessity be drawn from this source; because all the other notions we have of sensible things, as confused and obscure, can be of no avail in affording us the knowledge of anything out of ourselves, but must serve rather to impede it]. Thereupon, taking as my ground of inference the simplest and best known of the principles that have been implanted in our minds by nature, I considered the chief differences that could possibly subsist between the magnitudes, and figures, and situations of bodies insensible on account of their smallness alone, and what sensible effects could be produced by their various modes of coming into contact; and afterwards, when I found like effects in the bodies that we perceive by our senses, I judged that they could have been thus produced, especially since no other mode of explaining them could be devised. And in this matter the example of several bodies made by art was of great service to me: for I recognise no difference between these and natural bodies beyond this, that the effects of machines depend for the most part on the agency of certain instruments, which, as they must bear some proportion to the hands of those who make them, are always so large that their figures and motions can be seen; in place of which, the effects of natural bodies almost always depend upon certain organs so minute as to escape our senses. And it is certain that all the rules of mechanics belong also to physics, of which it is a part or species, [so that all that is artificial is withal natural]: for it is not less natural for a clock, made of the requisite number of wheels, to mark the hours, than for a tree, which has sprung from this or that seed, to produce the fruit peculiar to it. Accordingly, just as those who are familiar with automata, when they are informed of the use of a machine, and see some of its parts, easily infer from these the way in which the others, that are not seen by them, are made; so from considering the sensible effects and parts of natural bodies, I have essayed to determine the character of their causes and insensible parts.

CCIV. That, touching the things which our senses do not perceive, it is sufficient to explain how they can be, [and that this is all that Aristotle has essayed].

But here some one will perhaps reply, that although I have supposed causes which could produce all natural objects, we ought not on this account to conclude that they were produced by these causes; for, just as the same artisan can make two clocks, which, though they both equally well indicate the time, and are not different in outward appearance, have nevertheless nothing resembling in the composition of their wheels; so doubtless the Su-

preme Maker of things has an infinity of diverse means at his
disposal, by each of which he could have made all the things of
this world to appear as we see them, without it being possible
for the human mind to know which of all these means he chose to
employ. I most freely concede this; and I believe that I have
done all that was required, if the causes I have assigned are
such that their effects accurately correspond to all the phenomena of nature, without determining whether it is by these or by
others that they are actually produced. And it will be sufficient
for the use of life to know the causes thus imagined, for medicine, mechanics, and in general all the arts to which the knowledge of physics is of service, have for their end only those
effects that are sensible, and that are accordingly to be
reckoned among the phenomena of nature. And lest it should be
supposed that Aristotle did, or professed to do, anything more
than this, it ought to be remembered that he himself expressly
says, at the commencement of the seventh chapter of the first
book of the Meteorologics, that, with regard to things which are
not manifest to the senses, he thinks to adduce sufficient reasons and demonstrations of them, if he only shows that they may
be such as he explains them.

CCV. That nevertheless there is a moral certainty that all
the things of this world are such as has been here shown they
may be.

But nevertheless, that I may not wrong the truth by supposing it less certain than it is, I will here distinguish two
kinds of certitude. The first is called moral, that is, a certainty sufficient for the conduct of life, though, if we look to
the absolute power of God, what is morally certain may be false.
[Thus, those who never visited Rome do not doubt that it is a
city of Italy, though it might be that all from whom they got
their information were deceived]. Again, if any one, wishing to
decipher a letter written in Latin characters that are not placed
in regular order, bethinks himself of reading a B wherever an A
is found, and a C wherever there is a B, and thus of substituting
in place of each letter the one which follows it in the order of
the alphabet, and if by this means he finds that there are certain Latin words composed of these, he will not doubt that the
true meaning of the writing is contained in these words, although
he may discover this only by conjecture, and although it is possible that the writer of it did not arrange the letters on this
principle of alphabetical order, but on some other, and thus
concealed another meaning in it: for this is so improbable
[especially when the cipher contains a number of words] as to
seem incredible. But they who observe how many things regarding
the magnet, fire, and the fabric of the whole world, are here
deduced from a very small number of principles, though they deemed
that I had taken them up at random and without grounds, will yet
perhaps acknowledge that it could hardly happen that so many
things should cohere if these principles were false.

CCVI. That we possess even more than a moral certainty of
it.

Besides, there are some, even among natural, things which we
judge to be absolutely certain. [Absolute certainty arises when

we judge that it is impossible a thing can be otherwise than as
we think it]. This certainty is founded on the metaphysical
ground, that, as God is supremely good and the source of all
truth, the faculty of distinguishing truth from error which he
gave us, cannot be fallacious so long as we use it aright, and
distinctly perceive anything by it. Of this character are the
demonstrations of mathematics, the knowledge that material things
exist, and the clear reasonings that are formed regarding them.
The results I have given in this treatise will perhaps be admitted to a place in the class of truths that are absolutely certain, if it be considered that they are deduced in a continuous
series from the first and most elementary principles of human
knowledge; especially if it be sufficiently understood that we
can perceive no external objects unless some local motion be
caused by them in our nerves, and that such motion cannot be
caused by the fixed stars, owing to their great distance from us,
unless a motion be also produced in them and in the whole heavens
lying between them and us: for these points being admitted, all
the others, at least the more general doctrines which I have
advanced regarding the world or earth [e.g., the fluidity of the
heavens, Part III., §XLVI.], will appear to be almost the only
possible explanations of the phenomena they present.

CCVII. That, however, I submit all my opinions to the
authority of the church.

Nevertheless, lest I should presume too far, I affirm
nothing, but submit all these my opinions to the authority of the
church and the judgment of the more sage; and I desire no one to
believe anything I may have said, unless he is constrained to
admit it by the force and evidence of reason.

C.   Robert Boyle, *The Excellency and Grounds of the Mechanical Hypothesis**

Robert Boyle (1627-1691) was, in many ways, the true father of the mechanical philosophy for it was he who was able to bring it down to earth through experiment.   Boyle devoted his scientific life to devising experiments to illustrate the mechanical philosophy and it was through his work that the mechanical philosophy could be regarded as a serious scientific theory.   In his The Excellency and Grounds of the Mechanical Hypothesis *(1674), Boyle explained the scientific strength of the mechanical philosophy.*

Of the Excellency and Grounds of
the Corpuscular or Mechanical Philosophy

By embracing the corpuscular or mechanical philosophy, I am far from supposing with the Epicureans that atoms accidentally meeting in an infinite vacuum were able, of themselves, to produce a world and all its phenomena: nor do I suppose, when God had put into the whole mass of matter an invariable quantity of motion, he needed do no more to make the universe; the material parts being able, by their own unguided motions, to throw themselves into a regular system.   The philosophy I plead for reaches but to things purely corporeal; and distinguishing between the first origin of things and the subsequent course of nature, teaches that God indeed gave motion to matter; but that, in the beginning, he so guided the various motion of the parts of it as to contrive them into the world he designed they should compose; and established those rules of motion, and that order amongst things corporeal, which we call the laws of nature.   Thus the universe being once framed by God and the laws of motion settled and upheld by his perpetual concourse and general providence; the same philosophy teaches, that the phenomena of the world are physically produced by the mechanical properties of the parts of matter, and, that they operate upon one another according to mechanical laws.   'Tis of this kind of corpuscular philosophy, that I speak.
And the first thing that recommends it is the intelligibleness or clearness of its principles and explanations.   Among the peripatetics there are many intricate disputes about matter, privation, substantial forms, their educations, etc.   And the chymists are puzzled to give such definitions, and accounts, of their hypostatical principles as are consistent with one another, and to some obvious phenomena: and much more dark and intricate are their doctrines about the Archeus, Astral Beings, and other odd notions; which perhaps, have in part occasioned the darkness and ambiguity of their expressions, that could not be very clear,

---

*Robert Boyle, *The Excellency and Grounds of the Mechanical Hypothesis* in Peter Shaw, *The Philosophical Works of the Hon. Robert Boyle*, 3 vols., London, 1725, *1*, 187-96.

when the conceptions were obscure. And if the principles of the Aristotelians and chymists are thus obscure, it is not to be expected that the explications made by the help of such principles only should be intelligible. And, indeed, many of them are so general and slight, or otherwise so unsatisfactory, that, granting their principles, 'tis very hard to understand or admit their applications of them to particular phenomena. And, me-thinks, even in some of the more ingenious and subtle of the peripatetic discourses, the authors, upon their superficial and narrow theories, have acted more like painters than philosophers; and only shown their skill in making men fancy they see castles, cities, and other structures, that appear solid, magnificent, and extensive; when the whole piece is superficial, artificially made up of colours, and comprized within a frame. But, as to the corpuscular philosophy, men do so easily understand one another's meaning, when they talk of local motion, rest, magni-tude, shape, order, situation, and contexture, of material substances; and these principles afford such clear accounts of those things, that are rightly deduced from them alone; that, even such peripatetics or chymists, as maintain other principles, acquiesce in the explications made by these, when they can be had; and seek no further: though, perhaps, the effect be so admirable, as to make it pass for that of a hidden form, or an occult quality. Those very Aristotelians, who believe the celes-tial bodies to be moved by intelligences, have no recourse to any peculiar agency of theirs to account for eclipses! and we laugh at those East Indians who, to this day, go out in multi-tudes, with some instruments, to relieve the distressed luminary; whose loss of light, they fancy, proceeds from some fainting fit; out of which it must be roused. For no intelligent man, whether chymist or peripatetic, flies to his peculiar principles, after he is informed that the moon is eclipsed, by the interposition of the earth betwixt her, and it; and the sun, by that of the moon, betwixt him and the earth. And, when we see the image of a man cast into the air by a concave spherical speculum; though most men are amazed at it, and some suspect it to be no less than an effect of witchcraft, yet he who is skilled enough in catop-trics will, without consulting Aristotle or Paracelsus or flying to hypostatical principles or substantial forms, be satisfied that the phenomenon is produced by rays of light reflected and made to converge according to optical and mathematical laws.

I next observe that there cannot be fewer principles than the two grand ones of our philosophy, matter and motion; for matter alone, unless it be moved, is wholly unactive; and, whilst all the parts of a body continue in one state, without motion, that body will not exercise any action, or suffer any alteration; though it may, perhaps, modify the action of other bodies that move against it.

Nor can we conceive any principles more primary than matter and motion: for either both of them were immediately created by God; or, if matter be eternal, motion must either be produced by some immaterial supernatural agent; or it must immediately flow, by way of emanation, from the nature of the matter it appertains to.

There cannot be any physical principles more simple than matter and motion; neither of them being resoluble into any other thing.

The next thing which recommends the corpuscular principles is their extensiveness. The genuine and necessary effect of the strong motion of one part of matter against another is either to drive it on, in its entire bulk, or to break and divide it into particles of a determinate motion, figure, size, posture, rest, order or texture. The two first of these, for instance, are each of them capable of numerous varieties: for the figure of a portion of matter may either be one of the five regular geometrical figures, some determinate species of solid figures, or irregular, as the grains of sand, feathers, branches, files etc. And, as the figure, so the motion of one of these particles may be exceedingly diversified, not only by the determination to a particular part of the world but by several other things: as by the almost infinitely different degrees of celerity; by the manner of its progression, with or without rotation, etc. and more yet by the line wherein it moves; as circular, elliptical, parabolical, hyperbolical, spiral, etc. For, as later geometricians have shown that these curves may be compounded of several motions, that is, described by a body whose motion is mixed, and results from two or more simple motions; so, how many more curves may be made by new compositions, and recompositions of motion, is not easy to determine.

Now, since a single particle of matter, by virtue of only two mechanical properties that belong to it, may be diversified so many ways; what a vast number of variations may we suppose capable of being produced by the compositions, and recompositions of myriads of single invisible corpuscles, that may be contained and concreted in one small body; and each of them be endued with more than two or three of the fertile, universal principles above-mentioned? And the aggregate of those corpuscles may be further diversified by the texture resulting from their convention into a body; which, as so made up, has its own magnitude, shape, pores, and many capacities of acting and suffering, upon account of the place it holds among other bodies, in a world constituted like ours: so that, considering the numerous diversifications that compositions and re-compositions may make of a small number, those who think the mechanical principles may serve, indeed, to account for the phenomena of some particular part of natural philosophy, as statics, the theory of planetary motions etc. but prove unapplicable to all the phenomena of things corporeal seem to imagine, that by putting together the letters of the alphabet one may, indeed, make up all the words to be found in Euclid or Virgil, or in the Latin or English language, but that they can by no means supply words to all the books of a great library; much less, to all the languages in the world.

There are other philosophers, who, observing the great efficacy of magnitude, situation, motion, and connection in engines are willing to allow those mechanical principles a great share in the operations of bodies of a sensible bulk and manifest mechanism; and, therefore, to be usefully employed, in accounting for the effects and phenomena of such bodies: though they will not

admit that these principles can be applied to the hidden transactions among the minute particles of bodies; and, therefore,
think it necessary to refer these to what they call nature, substantial forms, real qualities, and the like unmechanical agents.
But this is not necessary: for the mechanical properties of
matter are to be found, and the laws of motion take place, not
only in the great masses and the middle-sized lumps, but in the
smallest fragments of matter: a less portion of it being as much
a body as a greater, must as necessarily as the other have its
determinate bulk and figure. And whoever views sand through a
good microscope will easily perceive that each minute grain has
as well its own size and shape as a rock or a mountain. Thus
too, when we let fall a large stone, and a pebble, from the top
of a high building, they both move comfortable to the laws of
acceleration, in heavy descending bodies: and the rules of
motion are observed, not only in cannon-bullets, but in small
shot; and the one strikes down a bird, according to the same laws,
as the other batters a wall. And though nature works with much
finer materials, and employs more curious contrivances, than art;
yet an artist, according to the quantity of the matter he employs, the exigency of the design he undertakes, and the magnitude and shape of the instruments he uses, is able to make
pieces of work of the same nature or kind, of extremely different
bulks where yet the like art, contrivance, and motion may be
observed. Thus a smith who, with a hammer and other large instruments can, out of masses of iron, forge great bars or wedges
to make strong and ponderous chains to secure streets and gates
may, with lesser instruments, make smaller nails, and filings,
almost as minute as dust; and with yet finer tools, make links
wonderfully light and slender. And therefore, to say that though
in natural bodies, whose bulk is manifest and their structure
visible, the mechanical principles may be usefully admitted but
are not to be extended to such portions of matter, whose parts
and texture are invisible, is like allowing that the laws of
mechanism may take place in a town-clock, and not in a pocket-
watch: or, because the terraqueous globe is a vast magnetical
body, one should affirm that magnetical laws are not to be expected manifest in a small spherical piece of loadstone; yet
experience shows us that, notwithstanding the immense dispropor-
tion betwixt these two spheres, the terella as well as the earth,
hath its poles, equator, and meridians; and in several other
magnetical properties resembles the terrestrial globe.
    When, to solve the phenomena of nature, agents are made use
of which, though they involve no contradiction in their notions,
as many think substantial forms and real qualities do, yet are
such that we conceive not how they operate to produce effects;
such agents I mean, as the soul of the world, the universal
spirit, the plastic power etc., the curiosity of an inquisitive
person is not satisfied hereby; who seeks not so much to know
what is the general agent that produces a phenomenon, as by what
means, and after what manner, it is produced. Sennertus, and
other physicians, tell us of diseases which proceed from incanta-
tion; but sure, it is very trivial to a sober physician, who
comes to visit a patient reported to be bewitched, to hear only
that the strange symptoms he meets with, and would have an ac-

count of, are produced by a witch or the devil; and he will never be satisfied with so short an answer, if he can by any means reduce those extravagant symptoms to any more known and stated diseases; as epilepsies, convulsions, hysteric fits, etc. and if he cannot, he will confess his knowledge of this distemper to come far short of what might be expected and attained in other diseases, wherein he thinks himself bound to search into the morbific matter; and will not be satisfied, till he can, probably, deduce from that, and the structure of the human body, and other concurring physical causes, the phenomena of the malady. And it would be of little satisfaction to one who desires to understand the causes of the phenomena in a watch, and how it comes to point at and strike the hours to be told that a certain watch-maker so contrived it: or, to him who would know the true causes of an echo, to be answered that it is a man, a vault, or a wood, that makes it.

I come now to consider that which I observe most alienates other sects from the mechanical philosophy; viz. a supposition, that it pretends to have principles so universal and mathematical that no other physical hypothesis can be tolerated by it.

This I look upon as an easy, indeed but an important mistake: for the mechanical principles are so universal, and appliable to so many purposes, that they are rather fitted to take in, than to exclude, any other hypothesis founded on nature. And such hypotheses, if prudently considered, will be found, as far as they have truth on their side, to be either legitimately deducible from the mechanical principles or fairly reconcileable to them. For such hypotheses will, probably, attempt to account for the phenomena of nature, either by the help of a determinate number of material ingredients, such as the tria prima of the chymists, or else by introducing some general agents, as the Platonic soul of the world, and the universal spirit, asserted by some chymists; or, by both these ways together.

Now, the chief thing that a philosopher should look after, in explaining difficult phenomena, is not so much what the agent is or does as, what changes are made in the patient, to bring it to exhibit the phenomena proposed; and by what means, and after what manner, those changes are effected. So that the mechanical philosopher being satisfied, one part of matter can act upon another, only by virtue of local motion, or the effects and consequences thereof; he considers, if the proposed agent be not intelligible and physical, it can never physically explain the phenomena; and if it be intelligible and physical, it will be reducible to matter and some or other of its universal properties. And the indefinite divisibility of matter, the wonderful efficacy of motion, and the almost infinite variety of coalitions and structures that may be made of minute and insensible corpuscles being duly weighed; why may not a philosopher think it possible to make out, by their help, the mechanical possibility of any corporeal agent, how subtle, diffused, or active soever, that can be solidly proved to have a real existence in nature? Though the Cartesians are mechanical philosophers, yet their subtle matter, which the very name declares to be a corporeal substance, is, for ought I know, little less diffused through the universe, or less active in it, than the universal spirit of some chymists; not to say the world soul of the Platonists. But

whatever be the physical agent, whether it be inanimate, or
living, purely corporeal, or united to an intellectual substance;
the above-mentioned changes, wrought in the body made to exhibit
the phenomena, may be effected by the same, or the like means; or
after the same, or the like manner: as, for instance, if corn be
reduced to meal, the materials and shape of the mill-stones and
their peculiar motion and adaptation will be much of the same
kind; and, to be sure, the grains of corn will suffer a various
attrition, and comminution in their passage to the form of meal,
whether the corn be ground by a watermill, or a windmill, a
horsemill, or a handmill; that is, a mill, whose stones are
turned by inanimate, by brute, or by rational agents. And if an
angel himself should work a real change in the nature of a body,
'tis scarce conceivable to men how he could do it without the
assistance of local motion; since, if nothing were displaced, or
otherwise moved than before it is hardly conceivable how it
should be, in itself, different from what it was before.
     But if the chymists, or others, who would deduce a compleat
natural philosophy from salt, sulphur, and mercury, or any determined number of ingredients of things, would well consider what
they undertake, they might easily discover that the material
parts of bodies can reach but to a few phenomena of nature,
whilst these things [ingredients] are considered but as quiescent
things, whence, they would find themselves to suppose them active;
and that things purely corporeal cannot but by means of local
motion, and the effects that may result from it, be very variously shaped, sized, and combined parts of matter: so that the
chymists must leave the greatest part of the phenomena of the
universe unexplained, by means of the ingredients of bodies,
without taking in the mechanical and more comprehensive properties of matter, especially local motion. I willingly grant that
salt, sulphur, and mercury, or some substances analogous to them,
are obtainable, by the action of the fire, from a very great many
dissipable bodies here below. Nor do I deny that in explaining
several phenomena of such bodies, it may be of use to a natural-
ist to know and consider that as sulphur, for instance, abounds
in the body proposed, it may be, thence, probably argued that
the qualities usually attending that principle , when predomi-
nant, may be also upon its account found in the body that so
largely partakes of it. But, though chymical explications are,
sometimes, the most obvious, yet they are not the most fundamental and satisfactory: for the chymical ingredient itself,
whether sulphur, or any other must owe its nature and other
qualities to the union of insensible particles, in a convenient
size, shape, motion, or rest, and texture; all which are but
mechanical properties of convening corpuscles. And this may be
illustrated by what happens in artificial fire-works. For,
though in most of those sorts, made either for war, or recreation,
gun-powder be a principal ingredient; and many of the phenomena
may be derived from the greater or less proportion wherein it
enters the compositions: yet there may be fire-works made without gun-powder, as appears by those of the ancient Greeks and
Romans. And gun-powder owes its aptness to fire, and to be ex-
ploded, to the mechanical texture of more simple portions of

matter, nitre, charcoal, and sulphur. And sulphur itself, though
it be by many chymists mistaken for an hypostatical [essential]
principle, owes its inflammability to the union of still more
simple and primary corpuscles; since chymists confess that it had
an inflammable ingredient: and experience shows that it very
much abounds with an acid and uninflammable salt and is not
destitute of a terrestrial part. It may, indeed, be here alleged
that the productions of chymical analyses are simple bodies; and,
upon that account, irresoluble; but that several substances,
which chymists call the salts, sulphurs, or mercuries of the
bodies that afford them, are not simple and homogeneous is demonstrable. Nor is their not being easily dissipable, or resoluble,
a clear proof of their not being made up of more primitive portions of matter. For compounded bodies may be as difficultly
resoluble as most of those that chymists obtain by the fire:
witness common greenglass, which is far more durable, and irresoluble, than many of those which pass for hypostatical substances. And some enamels will, for several times, even vitrify
in the forge, without losing their nature or often so much as
their colour: yet, enamel consists of salt, powder of pebbles,
or sand, and calcined tin; and, if not white, usually of some
tinging metal or mineral. But how indestructible soever the
chymical principles are supposed, several of the operations ascribed to them will never be made appear without the help of
local motion: were it not for this, we can but little better
solve the phenomena of many bodies by knowing what ingredients
compose them than we can explain the operations of a watch by
knowing of how many and of what metals, the balance, the wheels,
the chain, and otherparts consist; or than we can derive the
operations of a windmill from barely knowing that it is made up
of wood, stone, canvas, and iron. And here let me add that it
would not at all overthrow the corpuscularian hypothesis, though,
either by more exquisite purifications or by some other operations, than the usual analysis by fire, it should appear that the
material principles of mixed bodies are not the tria prima of
the vulgar chymists; but, either substances of another nature, or
fewer in number; of, if it were true that the Helmontians had
such a resolving menstruum as their master's alkahest, by which he
affirms that he could reduce stones into salt, of the same weight
with the mineral; and bring both that salt, and all other mixed
and tangible bodies, into insipid water. For whatever be the
number or qualities of the chymical principles, if they really
exist in nature, it may very possibly be shown that they are made
up of insensible corpuscles, of determinate bulks and shapes:
and, by the various coalitions and textures of such corpuscles,
many material ingredients may be composed, or made to result.
But though the alkahestical reductions, newly mentioned, should
be admitted, yet the mechanical principles might well be accommodated even to them. For the solidity, taste, etc. of salt may
be fairly accounted for by the stiffness, sharpness, and other
mechanical properties of the minute particles whereof salt consists: and if, by a farther action of the alkahest, the salt, or
any other solid body, be reduced into insipid water, this also
may be explained by the same principles; supposing a farther

comminution of its parts, and such an attrition as wears off the
edges and points that enabled them to strike briskly upon the
organ of taste: for as to fluidity and firmness, they, principally, depend upon two of our grand principles, motion and rest.
And 'tis certain that the agitation, or rest, and the looser
contact, or closer cohesion of the particles, is able to make the
same portion of matter at one time a firm and at another a fluid
body. So that, though future sagacity and industry of chymists
should obtain, from mixed bodies, homogeneous substances, different in number, nature, or both, from their vulgar salt, sulphur,
and mercury; yet the corpuscular philosophy is so general and
fertile as to be fairly reconcilable to such a discovery; and
also so useful, that these new material principles will, as well
as the old tria prima, stand in need of the more universal principles of the corpuscularians; especially of local motion. And,
indeed, whatever elements or ingredients men have pitched upon;
yet, if they take not in the mechanical properties of matter,
their principles are so deficient that I have observed both the
materialists and chymists not only leave many things unexplained,
to which their narrow principles will not extend; but, even in
the particulars they presume to give an account of, they either
content themselves to assign such common and indefinite causes as
are too general to be satisfactory; or, if they venture to give
particular causes, they assign precarious or false ones, liable
to be easily disproved by circumstances, or instances, whereto
their doctrines will not agree. The chymists, however, need not
be frightened from acknowledging the prerogative of the mechanical philosophy, since that may be reconcilable with the truth of
their own principles, so far as they agree with the phenomena
they are applied to: for these more confined hypotheses may be
subordinate to those more general and fertile principles; and
there can be no ingredient assigned that has a real existence in
nature but may be derived, either immediately or by a row of
compositions, from the universal matter, modified by its mechanical properties. For if with the same bricks, differently put
together and ranged, several bridges, vaults, houses, and other
structures may be raised merely by a various contrivance of parts
of the same kind; what a great variety of ingredients may be produced by nature from the various coalitions and contextures of
corpuscles, that need not be supposed, like bricks, all of the
same size and shape; but to have, both in the one and the other,
as great a variety as could be wished for? And the primary and
minute concretions that belong to these ingredients may, without
opposition from the mechanical philosophy, be supposed to have
their particles so minute and strongly coherent that nature of
herself scarce ever tears them asunder. Thus mercury and gold
may be successively made to put on a multitude of disguises; and
yet so retain their nature as to be reducible to their pristine
forms.
     From hence it is probable if, besides rational souls, there
be any immaterial substances, such as the heavenly intelligences,
and the substantial forms of the Aristotelians, that are regularly to be numbered among natural agents; their way of working
being unknown to us, they can only help to constitute and effect

things, but will very little help us to conceive how things are
effects; so that, by whatever principles natural things are
constituted, 'tis by the mechanical principles that their
phenomena must be clearly explained. For instance though we
grant, with the Aristotelians, that the planets are made of a
quintessential matter and moved by angels or immaterial intelligences; yet, to explain the stations, progressions and retro-
gradations, and other phenomena of the planets, we must have
recourse either to excentrics, epicycles, etc. or to motions,
made in elliptical, or other peculiar lines; and, in a word, to
theories wherein the motion, figure, situation and other mathematical, or mechanical properties are chiefly employed. But if
the principles proposed be corporeal, they will then be fairly
reducible or reconcilable to the mechanical principles; these
being so general and fertile that, among real material things,
there is none but may be derived from or reduced to them. And
when the chymists shall show that mixed bodies owe their qualities to the predominance of any one of their three grand ingredients, the corpuscularians will show that the very qualities of
this or that ingredient flow from its peculiar texture, and the
mechanical properties of the corpuscles that compose it. And to
affirm that because the chemical furnaces afford a great number
of uncommon productions, and phenomena, that there are bodies or
operations amongst things purely corporeal not derivable from or
reconcilable to the principles of mechanical philosophy is to
say, because there are many and various hymns, pavanes, threno-
dies, courants, gavottes, sarabands, etc. in a music book, many
of the tunes, or notes have no dependence on the scale of
music; or as if because excepting rhomboids, squares, pentagons,
chiliagons, and numerous other polygons, one should affirm there
are some rectilineal figures not reducible to triangles, or
that have properties which overthrow Euclid's doctrine of triangles and polygons.
    I shall only add that as mechanical principles and explana-
tions, where they can be had, are, for their clearness, preferred
by materialists themselves; so the sagacity and industry of
modern naturalists and mathematicians, having happily applied
them to several of those difficult phenomena which before were
referred to occult qualities it is probable that when this
philosophy is more scrutinized and farther improved, it will be
found applicable to the solution of still more phenomena of
nature. And 'tis not always necessary that he who advances an
hypothesis in astronomy, chymistry, anatomy, etc. be able, a
priori, to prove it true, or demonstratively to show that the
other hypothesis proposed about the same subject must be false;
for as Plato said that the world is God's epistle to mankind;
and might have added, in his own way, that it was written in
mathematical characters; so, in the physical explanations of the
parts of the system of the world, methinks there is somewhat like
what happens when men conjecturally frame several keys to read a
letter in ciphers. For though one man, by his sagacity, finds
the right key, it will be very difficult for him either to
prove, otherwise than by trial, that any particular word is not
such as 'tis guessed to be by others, according to their keys;

or to show, a priori, that theirs are to be rejected and his to be preferred; yet, if due trial being made, the key he proposes be found so agreeable to the characters of the letter, as to enable one to understand them, and make coherent sense of them, its suitableness to what it should decipher is, without either confutations or foreign positive proofs, alone sufficient to make it accepted as the right key of that cipher. Thus, in physical hypotheses, there are some that, without falling foul upon others, peacably obtain the approbation of discerning men only by their fitness to solve the phenomena for which they were devised, without thwarting any known observation or law of nature; and therefore, if the mechanical philosophy shall continue to explain corporeal things, as it has of late, 'tis scarce to be doubted but that in time unprejudiced persons will think it sufficiently recommended, by its being consistent with itself and applicable to so many phenomena of nature.

d.   Sir Isaac Newton

As with the new cosmology, it was Isaac Newton who built most firmly upon the foundations he inherited.   In the Principia, *Newton had laid out the mathematical framework of the new physics.   He had also indicated how it was possible, experimentally, to work with subsensible corpuscles.   In his rules of reason, Newton provided a methodological guide to the ultimate reality underlying the phenomenal world.   In his* Opticks, *Newton showed the world how to investigate the corpuscular world experimentally.   And, in the Queries that he added to the Opticks, Newton provided those who followed him with some very shrewd guesses about the nature of the atomic realm.   After Newton had done with it, the mechanical philosophy appeared to be a complete and true philosophy of nature.*

1.   Isaac Newton's Rules of Reasoning in Philosophy*

Book III.

In the preceding books I have laid down the principles of philosophy; principles not philosophical, but mathematical; such, to wit, as we may build our reasonings upon in philosophical enquiries.   These principles are the laws and conditions of certain motions, and powers or forces, which chiefly have respect to philosophy; but, lest they should have appeared of themselves dry and barren, I have illustrated them here and there with some philosophical scholiums, giving an account of such things as are of more general nature, and which philosophy seems chiefly to be founded on; such as the density and the resistance of bodies, spaces void of all bodies, and the motion of light and sounds. It remains that, from the same principles, I now demonstrate the frame of the System of the World.   Upon this subject I had, indeed, composed the third book in a popular method, that it might be read by many; but afterwards, considering that such as had not sufficiently entered into the principles could not easily discern the strength of the consequences, nor lay aside the prejudices to which they had been many years accustomed, therefore, to prevent the disputes which might be raised upon such accounts, I chose to reduce the substance of this book into the form of propositions (in the mathematical way), which should be read by those only who had first made themselves masters of the principles established in the preceding books: not that I would advise any one to the previous study of every proposition of those books; for they abound with such as might cost too much time, even to readers of good mathematical learning.   It is enough if one carefully reads the definitions, the laws of motions, and the first three sections of the first book.   He may then pass on to this book, and consult such of the remaining propositions of the first two books, as the references in this, and his occasions,

*The Mathematical Principles of Natural Philosophy *by Sir Isaac Newton.   Translated into English by Andrew Motte: to which are added Newton's System of the World; 3 Volumes (London: Sherwood, Neely and Jones, 1919), Vol II., pp. 159-162.   Also found in: Isaac Newton, *Principia *in Cajori, *op. cit.,* pp. 397-400.

shall require.

Rules of Reasoning in Philosophy.

Rule I.

We are to admit no more causes of natural things than such as are both true and sufficient to explain their appearances.

To this purpose the philosophers say that Nature does nothing in vain, and more is in vain when less will serve; for Nature is pleased with simplicity, and affects not the pomp of superfluous causes.

Rule II.

Therefore to the same natural effects we must, as far as possible, assign the same causes.

As to respiration in a man and in a beast; the descent of stones in Europe and in America; the light of our culinary fire and of the sun; the reflection of light in the earth and in the planets.

Rule III.

The qualities of bodies, which admit neither intension ͵or remission of degrees, and which are found to belong to all bodies within the reach of our experiments, are to be esteemed the universal qualities of all bodies whatsoever.

For since the qualities of bodies are only known to us by experiments, we are to hold for universal all such as universally agree with experiments; and such as are not liable to diminution can never be quite taken away. We are certainly not to relinquish the evidence of experiments for the sake of dreams and vain fictions of our own devising; nor are we to recede from the analogy of Nature, which is wont to be simple, and always consonant to itself. We no other way know the extension of bodies than by our senses, nor do these reach it in all bodies; but because we perceive extension in all that are sensible, therefore we ascribe it universally to all others also. That abundance of bodies are hard, we learn by experience; and because the hardness of the whole arises from the hardness of the parts, we therefore justly infer the hardness of the undivided particles not only of the bodies we feel but of all others. That all bodies are impenetrable, we gather not from reason, but from sensation. The bodies which we handle we find impenetrable, and thence conclude impenetrability to be an universal property of all bodies whatsoever. That all bodies are moveable, and endowed with certain powers (which we call *vires inertiæ*) of persevering in their motion, or in their rest, we only infer from the like properties observed in the bodies which we have seen. The extension, hardness, impenetrability, mobility, and *vis inertiæ* of the whole, result from the extension, hardness, impenetrability, mobility, and *vires inertiæ* of the parts; and thence we conclude the least particles of all bodies to be also all extended, and hard, and impenetrable, and moveable, and endowed with their proper *vires inertiæ*. And this is the foundation of all philosophy. Moreover, that the divided but continuous particles of bodies may be separated from one another, is matter of observation; and, in the particles that remain undivided, our minds are able to distinguish yet lesser parts, as is mathematically demonstrated. But whether the parts so distinguished, and not yet divided, may, by the powers of Nature, be actually divided and separated from one another, we cannot certainly determine. Yet, had we the proof of but one experiment that any undivided particle, in breaking a hard and solid body, suffered a division, we might by virtue of this rule conclude that the undivided as well as the divided particles may be divided and actually separated to infinity.

Lastly, if it universally appears, by experiments and astronomical observations, that all bodies about the earth gravitate towards the earth, and that in proportion to the quantity of matter which they severally contain; that the moon likewise, according to the quantity of its matter, gravitates towards the earth; that, on the other hand, our sea gravitates towards the moon; and all the planets mutually one towards another; and the comets in like manner towards the sun; we must, in consequence of this rule, universally allow that all bodies whatsoever are endowed with a principle of mutual gravitation. For the argument from the appearances concludes with more force for the universal gravitation of all bodies than for their impenetrability; of which, among those in the celestial regions, we have no experiments, nor any manner of observation. Not that I affirm gravity to be essential to bodies: by their *vis insita* I mean nothing but their *vis inertiæ*. This is immutable. Their gravity is diminished as they recede from the earth.

Rule IV.

In experimental philosophy we are to look upon propositions collected by general induction from phænomena as accurately or very nearly true, notwithstanding any contrary hypotheses that may be imagined, till such time as other phænomena occur, by which they may either be made more accurate, or liable to exceptions.

This rule we must follow, that the argument of induction may not be evaded by hypotheses.

2. Isaac Newton, *Opticks**

Propositions.
Prop. I. Theor. I.

Lights which differ in Colour, differ also in
Degrees of Refrangibility.

The Proof by Experiments.

Exper. I. I took a black oblong stiff Paper terminated by
Parallel Sides, and with a Perpendicular right Line drawn cross
from one Side to the other, distinguished it into two equal
Parts. One of these parts I painted with a red colour and the
other with a blue. The Paper was very black, and the Colours
intense and thickly laid on, that the Phænomenon might be more
conspicuous. This Paper I view'd through a Prism of solid Glass,
whose two Sides through which the Light passed to the Eye were
plane and well polished, and contained an Angle of about sixty
degrees; which Angle I call the refracting Angle of the Prism.
And whilst I view'd it, I held it and the Prism before a Window
in such manner that the Sides of the Paper were parallel to the
Prism, and both those Sides and the Prism were parallel to the
Horizon, and the cross Line was also parallel to it: and that
the Light which fell from the Window upon the Paper made an
Angle with the Paper, equal to that Angle which was made with
the same Paper by the Light reflected from it to the Eye.
Beyond the Prism was the Wall of the Chamber under the Window
covered over with black Cloth, and the Cloth was involved in
Darkness that no Light might be reflected from thence, which in
passing by the Edges of the Paper to the Eye, might mingle itself
with the Light of the Paper, and obscure the Phænomenon thereof.
These things being thus ordered, I found that if the refracting
Angle of the Prism be turned upwards, so that the Paper may
seem to be lifted upwards by the Refraction, its blue half will
be lifted higher by the Refraction than its red half. But if
the refracting Angle of the Prism be turned downward, so that the
Paper may seem to be carried lower by the Refraction, its blue
half will be carried something lower thereby than its red half.
Wherefore in both Cases the Light which comes from the blue half
of the Paper through the Prism to the Eye, does in like Circumstances suffer a greater Refraction than the Light which comes
from the red half, and by consequence is more refrangible.
Illustration. In the eleventh Figure, MN represents the
Window, and DE the Paper terminated with parallel Sides DJ and
HE, and by the transverse Line FG distinguished into two halfs,
the one DG of an intensely blue Colour, the other FE of an intensely red. And BACcab represents the Prism whose refracting
Planes ABba and ACca meet in the Edge of the refracting Angle Aa.

---

*Isaac Newton, *Opticks*, 4th ed., London, 1730. Dover Publications (G. Bell, London), New York, 1952. Pp. 20-3; 26-38; 45-8;
374-8; 382-3; 387-90; 397-406.

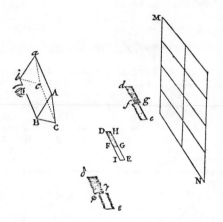

This Edge Aa being upward, is parallel both to the Horizon, and to the Parallel-Edges of the Paper DJ and HE, and the transverse Line FG is perpendicular to the Plane of the Window. And de represents the Image of the Paper seen by Refraction upwards in such manner, that the blue half DG is carried higher to dg than the red half FE is to fe, and therefore suffers a greater Refraction. If the Edge of the refracting Angle be turned downward, the Image of the Paper will be refracted downward; suppose to δε, and the blue half will be refracted lower to δγ than the red half is to φε.

*   *   *   *   *

Prop. II.   Theor. II.

The Light of the Sun consists of Rays differently Refrangible.

The Proof by Experiments.

Exper. 3. In a very dark Chamber, at a round Hole, about one third Part of an Inch broad, made in the Shut of a Window, I placed a Glass Prism, whereby the Beam of the Sun's Light, which came in at that Hole, might be refracted upwards toward the opposite Wall of the Chamber, and there form a colour'd Image of the Sun. The Axis of the Prism (that is, the Line passing through the middle of the Prism from one end of it to the other end parallel to the edge of the Refracting Angle) was in this and the following Experiments perpendicular to the incident Rays. About this Axis I turned the Prism slowly, and saw the refracted Light on the Wall, or coloured Image of the Sun, first to descend, and then to ascend. Between the Descent and Ascent, when the Image

seemed Stationary, I stopp'd the Prism, and fix'd it in that
Posture, that it should be moved no more. For in that Posture
the Refractions of the Light at the two Sides of the refracting
Angle, that is, at the Entrance of the Rays into the Prism, and
at their going out of it, were equal to one another. So also in
other Experiments, as often as I would have the Refractions on
both sides the Prism to be equal to one another, I noted the
Place where the Image of the Sun formed by the refracted Light

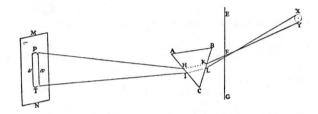

stood still between its two contrary Motions, in the common Period of its Progress and Regress; and when the Image fell upon that
Place, I made fast the Prism. And in this Posture, as the most
convenient, it is to be understood that all the Prisms are placed
in the following Experiments, unless where some other Posture is
described. The Prism therefore being placed in this Posture, I
let the refracted Light fall perpendicularly upon a Sheet of
white Paper at the opposite Wall of the Chamber, and observed the
Figure and Dimensions of the Solar Image formed on the Paper by
that Light. This Image was Oblong and not Oval, but terminated
with two Rectilinear and Parallel Sides, and two Semicircular
Ends. On its Sides it was bounded pretty distinctly, but on its
Ends very confusedly and indistinctly, the Light there decaying
and vanishing by degrees. The Breadth of this Image answered to
the Sun's Diameter, and was about two Inches and the eighth Part
of an Inch, including the Penumbra. For the Image was eighteen
Feet and an half distant from the Prism, and at this distance
that Breadth, if diminished by the Diameter of the Hole in the
Window-shut, that is by a quarter of an Inch, subtended an Angle
at the Prism of about half a Degree, which is the Sun's apparent
Diameter. But the Length of the Image was about ten Inches and a
quarter, and the Length of the Rectilinear Sides about eight
Inches; and the refracting Angle of the Prism, whereby so great a
Length was made, was 64 degrees. With a less Angle the Length of

the Image was less, the Breadth remaining the same. If the Prism
was turned about its Axis that way which made the Rays emerge
more obliquely out of the second refracting Surface of the Prism,
the Image soon became an Inch or two longer, or more; and if the
Prism was turned about the contrary way, so as to make the Rays
fall more obliquely on the first refracting Surface, the Image
soon became an Inch or two shorter. And therefore in trying this
Experiment, I was as curious as I could be in placing the Prism
by the above-mention'd Rule exactly in such a Posture, that the
Refractions of the Rays at their Emergence out of the Prism might
be equal to that at their Incidence on it. This Prism had some
Veins running along within the Glass from one end to the other,
which scattered some of the Sun's Light irregularly, but had no
sensible Effect in increasing the Length of the coloured Spectrum. For I tried the same Experiment with other Prisms with
the same Success. And particularly with a Prism which seemed
free from such Veins, and whose refracting Angle was 62 1/2 Degrees, I found the Length of the Image 9 3/4 or 10 Inches at the
distance of 18 1/2 Feet from the Prism, the Breadth of the Hole
in the Window-shut being 1/4 of an Inch, as before. And because
it is easy to commit a Mistake in placing the Prism in its due
Posture, I repeated the Experiment four or five Times, and always
found the Length of the Image that which is set down above. With
another Prism of clearer Glass and better Polish, which seemed
free from Veins, and whose refracting Angle was 63 1/2 Degrees,
the Length of this Image at the same distance of 18 1/2 Feet was
also about 10 Inches, or 10 1/8. Beyond these Measures for about
a 1/4 or 1/3 of an Inch at either end of the Spectrum the Light
of the Clouds seemed to be a little tinged with red and violet,
but so very faintly, that I suspected that Tincture might either
wholly, or in great Measure arise from some Rays of the Spectrum
scattered irregularly by some Inequalities in the Substance and
Polish of the Glass, and therefore I did not include it in these
Measures. Now the different Magnitude of the hole in the Window-
shut, and different thickness of the Prism where the Rays passed
through it, and different inclinations of the Prism to the Horizon, made no sensible changes in the length of the Image. Neither did the different matter of the Prisms make any: for in a
Vessel made of polished Plates of Glass cemented together in the
shape of a Prism and filled with Water, there is the like Success
of the Experiment according to the quantity of the Refraction.
It is farther to be observed, that the Rays went on in right
Lines from the Prism to the Image, and therefore at their very
going out of the Prism had all that Inclination to one another
from which the length of the Image proceeded, that is, the Inclination of more than two degrees and an half. And yet according to the Laws of Opticks vulgarly received, they could not
possibly be so much inclined to one another. For let EG
represent the Window-shut, F the hole made therein through which
a beam of the Sun's Light was transmitted into the darkened Chamber, and ABC a Triangular Imaginary Plane whereby the Prism is
feigned to be cut transversely through the middle of the Light.
Or if you please, let ABC represent the Prism it self, looking
directly towards the Spectator's Eye with its nearer end: And

let XY be the Sun, MN the Paper upon which the Solar Image or
Spectrum is cast, and PT the Image it self whose sides towards
v and *w* are Rectilinear and Parallel, and ends towards P and T
Semicircular. YKHP and XLJT are two Rays, the first of which
comes from the lower part of the Sun to the higher part of the
Image, and is refracted in the Prism at K and H, and the latter
comes from the higher part of the Sun to the lower part of the
Image, and is refracted at L and J. Since the Refractions on
both sides of the prism are equal to one another, that is, the Refraction at K equal to the Refraction at J, and the Refraction at
L equal to the Refraction at H, so that the Refractions of the
incident Rays at K and L taken together, are equal to the Refractions of the emergent Rays at H and J taken together: it follows
by adding equal things to equal things, that the Refractions at
K and H taken together, are equal to the Refractions at J and L
taken together, and therefore the two Rays being equally refracted, have the same Inclination to one another after Refraction
which they had before; that is, the Inclination of half a
Degree answering to the Sun's Diameter. For so great was the
inclination of the Rays to one another before Refraction. So
then, the length of the Image PT would by the Rules of Vulgar
Opticks subtend an Angle of half a Degree at the Prism, and by
Consequence be equal to the breadth *vw* ; and therefore the Image
would be round. Thus it would be were the two Rays XLJT and YKHP,
and all the rest which form the Image P*w*T*v*, alike refrangible.
And therefore seeing by Experience it is found that the Image is
not round, but about five times longer than broad, the Rays which
going to the upper end P of the Image suffer the greatest Refraction, must be more refrangible than those which go to the lower
end T, unless the Inequality of Refraction be casual.

　　This Image or Spectrum PT was coloured, being red at its
least refracted end T, and violet at its most refracted end P,
and yellow green and blue in the intermediate Spaces. Which
agrees with the first Proposition, that Lights which differ in
Colour, do also differ in Refrangibility. The length of the
Image in the foregoing Experiments, I measured from the faintest
and outmost red at one end, to the faintest and outmost blue at
the other end, excepting only a little Penumbra, whose breadth
scarce exceeded a quarter of an Inch, as was said above.

　　Exper. 4. In the Sun's Beam which was propagated into the
Room through the hole in the Window-shut, at the distance of some
Feet from the hole, I held the Prism in such a Posture, that its
Axis might be perpendicular to that Beam. Then I looked through
the Prism upon the hole, and turning the Prism to and fro about
its Axis, to make the Image of the Hole ascend and descend, when
between its two contrary Motions it seemed Stationary, I stopp'd
the Prism, that the Refractions of both Sides of the refracting
Angle might be equal to each other, as in the former Experiment.
In this situation of the Prism viewing through it the said Hole,
I observed the length of its refracted Image to be many times
greater than its breadth, and that the most refracted part thereof appeared violet, the least refracted red, the middle parts
blue, green and yellow in order. The same thing happen'd when I
removed the Prism out of the Sun's Light, and looked through it

upon the hole shining by the Light of the Clouds beyond it. And
yet if the Refraction were done regularly according to one certain Proportion of the Sines of Incidence and Refraction as is
vulgarly supposed, the refracted Image ought to have appeared
round.

So then, by these two Experiments it appears, that in Equal
Incidences there is a considerable inequality of Refractions.
But whence this inequality arises, whether it be that some of the
incident Rays are refracted more, and others less, constantly, or
by chance, or that one and the same Ray is by Refraction disturbed, shatter'd, dilated, and as it were split and spread into
many diverging Rays, as *Grimaldo* supposes, does not yet appear
by these Experiments, but will appear by those that follow.

Exper. 5. Considering therefore, that if in the third Experiment the Image of the Sun should be drawn out into an oblong
Form, either by a Dilatation of every Ray, or by any other casual
inequality of the Refractions, the same oblong Image would by a
second Refraction made sideways be drawn out as much in breadth
by the like Dilatation of the Rays, or other casual inequality
of the Refractions sideways, I tried what would be the Effects of
such a second Refraction. For this end I ordered all things as
in the third Experiment, and then placed a second Prism immediately after the first in a cross Position to it, that it might
again refract the beam of the Sun's Light which came to it
through the first Prism. In the first Prism this beam was refracted upwards, and in the second sideways. And I found that by
the Refraction of the second Prism, the breadth of the Image was
not increased, but its superior part, which in the first Prism
suffered the greater Refraction, and appeared violet and blue,
did again in the second Prism suffer a greater Refraction than
its inferior part, which appeared red and yellow, and this without any Dilatation of the Image in breadth.

Illustration. Let S represent the Sun, F the hole in the
Window, ABC the first Prism, DH the second Prism, Y the round
Image of the Sun made by a direct beam of Light when the Prisms

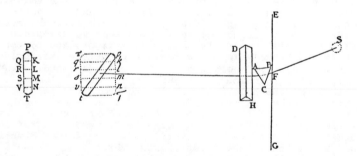

are taken away, PT the oblong Image of the Sun made by that beam
passing through the first Prism alone, when the second Prism is
taken away, and *pt* the Image made by the cross Refractions of
both Prisms together. Now if the Rays which tend towards the

several Points of the round Image Y were dilated and spread by
the Refraction of the first Prism, so that they should not any
longer go in single Lines to single Points, but that every Ray
being split, shattered, and changed from a Linear Ray to a Superficies of Rays diverging from the Point of Refraction, and lying
in the Plane of the Angles of Incidence and Refraction, they
should go in those Planes to so many Lines reaching almost from
one end of the Image PT to the other, and if that Image should
thence become oblong: those Rays and their several parts tending
towards the several Points of the Image PT ought to be again
dilated and spread sideways by the transverse Refraction of the
second Prism, so as to compose a four square Image, such as is
represented at πτ. For the better understanding of which, let
the Image PT be distinguished into five equal parts PQK, KQRL,
LRSM, MSVN, NVT. And by the same irregularity that the orbicular
Light Y is by the Refraction of the first Prism dilated and drawn
out into a long Image PT, the Light PQK which takes up a space of
the same length and breadth with the Light Y ought to be by the
Refraction of the second Prism dilated and drawn out into the
long Image πqkp, and the Light KQRL into the long Image kqrl
and the Lights LRSM, MSVN, NVT, into so many other long Images
lrøm, møvn, nvtτ ; and all these long Images would compose the
four square Image πτ. Thus it ought to be were every Ray dilated by Refraction, and spread into a triangular Superficies of
Rays diverging from the Point of Refraction. For the second Refraction would spread the Rays one way as much as the first doth
another, and so dilate the Image in breadth as much as the first
doth in length. And the same thing ought to happen, were some
rays casually refracted more than others. But the Event is
otherwise. The Image PT was not made broader by the Refraction
of the second Prism, but only became oblique, as 'tis represented
at pt, its upper end P being by the Refraction translated to a
greater distance than its lower end T. So then the Light which
went towards the upper end P of the Image, was (at equal Incidences) more refracted in the second Prism, than the Light which
tended towards the lower end T, that is the blue and violet, than
the red and yellow; and therefore was more refrangible. The same
Light was by the Refraction of the first Prism translated farther
from the place Y to which it tended before Refraction; and therefore suffered as well in the first Prism as in the second a
greater Refraction than the rest of the Light, and by consequence
was more refrangible than the rest, even before its incidence on
the first Prism.

*   *   *   *   *

Exper. 6. In the middle of two thin Boards I made round
holes a third part of an Inch in diameter, and in the Window-shut
a much broader hole being made to let into my darkened Chamber a
large Beam of the Sun's Light; I placed a Prism behind the Shut
in that beam to refract it towards the opposite Wall, and close
behind the Prism I fixed one of the Boards, in such manner that
the middle of the refracted Light might pass through the hole
made in it, and the rest be intercepted by the Board. Then at

the distance of about twelve Feet from the first Board I fixed
the other Board in such manner that the middle of the refracted
Light which came through the hole in the first Board, and fell
upon the opposite Wall, might pass through the hole in this other
Board, and the rest being intercepted by the Board might paint
upon it the coloured Spectrum of the Sun. And close behind this
Board I fixed another Prism to refract the Light which came
through the hole. Then I returned speedily to the first Prism,
and by turning it slowly to and fro about its Axis, I caused the
Image which fell upon the second Board to move up and down upon
that Board, that all its parts might successively pass through the
hole in that Board and fall upon the Prism behind it. And in the
mean time, I noted the places on the opposite Wall to which that
Light after its Refraction in the second Prism did pass; and by
the difference of the places I found that the Light which being
most refracted in the first Prism did go to the blue end of the
Image, was again more refracted in the second Prism than the
Light which went to the red end of that Image, which proves as
well the first Proposition as the second. And this happened
whether the Axis of the two Prisms were parallel, or inclined to
one another, and to the Horizon in any given Angles.

    Illustration. Let F be the wide hole in the Window-shut,
through which the Sun shines upon the first Prism ABC, and let
the refracted Light fall upon the middle of the Board DE, and the
middle part of that Light upon the hole G made in the middle part

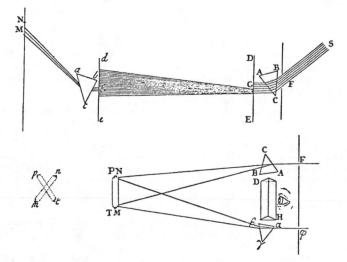

of that Board. Let this trajected part of that Light fall again
upon the middle of the second Board *de*, and there paint such an
oblong coloured Image of the Sun as was described in the third
Experiment. By turning the Prism ABC slowly to and fro about its
Axis, this Image will be made to move up and down the Board *de*,

and by this means all its parts from one end to the other may be
made to pass successively through the hole *g* which is made in the
middle of that Board. In the mean while another Prism *abc* is to
be fixed next after that hole *g*, to refract the trajected Light
a second time. And these things being thus ordered, I marked the
places M and N of the opposite Wall upon which the refracted
Light fell, and found that whilst the two Boards and second Prism
remained unmoved, those places by turning the first Prism about
its Axis were changed perpetually. For when the lower part of
the Light which fell upon the second Board *de* was cast through
the hole *g*, it went to a lower place M on the Wall and when the
higher part of that Light was cast through the same hole *g*, it
went to a higher place N on the Wall, and when any intermediate
part of the Light was cast through that hole, it went to some
place on the Wall between M and N. The unchanged Position of the
holes in the Boards, made the Incidence of the Rays upon the second Prism to be the same in all cases. And yet in that common
Incidence some of the Rays were more refracted, and others less.
And those were more refracted in this Prism, which by a greater
Refraction in the first Prism were more turned out of the way,
and therefore for their Constancy of being more refracted are
deservedly called more refrangible.

*   *   *   *   *

Quest. 30. Are not gross Bodies and Light convertible into
one another, and may not Bodies receive much of their Activity
from the Particles of Light which enter their Composition? For
all fix'd Bodies being heated emit Light so long as they continue
sufficiently hot, and Light mutually stops in Bodies as often as
its Rays strike upon their Parts, as we shew'd above. I know no
Body less apt to shine than Water; and yet Water by frequent
Distillations changes into fix'd Earth, as Mr. *Boyle* has try'd;
and then this Earth being enabled to endure a sufficient Heat,
shines by Heat like other Bodies.

The changing of Bodies into Light, and Light into Bodies, is
very conformable to the Course of Nature, which seems delighted
with Transmutations. Water, which is a very fluid tasteless Salt,
she changes by Heat into Vapour, which is a sort of Air, and by
Cold into Ice, which is a hard, pellucid, brittle, fusible Stone;
and this Stone returns into Water by Heat, and Vapour returns
into Water by Cold. Earth by Heat becomes Fire, and by Cold returns into Earth. Dense Bodies by Fermentation rarify into
several sorts of Air, and this Air by Fermentation, and sometimes
without it, returns into dense Bodies. Mercury appears sometimes
in the form of a fluid Metal, sometimes in the form of a hard
brittle Metal, sometimes in the form of a corrosive pellucid Salt
call'd Sublimate, sometimes in the form of a tasteless, pellucid,
volatile white Earth, call'd *Mercurius Dulcis*; or in that of a
red opake volatile Earth, call'd Cinnaber; or in that of a red or
white Precipitate, or in that of a fluid Salt; and in Distilla-
tion it turns into Vapour, and being agitated *in Vacuo*, it shines
like Fire. And after all these Changes it returns again into its
first form of Mercury. Eggs grow from insensible Magnitudes, and

change into Animals; Tadpoles into Frogs; and Worms into Flies.
All Birds, Beasts and Fishes, Insects, Trees, and other Vege-
tables, with their several Parts, grow out of Water and watry
Tinctures and Salts, and by Putrefaction return again into watry
Substances. And Water standing a few Days in the open Air,
yields a Tincture, which (like that of Malt) by standing longer
yields a Sediment and a Spirit, but before Putrefaction is fit
Nourishment for Animals and Vegetables. And among such various
and strange Transmutations, why may not Nature change Bodies into
Light, and Light into Bodies?

 Quest. 31. Have not the small Particles of Bodies certain
Powers, Virtues, or Forces, by which they act at a distance, not
only upon the Rays of Light for reflecting, refracting, and in-
flecting them, but also upon one another for producing a great
Part of the Phænomena of Nature? For it's well known, that
Bodies act one upon another by the Attractions of Gravity, Magnetism, and Electricity; and these Instances shew the Tenor and
Course of Nature, and make it not improbable but that there may
be more attractive Powers than these. For Nature is very consonant and conformable to her self. How these Attractions may be
perform'd, I do not here consider. What I call Attraction may be
perform'd by impulse, or by some other means unknown to me. I
use that Word here to signify only in general any Force by which
Bodies tend towards one another, whatsoever be the Cause. For
we must learn from the Phænomena of Nature what Bodies attract
one another, and what are the Laws and Properties of the Attraction, before we enquire the Cause by which the Attraction is
perform'd. The Attractions of Gravity, Magnetism, and Electricity, reach to very sensible distances, and so have been observed
by vulgar Eyes, and there may be others which reach to so small
distances as hitherto escape Observation; and perhaps electrical
Attraction may reach to such small distances, even without being
excited by Friction.

 For when Salt of Tartar runs *per Deliquium*, is not this done
by an Attraction between the Particles of the Salt of Tartar, and
the Particles of the Water which float in the Air in the form of
Vapours? And why does not common Salt, or Salt-petre, or Vitriol,
run *per Deliquium*, but for want of such an Attraction? Or why
does not Salt of Tartar draw more Water out of the Air than in a
certain Proportion to its quantity, but for want of an attractive
Force after it is satiated with Water? And whence is it but from
this attractive Power that Water which alone distils with a gentle luke-warm Heat, will not distil from Salt of Tartar without
a great Heat? And is it not from the like attractive Power between the Particles of Oil of Vitriol and the Particles of Water,
that Oil of Vitriol draws to it a good quantity of Water out of
the Air, and after it is satiated draws no more, and in Distilla-
tion lets go the Water very difficultly? And when Water and Oil
of Vitriol poured successively into the same Vessel grow very
hot in the mixing, does not this Heat argue a great Motion in
the Parts of the Liquors? And does not this Motion argue, that
the Parts of the two Liquors in mixing coalesce with Violence,
and by consequence rush towards one another with an accelerated
Motion? And when *Aqua fortis*, or Spirit of Vitriol poured upon

Filings of Iron dissolves the Filings with a great Heat and
Ebullition, is not this Heat and Ebullition effected by a violent
Motion of the Parts, and does not that Motion argue that the acid
Parts of the Liquor rush towards the Parts of the Metal with
violence, and run forcibly into its Pores till they get between
its outmost Particles, and the main Mass of the Metal, and surrounding those Particles loosen them from the main Mass, and set
them at liberty to float off into the Water? And when the acid
Particles, which alone would distil with an easy Heat, will not
separate from the Particles of the Metal without a very violent
Heat, does not this confirm the Attraction between them?

         *   *   *   *   *

When *Aqua fortis* dissolves Silver and not Gold, and *Aqua
regia* dissolves Gold and not Silver, may it not be said that *Aqua
fortis* is subtil enough to penetrate Gold as well as Silver, but
wants the attractive Force to give it Entrance; and that *Aqua
regia* is subtil enough to penetrate Silver as well as Gold, but
wants the attractive Force to give it Entrance? For *Aqua regia*
is nothing else than *Aqua fortis* mix'd with some Spirit of Salt,
or with Sal-armoniac; and even common Salt dissolved in *Aqua
fortis*, enables the *Menstruum* to dissolve Gold, though the Salt
be a gross Body. When therefore Spirit of Salt precipitates Silver out of *Aqua fortis*, is it not done by attracting and mixing
with the *Aqua fortis*, and not attracting, or perhaps repelling
Silver? And when Water precipitates Antimony out of the Sublimate of Antimony and Sal-armoniac, or out of Butter of Antimony,
is it not done by its dissolving, mixing with, and weakening the
Sal-armoniac or Spirit of Salt, and its not attracting, or perhaps repelling the Antimony? And is it not for want of an
attractive virtue between the Parts of Water and Oil, of Quick-
silver and Antimony, of Lead and Iron, that these Substances do
not mix; and by a weak Attraction, that Quick-silver and Copper
mix difficultly; and from a strong one, that Quick-silver and
Tin, Antimony and Iron, Water and Salts, mix readily? And in
general, is it not from the same Principle that Heat congregates
homogeneal Bodies, and separates heterogeneal ones?

         *   *   *   *   *

If a very small quantity of any Salt or Vitriol be dissolved
in a great quantity of Water, the Particles of the Salt or Vitriol will not sink to the bottom, though they be heavier in Specie
than the Water, but will evenly diffuse themselves into all the
Water, so as to make it as saline at the top as at the bottom.
And does not this imply that the Parts of the Salt or Vitriol
recede from one another, and endeavour to expand themselves, and
get as far asunder as the quantity of Water in which they float,
will allow? And does not this Endeavour imply that they have a
repulsive Force by which they fly from one another, or at least,
that they attract the Water more strongly than they do one
another? For as all things ascend in Water which are less attracted than Water, by the gravitating Power of the Earth; so all

the Particles of Salt which float in Water, and are less attracted than Water by any one Particle of Salt, must recede from
that Particle, and give way to the more attracted Water.

When any saline Liquor is evaporated to a Cuticle and let
cool, the Salt concretes in regular Figures; which argues, that
the Particles of the Salt before they concreted, floated in the
Liquor at equal distances in rank and file, and by consequence
that they acted upon one another by some Power which at equal
distances is equal, at unequal distances unequal. For by such a
Power they will range themselves uniformly, and without it they
will float irregularly, and come together as irregularly. And
since the Particles of Island-Crystal act all the same way upon
the Rays of Light for causing the unusual Refraction, may it
not be supposed that in the Formation of this Crystal, the
Particles not only ranged themselves in rank and file for concre-
ting in regular Figures, but also by some kind of polar Virtue
turned their homogeneal Sides the same way.

The Parts of all homogeneal hard Bodies which fully touch
one another, stick together very strongly. And for explaining
how this may be, some have invented hooked Atoms, which is beg-
ging the Question; and others tell us that Bodies are glued together by rest, that is, by an occult Quality, or rather by
nothing; and others, that they stick together by conspiring
Motions, that is, by relative rest amongst themselves. I had
rather infer from their Cohesion, that their Particles attract
one another by some Force, which in immediate Contact is exceeding strong, at small distances performs the chymical Operations
above-mention'd, and reaches not far from the Particles with any
sensible Effect.

All Bodies seem to be composed of hard Particles: For
otherwise Fluids would not congeal; as Water, Oils, Vinegar, and
Spirit or Oil of Vitriol do by freezing; Mercury by Fumes of
Lead; Spirit of Nitre and Mercury, by dissolving the Mercury
and evaporating the Flegm; Spirit of Wine and Spirit of Urine,
by deflegming and mixing them; and Spirit of Urine and Spirit of
Salt, by subliming them together to make Sal-armoniac. Even the
Rays of Light seem to be hard Bodies; for otherwise they would
not retain different Properties in their different Sides. And
therefore Hardness may be reckon'd the Property of all uncom-
pounded Matter. At least, this seems to be as evident as the
universal Impenetrability of Matter. For all Bodies, so far as
Experience reaches, are either hard, or may be harden'd; and we
have no other Evidence of universal Impenetrability, besides a
large Experience without an experimental Exception. Now if compound Bodies are so very hard as we find some of them to be, and
yet are very porous, and consist of Parts which are only laid
together; the simple Particles which are void of Pores, and were
never yet divided, must be much harder. For such hard Particles
being heaped up together, can scarce touch one another in more
than a few Points, and therefore must be separable by much less
Force than is requisite to break a solid Particle, whose Parts
touch in all the Space between them, without any Pores or
Interstices to weaken their Cohesion. And how such very hard
Particles which are only laid together and touch only in a few

Points, can stick together, and that so firmly as they do, without the assistance of something which causes them to be attracted
or press'd towards one another, is very difficult to conceive.

*   *   *   *   *

And thus Nature will be very conformable to her self and
very simple, performing all the great Motions of the heavenly
Bodies by the Attraction of Gravity which intercedes those
Bodies, and almost all the small ones of their Particles by some
other attractive and repelling Powers which intercede the Particles. The *Vis inertiæ* is a passive Principle by which Bodies
persist in their Motion or Rest, receive Motion in proportion to
the Force impressing it, and resist as much as they are resisted.
By this Principle alone there never could have been any Motion
in the World. Some other Principle was necessary for putting
Bodies into Motion; and now they are in Motion, some other Principle is necessary for conserving the Motion. For from the
various Composition of two Motions, 'tis very certain that there
is not always the same quantity of Motion in the World. For if
two Globes joined by a slender Rod, revolve about their common
Center of Gravity with an uniform Motion, while that Center moves
on uniformly in a right Line drawn in the Plane of their circular
Motion; the Sum of the Motions of the two Globes, as often as the
Globes are in the right Line described by their common Center of
Gravity, will be bigger than the Sum of their Motions, when they
are in a Line perpendicular to that right Line. By this Instance
it appears that Motion may be got or lost. But by reason of the
Tenacity of Fluids, and Attrition of their Parts, and the Weakness of Elasticity in Solids, Motion is much more apt to be lost
than got, and is always upon the Decay. For Bodies which are
either absolutely hard, or so soft as to be void of Elasticity,
will not rebound from one another. Impenetrability makes them
only stop. If two equal Bodies meet directly *in vacuo*, they
will by the Laws of Motion stop where they meet, and lose all
their Motion, and remain in rest, unless they be elastick, and
receive new Motion from their Spring. If they have so much
Elasticity as suffices to make them re-bound with a quarter, or
half, or three quarters of the Force with which they come together, they will lose three quarters, or half, or a quarter of
their Motion. And this may be try'd, by letting two equal Pendulums fall against one another from equal heights. If the
Pendulums be of Lead or soft Clay, they will lose all or almost
all their Motions: If of elastick Bodies they will lose all but
what they recover from their Elasticity. If it be said, that
they can lose no Motion but what they communicate to other
Bodies, the consequence is, that *in vacuo* they can lose no Motion, but when they meet they must go on and penetrate one
another's Dimensions. If three equal round Vessels be filled,
the one with Water, the other with Oil, the third with molten
Pitch, and the Liquors be stirred about alike to give them a
vortical Motion; the Pitch by its Tenacity will lose its Motion
quickly, the Oil being less tenacious will keep it longer, and
the Water being less tenacious will keep it longest, but yet will

lose it in a short time. Whence it is easy to understand, that
if many contiguous Vortices of molten Pitch were each of them as
large as those which some suppose to revolve about the Sun and
fix'd Stars, yet these and all their Parts would, by their Tenacity and Stiffness, communicate their Motion to one another till
they all rested among themselves. Vortices of Oil or Water, or
some fluider Matter, might continue longer in Motion; but unless
the Matter were void of all Tenacity and Attrition of Parts, and
Communication of Motion, (which is not to be supposed,) the
Motion would constantly decay. Seeing therefore the variety of
Motion which we find in the World is always decreasing, there is
a necessity of conserving and recruiting it by active Principles,
such as are the cause of Gravity, by which Planets and Comets
keep their Motions in their Orbs, and Bodies acquire great Motion in falling; and the cause of Fermentation, by which the
Heart and Blood of Animals are kept in perpetual Motion and Heat;
the inward Parts of the Earth are constantly warm'd, and in some
places grow very hot; Bodies burn and shine, Mountains take fire,
the Caverns of the Earth are blown up, and the Sun continues
violently hot and lucid, and warms all things by his Light. For
we meet with very little Motion in the World, besides what is
owing to these active Principles. And if it were not for these
Principles, the Bodies of the Earth, Planets, Comets, Sun, and
all things in them, would grow cold and freeze, and become inactive Masses; and all Putrefaction, Generation, Vegetation and
Life would cease, and the Planets and Comets would not remain in
their Orbs.

All these things being consider'd, it seems probable to me,
that God in the Beginning form'd Matter in solid, massy, hard,
impenetrable, moveable Particles, of such Sizes and Figures, and
with such other Properties, and in such Proportion to Space, as
most conduced to the End for which he form'd them; and that these
primitive Particles being Solids, are incomparably harder than
any porous Bodies compounded of them; even so very hard, as never
to wear or break in pieces; no ordinary Power being able to divide what God himself made one in the first Creation. While the
Particles continue entire, they may compose Bodies of one and the
same Nature and Texture in all Ages: But should they wear away,
or break in pieces, the Nature of Things depending on them, would
be changed. Water and Earth, composed of old worn Particles and
Fragments of Particles, would not be of the same Nature and Texture now, with Water and Earth composed of entire Particles in
the Beginning. And therefore, that Nature may be lasting, the
Changes of corporeal Things are to be placed only in the various
Separations and new Associations and Motions of these permanent
Particles; compound Bodies being apt to break, not in the midst
of solid Particles, but where those Particles are laid together,
and only touch in a few Points.

It seems to me farther, that these Particles have not only a *Vis inertiæ*, accompanied with such passive Laws of Motion
as naturally result from that Force, but also that they are moved
by certain active Principles, such as is that of Gravity, and
that which causes Fermentation, and the Cohesion of Bodies.
These Principles I consider, not as occult Qualities, supposed to

result from the specifick Forms of Things, but as general Laws of
Nature, by which the Things themselves are form'd; their Truth
appearing to us by Phænomena, though their Causes be not yet
discover'd. For these are manifest Qualities, and their Causes
only are occult. And the *Aristotelians* gave the Name of occult
Qualities, not to manifest Qualities, but to such Qualities only
as they supposed to lie hid in Bodies, and to be the unknown
Causes of manifest Effects: Such as would be the Causes of Gravity, and of magnetick and electrick Attractions, and of Fermenta-
tions, if we should suppose that these Forces or Actions arose
from Qualities unknown to us, and uncapable of being discovered
and made manifest. Such occult Qualities put a stop to the Improvement of natural Philosophy, and therefore of late Years have
been rejected. To tell us that every Species of Things is endow'd with an occult specifick Quality by which it acts and produces manifest Effects, is to tell us nothing: But to derive two
or three general Principles of Motion from Phænomena, and afterwards to tell us how the Properties and Actions of all corporeal
Things follow from those manifest Principles, would be a very
great step in Philosophy, though the Causes of those Principles
were not yet discover'd: And therefore I scruple not to propose
the Principles of Motion above-mention'd, they being of very
general Extent, and leave their Causes to be found out.

Now by the help of these Principles, all material Things
seem to have been composed of the hard and solid Particles above-
mention'd, variously associated in the first Creation by the
Counsel of an intelligent Agent. For it became him who created
them to set them in order. And if he did so, it's unphilosophi-
cal to seek for any other Origin of the World, or to pretend that
it might arise out of a Chaos by the mere Laws of Nature; though
being once form'd, it may continue by those Laws for many Ages.
For while Comets move in very excentrick Orbs in all manner of
Positions, blind Fate could never make all the Planets move one
and the same way in Orbs concentrick, some inconsiderable Irregularities excepted, which may have risen from the mutual Actions
of Comets and Planets upon one another, and which will be apt to
increase, till this System wants a Reformation. Such a wonderful
Uniformity in the Planetary System must be allowed the Effect of
Choice. And so must the Uniformity in the Bodies of Animals,
they having generally a right and a left side shaped alike, and
on either side of their Bodies two Legs behind, and either two
Arms, or two Legs, or two Wings before upon their Shoulders, and
between their Shoulders a Neck running down into a Back-bone, and
a Head upon it; and in the Head two Ears, two Eyes, a Nose, a
Mouth, and a Tongue, alike situated. Also the first Contrivance
of those very artificial Parts of Animals, the Eyes, Ears, Brain,
Muscles, Heart, Lungs, Midriff, Glands, Larynx, Hands, Wings,
swimming Bladders, natural Spectacles, and other Organs of
Sense and Motion; and the Instinct of Brutes and Insects, can be
the effect of nothing else than the Wisdom and Skill of a powerful ever-living Agent, who being in all Places, is more able by
his Will to move the Bodies within his boundless uniform Sensorium, and thereby to form and reform the Parts of the Universe,
than we are by our Will to move the Parts of our own Bodies. And

yet we are not to consider the World as the Body of God, or the
several Parts thereof, as the Parts of God. He is an uniform Being, void of Organs, Members or Parts, and they are his Creatures
subordinate to him, and subservient to his Will; and he is no
more the Soul of them, than the Soul of Man is the Soul of the
Species of Things carried through the Organs of Sense into the
place of its Sensation, where it perceives them by means of its
immediate Presence, without the Intervention of any third thing.
The Organs of Sense are not for enabling the Soul to perceive
the Species of Things in its Sensorium, but only for conveying
them thither; and God has no need of such Organs, he being every
where present to the Things themselves. And since Space is divisible *in infinitum*, and Matter is not necessarily in all places,
it may be also allow'd that God is able to create Particles of
Matter of several Sizes and Figures, and in several Proportions
to Space, and perhaps of different Densities and Forces, and
thereby to vary the Laws of Nature, and make Worlds of several
sorts in several Parts of the Universe. At least, I see nothing
of Contradiction in all this.

As in Mathematicks, so in Natural Philosophy, the Investigation of difficult Things by the Method of Analysis, ought ever to
precede the Method of Composition. This Analysis consists in
making Experiments and Observations, and in drawing general Conclusions from them by Induction, and admitting of no Objections
against the Conclusions, but such as are taken from Experiments,
or other certain Truths. For Hypotheses are not to be regarded
in experimental Philosophy. And although the arguing from Experiments and Observations by Induction be no Demonstration of general
Conclusions; yet it is the best way of arguing which the Nature of
Things admits of, and may be looked upon as so much the stronger,
by how much the Induction is more general. And if no Exception
occur from Phænomena, the Conclusion may be pronounced generally.
But if at any time afterwards any Exception shall occur from
Experiments, it may then begin to be pronounced with such Exceptions as occur. By this way of Analysis we may proceed from
Compounds to Ingredients, and from Motions to the Forces producing them; and in general, from Effects to their Causes, and
from particular Causes to more general ones, till the Argument
end in the most general. This is the Method of Analysis: And
the Synthesis consists in assuming the Causes discover'd, and
establish'd as Principles, and by them explaining the Phænomena
proceeding from them, and proving the Explanations.

In the two first Books of these Opticks, I proceeded by this
Analysis to discover and prove the original Differences of the
Rays of Light in respect of Refrangibility, Reflexibility, and
Colour, and their alternate Fits of easy Reflexion and easy
Transmission, and the Properties of Bodies, both opake and pellu-
cid, on which their Reflexions and Colours depend. And these
Discoveries being proved, may be assumed in the Method of Com-
position for explaining the Phænomena arising from them: An
Instance of which Method I gave in the End of the first Book.
In this third Book I have only begun the Analysis of what remains
to be discover'd about Light and its Effects upon the Frame of
Nature, hinting several things about it, and leaving the Hints to
be examin'd and improv'd by the farther Experiments and Observa-

tions of such as are inquisitive. And if natural Philosophy in
all its Parts, by pursuing this Method, shall at length be perfected, the Bounds of Moral Philosophy will be also enlarged.
For so far as we can know by natural Philosophy what is the first
Cause, what Power he has over us, and what Benefits we receive
from him, so far our Duty towards him, as well as that towards
one another, will appear to us by the Light of Nature. And no
doubt, if the Worship of false Gods had not blinded the Heathen,
their moral Philosophy would have gone farther than to the four
Cardinal Virtues; and instead of teaching the Transmigration of
Souls, and to worship the Sun and Moon, and dead Heroes, they
would have taught us to worship our true Author and Benefactor,
as their Ancestors did under the Government of *Noah* and his Sons
before they corrupted themselves.

C. THE ASSESSMENT OF THE SCIENTIFIC REVOLUTION

It is now generally recognized that the Scientific Revolution was an event in the history of Western Civilization of fundamental importance. Historians, therefore, have increasingly focused their attention upon it and tried to discover its source and its meaning. There is, today, a vigorous debate going on which can only be dimly reflected in the selections that follow. These should reveal, however, how wide is the disagreement and how far modern scholarship still is from a consensus.

1.

Robert K. Merton in his article on "Science and Economy of 17th Century England"* probably presented the thesis which is held by most people in the West today; namely that the Scientific Revolution was the intellectual response to increasingly important economic and social needs in the seventeenth century. This interpretation is seductive in that it emphasizes the practical nature of the new science which certainly did gain its advocates even in the seventeenth century.

The interplay between socio-economic and scientific development is scarcely problematical. To speak of socio-economic influences upon science in general unanalyzed terms, however, barely poses the problem. The sociologist of science is specifically concerned with the *types* of influence involved (facilitative and obstructive), the *extent* to which these types prove effective in different social structures, and the *processes* through which they operate. But these questions cannot be answered even tentatively without a clarification of the conceptual tools employed. All too often, the sociologist who repudiates the mythopoeic or heroic interpretation of the history of science lapses into a vulgar materialism which seeks to find simple parallels between social and scientific development. Such misguided efforts invariably result in a seriously biased and untenable discussion.

Formulation of the Problem

At least three common but unsound postulates must be avoided. The first and most illusive is the identification of personal utilitarian motivation of scientists with the structural determinants of their research. Second is the belief that socio-economic factors serve to account exhaustively for the entire complex of scientific activity; and third is the imputation of

---

* Robert K. Merton, *Social Theory and Social Structure*, Macmillan Co. 1949 (Free Press). Pp. 347-57; 361-3.

"social needs" where these needs are, in any significant sense, absent.

*   *   *   *   *

Motives may range from the desire for personal aggrandisement to a wholly "disinterested desire to know" without necessarily impugning the demonstrable fact that the thematics of science in seventeenth century England were in large part determined by the social structure of the time. Newton's own motives do not alter the fact that astronomical observations, of which he made considerable use, were a product of Flamsteed's work in the Greenwich Observatory, which was constructed at the command of Charles II for the benefit of the Royal Navy. Nor do they vitiate the striking influence upon Newton's work of such practically-oriented scientists as Halley, Hooke, Wren, Huyghens and Boyle. . . . It is neither an idle nor unguarded generalization that *every English scientist of this time* who was of sufficient distinction to merit mention in general histories of science at one point or another explicitly related at least some of his scientific research to immediate practical problems. But in any case, analysis exclusively in terms of (imputed) motives is seriously misleading and tends to befog the question of the modes of socio-economic influence upon science.

Thus it is important to distinguish the personal attitudes of individual men of science from the social role played by their research. Clearly, some scientists were sufficiently enamored of their subject to pursue it "for its own sake," at times with little consideration of its practical bearings. Nor need we assume that *all* individual researches are directly linked to technical tasks. The relation between science and social needs is two-fold: direct, in the sense that some research is advisedly and deliberately pursued for utilitarian purposes; and indirect, insofar as certain problems and materials for their solution come to the attention of scientists although they need not be cognizant of the practical exigencies from which they derive.

*   *   *   *   *

There remains the third problem--of ascertaining social needs--which can best be handled in specific empirical terms. The widely accepted notion that need precipitates appropriate inventions and canalizes scientific interests demands careful restatement. Specific emergencies have often focused attention upon certain fields, but it is equally true that a multitude of "human needs" have gone unsatisfied throughout the ages. In the technical sphere, needs far from being exceptional, are so general that they explain little. Each invention *de facto* satisfies a need or is an attempt to achieve such satisfaction. It is necessary to realize that certain needs may not exist for the society under observation, precisely because of its particular social structure. It is only when the goal is actually part and parcel of the culture in question, only when it is actually perceived as such by some members of the society, that one may

properly speak of a need directing scientific and technological
interest in certain channels. Moreover, economic needs may be
satisfied not only technologically but also by changes in social
organization. But given the routine of fulfilling certain types
of needs by technologic invention, a pattern which was becoming
established in the seventeenth century; given the prerequisite
accumulation of technical and scientific knowledge which provides
the basic fund for innovation; given (in this case) an *expanding*
capitalistic economy; and it may be said that necessity is the
(foster) mother of invention and the grandparent of scientific
advance.

Transport and Science

The burgeoning of capitalistic enterprise in seventeenth
century England intensified interest in more adequate means of
transport and communication. St. Helena, Jamaica, North America
were but the beginnings of England's great colonial expansion.
This and the relatively low cost of water-transport led to the
marked growth of the merchant marine. More than forty per cent
of the English production of coal was carried by water. Similarly, internal trade enhanced the need for improved facilities for
land and river transport. Proposals for turnpikes and canals
were common throughout the century.

Foreign trade was assuming world-wide proportions. The
best available, though defective, statistics testify to these
developments. Imports and exports increased by almost 300 per
cent between 1613 and 1700.

*   *   *   *   *

These developments were accompanied by increased emphasis
upon a number of technical problems. Above all, the increase of
commercial voyages to distant points--India, North America,
Africa, Russia--stressed anew the need for accurate and expedient
means of determining position at sea, of finding latitude and
longitude. Scientists were profoundly concerned with possible
solutions to these problems. Both mathematics and astronomy were
signally advanced through research oriented in this direction.

Napier's invention of logarithms, expanded by Henry Briggs,
Adrian Vlacq (in Holland), Edmund Gunter and Henry Gellibrand,
was of incalculable aid to astronomer and mariner alike. Adam
Anderson possibly reflects the general attitude toward this
achievement when he remarks that "logarithms are of great special
utility to mariners at sea in calculations relating to their
course, distance, latitude, longitude, etc." Sprat, the genial
historiographer of the Royal Society, asserted that the advancement of navigation was one of the chief aims of the group.

*   *   *   *   *

A ballad written shortly after the Society began to meet at
Gresham College reflects the popular appreciation of this interest, as is manifest in the following excerpt:

This College will the whole world measure
Which most impossible conclude,
And navigation make a pleasure,
By finding out the longitude:
Every Tarpaulian shall then with ease
Saile any ship to the Antipodes.

Meeting officially as the Royal Society or foregathering at coffee-houses and private quarters, the scientific coterie discussed without end technical problems of immediate concern for the profit of the realm. Hooke's recently published diary discloses the varied pressures exerted upon him by the Society, the King and interested nobles to devote his studies to "things of use." He would frequently repair to Garaways or Jonathans, the coffee-houses in Change Alley, where, with Christopher Wren and others of their company, he would "discourse about Celestiall Motions" over a pot of tea while at nearby tables more mundane speculations engrossed the attention of stockjobbers and lottery touts. Problems considered at Garaways were often made the object of special inquiry by the Society. In short, the prevailing picture is not that of a group of "economic men" jointly or severally seeking to improve their economic standing, but one of a band of curious students cooperatively delving into the arcana of nature. The demands of economically-derived needs posed new questions and emphasized old, opening up fresh avenues of research and coupling with this a persistent pressure for the solution of these problems.

A Case: Problem of the Longitude

This engrossing problem of finding the longitude perhaps illustrates best the way in which practical considerations focused scientific interest upon certain fields. There can be no doubt that the contemporary astronomers were thoroughly impressed with the importance of discovering a satisfactory way of finding the longitude, particularly at sea. . . .

The various methods proposed for finding longitude led to the following investigations:

1. Computation of lunar distances from the sun or from a fixed star. First widely used in the first half of the sixteenth century and again in the latter seventeenth century.

2. Observations of the eclipses of the satellites of Jupiter. First proposed by Galileo in 1610; adopted by Hooke, Halley, G. D. Cassini, Flamsteed and others.

3. Observations of the moon's transit of the meridian. Generally current in the seventeenth century.

4. The use of pendulum clocks, and other chronometers, at sea, aided by Huyghens, Hooke, Halley, Messy, Sully, and others.

Newton clearly outlined these procedures, as well as the scientific problems which they involved, upon the occasion of Ditton's claim of the reward for an accurate method of determining longitude at sea. The profound interest of English scientists in this subject is marked by an article in the first volume of the *Philosophical Transactions*, describing the use of pendulum clocks at sea. As Sprat put it, the Society had taken the problem "into its peculiar care." Hooke attempted to improve the pendulum clock and, as he says, "the success of these [trials] made me further think of improving it for finding the Longitude, and . . . quickly led me to the use of Springs instead of Gravity for the making a Body vibrate in any posture. . . ." A notorious controversy then raged about Hooke and Huyghens concerning priority in the successful construction of a watch with spiral balance spring. Howsoever the question of priority be settled, the very fact that two such eminent men of science, among others, focused their attention upon this sphere of inquiry is itself significant. These simultaneous inventions are a resultant of two forces: the intrinsically scientific one which provided the theoretical materials employed in solving the problem in hand, and the non-scientific, largely economic, factor which served to direct interest toward the general problem. The limited range of practicable possibilities leads to independent duplicate inventions.

* * * * *

It is precisely these examples, with their acknowledged practical implications, which clearly illustrate the role of utilitarian elements in furthering scientific advance. For it may be said, upon ample documentary grounds, that Giovanni Domenico Cassini's astronomical discoveries were largely a result of utilitarian interests. In almost all of Cassini's papers in the *Transactions* he emphasizes the value of observing the moons of Jupiter for determining longitude, by means of the method first suggested by Galileo. It is perhaps not too much to say that from this interest derived his discovery of the rotation of Jupiter, the double ring of Saturn, and the third, fourth, fifth, sixth and eighth satellites of Saturn for, as he suggests, astronomical observations of this sort were "incited" because of their practical implications. . . .

Newton was likewise deeply interested in the same general problem. Early in his career, he wrote a now famous letter of advice to his friend, Francis Aston, who was planning a trip to the Continent, in which he suggested among other particulars that Aston "inform himself whether pendulum clocks be of any service in finding out the longitude." In a correspondence which we have reason to believe ultimately led Newton to the completion of the *Principia*, both Halley and Hooke urged Newton to continue certain phases of his research because of its utility for navigation.

* * * * *

Newton's lunar theory was the climactic outcome of scientific concentration on this subject. . . . Halley, who had decided that the various methods of determining longitude were all defective and had declared that "it would be scarce possible ever to find the Longitude at sea sufficient for sea uses, till such time as the Lunar Theory be fully perfected," constantly prompted Newton to continue his work. Flamsteed, and (from 1691 to 1739)

Halley also endeavored to rectify the lunar tables sufficiently to attain "the great objects, of finding the Longitude with the requisite degree of exactness." Observations of the eclipses of the moon were recommended by the Royal Society for the same purpose.

*　　　*　　　*　　　*　　　*

Thus we are led to see that the scientific problems emphasized by the manifest value of a method for finding longitude were manifold. If the scientific study of various possible means of achieving this goal was not invariably dictated by the practical utility of the desired result, it is clear that at least part of the continued diligence exercised in these fields was due to it. In the last analysis it is impossible to determine with exactitude the extent to which practical concern focused scientific attention upon certain problems. What can be conscionably suggested is a certain correspondence between the subjects most intensively investigated by the contemporary men of science and the problems raised or emphasized by economic developments. It is an inference--usually supported by the explicit statements of the scientists themselves--that these economic requirements or, more properly, the technical needs deriving from these requirements, provoked research in particular channels. The finding of the longitude was one problem which, engrossing the attention of many scientists, furthered profound developments in astronomy, geography, mathematics, mechanics, and the invention of clocks and watches.

*　　　*　　　*　　　*　　　*

The Extent of Economic Influence

In a sense, the foregoing discussion provides materials illustrative only of the connections we have been tracing. We still have to determine the extent to which socio-economic influences were operative. The minutes of the Royal Society as transcribed in Birch's *History of the Royal Society* provide one basis for such a study. A feasible, though in several manifest respects inadequate, procedure consists of a classification and tabulation of the researches discussed at these meetings, together with an examination of the context in which the various problems came to light. This should afford some ground for deciding *approximately* the extent to which extrinsic factors operated.

Meetings during the four years 1661, 1662, 1686 and 1687 will be considered. There is no reason to suppose that these did not witness meetings "typical" of the general period. The classification employed is empirical rather than logically symmetrical. Items were classified as "directly related" to socio-economic demands when the individual conducting the research explicitly indicated some such connection or when the immediate discussion of the research evidenced a prior appreciation of some such relation. Items classified as "indirectly related" comprise researches which had a clear-cut connection with current practical needs, intimated in the context, but which were not definite-

ly so related by the investigators. Researches which evidenced
no relations of this sort were classified as "pure science."
Many items have been classified in this category which have (for
the present-day observer) a conceivable relation to practical
exigencies but which were not so regarded explicitly in the
seventeenth century. Thus, investigations in the field of
meteorology could readily be related to the practical desirabil-
ity of forecasting the weather but when these researches were not
explicitly related to specific problems they were classified as
pure science. Likewise, much of the work in anatomy and physiology was undoubtedly of value for medicine and surgery, but the
same criteria were employed in the classification of these items.
It is likely, therefore, that if any bias was involved in this
classification, it was in the direction of over-estimating the
scope of "pure science."

Each research discussed was "counted" as one "unit." It is
obvious that this procedure provides only a gross approximation
to the extent of extrinsic influences upon the selection of subjects for scientific study, but when greater precision is impossible one must perforce rest temporarily content with less. The
results can merely suggest the relative extent of the influences
which we have traced in a large number of concrete instances.

From this tabulation it appears that less than half (41.3%)
of the investigations conducted during the four years in question
are classifiable as "pure science." If we add to this the items
which were but indirectly related to practical needs, then about
seventy percent of this research had no explicit practical
affiliations. Since these figures are but grossly approximate,
the results may be summarized by saying that from forty to seventy per cent occurred in the category of pure science; and conversely that from thirty to sixty percent were influenced by
practical requirements.

Again, considering only the research directly related to
practical needs, it appears that problems of marine transport
attracted the most attention. This is in accord with one's
impression that the contemporary men of science were well aware
of the problems raised by England's insular position--problems
both military and commercial in nature--and were eager to rectify
them. Of almost equal importance was the influence of military
exigencies. Not only were there some fifty years of actual
warfare during this century, but also the two greatest revolutions in English history. Problems of a military nature left
their impress upon the culture of the period, including scientific development.

Likewise, mining which developed so markedly during this
period, as we may see from the studies of Nef and other economic
historians, had an appreciable influence. In this instance, the
greater part of scientific, if one may divorce it from technologic, research was in the fields of mineralogy and metallurgy with
the aim of discovering new utilizable ores and new methods of
extracting metals from the ore.

It is relevant to note that, in the latter years considered
in this summary, there was an increasing proportion of investigation in the field of pure science. A conjectural explanation is

not far to seek. It is probable that at the outset the members
of the Society were anxious to justify their activities (to the
Crown and the lay public generally) by deriving practical results
as soon as possible. Hence, the initially marked orientation
toward practical problems. Furthermore, many of the problems
which were at first advisedly investigated because of their
utilitarian importance may later be studied with no awareness of
their practical implications. On the basis of the (perhaps
biased) criteria adopted in this compilation, some of the later
researches would arbitrarily be classified as pure science.

On the grounds afforded by this study it seems justifiable
to assert that the range of problems investigated by seventeenth
century English scientists was appreciably influenced by the
socio-economic structure of the period.

2. *Miss Frances Yates presents a much more unorthodox view of
    the origin of modern science in her article on "The
    Hermetic Tradition in Renaissance Science."* She examines
    the role magic may have played and brings a startling new
    perspective to the scholarly debate.*

"If there is any characteristic by which the Renaissance can
be recognised it is, I believe, in the changing conception of
Man's relation to the Cosmos." That is a quotation from a fairly
recent book on *Science and the Renaissance*, the writer of which
proceeds to inquire where we should look for the origins of a
change in the climate of opinion in western Europe which could
have produced this changed relation to the cosmos. He looks,
naturally, first of all in the movement known as "Renaissance
Neo-Platonism," originating in the renewed study of Plato and the
Platonists in the Florentine circle of Marsilio Ficino, but he
dismisses this movement as useless for his search. There is no
evidence, he thinks, that the Florentine academicians had any but
an incidental interest in the problem of knowledge of the external world or of the structure of the cosmos. Yet the movement
loosely known as "Renaissance Neo-Platonism" is the movement
which--coming in time between the Middle Ages and the seventeenth
century--ought to be the originator of the changed climate of
opinion, the change in man's attitude to the cosmos, which was to
be fraught with such momentous consequences. The difficulty has
been, perhaps, that historians of philosophy may have somewhat
misled us as to the nature of that movement. When treated as
straight philosophy, Renaissance Neo-Platonism may dissolve into
a rather vague eclecticism. But the new work done in recent
years on Marsilio Ficino and his sources has demonstrated that
the core of the movement was Hermetic, involving a view of the
cosmos as a network of magical forces with which man can operate.
The Renaissance magus had his roots in the Hermetic core of
Renaissance Neo-Platonism, and it is the Renaissance magus, I
believe, who exemplifies that changed attitude of man to the
cosmos which was the necessary preliminary to the rise of science.
    The word "Hermetic" has many connotations; it can be vaguely
used as a generic term for all kinds of occult practices, or it
can be used more particularly of alchemy, usually thought of as
the Hermetic science *par excellence*. This loose use of the word
has tended to obscure its historical meaning--and it is in the
historical sense alone that I use it. I am not an occultist, nor
an alchemist, nor any kind of a sorceress. I am only a humble
historian whose favorite pursuit is reading. In the course of
this reading and reading, I came to be immensely struck by the
phenomenon--to which scholars in Italy, in the United States, and

* Frances A. Yates, "The Hermetic Tradition in Renaissance Science," in Charles S. Singleton, ed., *Art, Science, and History in
the Renaissance*, The Johns Hopkins Press, Baltimore, 1968.
Pp. 255-62; 265-71.

in my own environment in the Warburg Institute had been drawing attention, namely the diffusion of Hermetic texts in the Renaissance.

I must very briefly remind you that the first work which Ficino translated into Latin at the behest of Cosimo de' Medici was not a work of Plato's but the *Corpus Hermeticum*, the collection of treatises going under the name of "Hermes Trismegistus." And I must also remind you that Ficino and his contemporaries believed that "Hermes Trismegistus" was a real person, an Egyptian priest, almost contemporary with Moses, a Gentile prophet of Christianity, and the source--or one of the sources with other *prisci theologi*--of the stream of ancient wisdom which had eventually reached Plato and the Platonists. It was mainly, I believe, in the Hermetic texts that the Renaissance found its new, or new-old, conception of man's relation to the cosmos. I illustrate this very briefly from two of the Hermetic texts.

The "Pimander," the first treatise of the *Corpus Hermeticum*, gives an account of creation which,although it seems to recall Genesis, with which Ficino of course compared it, differs radically from Genesis in its account of the creation of man. The second creative act of the Word in the "Pimander," after the creation of light and the elements of nature, is the creation of the heavens, or more particularly of the Seven Governors or seven planets on which the lower elemental world was believed to depend. Then followed the creation of man who "when he saw the creation which the demiurge had fashioned . . . wished also to produce a work, and permission to do this was given him by the Father. Having thus entered into the demiurgic sphere in which he had full power, the Governors fell in love with man, and each gave to him a part of their rule. . . ."

Contrast this Hermetic Adam with the Mosaic Adam, formed out of the dust of the earth. It is true that God gave him dominion over the creatures, but when he sought to know the secrets of the divine power, to eat of the tree of knowledge, this was the sin of disobedience for which he was expelled from the Garden of Eden. The Hermetic man in the "Pimander" also falls and can also be regenerated. But the regenerated Hermetic man regains the dominion over nature which he had in his divine origin. When he is regenerated, brought back into communion with the ruler of "the all" through magico-religious communion with the cosmos, it is the regeneration of a being who regains his divinity. One might say that the "Pimander" describes the creation, fall and redemption not of a man but of a magus--a being who has within him the powers of the Seven Governors and hence is in immediate and most powerful contact with elemental nature.

Here--in the Hermetic core of Ficinian Neo-Platonism--there was indeed a vast change in the conception of man's relation to the cosmos. And in the Hermetic *Asclepius*, the work which had been known all through the Middle Ages but which became most potently influential at the Renaissance through the respect accorded to the Egyptian Hermes Trismegistus and all his works, the magus man is shown in operation. The Egyptian priests who are the heroes of the *Asclepius* are presented as knowing how to capture the effluxes of the stars and through this magical knowledge

to animate the statues of their gods. However strange his operations may seem to us, it is man the operator who is glorified in
the *Asclepius*. As is now well known, it was upon the magical
passages in the *Asclepius* that Ficino based the magical practices
which he describes in his *De vita coelitus comparanda*. And it
was with a quotation from the *Asclepius* on man as a great miracle
that Pico della Mirandola opened his "Oration on the Dignity of
Man." With that oration, man as magus has arrived, man with
powers of operating on the cosmos through magia and through the
numerical conjurations of cabala.

I believe that the tradition which has seen in Pico della
Mirandola's oration and in his nine hundred theses a great turning point in European history has not been wrong, though sometimes wrongly interpreted. It is not as the advocate of
"humanism" in the sense of the revival of classical studies that
he should be chiefly regarded but as the spokesman for the new
attitude to man in his relation to the cosmos, man as the great
miracle with powers of acting on the cosmos. From the new
approach to them, Ficino and Pico emerge not primarily as "humanists," nor even primarily, I would say, as philosophers, but as
magi. Ficino's operations were timid and cautious; Pico came out
more boldly with the ideal of man as magus. And if, as I
believe, the Renaissance magus was the immediate ancestor of the
seventeenth-century scientist, then it is true that "Neo-
Platonism" as interpreted by Ficino and Pico was indeed the body
of thought which, intervening between the Middle Ages and the
seventeenth century, prepared the way for the emergence of
science.

*   *   *   *   *

It is convenient to consult the practical compendium for a
would-be magus compiled by Henry Cornelius Agrippa as a guide to
the classifications of Renaissance magic. Based on Ficino and the
Asclepius, and also making use of one of Ficino's manuscript
sources, the *Picatrix*, and based on Pico and Reuchlin for Cabalist magic, Agrippa distributes the different types of magic under
the three worlds of the Cabalists. The lowest or elemental world
is the realm of natural magic, the manipulation of forces in the
elemental world through the manipulation of the occult sympathies
running through it. To the middle celestial world of the stars
belongs what Agrippa calls mathematical magic. When a magician
follows natural philosophy and mathematics and knows the middle
sciences which come from them--arithmetic, music, geometry, optics, astronomy, mechanics--he can do marvelous things. There
follow chapters on Pythagorean numerology and on world harmony,
and on the making of talismans. To the highest or supercelestial
world belongs religious magic, and here Agrippa treats of magical
rituals and of the conjuring of angels.

The magical world view here expounded includes an operative
use of number and regards mechanics as a branch of mathematical
magic. The Hermetic movement thus encouraged some of the genuine
applied sciences, including mechanics, which Campanella was later
to classify as "real artificial magic." Many examples could be

given of the prevalent confusion of thought between magic and
mechanics. John Dee, for example, branded as the "great conjur-
or" for his angel-summoning magic, was equally suspect on account
of the mechanical Scarabaeus which he constructed for a play at
Trinity College, Cambridge. In his preface to Henry Billingsley's translation of Euclid, Dee bitterly protests against the
reputation for conjuring which his skill in mechanics has brought
him:

> And for . . . marueilous Actes and Feates, Naturally,
> Mathematically, and Mechanically wrought and contriued,
> ought any honest Student and Modest Christian Philoso-
> pher, be counted & called a Coniuror?

Yet there is no doubt that for Dee his mechanical operations,
wrought by number in the lower world, belonged into the same
world view as his attempted conjuring of angels by Cabalist numerology. The latter was for him the highest and most religious
use of number, the operating with number in the supercelestial
world.

Thus the strange mental framework outlined in Agrippa's *De
occulta philosophia* encouraged within its purview the growth of
those mathematical and mechanical sciences which were to triumph
in the seventeenth century. Of course it was through the recovery of ancient scientific texts, and particularly of Archimedes,
that the advance was fostered, but even here the Hermetic outlook may have played a part which has not yet been examined.
Egypt was believed to have been the home of mathematical and
mechanical sciences. The cult of Egypt, and of its great sooth-
sayer, Hermes Trismegistus, may have helped to direct enthusias-
tic attention toward newly recovered scientific texts. I can
only give one example of this.

In 1589 there was published in Venice a large volume by
Fabio Paolini entitled *Hebdomades*. D. P. Walker has said of this
work that it contains "not only the theory of Ficino's magic but
also the whole complex of theories of which it is a part: the
Neo-Platonic cosmology and astrology on which magic is based, the
prisca theologia and *magia*" and so on. It represents the impor-
tation of the Florentine movement into Venice and into the discussions of the Venetian academies. The movement has not yet
been adequately studied in its Venetian phase, in which it under-
went new developments. When speaking of the magical statues of
the Hermetic *Asclepius*, Paolini makes this remark: "we may refer
these to the mechanical art and to those machines which the
Greeks call *automata*, of which Hero has written." Paolini is
here speaking in the same breath of the statues described by Hermes Trismegistus in the *Asclepius*, which the Egyptian magicians
knew how to animate, and of the work on automata by Hero of
Alexandria which expounds mechanical or pneumatic devices for
making statues move and speak in theaters or temples. Nor is he
intending to debunk the magic statues of the *Asclepius* by showing
them up as mere mechanisms, for he goes on to speak with respect
of how the Egyptians, as described by Trismegistus, knew how to
compound their statues out of certain world materials and to draw
into them the souls of demons. There is a basic confusion in his

mind between mechanics as magic and magic as mechanics, which
leads him to a fascinated interest in the technology of Hero of
Alexandria. Such associations may also account for passages in
the *Hebdomades*, to which Walker has drawn attention, in which
Paolini states that the production of motion in hard recalcitrant
materials is not done without the help of the *anima mundi*, to
which he attributes, for example, the invention of clocks. Thus
even the clock, which was to become the supreme symbol of the
mechanistic universe established in the first phase of the scientific revolution, had been integrated into the animistic universe
of the Renaissance, with its magical interpretations of mechanics.

Among the great figures of the Renaissance who have been
hailed as initiators of modern science, one of the greatest is
Leonardo da Vinci. We are all familiar with the traditional reputation of Leonardo as a precursor, throwing off the authority
both of the schools and of rhetorical humanism to which he
opposed concrete experiment integrated with mathematics. In
two essays on Leonardo, published in 1965, Professor Eugenio
Garin argues, with his usual subtlety, that Vasari's presentation
of the great artist as a magus, a "divine" man, may be nearer the
truth. Garin points to Leonardo's citation of "Hermes the
philosopher" and to his definition of force as a spiritual essence. According to Garin, Leonardo's conception of spiritual
force "has little to do with rational mechanics but has a very
close relationship to the Ficinian-Hermetic theme of universal
life and animation." If as Garin seems to suggest, it is after
all within the Renaissance Hermetic tradition that Leonardo
should be placed, if he is a "divine" artist whose strong technical bent is not unmixed with magic and theurgy, whose mechanics
and mathematics have behind them the animist conception of the
universe, this would in no way diminish his stature as a man of
genius. We have to get rid of the idea that the detection of
Hermetic influences in a great Renaissance figure is derogatory
to the figure. Leonardo's extraordinary achievements would be,
on the hypothesis put forward by Garin, one more proof of the
potency of the Hermetic impulses toward a new vision of the
world, one more demonstration that the Hermetic core of Renaissance Neo-Platonism was the generator of a movement of which
the great Renaissance magi represent the first stage.

In the case of John Dee, we do not have to get rid of a
reputation for enlightened scientific advance, built up by
nineteenth-century admirers, in order to detect the Hermetic
philosopher behind the scientist. Dee's reputation has not been
at all of a kind to attract the enlightened. The publication in
1659 of Dee's spiritual diaries, with their strange accounts of
conferences with the spirits supposedly raised by Dee and Kelly
in their conjuring operations, ensured that it was as a conjuror,
necromancer, or deluded charlatan of the most horrific kind that
Dee's reputation should go down to posterity. Throughout the
nineteenth century this image of Dee prevailed, and it warned off
those in search of precursors of scientific enlightenment from
examining Dee's other works. Though Dee's reputation as a genuine scientist and mathematician has been gradually growing during
the present century, some survival of the traditional prejudice

against him may still account for the extraordinary fact that
Dee's preface to Billingsley's translation of Euclid (1570), in
which he fervently urges the extension and encouragement of
mathematical studies, has not yet been reprinted. While I suppose that practically every educated person either possesses one
of the many modern editions of Francis Bacon's *Advancement of
Learning* or has had easy access to them in some library, Dee's
mathematical preface can still only be read in the rare early
editions of the Euclid. (Fortunately this situation will not
long continue, for a long-awaited edition of the Euclid and its
preface is planned for publication in the near future.) Yet
Dee's preface is in English, like Bacon's *Advancement*, and in a
nervous and original kind of English; and as a manifesto for
the advancement of science it is greatly superior to Bacon's
work. For Dee most strongly emphasizes the central importance
of mathematics, while the neglect or relative depreciation of
mathematics is, as we all know, the fatal blind spot in Bacon's
outlook and the chief reason why his inductive method did not
lead to scientifically valuable results.

*   *   *   *   *

...That Dee goes back to the great Florentine movement for his
inspiration is suggested by the fact that he appeals, in his plea
for mathematics, to the "noble Earle of Mirandula" and quotes
from Pico's nine hundred theses the statement in the eleventh
mathematical conclusion that "by numbers, a way is to be had to
the searching out and understanding of euery thyng, hable to be
known." And it was certainly from Agrippa's compilation with
its classification of magical practices under the three worlds
that he drew the discussion of number in the three worlds with
which the preface opens. It may be noticed, too, that it is with
those mathematical sciences which Agrippa classifies as belonging
to the middle celestial world that the preface chiefly deals,
though there are many other influences in the preface, particularly an important influence of Vitruvius. This may raise in
our minds the curious thought that it was *because*, unlike
Francis Bacon, he was an astrologer and a conjuror, attempting
to put into practice the full Renaissance tradition of Magia and
Cabala as expounded by Agrippa, that Dee, unlike Bacon, was imbued with the importance of mathematics.

*   *   *   *   *

Francis Bacon is, in my opinion, one of those figures who
have been misunderstood and their place in history distorted by
those historians of science and philosophy who have seen in them
only precursors of the future without examining their roots in
the past. The only modern book on Bacon which makes, or so it
seems to me, the right historical approach is Paolo Rossi's
Francesco Bacone, published in Italian in 1957, and now translated into English. The significant subtitle of Rossi's book is
Dalla Magia alla Scienza [*From Magic to Science*]. Rossi begins
by outlining the Renaissance Hermetic tradition, pointing out

that Bacon's emphasis on the importance of technology cannot be disentangled from the Renaissance Hermetic tradition in which magic and technology are inextricably mingled. He emphasizes those aspects of Bacon's philosophy which show traces of Renaissance animism, and he argues that the two main planks of the Baconian position--the conception of science as power, as a force able to work on and modify nature, and the conception of man as the being to whom has been entrusted the capacity to develop this power--are both recognizably derivable from the Renaissance ideal of the magus. While urging that the approach to Bacon should take full cognizance of his roots in the Renaissance Hermetic tradition, Rossi emphasizes that such an approach does not diminish Bacon's great importance in the history of thought but should enable the historian to analyze and bring out his true position. In Rossi's opinion, Bacon's supreme importance lies in his insistence on the co-operative nature of scientific effort, on the fact that advance does not depend on individual genius alone but in pooling the efforts of many workers. He emphasizes, and this second point is related to the first one, Bacon's polemic against the habit of secrecy which was so strongly ingrained in the older tradition, his insistence that the scientific worker must not veil his knowledge in inscrutable riddles but communicate it openly to his fellow workers. And finally he draws attention to Bacon's dislike of illuminism and of the pretensions of a magus to knowledge of divine secrets, his insistence that it is not through such proud claims but through humble examination and experiment that nature is to be approached.

I believe that Rossi has indicated the right road for further research on Bacon, who should be studied as a Rosicrucian type but of a reformed and new kind, reformed on the lines indicated by Rossi, through which the Rosicrucian type abandons his secrecy and becomes a scientist openly co-operating with others in the future Royal Society, and abandons also his pretensions to illuminism, to being the "divine" man admired in the Hermetic tradition, with its glorification of the magus, for the attitude of a humble observer and experimentalist. The interesting point emerges here that the humble return to nature in observation and experiment advocated by Bacon takes on a moral character, as an attitude deliberately opposed to the sinful pride of a Renaissance magus with his claims to divine insights and powers.

Yet Bacon's reactions against the magus type of philosopher or scientist themselves belong into a curious context. Rossi has emphasized that Bacon regarded his projected *Instauratio Magna* of the sciences as a return for man of that dominion over nature which Adam had before the Fall but which he lost through sin. Through the sin of pride, Aristotle and Greek philosophers generally lost immediate contact with natural truth, and in a significant passage Bacon emphasizes that this sin of pride has been repeated in recent times in the extravagances of Renaissance animist philosophers. The proud fantasies of the Renaissance magi represent for Bacon something like a second Fall through which man's contact with nature has become even more distorted than before. Only by the humble methods of observation and ex-

periment in the Great Instauration will this newly repeated sin
of pride be redeemed, and the reward will be a new redemption of
man in his relation to nature. Thus Bacon's very reaction
against the magi in favor of what seems a more modern conception
of the scientist contained within it curious undercurrents of
cosmic mysticism. Though Bacon's attitude would seem to dethrone
the Hermetic Adam, the divine man, his conception of the regenerated Mosaic Adam, who is to be in a new and more immediate and
more powerful contact with nature after the Great Instauration
of the sciences, seems to bring us back into an atmosphere which
is after all not so different from that in which the magus lived
and moved and had his being. In fact, Cornelius Agrippa repeat-
edly asserts that it is the power over nature which Adam lost by
original sin that the purified soul of the illuminated magus will
regain. Bacon rejected Agrippa with contempt, yet the Baconian
aim of power over nature and the Baconian Adam mysticism were
both present in the aspirations of the great magician. Though
for Bacon, the claim of the magus to Illuminism would itself
constitute a second Fall through pride.

Bacon's reaction against the animist philosophers as proud
magi who have brought about a second Fall is extremely important
for the understanding of his position as a reformed and humble
scientific observer, and I would even go further than Rossi and
suggest that some of Bacon's mistakes may have been influenced
by his desire to rationalize and make respectable a tradition
which was heavily suspected by its opponents, by the Aristotelians of the schools and by the humanists of the rhetoric tradition. Bacon's admirers have often been puzzled by his rejection
of Copernican heliocentricity and of William Gilbert's work on
the magnet. I would like to suggest, though there is hardly time
to work this out in detail, that these notions might have seemed
to Bacon heavily engaged in extreme forms of the magical and
animist philosophy or like the proud and erroneous opinions of
a magus.

In the sensational works published by Giordano Bruno during
his visit to England, of which Bacon must have been well aware,
Bruno had made use of heliocentricity in connection with the
extreme form of religious and magical Hermetism which he preached
in England. Bruno's Copernicanism was bound up with his magical
view of nature; he associated heliocentricity with the Ficinian
solar magic and based his arguments in favor of earth movement
on a Hermetic text which states that the earth moves because it
is alive. He had thus associated Copernicanism with the animist
philosophy of an extreme type of magus. When Bacon is deploring
the sinful pride of those philosophers who have brought about the
second Fall, who, believing themselves divinely inspired, invent
new philosophical sects which they create out of their individual
fantasy, imprinting their own image on the cosmos instead of hum-
bly approaching nature in observation and experiment, he mentions
Bruno by name as an example of such misguided Illuminati, together with Patrizi, William Gilbert, and Campanella. Is it possible
that Bacon avoided heliocentricity because he associated it with
the fantasies of an extreme Hermetic magus, like Bruno? And is
it further possible that William Gilbert's studies on the magnet,

and the magnetic philosophy of nature which he associated with
it, also seemed to Bacon to emanate from the animistic philosophy
of a magus, of the type which he deplored?

The magnet is always mentioned in textbooks of magic as an
instance of the occult sympathies in action. Giovanni Baptista
Porta, for example, in his chapters on the occult sympathies and
how to use them in natural magic constantly mentions the load-
stone. The animist philosophers were equally fond of this illustration; Giordano Bruno when defending his animistic version of
heliocentricity in the *Cena de le ceneri* brings in the magnet.
I think that it has not been sufficiently emphasized how close to
Bruno's language in the *Cena de le ceneri* is Gilbert's defense of
heliocentricity in the *De magnete*. Gilbert, like Bruno, actually
brings in Hermes and other *prisci theologi* who have stated that
there is a universal life in nature when he is defending earth
movement. There are passages in the *De magnete* which sound
almost like direct quotations from Bruno's *Cena de le ceneri*.
The magnetic philosophy which Gilbert extends to the whole universe is, it seems to me, most closely allied to Bruno's philosophy, and it is therefore not surprising that Bacon should list
Gilbert with Bruno as one of the proud and fantastic animist
philosophers or that notions about heliocentricity or magnetism
might seem to him dangerous fantasies of the Illuminati, to be
avoided by a humble experimentalist who distrusts such proud
hypotheses.

Finally, there is the suggestion at which I hinted earlier.
Is it possible that the reputation of John Dee, the conjuror,
conjuring angels with number in the supercelestial world with a
magus-like lack of humility of the kind which Bacon deplored,
might have made the Lord Verulam suspicious also of too much
operating with number in the lower worlds? Was mathematics, for
Bacon, too much associated with magic and with the middle world
of the stars, and was this one of the reasons why he did not
emphasize it in his method? I am asking questions here, obviously somewhat at random, but they are questions which have never
been asked before, and one object in raising them is to try to
startle historians of science into new attitudes to that key
figure, Francis Bacon. To see him as emerging from the Renaissance Hermetic tradition and as anxious to dissociate himself
from what he thought were extreme and dangerous forms of that
tradition may eventually lead to new adjustments in the treatment
both of his own thought and of his attitude toward contemporaries.
It would be valuable if careful comparisons could be organized
between the works of Dee, Bacon, and Fludd. The extreme Rosicrucian types, Dee and Fludd, might come out of such an examination with better marks as scientists than Bacon. Dee certainly
would, and even Fludd might do better than expected.

Nevertheless, all this does not do away with Bacon's great
importance. As compared with Dee and Fludd, Bacon has unques-
tionably moved into another era in his conception of the role of
the scientist and of the character of the scientist. Though
Bacon descends from the magus in his conception of science as
power and of man as the wielder of that power, he also banishes
the old conception of the magus in favor of an outlook which can

be recognized as modern, if the Adamic mysticism behind the Great Instauration is not emphasized. Bacon obviously qualifies as a member of the future Royal Society, though one with surviving affiliations with the occult tradition--as was the case with many early members of the Society. The figure of Bacon is a striking example of those subtle transformations through which the Renaissance tradition takes on, almost imperceptibly, a seventeenth-century temper and moves on into a new era.

I would thus urge that the history of science in this period, instead of being read solely forwards for its premonitions of what was to come, should also be read backwards, seeking its connections with what had gone before. A history of science may emerge from such efforts which will be exaggerated and partly wrong. But then the history of science from the solely forward-looking point of view has also been exaggerated and partly wrong, misinterpreting the old thinkers by picking out from the context of their thought as a whole only what seems to point in the direction of modern developments. Only in the perhaps fairly distant future will a proper balance be established in which the two types of inquiry, both of which are essential, will each contribute their quota to a new assessment. In the meantime, let us continue our investigations in which the detection of Hermetic influences in some great figure and acknowledged precursor should be a parallel process to the detection of genuine scientific importance in figures who have hitherto been disregarded as occultists and outsiders.

*   *   *   *   *

...The emergence of modern science should perhaps be regarded as proceeding in two phases, the first being the Hermetic or magical phase of the Renaissance with its basis in an animist philosophy, the second being the development in the seventeenth century of the first or classical period of modern science. The two movements should, I suggest, be studied as inter-related; gradually the second phase sheds the first phase, a process which comes out through the double approach of detecting intimations of the second phase in the first and survivals of the first phase in the second. Even in Isaac Newton, as is now well known, there are such survivals, and if Professor Garin is right, even in Galileo, while Kepler provides the obvious example of a great modern figure who still has one foot in the old world of universal harmony which sheltered the magus.

3.   *In their article on "Newton and the 'Pipes of Pan,'"* J. E.
      McGuire and P. M. Rattansi apply Miss Yates' thesis to the
      philosophy of Isaac Newton with rather surprising results.*

> What is it, by means of wch, bodies act on one another
> at a distance. And to what Agent did the Ancients
> attribute the gravity of their atoms and what did they
> mean by calling God an harmony and comparing him & matter
> (the corporeal part of the Universe) to the God Pan and
> his Pipe. Can any space be without something in it &
> what is that something in space void of matter (& what
> are its properties & operations on matter).
>   Draft of Query 27 of *Opticks*

Newtonian scholars have long been aware of a set of draft
Scholia to Propositions IV to IX of Book III of the *Principia*.
These were composed in the 1690's, as part of an unimplemented
plan for a second edition of the work. Since they describe
supposed anticipations of Newton's doctrines in the thought of
Graeco-Roman antiquity, they have become known as the 'classical'
Scholia. The analogies and parallels drawn in them are so
strained, as judged by modern standards of scholarship, that it
is tempting to consider them as merely literary embellishments
of a scientific work.

However, the sheer bulk of the manuscripts, the number of
copies and variants, their relation to Newton's other writings,
and the testimony of Newton's associates together with their
publication of some of the materials, all make it certain that
he considered the arguments and conclusions of the Scholia an
important part of his philosophy.

It would perhaps be possible to interpret the Scholia, with
their discussions of legendary figures and their references to a
'mystical' philosophy, as the work of the 'magical' (and hence
aberrant) Newton--as eccentric productions that possess little
significance for the reconstruction of his genuinely scientific
work, but merely throw light on his esoteric and occult interests. To us, however, this interpretation appears untenable. It
is now amply clear that Newton's serious enquiries were not
restricted to natural philosophy, investigated by an experimental-
mathematical method. His studies of theology and ancient chrono-
logy were of equal importance to him, and were pursued in as
rigorous a fashion as his scientific work. There is sufficient
evidence, even in his published writings, to show that he did not
regard these different sorts of enquiry as unrelated exercises.
Rather, he shared the belief, common in the seventeenth century,
that natural and divine knowledge could be harmonized and shown
to support each other.

We shall first describe the contents of these Scholia, and

---

* J. E. McGuire and P. M. Rattansi, "Newton and the 'Pipes of
Pan,'" *Notes and Records of the Royal Society*, 21 (1966), pp.
108-23; 126-31; 134-8.

interpret them in the light of the statements of Newton's associates, and of other works by Newton. These materials will provide the basis for a re-examination of parts of the *General Scholium* and the *Opticks*. At that time, as is well known, Newton believed that he knew how God's agency operated in His created world, particularly in the cause of gravitation. Our analysis of the Scholia will show that Newton held (at least at the time of their composition) an equally firm belief about his own place among the *prisci theologi* who had possessed such knowledge. He believed, in brief, that God had once revealed these and other truths, but they had soon been obscured and had been partially rediscovered by certain antique sages. In this respect, Newton's work has close similarities with that of the Cambridge Platonists. These similarities may be more significant than the well-known similarity between Newton's doctrine of absolute space and that of Henry More. In reexamining Newton's relation to the Cambridge Platonists, we shall see that he did not merely borrow ideas from them, but was engaged in a private dialogue whose terms were set by a certain intellectual tradition.

The study of the 'classical' Scholia should therefore deepen our understanding of the Newton's philosophical endeavour, and make it possible to relate his work to its contemporary English natural-philosophical and theological context with greater precision.

*   *   *   *   *

I

In May 1694, David Gregory visited Newton in Cambridge, and made 'Annotations Physical, Mathematical and Theological' from their conversations. Notes on the three topics follow each other in an indiscriminate sequence. Concerning the *prisca*, Gregory records:

> He will spread himself in exhibiting the agreement of this philosophy with that of the ancients, and principally with that of Thales. The philosophy of Epicurus and Lucretius is true and old, but was wrongly interpreted by the ancients as atheism.
>
> It is clear from the names of the planets given by Thoth (the Egyptian Mercury)--he gave them, in fact, the names of his predecessors whom he wished to be accepted as Gods--that he was a believer in the Copernican system.

There can be no doubt that Newton intended to incorporate such material into the revised version of the *Principia*; in July 1694 a memorandum of Gregory described the extensive changes planned by Newton, and mentioned:

> By far the greatest changes will be made to Book III. He will make a big change in Hypothesis III. page 402. He will show that the most ancient philosophy is in agreement with this hypothesis of his as much because the Egyptians and others taught the Copernican system, as he shows from their religion and hieroglyphics and images of the Gods, as because Plato and others--Plutarch and Galileo refer to it--observed the gravitation of all bodies towards all.

Some of the materials which Newton then intended for inclusion in the revised edition of the *Principia* have survived in a reasonably complete state. The main body of text is a set of fifteen folio sheets in Newton's hand, in the Library of the Royal Society. Their contents are Scholia on Propositions IV to IX of the Third Book of the *Principia*, where the essentials of Newton's doctrine of gravitation are set out. The material includes many references to, and quotations from, the ancients on the nature of the physical world. There is not space to present the material of these 'classical' Scholia *in extenso*. We shall, however, give an indication of its character, and present important passages which he took to support these key propositions of the Third Book. Newton gave the manuscript to Gregory, probably on the visit of May 1694, either as a gift or as a loan. Gregory drew from it extensively for the preface to his *Astronomia Physicae et Geometricae Elementa*, some paragraphs being almost identical with the manuscript.

The Propositions of Book III, for which the Scholia were intended, exhibit a carefully developed structure. The Book starts with six solar Phaenomena, obtained through astronomical observation and calculation. Then the first three Propositions state that the circumjovial planets, the primary planets, and the moon, are all retained in their orbits by a force which is mathematically described by the inverse-square law. The proof of this is supplied by the first four Propositions of the First Book.

So far we are at the level of the mathematical description of the phenomena. But Proposition IV states that the forces mentioned in the first three Propositions are the force of gravity. Thus it is a statement about a real force in the physical world, embodying the famous proof that the gravitational force which pulls terrestrial objects to the Earth is the same as that which pulls the moon from its inertial path. By induction and by appeal to Rules 1 and 2, Propositions V and VI extend the reasoning to cover the primary planets and then all celestial bodies. Proposition VI also introduces the proportionality of gravity to the quantity of matter in a body, which leads to a discussion of the interstitial void in the corrollaries. But more importantly, Proposition VI not only asserts the generality of the action of gravity in affecting all sensible bodies, but it implies that sub-sensible particles gravitate as well. This latter doctrine is explicitly treated in Proposition VII. The inverse-square law of attraction is shown, in Proposition VIII, to apply not only to celestial bodies but also to their component particles. Finally, Proposition IX asserts the law of action of the real force of gravity *within* celestial bodies. Thus, by this series of extensions, gravity is concluded to be a completely universal force.

The central purpose of the 'classical' scholia was to support the doctrine of universal gravitation as developed in these Propositions, and to enquire into its nature as a cosmic force. This doctrine is shown by Newton to be identifiable in the writings of the ancients. As will become clear, he is not using this historical evidence in a random fashion, or merely for literary ornamentation. Rather, the evidence is used in a serious and systematic fashion, as support for, and justification of, the

components of Newton's theory of matter, space and gravitation.
The evidence is used to establish four basic theses, which correspond to the matter of the Propositions IV to IX. These are,
that there was an ancient knowledge of the truth of the following
four principles: that matter is atomic in structure and moves by
gravity through void space; that gravitational force acts universally; that gravity diminishes in the ratio of the inverse square
of the distance between bodies; and that the true cause of gravity is the direct action of God. We shall analyse these in turn,
using supporting texts from some associates of Newton, and from
Newton's other writings.

*   *   *   *   *

    In Proposition VII, Newton is explicitly concerned with the
doctrine that the gravity of any composite body is the sum of its
component parts which are held together by mutual gravitation.
By analogy, he concludes that it follows that all celestial
bodies mutually gravitate as the inverse square of the distance
with respect to their components. Apart from the draft scholia
in the Royal Society manuscript, there is another in the Ports-
mouth collection which is, in part, a summary of the longer set of
Scholia and which was probably intended as an alternative. Both
documents are concerned with the absolute universality of gravitation. In the Royal Society manuscript there is a passage directly
relevant to the main doctrine of Proposition VII, namely, that the
quantity of matter of any body is a function of its parts:

> Therefore just as the attractive force of the whole Mag-
> net is composed of the attractive forces of the individu-
> al particles of which the Magnet consists, even so the
> ancient opinion was that Gravity towards the whole Earth
> arises from the gravity towards its individual parts.
> For that reason, if the whole Earth were divided into
> several globes, gravity, by the mind of the ancients,
> would have to be extended towards each several globe, in
> the same way as magnetic attraction is extended towards
> individual fragments of the magnet. And the ratio of
> gravity is equally towards all bodies whatever.
>
> Hence Lucretius teaches that there exists no centre
> of the universe, and no lowest place, but that there are
> in infinite space worlds similar to this of ours, and in
> addition to this he argues for the infinity of things in
> these terms.

Following this is another passage from Lucretius, containing an
argument for the infinity of the universe:

> . . . if all the space in the universe stood contained
> within fixed boundaries on all sides and were limited,
> by this time the store of matter would by its solid
> weight have run together from all sides to the
> bottom. . . .

In the same document, Newton dates the atomic succession back to
Moschus the Phoenician.

> That all matter consists of atoms was a very ancient
> opinion. This was the teaching of the multitude of

philosophers who preceded Aristotle, namely Epicurus,
Democritus, Ecphantus, Empedocles, Zenocrates,Heraclides,
Asclepiades, Diodorus, Metrodorus of Chios, Pythagoras,
and previous to these Moschus the Phoenician whom Strabo
declares older than the Trojan war. For I think that
same opinion obtained in that mystic philosophy which
flowed down to the Greeks from Egypt and Phoenicia, since
atoms are sometimes found to be designated by the mystics
as monads. For the mysteries of numbers equally with the
rest of hieroglyphics had regard to the mystical philosophy.

Newton goes on to say that such 'immutable seeds' account for the
fact that 'the species of objects are conserved in perpetuity'.

It may be difficult for the modern reader to imagine Sir
Isaac Newton being serious about such supposed 'anticipations' of
his views. Indeed, were it not for the testimony of Fatio and
Gregory, one would most naturally interpret them as adding a
classical flourish to a scientific treatise. But the draft
Scholium to Proposition VIII cannot be interpreted in such a
fashion. For here Newton asserts unequivocally that Pythagoras
discovered by experiment an inverse-square relation in the vibrations of strings (unison of two strings when tensions are reciprocally as the squares of lengths); that he extended such a relation to the weights and distances of the planets from the sun;
and that this true knowledge, expressed esoterically, was lost
through the misunderstanding of later generations. This is an
instance of a fully developed *prisca sapientia*, and as such
merits extended quotation.

By what proportion gravity decreases by receding from
the Planets the ancients have not sufficiently explained.
Yet they appear to have adumbrated it by the harmony of
the celestial spheres, designating the Sun and the remaining six planets, Mercury, Venus, Earth, Mars, Jupiter, Saturn, by means of Apollo with the Lyre of seven
strings, and measuring the intervals of the spheres by
the intervals of the tones. Thus they alleged that seven
tones are brought into being, which they called the harmony diapason, and that Saturn moved by the Dorian
phthong, that is, the heavy one, and the rest of the
Planets by sharper ones (as Pliny, bk. I, ch. 22 relates,
by the mind of Pythagoras) and that the Sun strikes the
strings. Hence Macrobius, bk. I, ch. 19, says:
'Apollo's Lyre of seven strings provides understanding of
the motions of all the celestial spheres over which
nature has set the Sun as moderator.' And Proclus on
Plato's Timaeus, bk. 3, page 200, 'The number seven they
have dedicated to Apollo as to him who embraces all sym-
phonies whatsoever, and therefore they used to call him
the God the Hebdomagetes', that is the Prince of the number Seven. Likewise in Eusebius' Preparation of the
Gospel, bk. 5, ch. 14, the Sun is called by the oracle of
Apollo the King of the seven sounding harmony. But by
this symbol they indicated that the Sun by his own force
acts upon the planets in that harmonic ratio of distances

by which the force of tension acts upon strings of different lengths, that is reciprocally in the duplicate ratio of the distances. For the force by which the same tension acts on the same string of different lengths is reciprocally as the square of the length of the string.

The same tension upon a string half as long acts four times as powerfully, for it generates the Octave, and the Octave is produced by a force four times as great. For if a string of given length stretched by a given weight produces a given tone, the same tension upon a string thrice as short acts nine times as much. For it produces the twelfth, and a string which stretched by a given weight produces a given tone needs to be stretched by nine times as much weight so as to produce the twelfth. And, in general terms, if two strings equal in thickness are stretched by weights appended, these strings will be in unison when the weights are reciprocally as the squares of the lengths of the strings. Now this argument is subtle, yet became known to the ancients. For Pythagoras, as Macrobius avows, stretched the intestines of sheep or the sinews of oxen by attaching various weights, and from this learned the ratio of the celestial harmony. Therefore, by means of such experiments he ascertained that the weights by which all tones on equal strings . . . were reciprocally as the squares of the length of the string by which the musical instrument emits the same tones. But the proportion discovered by these experiments, on the evidence of Macrobius, he applied to the heavens and consequently by comparing those weights with the weights of the Planets and the lengths of the strings with the distances of the Planets, he understood by means of the harmony of the heavens that the weights of the Planets towards the Sun were reciprocally as the squares of their distances from the Sun.

But the Philosophers loved so to mitigate their mystical discourses that in the presence of the vulgar they foolishly propounded vulgar matters for the sake of ridicule, and hid the truth beneath discourses of this kind. In this sense Pythagoras numbered his musical tones from the Earth, as though from here to the Moon were a tone, and thence to Mercury a semitone, and from thence to the rest of the Planets other musical intervals. But he taught that the sounds were emitted by the motion and attrition of the solid spheres, as though a greater sphere emitted a heavier tone as happens when iron hammers are smitten. And from this, it seems, was born the Ptolemaic system of solid orbs, when meanwhile Pythagoras beneath parables of this sort was hiding his own system and the true harmony of the heavens.

*　　　*　　　*　　　*　　　*

The same theme was mentioned in a draft variant to Query 23 of the Latin edition of the *Opticks* of 1706:

> By what means do bodies act on one another at a distance? The ancient Philosophers who held Atoms and Vacuum attributed gravity to atoms without telling us the means unless in figures: as by calling God Harmony representing him & matter by the God Pan and his Pipe, or by calling the Sun the prison of Jupiter because he keeps the Planets in their Orbs. Whence it seems to have been an ancient opinion that matter depends upon a Deity for its laws of motion as well as for its existence.

This passage serves us as a bridge to the material of the Scholium intended for Proposition IX. We notice that at the end, Newton states the *cause* of gravity, for the ancients, was God. In this draft variant, Newton develops the idea further. After stating that matter is passive and non-active, he says:

> These are passive laws and to affirm that there are no others is to speak against experience. For we find in ourselves a power of moving our bodies by our thought. Life and will are active principles by which we move our bodies and thence arise other laws of motion unknown to us.

> And since all matter duly formed is attended with signes of life and all things are framed with perfect art and wisdom and nature does nothing in vain; if there be an universal life and all space by the sensorium of a thinking being who by immediate presence perceives all things in it, as that which thinks in us, perceives their pictures in the brain: those laws of motion arising from life or will may be of universal extent. To some such laws the ancient Philosophers seem to have alluded when they called God Harmony and signified his actuating matter harmonically by the God Pan's playing upon a Pipe and attributing musick to the spheres made the distances and motions of the heavenly bodies to be harmonical, and represented the Planets by the seven strings of Apollo's Harp.

The personal testimony of David Gregory confirms the importance of this set of ideas for Newton's philosophy. His memorandum of 21 December 1705 tells us that Newton would answer the question, 'What cause did the ancients assign to gravity?' (in the projected Latin edition of the *Opticks*) by saying that, 'they reckoned God the cause of it, nothing else, that is no body being the cause; since every body is heavy'. Thus we have in the intended Query, an expression of the Newtonian distinction between passive and active principles in an orderly universe, and the complete dependence of matter, for its existence and motion, on the will of God; and all of this expressed by the ancients through the idea of 'Harmony'.

The draft Scholium to Proposition IX develops the same theme in greater detail. It starts with Newton's customary abjuring of causal explanations, and concludes with an eloquent passage in which the ancient dieties are assimilated into the one true God.

> So far I have expounded the properties of gravity. Its cause I by no means recount. Yet I shall say what

the ancients thought about this subject. Thales regarded
all bodies as animate, deducing that from magnetic and
electrical attractions. And by the same argument he
ought to have referred the attraction of gravity to the
soul of matter. Hence he taught that all things are full
of Gods, understanding by Gods animate bodies. He held
the sun and the Planets for Gods. And in the same sense
Pythagoras, on account of its immense force of attraction,
said that the sun was the prison of Zeus, that is, a body
possessed of the greatest circuits. And to the mystical
philosophers Pan was the supreme divinity inspiring this
world with harmonic ratio like a musical instrument and
handling it with modulation, according to that saying of
Orpheus 'striking the harmony of the world in playful
song'. Thence they named harmony God and soul of the
world composed of harmonic numbers. But they said that
the Planets move in their circuits by force of their own
souls, that is, by force of the gravity which takes its
origin from the action of the soul. From this, it seems,
arose the opinion of the Peripatetics concerning Intelligences moving solid globes. But the souls of the sun
and of all the Planets the more ancient philosophers held
for one and the same divinity exercising its powers in
all bodies whatsoever, according to that of Orpheus in
the Bowl.
Cylennius himself is the interpreter of divinity to all:
The nymphs are water. Ceres corn, Vulcan is fire.
Neptune is the sea striking the foaming shores.
Mars is war, kindly Venus is peace, the Bull-born
Horned Bacchus frequenting gladsome feasts
Is to mortals and to gods relief of mind from care.
Golden Themis is guardian of Justice and right
Next Apollo is the Sun, hurling his darts
From afar, circling round, the Divines and the Soothsayers
The Epidaurian God is the expeller of diseases: these
    things
All are one thing, though there be many names.
   For the material of this passage, Newton drew heavily on
Macrobius, Cicero, Virgil, Porphyry, and the Orphic hymns. In
it, he completes the view of nature which was developed in the
earlier Scholia. In those, the universe was seen as comprising
innumerable worlds, composed of immutable atoms, held together
by gravity, moving in an absolute void. Now the immaterial,
'immechanical' cause of it, is seen to be God himself. Newton
states this conception clearly in another manuscript intended for
the same unimplemented edition of the 1690's:
    . . . those ancients who more rightly held unimpaired the
    mystical philosophy as Thales and the Stoics, taught that
    a certain infinite spirit pervades all space *into infin-*
    ity, and contains and vivifies the entire world. And
    this spirit was their supreme divinity, according to the
    Poet cited by the Apostle. In him we live and move and
    have our being.

       *   *   *   *   *

II

It seems clear from the 'classical' Scholia, and from the testimony of his intimate friends, that Newton considered it necessary to complement his endeavours in natural philosophy by an investigation of the sources of the ancient knowledge that he believed himself to be re-discovering; and also that in that ancient tradition God was conceived as being in the most intimate relation with His creation. The draft Scholia, running parallel to the Propositions of Book III of the *Principia*, begin with classical views on matter, void, and gravity, and culminate in an affirmation of the ancient knowledge of the divine harmony by which God moved all bodies in the cosmos. Since a 'classical' edition of the *Principia*, incorporating these annotations, was never published, it may plausibly be argued that Newton considered these enquiries too speculative, or too incongruous with his inductive natural philosophy, to be made public.

Newton's thoughts on these matters were not, however, kept completely concealed. He permitted David Gregory to use the material extensively in a long historical preface to his *Astronomia physicae et geometricae elementa* (1702), if without attribution. (It was also available to Maclaurin for his much later work.) More important, the basic thesis of the Scholia is set out, more or less explicitly, in important sections of his two most important scientific works. These passages enable us to conclude that Newton was convinced of the importance of the *prisca* tradition for his philosophy, and that he believed his inductive method would yield as much certainty in historical and theological as in natural-philosophical studies. In both the *General Scholium* to the second edition of the *Principia* (1703) as well as the concluding pages of the *Opticks* (1704), a discussion of God's causal agency in the natural world ends with allusions to the suppressed material of the 'classical' Scholia.

In the *General Scholium*, Newton's special doctrines of the near-identification of infinite space with God and the assertion of His continuous intervention in His Creation end, not with a characteristic disclaimer, but with the affirmation:

> And thus much concerning God, to discourse of whom from the appearance of things does certainly belong to natural philosophy.

This extension of the scope of natural philosophy is significant. It implies that the sequence of ever more fundamental causes in nature does not stop short of the First Cause, but includes Him as a legitimate part of a natural-philosophical inquiry. That is already implicit in the use of God's attributes to establish the properties of atoms; and it justifies the attempt to define the mode of God's causal agency, as in the 'harmony' mentioned in the *Scholium* to Proposition IX.

Newton's belief in a *prisca* tradition is expressed in the same passages. In the *General Scholium*, a lengthy discussion of the divine attributes is concluded with the remarks:

> And from his true dominion it follows that the true God is a living, intelligent, and powerful Being; and, from His other perfections, that He is supreme, or most per-

fect. God is the same God, always and everywhere. He is omnipresent, not *virtually* but also *substantially*; for virtue cannot subsist without substance. In Him are all things contained and moved.

Newton's marginal note to the passage cites some of the main sources of the 'classical' Scholia:

This was the opinion of the Ancients. So *Pythagoras*, in Cicer. *de Nat. Deo. Lib.* I. *Thales, Anaxagoras, Virgil* Georg. Lib. IV. Ver. 220; and the *Aeneid*, lib. VI, ver. 721. *Philo Allegor*, at the beginning of Lib. I. *Aratus*, in his *Phaenom*, at the beginning. So also the sacred writers: as *St. Paul, Acts* xvii, ver. 27, 28. *St. John's* Gosp. Chap. xiv, ver. 2. *Moses*, *Deut*. iv, ver. 39; and x, ver. 14. *David, Psal.cxxxix*, ver. 7, 8, 9. *Solomon, I, Kings*, viii, ver. 27. *Job*, xxii, ver. 12, 13, 14. *Jeremiah*, xxiii, ver. 23,24. The Idolators supposed the sun, moon, and stars, the souls of men, and other parts of the world, to be parts of the Supreme God, and therefore to be worshipped; but erroneously.

Newton is asserting here a *prisca theologia*, an original conception of divinity from which 'the Idolators' had departed. A parallel *prisca* is described in a concluding passage of the *Opticks*. After examining the attributes of God and emphasizing His power to vary the laws of nature in different parts of the universe, he seems to pass by an abrupt transition to a review of his method of Analysis and the manner in which it was employed in the treatise. He then reverts to the theological considerations, for

. . . if Natural Philosophy in all its parts, by pursuing this method, shall at length be perfected, the bounds of Moral Philosophy will be also enlarged. For so far as we can know by Natural Philosophy what is the first cause, what power He has over us, and what benefits we receive from Him, so far our duty towards Him, as well as that towards one another, will appear to us by the Light of Nature. And no doubt, if the worship of false gods had not blinded the heathen, their Moral Philosophy would have gone farther than to the four cardinal virtues; and instead of teaching the transmigration of souls, and to worship the sun and moon and dead heroes, they would have taught us to worship our true Author and Benefactor, as their ancestors did under the government of Noah and his sons before they corrupted themselves.

The *prisca sapientia* and the *prisca theologia* is implicit in the closing passage of Newton's great scientific treatise. A true natural philosophy must lead to a surer knowledge of God, and thence to a firmly-grounded moral philosophy. The curious reference to Noah and his sons can be explained only by the assumption that, if true religion follows from true natural philosophy, then the latter must have served as the foundation for the former in the pristine age before the corruption of Noah and his sons. The supporting evidence from the unpublished material would appear to make that conclusion certain.

Finally, certain stylistic features of the concluding section of the *Opticks*, quoted above, make it plain that when Newton undertook to 'discourse' of God within natural philosophy, he believed that could be done by the same rigorous methods as those employed in mathematics and experimental philosophy. As mentioned above, in the last pages of the *Opticks*, a discussion of God's attributes and power is interrupted by a discussion of Newton's method of 'Analysis', consisting in a careful sequence of inductions from observations and experiment. The sequence of causes yielded by this method, could be pursued 'Till the argument end in the most general'. Newton seems to be alluding here to the First Cause or God. That interpretation is strengthened by the succeeding passage, quoted above. The perfection of natural knowledge must lead to a more perfect knowledge of God, with its attendant moral benefits.

* * * * *

III

The weight attached by Newton to his historical Scholia must appear curious and anachronistic in the light of the generally-accepted view of the intellectual milieu in late seventeenth- and early eighteenth-century England. The 1690's witnessed a decisive confrontation in England in a literary battle that had raged through much of the century: the 'battle of books' between those who championed and those who contested the superiority of the moderns over the ancients. In 1694 the young William Wotton published his *Reflections on Ancient and Modern Learning*, a work which gave a careful account of the scientific achievements of the century, and, while on the whole acknowledging the superiority of the ancients in literature, insisted that the moderns had far surpassed them in natural philosophy. Wotton's work was a reply to Sir William Temple's defence of the ancients in his *Essay upon the Ancient and Modern Learning* (1690). The controversy has been regarded as an indication of the extent to which the idea of progress had permeated the general intellectual consciousness by this time, as compared with Temple's circular view of history. Newton's defence of his *systema mundi* by representing it as no more than a return to the views of the ancients appears reactionary against that background, and not easily reconcilable with the idea of progress.

The discrepancy seems most glaring in Newton, since his system of the world came to be regarded as the most important argument for the superiority of the moderns over the ancients. Was Newton, in poring over the fragments of the ancients and elaborating dubious genealogies for his doctrines, reflecting a backward-looking attitude peculiar to him and his circle of intimates at Cambridge? It would be misleading to accept such a view of Newton's relations to the general intellectual currents of his time. Though a new conception of human progress had been gaining ground through the seventeenth century, there were other conceptions of the development of human knowledge whose role can easily be overlooked or minimized if we fix our gaze wholly on the 'idea of progress'. Through them Newton is linked to a certain Renaissance tradition, and, beyond the thinkers of the Renaissance, to the early Greek Church Fathers on whom he relied so considerably in discovering intimations of his physical doctrines among the ancients.

'Rebirth', 'rediscovery', not absolute originality but a return to truths well known to men in earlier ages, corrupted and obscured through the centuries: that is recognized as a cardinal characteristic of the Italian Renaissance. The broad similarity of Newton's scholia with that approach is immediately obvious. A more precise understanding of various *prisca* traditions and their modifications is necessary before we can place Newton's views in their historical context.

During the Renaissance, the ideal of classical antiquity aided the emergence and legitimation of a new sensibility and a new view of the world and of man. Innovation and experiment, the break with the traditional culture of the time, could be justified by a doctrine of the 'imitation' of the ancients, whose civilization typified the perfect models of conduct, arts, philosophy and polity. By the sixteenth century, the 'prisca' concept served, at least for the more critical humanists as a way of drawing attention to the undoubted superiority which classical antiquity had enjoyed over medieval Europe in civilization and refinement. But there were other thinkers who interpreted the concept much more literally. They wished to demonstrate that the best of pre-Christian thought owed its excellence to the fact that it represented fragments of the only major non-Christian revelation which a Christian could acknowledge, the Mosaic one enshrined in the Old Testament. Others postulated a series of partial revelations to humanity, preceding the Christian one, through a chain of *prisci theologi*. is not surprising that the most elaborately developed Renaissance *prisca* doctrine is to be found in the works of leading thinkers of the Platonic Academy at Florence in the late fifteenth century, Marsilio Ficino (1433-1499) and Pico della Mirandola (1463-1494), since their interest was centred upon writings and practices which the Church had traditionally regarded as heretical and diabolic: the magical works of late antiquity, and especially the newly-recovered *Corpus Hermeticum*. Through Ficino's Latin translation of the *Poemander* and *Asclepius* of Hermes Trismegistus, supposedly an Egyptian contemporary of Moses, these opinions came to be widely diffused in the sixteenth and seventeenth centuries.

Tracing pagan wisdom back to Moses was far more cautious and compatible with orthodoxy than postulating a series of partial revelations, since the unique status of Old Testament was thus safeguarded. In practice, the two approaches were not kept quite distinct. Ficino, for example, had accused the Neo-Platonists of having stolen from the apostles and apostolic disciples 'anything sublime that they have said about the divine mind, angels, and other things pertaining to theology'. But the tendency was pursued to such an extreme by other thinkers that every great pagan philosopher, including Plato, was placed in the debt of 'Egyptian wisdom'. The attribution was not original. The cult of 'Egyptian wisdom' found many votaries at Hellenistic Alexandria in late antiquity. Jewish thinkers of the Alexandrian school

sought to reconcile their own religious traditions with the Greek
doctrines to which they had been exposed by attributing a Hebraic
origin to Greek philosophy. Even before Philo, a host of treatises had convicted the Greek philosophers of having stolen from
the Hebrews, until Plato (in a famous saying attributed to
Numneius) became nothing but 'an Attic Moses'. The Egyptian
priests themselves began to claim an Egyptian origin for the doctrines, arts and institutions of the Greeks. Pythagoras had
derived his theory of numbers, and Democritus his supposed knowledge of astronomy from the Egyptians and had transmitted these
to the Hellenes. The Alexandrian Christians gave the Hebraic
tradition an important place in Christian apologetics.

*   *   *   *   *

In the sixteenth century, the many authors who adhered to
these *prisca* traditions drew upon the authority of these patris-
tic works. By a curious shift, a tactic originally employed to
secure the authority of the Christian revelation against pagan
philosophy was now used by Renaissance apologists for pagan
philosophy. Since what was best in the philosophy of Greece and
Rome was borrowed from the Mosaic revelation, Christianity had
nothing to fear from the study of pagan doctrines.
The history of *prisca* doctrines in the sixteenth century
is complicated by the Reformation and Counter-Reformation, and
the doctrinal strife between Protestants and Catholics and among
the various Protestant sects. The Protestant stress on the Bible
at the expense of the mediating Church may be expected to have
diminished Catholic enthusiasm for the naked text of the Scripture as the sole repository of God's revelation to mankind. It
is certainly true that Catholic writers who continued to concern
themselves with the *prisca* in the post-Reformation period came to
be regarded with increasing suspicion by the orthodox. An over-
emphasis on the *prisca* could lead to a depreciation of the
uniqueness of the Christian revelation. In the closing years of
the sixteenth century, two heretic south-Italian Dominicans, each
in his own way, conceived it as their mission to restore the
true Hermetic religion. One of these was Tommaso Campanella
(1558-1639), who spent twenty-five years in the prison of the
Inquisition for his part in a Calabrian revolt aiming to set up
an Hermetic 'City of the Sun'. The other was Giordano Bruno
(1548-1600), burnt at the stake in Rome, who planned to restore
the true Egyptian 'religion of the world', Christianity having
been a falling away from that true religion. That is probably
the reason for Francesco Patrizi's much less socially revolutionary ideas in his *Nova de universis philosophia* (1591) being
placed on the Index in 1594.
The *prisca* doctrines discussed so far were not without significance for natural philosophy, in as much as its adherents
wished to substitute a Neo-Platonic explanation, based on secret
sympathies and antipathies, stellar virtues, and the microcosm-
macrocosm analogy, for the Aristotelian qualitative physics. A
prisca variant more directly concerned with natural philosophy
made its appearance in the late sixteenth century. There was a
growing interest in the teachings of the earliest Greek natural

go round in the same orbit, unless it be of the same density with the fluid. But we have shewn in that case that it would revolve according to the same law with those parts of the fluid that are at the same or equal distances from the centre of the vortex.

 COR. 1. Therefore a solid revolving in a vortex, and continually going round in the same orbit, is relatively quiescent in the fluid that carries it.

 COR. 2. And if the vortex be of an uniform density, the same body may revolve at any distance from the centre of the vortex.

Scholium.

 Hence it is manifest that the planets are not carried round in corporeal vortices; for, according to the *Copernican* hypothesis, the planets going round the sun revolve in ellipses, having the sun in their common focus; and by radii drawn to the sun describe areas proportional to the times. But now the parts of a vortex can never revolve with such a motion. Let AD, BE, CF, represent

three orbits described about the sun S, of which let the utmost circle CF be concentric to the sun; and let the aphelia of the two innermost be A, B; and their perihelia D, E. Therefore a body revolving in the orb CF, describing, by a radius drawn to the sun, areas proportional to the times, will move with an uniform motion. And, according to the laws of astronomy, the body revolving in the orb BE will move slower in its aphelion B, and swifter in its perihelion E; whereas, according to the laws of mechanics, the matter of the vortex ought to move more swiftly in the narrow space between A and C than in the wide space between D and F; that is, more swiftly in the aphelion than in the perihelion. Now these two conclusions contradict each other. So at the beginning of the sign of Virgo, where the aphelion of Mars is at present, the distance between the orbits of Mars and Venus is to the distance between the same orbits, at the beginning of the sign of Pisces, as about 3 to 2; and therefore the matter of the vortex between those orbits ought to be swifter at the beginning of Pisces than at the beginning of Virgo in the ratio of 3 to 2; for the narrower the space is through which the same quantity of matter passes in the same time of one revolution, the greater will be the velocity with which it passes through it. Therefore if the earth being relatively at rest in this celestial matter should be introduced him to the Gassendist approach, sifting the opinions of the ancients to establish their concordance with his own philosophy. At the same time, the early writings of Henry More would have acquainted him with a much more fundamentalist *prisca*, tracing the new mechanical philosophy to Moses, and making it an essential part of a new theological synthesis.

Much later, when Newton was developing his 'classical' annotations, he drew considerably on Cudworth's erudite *True Intellectual System*. His extant notes on the *System* reproduce almost verbatim Cudworth's account of Moschus and of the atomic succession from him. There was a large body of shared assumptions between Newton and Cudworth. From the earliest period of his intellectual development, Newton held a view of the world as comprising both active and passive principles, with the technique later presented in the *Principia* applying only to inert matter. He believed that conceiving matter as independent of God, or endowed with self-activity, led to atheism. Like Cudworth, he seems to have had the mechanical philosophies of Hobbes and of Descartes, and the 'hylozoistic atheism' of various English freethinkers in mind.

*   *   *   *   *

The most important difference between More and Cudworth on the one hand, and Newton on the other, lay in Newton's conviction that not the Cartesian philosophy (as More had once held), nor the 'mechanical philosophy' (in Cudworth's basically Cartesian interpretation), but his own system of the world represented the restoration of the true and original natural philosophy, as revealed by God even before the Flood.

In concluding this outline of the main points of agreement and disagreement between Newton and the Cambridge Platonists, attention must again be drawn to the fact that the terms of the dialogue were set by a certain theological-philosophical tradition. Only against that tradition can Newton's 'classical' endeavour be understood and explained. Newton's relation to that tradition becomes clearer if we remember that his interpretation of the texts of ancient natural philosophy was not the only 'exegetical' exercise which had engaged his attention. He had spent much time and labour on two other fields which demanded highly-developed techniques of interpretation. One was alchemy, whose practitioners wrapped up their supposed knowledge in a complex symbolism, designed to obscure it from the uninitiated. During the early seventeenth century, Michael Maier (1568-1622), whose works were deeply studied by Newton, had undertaken a survey of the entire Greek mythology to demonstrate that they represented alchemical secrets. Newton's interpretation of the 'harmony of the spheres' is analogous, in that it sees it as a symbolical representation of 'physical' secrets. The other major field employing exegetical techniques was that of biblical studies, which absorbed Newton throughout his life. In interpreting the prophetical books of the Old Testament, Newton attempted to show that the prophecies had been fulfilled down to the minutest details.

Both alchemy, as well as biblical exegetics, rested on the

assumption that a true body of knowledge had been available to
wise men in the remotest antiquity, and that the knowledge was
couched in an enigmatical, symbolical form to conceal it from
the vulgar. It is evident that the same assumptions underlie
Newton's exegesis of the natural philosophy of the ancients. His
tortuous interpretation of the Lyre of Apollo, the Pipes of Pan,
and the 'Harmony of the Spheres' rests on the belief that the
true system of the world was known to the ancients, but had been
turned into 'a great mystery' which only the initiates could
penetrate. In his studies of the Old Testament prophecies,
Newton was tracing the pristine knowledge of the historical
events of future ages; in his alchemical studies, the pristine
knowledge of the constitution of things; in his studies of ancient natural philosophy, the pristine knowledge of physical
nature and the system of the world. The true meaning of the Old
Testament prophecies would only become clear in retrospect, in
the light of historical experience. In the same way, the authen-
tic meaning of the ancient natural philosophy would only be revealed when the truths it embodied had been independently discovered by experimental investigation; it was thus that
Pythagoras--and Newton--had unravelled the mystery of the most
ancient 'harmony of the spheres'.

It should be quite clear that Newton's textual analysis of
ancient natural philosophy was not based on a consciously *post
hoc* procedure: reading into ancient texts truths arrived at in
the course of his scientific work. For him, they represented a
deeper penetration into the *prisca sapientia*, possible only when
the preliminary work had been accomplished through experience.
Besides this overriding justification, these investigations could
perform a number of different functions. They could provide a
pedigree for his own doctrines, to legitimate them for an audience which still widely accepted the idea of a *prisca sapientia*.
He could use them as a direct defence for his own doctrines, as
he does in the *Opticks*, and, on one occasion, during the controversy with Leibniz. Furthermore, the documents dealt with in
this paper do not tell us whether his own adoption of the doctrines he ascribes to the ancients preceded his textual studies.
Such basic problems as the existence of the void, the properties
of matter, and the character of the divine agency lay beyond the
experimental procedures he could deploy. Newton's solutions to
some of these problems are explained and defended by the analo-
gical reasoning whose patterns he defined in the *Regulae*. But
the possibility that the ancient texts might have provided clues,
and guided his thoughts in one direction or another, can by no
means be excluded.

It is also possible to discern the function of the *prisca*
arguments in Newton's more general philosophical concerns. Like
Cudworth, he wished to confute 'Hobbists', Deists, and
'hylozoistick atheists', on the basis of *prisca* arguments. His
own variant of the history of the original natural philosophy,
with its insistence on absolutely dead matter, would be his
contribution to the debate. On the struggle which was taking
place on another front, concerning the authenticity and reliability of the Old Testament, Newton's demonstration of a pre-Noachian

But further; the weights of all the parts of every planet towards any other planet are one to another as the matter in the several parts; for if some parts did gravitate more, others less, than for the quantity of their matter, then the whole planet, according to the sort of parts with which it most abounds, would gravitate more or less than in proportion to the quantity of matter in the whole. Nor is it of any moment whether these parts are external or internal; for if, for example, we should imagine the terrestrial bodies with us to be raised up to the orb of the moon, to be there compared with its body; if the weights of such bodies were to the weights of the external parts of the moon as the quantities of matter in the one and in the other respectively, but to the weights of the internal parts in a greater or less proportion, then likewise the weights of those bodies would be to the weight of the whole moon in a greater or less proportion; against what we have shewed above.

COR. 1. Hence the weights of bodies do not depend upon their forms and textures; for if the weights could be altered with the forms, they would be greater or less, according to the variety of forms, in equal matter; altogether against experience.

COR. 2. Universally, all bodies about the earth gravitate towards the earth; and the weights of all, at equal distances from the earth's centre, are as the quantities of matter which they severally contain. This is the quality of all bodies within the reach of our experiments; and therefore (by rule 3) to be affirmed of all bodies whatsoever. If the *œther*, or any other body, were either altogether void of gravity, or were to gravitate less in proportion to its quantity of matter, then, because (according to *Aristotle*, *Des Cartes*, and others) there is no difference betwixt that and other bodies but in *mere* form of matter, by a successive change from form to form, it might be changed at last into a body of the same condition with those which gravitate most in proportion to their quantity of matter; and, on the other hand, the heaviest bodies, acquiring the first form of that body, might by degrees quite lose their gravity. And therefore the weights would depend upon the forms of bodies, and with those forms might be changed: contrary to what was proved in the preceding corollary.

COR. 3. All spaces are not equally full; for if all spaces were equally full, then the specific gravity of the fluid which fills the region of the air, on account of the extreme density of the matter, would fall nothing short of the specific gravity of quicksilver, or gold, or any other the most dense body; and, therefore, neither gold, nor any other body, could descend in air; for bodies do not descend in fluids, unless they are specifically heavier than the fluids. And if the quantity of matter in a given space can, by any rarefaction, be diminished, what should hinder a diminution to infinity?

COR. 4. If all the solid particles of all bodies are of the same density, nor can be rarefied without pores, a void, space, or vacuum, must be granted. By bodies of the same density, I mean those whose *vires inertiæ* are in the proportion of their bulks.

COR. 5. The power of gravity is of a different nature from the power of magnetism; for the magnetic attraction is not as the matter attracted. Some bodies are attracted more by the magnet;

4. *Professor A. Rupert Hall of Imperial College, London, sums up both the issues involved and the current state of the question in a recent article "On the Historical Singularity of the Scientific Revolution of the Seventeenth Century."**

Even before the seventeenth century ended it was becoming customary to contrast the slow progress of scientific knowledge after its inception among the Ancients, with the profound and swiftly-succeeding achievements of the Moderns since the 'revival of learning'. No reader of William Wotton's *Reflections upon Ancient and Modern Learning* (1694) could doubt where the superiority lay. . . .

*   *   *   *   *

The scientific revolution that was already passing into history had itself by no means lacked historical consciousness. While indebtedness to scholastic subtlety was scarcely ever avowed by its leaders--one finds no trace of medieval debates about the possible motion of the earth in Copernicus and no explicit allusions to medieval kinematics in Galileo--inspiration rather than authoritative precedent was drawn from the Greeks. Not to insist upon Copernicus's open statement of the Pythagoreans' precedence (so well known that he was not infrequently stated even by his best supporters to have 'revived' their hypothesis), or Galileo's frequent invocations of Archimedes, or Harvey's Aristotelianism, there was a still more striking recognition of the *prisci theologi* by Newton and his followers. In the words of J. T. Desaguliers, 'The System of the Universe, as taught by Pythagoras, Philolaus, and others of the Ancients, is the same, which was since reviv'd by Copernicus, allow'd by all the unprejudic'd of the Moderns, and at last demonstrated by Sir Isaac Newton.' No one in the seventeenth century could feel quite certain that science was treading wholly new paths, rather than retreading an old course. Yet, on the other hand, though the notion of a past Golden Age must entail a subsequent decline, there was an uneasy admission that so far as techniques were concerned, the barbaric Middle Ages had seen the appearance of the ocean-going sailing-ship and its magnetic compass, of the windmill, of gunpowder, of paper and printing. If, as Bacon held, there was a relation between scientific originality and technical ingenuity, the theory of barbarism must look a bit thin.

These complexities, however, were hardly important enough to modify the conventional historical judgment that natural science

* A. Rupert Hall, "On the Historical Singularity of the Scientific Revolution of the Seventeenth Century," in *The Diversity of History, Essays in Honour of Sir Herbert Butterfield*, edited by J. H. Elliott and H. G. Koenigsberger, Cornell U. Press, Ithaca, N.Y. Copyright held by Routledge & Kegan Paul Ltd., London. Pp. 201-14; 217-21.

had been virtually re-created by the seventeenth century. When
William Whewell came to compose his *History of the Inductive
Sciences*, though he could write (of Leonardo da Vinci) that
'both the heliocentric doctrine and [the] truths of mechanics
were fermenting in the minds of intelligent men, and gradually
assuming clearness and strength, some time before they were
publicly asserted', he had no doubt of a 'mental declension' produced by an obscurantist religion causing 'the almost complete
blank which the history of physical science offers, from the
decline of the Roman Empire, for a thousand years'. Only in the
seventeenth century arrived 'the grand completion of the history
of the most ancient and prosperous province of human knowledge'.
One might have supposed that, a little later in the nineteenth
century, the final collapse of the fluid theory of heat (following on the previous downfall of the phlogiston concept) would
have suggested the notion that even modern science was not necessarily infallible, especially as the great Newton's speculations
about the nature of light were now known to have been mistaken.
However, positivist preconceptions ensured the prevalence of the
alternative historical explanation that these false theories
were really mere aberrations, speculative deviations from the
true inductive line of progress, a view borne out by the stability of the empirical and mathematical parts of Newton's optics.
Indeed, it was feasible to see the relatively late ascendancy of
inductive methods and positive knowledge in such sciences as
chemistry, heat or geology as produced by the strong forces of
conservatism, in turn delaying the full 'modernization' of these
branches of science.

It was not until the late nineteenth or indeed the twentieth
century that the inconsistencies latent in the orthodox historiography were properly explored, and the great body of neglected
evidence submitted to honest examination. The causes of this
fresh interest were varied. The powerful historicism of the late
nineteenth century must be reckoned among them, as well as an
anxiety (created by the specialization and expansion of science
itself) to prove that the study of Nature was indeed a culture.
Marcellin Berthelot, Raffaello Caverni, Emil Wohlwill and Pierre
Duhem in the physical sciences, Karl Sudhoff and others in
medicine, followed by Sarton, Singer, Thorndike and many more
went back to the medieval sources, both Arabic and Latin. The
earlier concentration was on alchemy, medicine, and mechanics;
medieval astronomy and optics came in for attention rather later.
From the early work, in which the most important historiographi-
cal influence was that of Duhem, three chief conclusions emerged:
(1) the discussions of scientific questions in the Middle Ages
were not wholly or even largely trivial or obtuse; (2) certain
features or statements of 'classical' science had been anticipated in the Middle Ages; (3) there was a discernible continuity
of thought extending from medieval philosophy and science into
the beginnings of the scientific revolution itself.

Obviously, irrespective of the accuracy or otherwise of each
of these conclusions, the first and second are more readily
capable of historical verification than the last. Half a century's further effort, in which medieval texts have been elabor-

ately surveyed, edited, and translated, has put them beyond
reasonable doubt. The virtually axiomatic belief of almost three
centuries after Francis Bacon that medieval philosophy was meaningless verbiage is no longer held; we now know that medieval
men were exacting, even adventurous, in their attempts to confirm
and apply their intellectual inheritance. We know too that, in a
few respects, through their critical appraisal and attention to
phenomena, they formulated propositions whose real significance
was understood much later. But whether or not such historical
re-evaluations of medieval science also entail the replacement of
the scientific revolution by a gradual process of change is
another question. It is possibly not altogether a historical
question. For, apart from interpretation of the historical evidence in this particular case, there seems to be good reason to
believe that the rejection of conceptions long firmly held,
justified by reason and even sanctified by religion, and their
replacement by antithetic ones, must normally be a sudden and
even violent process. Where the inertial mass is large, and the
applied force becomes great, change can only occur through a
crisis.

Pierre Duhem, however, threw his influence wholly in favour
of gradualism. . . . Later, in studying kinematics, he was
impressed by the Aristotelian reaction and 'superstitious
archaism' of the Renaissance, delaying the fruition of medieval
mechanics to the time of Galileo. But to see the beginnings of
modern mechanics with Galileo and his contemporaries as a genuine
creation was, Duhem argued, an historical error; there was no
swift triumph of modern science over medieval error; one sees
rather the victory of the science born in Paris in the fourteenth
century over the doctrines of Aristotle and Averroës honoured by
the Italian Renaissance.

Subsequent criticism has modified the status of the
fourteenth-century nominalists from that of 'creators' of modern
science to that of 'precursors'. While it is difficult to express this idea with precision, most historians of science nowa-
days would agree that 'modern science was not suddenly born with
Galileo, but rather emerged about that time after a long period
of incubation', or with Herbert Butterfield that the scientific
revolution reached 'back in an unmistakably continuous line to a
period much earlier' than the Renaissance, without denying that
a real intellectual revolution took place. No one now supposes
that, in mechanics, the medieval concepts of inertia and acceleration were identical with those formulated in the seventeenth
century, or that the world-view of Oresme was identical with
that of Newton; rather, the recent view maintains that there were
varying degrees of analogy between the two. Consequently, no
historian would now argue that seventeenth-century science was a
mere reformulation of that of the fourteenth. For example, it is
now recognized that many of the more adventurous notions of the
high Middle Ages were never advanced as true, or even credible.
No one before Copernicus believed that in physical and theological reality the earth moves. As Dr Edward Grant has pointed out,
Copernicus's acceptance of this motion as a reality was a result
of 'his conception of the function and role of an hypothesis',

which itself entailed so great an epistemological revolution that
it marks Copernicus's 'drastic departure from the scholastic
tradition almost as much as his new cosmological system'. Like
E. A. Burtt (1925), like Herbert Butterfield (1949), and indeed
like many other historians, Dr Grant emphasizes the importance of
the scientific revolution, not as the sum of particular scientific propositions, but as a total modification of what Collingwood
called the 'idea of nature'--that is, an *a priori* redefinition of
the objects of philosophical and scientific inquiry.

In 1953 the scholastic contribution towards the scientific
revolution was stated afresh by Dr A. C. Crombie in an important
book which emphasized the medieval approximation towards experimental method, exemplified rather by optics than mechanics.
Robert Grosseteste and the Origins of Experimental Science asserted the case for gradualism against the traditional concept of
the scientific revolution in strong terms, in that it seemed to
be maintaining (in parallel to Duhem) the *identity* of medieval
empiricism with that of the seventeenth century, and the *identity*
of medieval optical theory at its height with that of Descartes.
Dr Crombie seemed almost prepared to claim, with Duhem, that the
seventeenth century had only to pick up where the fourteenth
century had left off. In his subsequent writings, however,
Crombie's views appear in a softer form; while marshalling in a
telling way the evidence for gradualism (in 1969 hardly longer in
dispute), and claiming what is no more than just, that medieval
science was neither trivial nor without succession, Crombie has
made it clear that, nevertheless, the scientific revolution did
occur as the climax to a more tentative process of change and
development.

The historiography of *Robert Grosseteste and the Origins of
Experimental Science* did not pass without criticism, on the one
hand from those who have doubted whether the medieval contributions to optics discussed by Crombie were as advanced, or as influential, as the author supposed: and by those who hold
(contrary, of course, to what one might call the old English
tradition) that experimenting did not provide the sole,or perhaps even the major, entrance to the new world of science.
Probably there can hardly be question of Descartes's
'copying' from Theodoric of Freiberg than of Galileo's 'copying'
from Nicole Oresme. It is more important that during the last
twenty years historians of science and technology have demonstrated, beyond dispute, that in the later Middle Ages rich and
fertile capacities for innovation were at work. This was no
period of sterile abstraction. On the contrary, it was a time
of acquisition, transmission, assimilation and experiment.
Whatever is to be said of the period between the fifth century
and the twelfth--in which the historian of science at any rate
can as yet claim no major accomplishment--when taking a general
view over several centuries from the twelfth onwards it is difficult not to perceive amid all vicissitudes a continuing extension
of civilization and intellect. In this historical process the
maturity of scholasticism appears as a plateau, the scientific
revolution as another sharp, upwards slope.

If medieval studies have, in the end, left the concept of

the unique scientific revolution in the seventeenth century relatively unscathed, though rendering its occurrence less abrupt,
another kind of historiography would destroy its historical
character by assimilating it into a succession of such events.
Whereas all participants in the older argument agreed (roughly)
that there was something called 'modern science' that came into
existence, either swiftly or gradually, over a definable stretch
of time, in basic outline the new interpretation sees nothing but
periods of relative quiescence within which ideas on any topic
remain constant, separated by shorter intervals of rapid transition from one 'paradigm' to another. The argument requires the
following moves to be made: firstly, the series of historical
events embraced under the term 'scientific revolution' are fragmented into the Vesalian revolution, the Copernican revolution,
the Harveian revolution, the Galilean revolution, and so on, as
a series of discrete episodes; secondly, it is to be recognized
that 'revolutions' (of sometimes greater effect) have occurred
in the eighteenth century and later, linked with the names of
Lavoisier, Young-Fresnel, Darwin, Joule-Clausius, Faraday-Maxwell,
Einstein, Planck, and so forth. Finally, it is argued that science is not concerned with a search for reality, but rather (to
use a convenient phrase) with 'probable stories'; the scientist
at any period of history (including the present, of course) cannot say whether or not any particular proposition corresponds
to the real structure of the Universe, but can only explain why
this proposition seems more credible than others and how it is
consonant with all or most of the relevant data. As the reasons
for finding any particular proposition acceptable vary, and the
data change, so do scientific propositions.

These revisions of the conventional historiography of science are salutary in several respects. They remind us that
chemistry, geology, the biological sciences, did not assume a
'classical' form in the seventeenth century, as mechanics did;
and that 'classical' mechanics was itself but an episode in the
history of science. They draw attention, too, to the Whiggism
of a historical narrative directed solely to tracing the lines
along which the 'classical' forms of the sciences were evolved.
If these 'classical' forms are no more than intermediates between Greek science and recent science (as represented by rela-
tivistic cosmology, quantum mechanics and molecular biology) then
the scientific revolution can hardly be described as bringing in
modern science.

Nevertheless, the scientific revolution seems to remain as
an historical reality. It refuses to dissolve into fragments,
nor is modern science (1500-1900) so episodic as the analysis
suggests. In the Renaissance period particularly there was an
unbroken and interlocking series of new discoveries combined with
changes in ideas, and it is quite arbitrary to resolve this into
chapters concerned with discrete problems. The Copernican issue
was still unsettled--indeed, the conservative view was still
ascendant--when it was modified by the new physical interpretations of the Universe put forward by Tycho Brahe and Galileo, and
given a fresh twist by Kepler; it was still unsettled when Galileo and Descartes (in their several ways) set this cosmological

debate in a mechanical context. That early seventeenth-century interest in the science of mechanics was integrally related to the problems of the earth's movement or rest is obvious, Galileo's *Dialogue on the Two Chief Systems of the World* (1632) being the *locus classicus*. It would be trivial to point out how all this meshed with the development of pure mathematics, of optics and scientific instruments, and of experimental physics to become negatively an attack on the whole of scholastic philosophy, and positively a universal front of investigation into Nature. Newton (mathematician, experimental physicist, theoretician) did not inherit two or three half-solved problems from his predecessors, but an evolving physical science that was in a state of flux at every point. Again, the scientific revolution was united by deeper and by now well-known intellectual characteristics that appear as common elements in many individuals and varied researches. Apart from a virtually ubiquitous contempt for argument about terms and mere book-learning that led many men to emphasize the empirical foundations of knowledge; apart from the frequent distinction drawn between primary and secondary qualities and, still more, the prevalence of the 'mechanical philosophy'; and apart from the fundamental conception that Nature is 'everywhere uniform and consonant to herself' (a conception that in itself destroyed the basis of Aristotelian science)--on all of which generalities physicists and biologists agreed--there was the mathematical analysis of phenomena which, in the opinion of Alexandre Koyré, constituted the core of the scientific revolution.

In 1939, in the first of his *Etudes Galiléennes,* Koyré made clear his commitment to the notion of a 'révolution scientifique du dix-septième siècle, profonde transformation intellectuelle dont la physique moderne, ou plus exactement classique, fut à la fois l'expression et le fruit', describing it as possibly the most important mutation in human thought since the Greek invention of the Cosmos. It was no matter of overthrowing insufficient or false theories [in discrete episodes], but of transforming 'les cadres de l'intelligence elle-même' in the replacement of one intellectual attitude, plausible enough, by another of far less plausible appearance. In particular, the scientific revolution involved a 'géométrisation de l'espace', a substitution for Aristotle's and Ptolemy's concrete cosmos of the abstract space of Euclid. Over the years Koyré widened and intensified his conception that the crucial difference between the Greco-medieval and the classical concepts of physics was the latter's mathematicism. Galileo, he argued, was a Platonist, Kepler a Pythagorean, Descartes both a Platonist and a Pythagorean. Hence he insisted again and again that the changes that had brought classical science into being were neither socio-economic nor technological, nor concerned with the methodology of science (empirical or otherwise), but solely changes in the way the human mind reflected upon its natural environment. . . . And no student of Koyré's work can doubt that he regarded mathematical thinking as the supreme form of scientific thought.

Such an expression of the totality of intellectual change during the late Renaissance (which I find extremely convincing) compels an historian to see the scientific revolution as a great historical drama, which has its subplots and convolutions as all grand dramas do, one that works slowly towards the climax of accomplishment in the mid- to late seventeenth century. Yet to insist excessively on the role of mathematics (in the later stages of the scientific revolution particularly) may be to court the objection that the drama was partial; for if it concerned only the mathematical sciences, it could hardly have dominated the intellectual life of the age. But even the most idealist historian of science, it seems to me, need not so restrict a claim for the transcendent role of the scientific revolution, particularly in its later stages. The biological sciences were indeed transformed, though in them empiricism took the place of mathematics. There is no contradiction here, for it is obvious that significant observation and experimentation are neither random, nor mechanical, nor undirected by ideas. On the contrary, it is certain that the mathematization of astronomy and optics could not have proceeded without observation and experiment, while in some aspects of physical science ideas of structure, organization and arrangement were more significant than ideas of number. There was as it were a methodological spectrum in the scientific revolution, relating rather to height of achievement than to profundity of conceptual change, from the combination of weak empiricism with much mathematicism, to that of strong empiricism with little mathematics. In general, the importance of empiricism increased throughout the seventeenth century.

*   *   *   *   *

The question now remains: if the scientific revolution directed (or redirected) intellectual energy towards the comprehension of reality, was this--to put it crudely--an aberration that the recent philosophy of scientists has reversed? To take the last part of this question first, it seems to me that for a historian (at any rate) to be easily persuaded that recent science has not been concerned with realities, but only with figments, 'probable stories', or, as the Greeks said, 'saving the appearances' might be perilous. Taking for granted all the well-known limitations on the certainty of knowledge, the difference is that between the investigator who believes that there is a reality towards which scientific propositions may successively approximate, and one who regards these propositions as intellectual constructs and reality as for ever unknowable--indeed, the discussion of its nature as meaningless. Perhaps there can be no final knowledge of matter or energy as ultimate realities. For Newton and his successors knowledge of matter passed into knowledge of God, since the Universe existed under divine law and would one day be reshaped into the Heavenly City. In recent physics, banishing for ever such realities of the last century as atoms and the aether, the ultimate realities appear to be mathematical expressions about which the purest of mathematicians are themselves somewhat unhappy. Very few scientists or philosophers have chosen to deify matter, to make it final and eternal. But to refuse to do that is not to deny that ordinary exploration of the Universe is, at other levels, devoted to the pursuit of reality, and that its results are taken to be (with all the restrictions hinted at above) true and not merely conventional; the major atomic particles, the molecular structure of materials, including the living cell, the evolutionary modification of organisms by natural selection and the nuclear processes governing the life of a star--these do not seem to be regarded by those who study them (or by the world at large) as less true than any contingent proposition whatsoever.

It is generally agreed that in this respect the scientific revolution made a profound and widespread change. Ancient mathematical science, particularly, 'saved appearances', and to Aristotelians reality could not be apprehended through mathematics. Upon these ideas the Middle Ages grafted the notion that in the highest sense only revealed truth is real, and is sufficient for man. Rational enquiry could be too easily defrauded by the frailty of the human mind. What was true to sense and reason might well be supernaturally false. On theological grounds alone, Nicole Oresme in the late fourteenth century rejected the hypothesis of the earth's mobility that he found most rational. After William of Ockham had categorized the idea of 'double truth' still further into the belief that statements in science are mere hypotheses or at best statements of what might be without assertion of what is, nominalist physics became an exercise in 'logic accompanied by explicit disavowals that the results or assumptions had application to physical reality'. In other words, philosophy was an intellectual game, only theology being concerned with truth.

Copernicus, unlike Oresme, believed in the physical reality of the earth's motions; this truth could not be demonstrated, but reason spoke for it; to believe the opposite was to credit an intellectual abomination, and this truth alone made God's cosmos simple and knowable. Like Einstein, Copernicus believed that God does not play at dice in Nature, or, as Galileo put it, God does not deceive His creation. Thus it was that in shifting the basis of reality from revelation to physical plausibility (in the words of Dr Edward Grant) Copernicus 'first mapped the new path and inspired the Scientific Revolution by bequeathing to it his own ardent desire for knowledge of physical realities'. And he remarks in a footnote that 'the significance of the quest for physical reality cannot be overestimated as a turning-point in the history of science'. To agree with this view does not commit one to positivism--indeed, quite the opposite--since it was shared by such a devoted idealist as Koyré, for whom science as the *itinerarium mentis in veritatem* was certainly a quest for reality, and for whom the 'ontologie mathématique inspirée de Platon' was linked with the modern science of Galileo and Descartes as that which tended towards a 'connaissance réelle, bien que naturellement partielle et provisoire, du monde réel. . .'. Indeed, the whole point of the distinction between mathematics and mathematical physics from Archimedes through Galileo to Newton--the whole structure of whose *Mathematical Principles of Natural Philosophy* was based on this distinction--is that physics is concerned with reality, so far as men may ascertain it.

Where did this concern for reality originate? It was opposed

to nominalism, it was not prompted by humanism, and it could not
have been produced by the renewed classicism of the Renaissance.
What other strands in contemporary thought were bridled neither
by theology nor by Aristotle? What other strands believed--to
fanaticism and absurdity--in the reality of its own truths? Are
they to be found, perhaps, in the Hermetic and Neoplatonic
traditions, which by this time had become one? Not to mention
the obvious appearance of Hermeticism in the writings of some of
the more mysterious, even 'uncanonical', figures of the scientific revolution (Paracelsus, Dee, Porta, Fludd), there are good
grounds for discerning it in such unimpeachable heroes as
Copernicus, Bruno, Francis Bacon, Kepler and Newton. Of course,
no one would wish to transfer all the honour of innovation once
accorded Oresme to Pico della Mirandola, or that accorded
Leonardo da Vinci to Marsilio Ficino. The Hermeticists were
not modern scientists; arithmetology is not mathematical physics.
The maximum claim is that the 'Renaissance *magus* . . . exemplifies that changed attitude of man to the cosmos which was the
necessary preliminary to the rise of science'. The direct and
positive contribution of the Renaissance *magus* to modern science
was virtually zero (the development of empiricism may show an
exception), and in the person of Robert Fludd he was opposed by
science in the person of Kepler and Mersenne. His contribution
was roundabout, indirect, and obscure. 'Paracelsus', as Walter
Pagel writes, 'though not "scientific" himself, produced scientific results from a non-scientific world of motives and thoughts.
In this lies the perennial interest of his work to the historian.'
The same might be said of others whose positive contribution was
even less than that of Paracelsus. The point here is not so much
whether Hermeticism was wrong and irrational (which it was), nor
whether it was a lineal precursor of modern science (which it was
not), but rather that it furnished an alternative *and real* conception of Nature. It was a conception promising man limitless
knowledge and power within the cosmos, one which unified the
cosmos that Aristotle had divided, and one that conduced both to
enquiry into the properties of things and to mathematicism. Yet
at the same time it countered both the naïve empiricism and the
sterile rationalism of scholastic philosophy. Perhaps one might
say crudely that Hermeticism was the 'bad side' of early modern
science, yielding in the seventeenth century the worst aspects of
alchemy, astrology and witchcraft, but if so it may well be that
this 'bad side' was indispensable to the emergence of the good,
exerting a constant catalytic or fermentative action.

What seems certain is the multifarious, perhaps in some
respects inconsistent, nature of the various factors ultimately
resulting in the scientific revolution. It was not simply a
succession of circumstances in which traditional beliefs were
first questioned and then, overwhelmed by the evidence against
them, rejected. Nor was it the consequence of a unique movement,
such as nominalist physics or late-medieval empiricism. Not even
the invocation of Platonic mathematicism will of itself explain
all its manifestations--and the ascendancy of Platonism has still
to be accounted for. Clearly the historian must be eclectic in
his choice of causal factors: to all those mentioned so far he

Machine metaphor, 6-7
Malpighi, Marcello (1628-94), 43
Mechanical philosophy, 39-40, 43-44, (Readings: p. 245-248, p. 249-273, p. 274-283, 335-336)
Moses, 2, 334-335

Navigation, 10, 308-309
Neo-Platonism, 2, 62-63, (Readings: p. 312-321, 347-348)
Newton, Sir Isaac (1642-1727), 2, 3, 26, 34, 36-40, 64, (Readings: p. 219-244, p. 284-286, p. 287-303, 322-332)
Nicholas of Cusa (1401-64), 1
Nifo, Agostino (fl. 1506), 56-59

Oresme, Nicholas (d. 1382), 1, 346

Paul of Venice (1429), 56
Peuerbach, George (1423-69), 14-15
Pietro d'Abano (fl. 1310), 52-54
Plato (427-347 B.C.), 2, 8
Ptolemy (fl. ca. A.D. 150), 9, 13-14, 17

Ray, John (1627-1705), 46-47
Reformation, 11-12

Scientific Revolution, 1-3, (Readings: p. 304-311, p. 339-348)
Servetius, Michael (ca. 1511-53), 41
Stellar parallax, 19

Tartaglia, Niccolo (1500-57), 32
Tournefort, Joseph Pitton de (1656-1708), 46

Vesalius, Andreas (1514-64), 40-41
Viete, Francois (1540-1603), 32

Zabarella, 59-63